Readings in the

Philosophy of Education:

A Study of Curriculum

Readings in the
Philosophy of Education:
A Study of Curriculum

edited by JANE R. MARTIN

ALLYN AND BACON, INC.
BOSTON

To my husband

CONTENTS

PREFACE

All the essays in this volume have to do with curriculum, and all are philosophical in approach. Otherwise they are a varied lot brought together for the twofold purpose of stimulating philosophers interested in education to pay more attention than they have in the recent past to questions directly connected with curriculum and drawing the attention of educators actively engaged in curriculum planning and theorizing to some of the philosophical problems to which their work gives rise. There is today a wide gulf between these two groups. In the last few years philosophy of education has changed radically. It has, in effect, turned back to the mainstream of general philosophy. A decade or so ago general philosophy and philosophy of education constituted two separate worlds, but those worlds have begun to merge: so-called philosophers of education are taking the methods and findings of general philosophy seriously.

Whereas this change in philosophy of education is undoubtedly to the good, one wonders if it may not have had at least one unfortunate consequence. For philosophers of education have been so busy trying to speak to general philosophers, one suspects that they have minimized the importance of speaking to educational practitioners and theorists; indeed, that they have tended to ignore many of the problems which are of most concern to educational practitioners and theorists. This book should be viewed as one attempt to bring together philosophers of education and those educational practitioners and theorists concerned with curriculum. The hope is neither that curriculum planners and theorists will turn into philosophers nor that philosophers will turn out curriculum packets. The hope is rather that curriculum planners and theorists will find philosophy of education, now that it is merging with general philosophy, to be relevant to their work and that philosophers of education will begin to study more closely and systematically than previously curriculum practice and theory.

I wish to thank Professor Israel Scheffler for his encouragement in this project and Professor William K. Frankena for some very helpful suggestions. I am grateful also to the authors and publishers for their cooperation. Finally, and most of all, I want to thank my husband, for if this book was not his idea — and it may have been — it was he who prodded me into doing it and who saw to it that I had the time to do it.

Jane R. Martin

Readings in the

Philosophy of Education:

A Study of Curriculum

INTRODUCTION

The Problem of Definition

What is curriculum? Perhaps the readings in this book will shed some light on this question. It should not be supposed, however, that they will provide us with an adequate answer to it. Philosophers have scarcely begun to explore the concept of curriculum; its "logical geography" is yet to be mapped.[1] What, for example, is the relationship between curriculum and teaching methods? Is there a sharp distinction between the two or, as some suggest, does a curriculum "imply" or "dictate" some method of teaching? Are aims or objectives a part of curriculum or are they distinct from it? Can there be a curriculum which has no subject matter? A curriculum for which there is no teacher? A curriculum for which there is no learner? Insofar as a curriculum is for someone, is it necessarily for people, or can there be a curriculum for, say, circus animals or Seeing Eye dogs? What exactly is the connection between the notion of a curriculum and the notion of a school: does every school necessarily have a curriculum? Is the institutional setting for a curriculum necessarily a school? And, for that matter, what are we talking about when we use the term 'curriculum' — a plan (blueprint, description, etc.) of what is expected or intended to take place or what actually takes place?

The issues are many and complex. The essays in this volume touch on some of them, but what is needed is something that goes far beyond the present book of readings: namely, detailed studies of a whole cluster of concepts. To date, philosophers of education have paid relatively little attention to this cluster, while they have dwelt at length — and very profitably — on such concepts as teaching and learning, knowledge and belief, work and leisure, freedom and equality.[2] To be sure, some of these concepts may belong to the curriculum cluster and others may be related to it, but to the extent that members of the cluster and close relations have been

---

1. Gilbert Ryle discusses the logical geography of concepts in *The Concept of Mind* (London: Hutchinson & Co. Ltd., 1949), pp. 7–9. His book represents an attempt to rectify "the logical geography of the knowledge we already possess" about minds. For another example of an attempt to map the logical geography of a concept see H. L. A. Hart, *The Concept of Law* (London: Oxford University Press, 1961).

2. See, for example, Donald Arnstine, *Philosophy of Education: Learning and Schooling* (New York: Harper & Row, 1967); Thomas F. Green, *Work, Leisure, and the American Schools* (New York: Random House, 1968); B. Paul Komisar and Jerrold R. Coombs, "The Concept of Equality in Education," *Studies in Philosophy and Education, 3,* pp. 223–244, and the replies to this paper in Vols. 3 and 4 of that journal; B. Paul Komisar and C. B. J. Macmillan (Eds.), *Psychological Concepts in Education* (Chicago: Rand McNally, 1967); Paul Nash, *Authority and Freedom in Education* (New York: John

examined by philosophers, they have still not been studied as members of the cluster or as close relations. Thus, although we may well be clearer today than we ever were before on the nature of teaching and learning, for example, we seem to be no clearer than we ever were about the nature of curriculum.

Almost every writer on curriculum begins his discussion with a definition of the term. However, these definitions are normally designed to set the stage for the discussion which follows and are not intended as descriptions of the way 'curriculum' functions in educational discourse, let alone intended to provide us with a general understanding of curriculum, its friends and relations.[3] Of course the discussions of curriculum which these definitions serve to introduce do in some cases themselves shed light on the concept,[4] but a curriculum theorist who needs to get on with his theorizing is not in the best position to investigate the foundations of his own enterprise. Indeed, if he were to investigate them in the way they need to be investigated, he might find that he had no time left for his theorizing. This is not to say that he ought not reflect on them or that the study of the foundations of his enterprise has no value for him. On the contrary, one aim of this book is to acquaint curriculum planners and theorists with what little philosophical inquiry into their enterprise there is, in the hope that such acquaintance will lead to reflection, further study, and perhaps in some cases to philosophical investigation. But philosophical inquiry is itself a full-time job; the aim here is not to recruit practitioners in it, but simply to help bring practitioners in curriculum and practitioners in philosophy into closer communication.

Yet if we do not know the answer to the question "What is curriculum?" how can we possibly carry on an intelligent discussion about curriculum? Must not discourse on any topic begin with a definition if the discussants are to talk to each other and not past each other? The belief that one must define one's terms at the outset if one is to avoid being misunderstood is widespread; however, we all talk about chairs, dogs, and airplanes and recognize instances of each without benefit of definition. Indeed, many of us would be hard pressed to give a definition of 'chair' even when sitting on one, of 'dog' even when patting one, of 'airplane' even when spotting one. The case is no different for more abstract things like law, art, education, except that here we may find it even more difficult to come up with adequate definitions. To be sure, disagreements over cases may arise:

Wiley & Sons, 1966); R. S. Peters, *Ethics and Education* (London: George Allen & Unwin Ltd., 1966); Israel Scheffler, *The Language of Education* (Springfield, Ill.: Charles C. Thomas, 1960) and *Conditions of Knowledge* (Chicago: Scott, Foresman, 1965); B. Othanel Smith and Robert H. Ennis (Eds.), *Language and Concepts in Education* (Chicago: Rand McNally, 1961).

3. For a discussion of definitions in education with particular reference to the term 'curriculum' see Scheffler, *The Language of Education,* Chapter 1.

4. See, for example, Hilda Taba, *Curriculum Development: Theory and Practice.* (New York: Harcourt Brace & World, 1962).

one person may consider a painting a work of art and another may not; one person may call an avant-garde piece of furniture a chair and another may not. But disputes of this sort can arise even when a definition is provided. The point is that we can and do recognize things and talk about them without necessarily being able to define them and that in this respect curriculum is no exception.

We can point to actual curricula, notice changes in curricula, propose new curricula, talk about the differences among curricula all quite apart from our ability to define the term 'curriculum.' This is not to say that we would not be better off if we could satisfactorily answer the question "What is curriculum?" but simply that we can proceed even if we cannot answer it. As a matter of fact we do not even know if the question "What is curriculum?" and its counterpart "What is the definition of curriculum?" are the right ones to ask. Perhaps we would do better to follow the lead of H. L. A. Hart who, in his study *The Concept of Law,* substitutes several more specific questions for the question "What is law?"[5] Questions of the form "What is X?" or "What is the definition of X?" cry for concise answers, but we simply do not know if in the case of curriculum a concise answer will be an illuminating one. Hart is convinced that a concise definition of the term 'law' will not provide the desired illumination and asks instead: How does law differ from and how is it related to orders backed by threats? How does legal obligation differ from and how is it related to moral obligation? What are rules and to what extent is law an affair of rules? We can be sure that he did not arrive at these questions overnight. If, as may be suspected, the question "What is curriculum?" has some of the defects of the question "What is law?" hard philosophical investigation will be required if we are to come up with good substitutes, let alone good answers to them. In the long run, however, such investigation may be worth the trouble.

But now it may be asked if we really need to answer the question "What is curriculum?" or seek substitute questions. If it is true that we can talk about curriculum although we have no maps of its logical geography, what need have we for such maps? Why should we be calling for their construction? Strictly speaking, of course, such maps are not necessary. But if philosophical inquiry had to meet some criterion of necessity before proceeding, it would scarcely ever get under way. Conceptual clarity is probably not necessary but it is surely desirable and if nothing else was yielded by extended philosophical investigation of curriculum and related concepts, the resulting clarity would seem to be enough to justify it. Besides yielding clarity we would expect such investigation to give to our pre-analytic ideas about curriculum some order and consistency. However, the greatest benefit to accrue from philosophical inquiry in curriculum is neither clarity

5. Chapter 1.

nor order but rather the freshness of a new perspective. If old questions are given new forms, if old problems are studied from new points of view, if long-standing assumptions are brought to light, the field of curriculum and the field of philosophy stand to gain.

Curriculum Questions

It is often assumed that the question made famous by Herbert Spencer, "What knowledge is of most worth?" is *the* curriculum question.[6] No one would deny that Spencer's question is one curriculum question, but it is important to recognize that it is neither the only curriculum question nor the only important or crucial or central curriculum question. To assume that it is *the* curriculum question is, first of all, to overlook the sort of question we have just been discussing. Of course there is a great difference between the question "What knowledge is of most worth?" and the question "What is curriculum?" Some might want to call the latter a question *about* curriculum and the former a question *in* curriculum.[7] However, even if we accept this distinction and, moreover, limit what will count as curriculum questions to questions *in* curriculum, it is a mistake to view Spencer's question as *the* curriculum question. For to assume that it is *the* curriculum question is to assume a particular answer — "Knowledge and only knowledge" — to a prior curriculum question, namely "What is of most educational worth?"

As it stands this prior question is very general — indeed so general one wonders if a decent answer can be given it. Can we really decide what is of most educational worth if we do not specify such things as person, place, time, institutional setting, level of educational development, educational purpose?[8] If we cannot, if we must narrow down the prior question by making it relative in a number of ways — for example, "What is of educational worth to person P at time t, and place L?" — then perhaps there will be contexts in which the answer to it is "Knowledge and only knowledge is of most worth." But of course there will just as surely be contexts in which the answer is something else. And it should be clear that to the extent that

6. Herbert Spencer, "What Knowledge Is of Most Worth?" *The Westminster Review, XVI* (July and October, 1859). For an interesting account of the context in which Spencer asked this question see Andreas M. Kazemias, " 'What Knowledge Is of Most Worth?': An Historical Conception and a Modern Sequel," *Harvard Educational Review, 30,* (Fall, 1960).

7. Broudy, Smith, and Burnett, in calling their book a study *in* curriculum theory and not an account *of* curriculum theory, draw a distinction like the one being drawn here although perhaps not identical to it. See *Democracy and Excellence in American Secondary Education* (Chicago: Rand McNally, 1964), p. 10.

8. In the course of a discussion of Spencer's question Arnstine, (*op. cit.,* Chapter 10) has some interesting things to say about educational purpose.

there are such contexts, even if the question in its most general form admits of an answer, it cannot be answered by "Knowledge and only knowledge."

No doubt some knowledge is of worth in almost every (if not every) educational context, and no doubt in some educational contexts only knowledge is of worth. But to suppose that in every educational context knowledge and only knowledge is of worth is to take a much too narrow view of education and the curriculum — or else to take a much too broad view of knowledge. One can of course define 'knowledge' in such a way that everything having educational worth qualifies as knowledge. But on the one hand this is misleading in that things that are clearly not knowledge in the ordinary sense of the term (attitudes, activities, habits, for example) are called knowledge, and on the other hand the concept of knowledge loses whatever power it is intended to have in curriculum theorizing if it is made too broad.

Perhaps it is because Spencer's question has been taken to be *the* curriculum question that philosophical problems arising in connection with curriculum have sometimes been viewed as being primarily epistemological. For, or so at least it might be argued, one's answer to the question "What knowledge is of most worth?" will depend on one's view of the nature of knowledge, and this, in turn, is an epistemological problem. If, however, 'knowledge' is defined so broadly that everything or else everything of educational worth is knowledge, epistemology will have no special claim on curriculum: the knowledge that curriculum planners and theorists would be talking about would not be the knowledge epistemologists discuss. If epistemology is to have relevance to curriculum, knowledge must not be construed in an overly broad way. And if it is not so construed, then it cannot legitimately be maintained that no matter what the context, knowledge is the only thing having educational worth.

Suppose, however, that knowledge were the only thing having educational worth. It would not be the case even then that all philosophical problems arising in connection with curriculum were epistemological. The question at issue is after all a question about *worth,* a question about what *ought* to be included in the curriculum. It falls squarely within what William K. Frankena, in his paper in the first section of this volume, calls normative philosophy of education. As Frankena points out, answers to questions of this sort cannot rest on a sound basis if they rely on epistemological theory alone. To adapt his example to the present purpose, given that mathematical knowledge is tautological, it does not follow that it is of more worth than some nontautological knowledge, say historical knowledge. Questions of worth are value questions. Thus even if Spencer's question were *the* curriculum question, philosophy of curriculum would not be confined to epistemology.

But it is far from obvious that Spencer's question is *the* curriculum question even when we limit ourselves to questions *in* curriculum and prejudge the answer to the more general question of educational worth. For one thing, there are nonphilosophical questions of great importance in curriculum, for example questions of the form "Given knowledge *K,* which is of great worth, at what age is pupil *P* going to be able to grasp it?" Our concern here is with philosophical questions, however, so that questions calling for empirical research may not seem to compete for the spotlight with Spencer's, It is easy enough, though, to think of philosophical questions besides Spencer's which are *in* curriculum and of some importance. For example, we must ask what sort of mastery students ought to have of the knowledge we take to be of most worth. We must ask how that knowledge should be viewed; which elements of it should be emphasized; whether it should be presented in the abstract or in relation to practical problems. Like Spencer's, these questions and countless others may be considered to fall within normative philosophy of education for they are questions about what *ought* to be the case.

There are, moreover, other important questions arising in curriculum of a rather different nature. Given that we think our students ought to learn with understanding and not simply by rote whatever it is we take to be of educational worth, what is it to learn with understanding? Given that we want our students to be creative, that we want them to use their imaginations, what is imagination, what is creativity? Given that knowledge, even if it is not the only thing of educational worth, is at least one thing of educational worth, what constitutes knowledge? Do the humanities yield knowledge? Does common sense knowledge differ from technical knowledge? Is theoretical knowledge all of a piece or not? Countless questions like these can be asked. They do not call for curriculum recommendations although answers to them may have bearing on such recommendations. They call instead for analysis. They may be said to fall within what Frankena calls analytic (rather than normative) philosophy of education and in this respect they are like our earlier question "What is curriculum?" Yet while that question seemed clearly to be *about* curriculum, one is inclined to say that these questions, perhaps because they are so closely linked to normative questions in curriculum, are themselves *in* curriculum.

We ought not make too much of this in-about distinction, however. If it is felt that analytic questions of the sort under discussion here are *about*, not *in* curriculum, no great harm is done; if it is felt that they are not clearly classifiable under these headings because the headings themselves are not clear, no harm is done either. What is important is that we recognize that Spencer's question is just one of many, many philosophical questions which arise in connection with curriculum; that these questions range over a wide array of topics; and that some demand one kind of answer and some another.

Philosophy of Curriculum

Neither of the distinctions introduced into this discussion is sacrosanct, but each is helpful in pointing up the great variety of things which may be counted as philosophy of curriculum. The distinction between normative and analytic philosophy of education points up a difference in method or approach. The distinction between questions in and questions about curriculum points up a difference in subject matter. These distinctions cut across each other: questions about curriculum may be analytic ("What is curriculum?") or normative ("Ought the curriculum of a society be a reflection of its culture?"); questions in curriculum may be normative ("Should history be taught?") or analytic ("What constitutes historical understanding?"). They are, moreover, distinctions in theory, not practice. If they are to be useful at all we must of course be able to recognize clear cases of one or the other sort of question and clear cases of one or the other sort of philosophy when we meet them in practice. We must not, however, expect a given example of philosophical practice to fall into one and only one of our categories. It is a rare philosopher who does only analysis just as it is a rare philosopher who does no analysis. And, as the esssays in this volume illustrate, it is as rare to confine oneself to questions about curriculum without ever considering questions in it as it is rare to worry about questions in it to the exclusion of questions about it.

It may be very hard, then, to say of a particular essay in this volume that it is analytic or normative, about curriculum or in curriculum, for it may be all of these. Consider the essay by Michael Oakeshott in the first section of this volume. Its title, "The Study of 'Politics' in a University," would lead one to expect it to be a normative study in curriculum and, indeed, a part of it is devoted to a discussion of the way politics ought to be taught. Yet the essay is rich in discussion about curriculum — about the ways subjects should be studied given different levels or kinds of education, for example — and is by no means devoid of analysis. Oakeshott's essay is much longer than most, and therefore allows for more interplay of questions and approaches than a shorter work. Yet if we examine a very short essay, Paul A. Freund's "The Law and the Schools," we find it too combining recommendation and analysis. At first reading this essay may seem to combine them solely in the interest of answering questions in curriculum — questions having to do with the study of law in general education. If we are willing to put to one side the author's particular concern with the law, however, we can abstract from his discussion some important points about curriculum: for example, the too often ignored one that even when a particular thing is included as a subject in the curriculum, a decision must be made about the approach taken to it.

In general the essays in this volume, although addressed to one or another specific topic connected with curriculum, have interesting things to say on a number of issues. A reader might not care a bit about the uses and abuses of history yet find W. B. Gallie's essay on that subject of interest because of the author's discussion of the "principle of reserve" and the "all-or-nothing principle," or because of the way he goes about justifying the study of history. A reader might disagree with Ernest Nagel about the values of studying science yet find Nagel's views on liberal education or on the cognitive claims of the humanities illuminating. Nancy Gayer's thesis that values are imbedded in the terms of everyday language may be of more interest to some readers than her discussion of moral education; Hugh G. Petrie's discussions of structure and discovery may take precedence for some readers over his analysis of learning with understanding.

That an essay directs our attention to more issues than its title suggests is all to the good. Let the reader hereby be warned that he may find illumination on some topic of his interest in the most unlikely places in this volume. In this respect section headings are of little help: an essay which touches on a number of topics can be classified in a variety of ways. The divisions used here may be valuable in some respects but ought not to be taken too seriously. They ought not, for example, to keep one from reading J. Myron Atkin's paper on behavioral objectives included in Part I of this book entitled "The Logic of Curriculum" along with the essays in Part II entitled "Aims and Objectives"; or Michael Oakeshott's essay on politics in Part I along with the essays in Part IV entitled "Subjects and Subject Matter." Nor should the section divisions, for example, keep one from reading Paul H. Hirst's essay included in Part III, "The Nature of Knowledge," together with the paper "The Disciplines and the Curriculum" in Part I. There are any number of fruitful combinations and permutations of the papers included here, and the reader is urged to get what he can where he can without regard for such formalities as headings and titles.

As the reader proceeds he may note a wide variety in style and approach. Some of the essays in this volume are rather technical, others are not; some seem to be many degrees removed from educational practice but some – for example, those by J. P. White, Joanne Reynolds Bronars, and Stephen I. Brown – seem rather close to it; some are addressed to very general issues, some to quite specific ones. These essays testify to the fact that there is no one model to which philosophy of curriculum does or should conform. Philosophers who want to worry about matters connected with curriculum, and curriculum planners and theorists who want to worry philosophically, can do so in ways they find congenial.

They can, moreover, work in a variety of areas within philosophy. Each essay in this volume is an essay in philosophy of curriculum, itself a subsidiary of philosophy of education. But many of the essays draw on or contribute to some area of general philosophy as well. It might be expected that philosophical essays on a particular school subject would have some connection with the philosophy of that subject, if there is such a field. And indeed we find Walter H. Clark, Jr.'s essay "The Role of Choice in Aesthetic Education" to be at least in part an essay in aesthetics and Frederick A. Olafson's essay "Philosophy and the Humanities" to be at least in part an essay in the philosophy of the humanities. But an essay need not be about a particular school subject to have close connections with some branch of general philosophy. K. Charlton's "Imagination and Education," for example, may be considered at least in part an essay in philosophy of mind, Israel Scheffler's "Justifying Curriculum Decisions" at least in part an essay in ethics, R. S. Peters' " 'Mental Health' as an Educational Aim" at least in part an essay in philosophy of psychology, L. R. Perry's and May Brodbeck's essays at least in part essays in epistemology.

Epistemology, then, provides but one entry into philosophy of curriculum. Ethics provides another, but as we have just seen, by no means the only other. It might be supposed, however, that insofar as a curriculum question is normative, one must look to ethics for one's answer. Ethical theorists, after all, ask the question "What things are good in themselves?" and one would expect their answers to this question to bear on issues of educational worth. Yet ethics is not the only branch of philosophy to deal with value questions. Social and political philosophy have commerce with them also and those who worry about *educational* worth ignore these branches of philosophy at their peril. This is not to say that a theory of the good society automatically answers questions of educational worth or even that answers to such questions must be based in part on some theory of society. Rather it is to point out that ethics has no monopoly on the study of value problems, and that although ethical theory undoubtedly is relevant to questions of educational worth, we cannot assume that these questions are to be answered in terms of it alone.

Unfortunately, despite the relevance of social and political philosophy to matters of curriculum, no essay in this volume can really be considered to fall primarily in this area of philosophy. Several of the essays, for example W. B. Gallie's and Nancy Gayer's, do touch on issues of social and political philosophy, but if a reader were to take the essays in this volume as directives about the sort of philosophy relevant to philosophy of curriculum, this very important area would be slighted. So would other areas of philosophy. It is therefore important to recognize that although the essays to follow range over a number of fields within philosophy which are relevant to curriculum, they do not range over every such field. Similary, it should be noted that although they represent a variety of approaches to curriculum and to philosophy, they do not represent every approach or even every worthwhile approach. These essays may be considered to be guides to what can be done in philosophy of curriculum provided it is recognized that things can be done and approaches can be taken for which no guides are given here.

If these essays ought to be viewed as suggesting but not dictating approaches to philosophy of curriculum, they ought also to be viewed as suggesting but not dictating topics of interest and importance in that field, for the essays are very far from being exhaustive in this respect. Discussions of curriculum evaluation are conspicuously absent; so are discussions of curriculum in professional education and curriculum in so-called technical and vocational education; so are discussions of physical education and many other sorts of education. To a certain extent considerations of space have made it necessary to exclude some topics, while some topics have been omitted because they have been given their due elsewhere. It needs to be emphasized, however, that many of the topics missing from this volume are missing simply because neither philosophers nor nonphilosophers in their philosophical moments have addressed themselves to them. The absence of discussions of physical education, for example, ought not to be taken as a result of editorial prejudice toward either the topic of physical education or physical education itself but simply as a result of the scarcity of philosophically interesting work on this topic.[9]

The reader is urged, then, not merely to get what he can where he can but, where he cannot get, to do some philosophical thinking on his own. Indeed he is urged, encouraged, if necessary commanded, to do his own philosophical thinking on a topic even when one of our authors has seemed to do it for him. As often as not our authors' words are the first on a topic; but even when they are not the first, they are surely not the last.

In every case what is needed is neither unthinking approval nor polite acquiescence but rather hardheaded criticism based on attentive reading and on knowledge of curriculum matters. One who can find nothing to criticize in a philosophical discussion, who finds himself agreeing with everything, had better beware: seldom if ever is a philosophical discussion entirely free from legitimate criticism. Need it be emphasized that to advocate critical reading of philosophical essays, as opposed to passive acceptance, is not to advocate "negative" or "destructive" thinking? Surely if philosophy of curriculum is to flourish it must launch out in new directions. But it must also build on what is sound in what has already been done, and this in turn requires that what has been done be examined not only sympathetically but critically.

9. Note, however, that the subject of games has been of great interest to philosophers. Indeed, several discussions of games may be found in this volume.

Part I

THE LOGIC OF CURRICULUM

Introduction

In his essay "A Model for Analyzing a Philosophy of Education" William K. Frankena seeks to show how to analyze a normative philosophy of education. A normative philosophy of education, he says, is one that makes normative statements about what education should do or not do and about what the aims, content, methods, etc., of education should be or not be. Given this conception of the concerns of normative philosophy of education, we would expect Frankena's essay to help us analyze that part or branch of philosophy of education that may be called normative philosophy of curriculum. The Frankena essay is, then, a fitting one with which to begin this volume: it directs us to the various kinds of statements we may find in the essays to follow — at least in those which are primarily normative in character — and the roles we may find these various kinds of statements playing. It directs us also to some of the questions to which the essays to follow are addressed: those which are primarily analytic in character as well as those which are primarily normative.

Frankena makes it clear that one of the important tasks of a normative philosophy of education is that of justifying the recommendations it makes. Israel Scheffler, in his paper "Justifying Curriculum Decisions," attempts to clarify this task. He offers an analysis of the process of justification and then makes suggestions for justifying curriculum decisions. Scheffler distinguishes between two senses of justification: a relative sense and a nonrelative or general sense. He likens the former to the justification of moves in chess and the latter to the justification of beliefs. A move in chess, he argues, is justified if it conforms to the rules of chess; a belief is justified if it hangs together with the family of beliefs that as a whole commands our highest degree of confidence. According to Scheffler, educational decisions admit of both sorts of justification. For some purposes it is sufficient to show that an educational decision conforms to some set of rules or practices; for other purposes it is necessary to go beyond this to a justification by rules which are themselves "controlled by the mass of our initial commitments." What rules are in fact so controlled? Scheffler offers a list relating to decisions on curriculum and invites criticism of it.

In discussing the justification of curriculum decisions Scheffler speaks primarily of decisions governing the selection of content. J. Myron Atkin, in "Behavioral Objectives in Curriculum Design: A Cautionary Note," discusses the selection of objectives. Atkin is not concerned so much with the rather large-scale objectives which Frankena presumably has in mind when he (Frankena) says that the central task of a normative philosophy of education is to list and define dispositions to be fostered as he is with somewhat lesser objectives that might well fall into Frankena's category of means for fostering the large-scale objectives — for example, the attainment of specific skills or concepts. Atkin's discussion of the widely held thesis that curriculum objectives must be formulated in behavioral terms would seem, however, to bear on the issue of the nature of curriculum objectives regardless of their scale. Atkin criticizes the behavioral thesis on various grounds. He argues that the thesis is based on a mistaken assumption and sees it, when translated into practice, as having a number of unfortunate effects. In the course of all this, Atkin gives us an account of objectives in relation to curriculum development and instruction. On his view the matter is very complex and one of the shortcomings of the behavioral thesis is that it completely overlooks this complexity.

While Atkin throws doubt on the view that curriculum development is simply a matter of setting objectives and finding the best way to achieve them, if we read carefully "The Study of 'Politics' in a University" by Michael Oakeshott we will see that the view of curriculum development as simply a matter of selecting subjects to teach may also be open to the charge of oversimplification. Oakeshott asks the question "What study under the plausible name of 'Politics' is an appropriate component of a university education?" He finds it necessary to answer a number of very general questions in order to answer this rather specific one — questions about the nature of education, the character of university education, the respects in which it differs from vocational education and from schooling. He also finds it necessary to consider the way subjects can be viewed, the way they are prop-erly to be viewed in a given kind of education, and the way they are properly to be taught or imparted when viewed in a particular way in a given kind of education. Not every reader will agree with Oakeshott about the nature of education or the character of the various kinds of education he distinguishes; nor will everyone agree with his conclusions about the way subjects in general are to be studied in a university education, let alone with his observations on the study of politics. But there is much to be learned from his approach to his underlying question about politics, and one need not agree with his answer to it or to the other questions he poses to see that his essay reveals some of the many decisions besides that of school subject that enter into curriculum development.

Each kind of education in Oakeshott's scheme of things has its own specific character. Thus a university education is properly a study of explanatory "languages," i.e., modes of thinking, while schooling, although like a university education in that it too is an initiation into civilization, is an initiation into a stock of ideas, beliefs, and the like. It is interesting to contrast this view with the one reconstructed and criticized in the essay "The Disciplines and the Curriculum." This essay examines a normative theory of curriculum which gives to the disciplines a ruling hand. The Structure of the Disciplines as Inquiry theory of curriculum as set forth in this essay bears some important similarities to Oakeshott's theory of a university curriculum. Not all the advocates of the former theory, however, see it as applying to university education and only university education. Some see it as applying to nonspecialized or general education, be it Oakeshott's schooling or his university education. Indeed, Oakeshott's conception of schooling sounds very much like the "traditional education" that many advocates of the Structure of the Disciplines as Inquiry theory criticize severely. We see, then, that there is room for argument about something Oakeshott takes as given, namely that each kind of education – school, vocational, university – must have its own distinctive curriculum.

Each of the essays in this section speaks to some important question about curriculum. The Frankena essay speaks, albeit indirectly, about the structure of a normative philosophy of curriculum, the Scheffler essay about the process of justifying curriculum decisions, the Atkin essay about the nature of curriculum objectives, the final essay about the relationship between the curriculum and the disciplines. But what about the Oakeshott essay? Granted that it has things to say on the way subjects should be viewed, does it have enough to say about curriculum to warrant its inclusion in a section called "The Logic of Curriculum"? If we recognize that one very important question to ask about curriculum – a question whose answer will, if adequate, shed a good deal of light on the logic of curriculum – is "What curriculum decisions are there to be made?" then we begin to see the reason for including the Oakeshott essay here, for it brings to light a number of decisions having to do with educational content: decisions which for some purposes need not be made explicit but which certainly must be if we are to get clear on the logic of curriculum.

Oakeshott's essay on the study of politics helps us see that someone does not simply teach a subject to someone, or, to use the terms of the essay, someone does not simply study a subject. Rather, someone who is getting a certain sort of education studies a subject which is viewed in a particular way. Thus we may say that the essay makes it clear that the form "*P* studies *X*," where '*P*' names some person or persons and '*X*' some subject, needs to be expanded. It would seem at first glance as if Oakeshott's essay makes clear the need to expand it simply as follows: "*P* studies *X* as *A* in education *K*" where '*A*' names some way of viewing a subject and '*K*' names a specific sort or kind of education. But if we examine Oakeshott's conception of education of a specific sort, examples of which are university and vocational education, we realize that a variety of things are involved. University education, for example, has a specific character (it is elementary) and a specific function (initiation into civilization as capital); it takes place at a particular point in a person's development (after schooling) and in a particular institutional setting (a university). If our purpose is to get clear on what decisions having to do with educational content there are, we would do well to make these things explicit. Let us consider Oakeshott's essay, then, as suggesting the need for a more complicated form, one in which *K* is "unpacked": "*P* studies *X* as *A* in education with *C* and *F* at *D* in *I*," where '*C*' names some character of education, '*F*' some function, '*D*' some stage of educational development, and '*I*' some institutional setting.

Now Oakeshott's essay by no means reveals all the curriculum decisions having to do with educational content there are. But simply by complicating the curriculum picture it does us a service. For one thing, it counterbalances the essays in this section which in the interests of clarifying something else draw a simplified picture of the decisions to be made in relation to educational content. This is not to say that simplication has no value – of course it has; but so at times does a degree of complication. This essay also sets the stage for the essays in later sections of this volume that in the course of discussing questions in curriculum, introduce still more complications into the picture. The complications are there and, if nothing else, the Oakeshott essay when taken together with the other essays in this section serves as a good introduction to them.

A MODEL FOR ANALYZING
A PHILOSOPHY OF EDUCATION

William K. Frankena

There are two sorts of things that go by the name of philosophy of education today, one traditional and one newish. The newish sort of thing is what is called "analytical philosophy of education." It consists in the analysis of educational concepts, arguments, slogans, and statements. For example, if one tries to define what is meant by teaching, to distinguish teaching from indoctrination, and to relate teaching to learning, or if one tries to determine what is meant by the slogan "Learn by doing!" then one is doing analytical philosophy of education. The analytical philosophy of education consists entirely of such inquiries. Since I am here seeking to show how to analyze a philosophy of education, this essay is itself an example of analytical philosophy of education. I say that this sort of thing is newish because, although educational philosophers have always included some of it in their works, it is only recently that some of them have come to think that their work should include nothing else.

The other kind of philosophy of education is what educational philosophers have done historically and what some of them still do. I shall call it "normative philosophy of education." It may be eclectic or noneclectic; idealistic, realistic, or pragmatic; naturalistic or supernaturalistic; traditional or progressive. In all its forms, however, what distinguishes it from analytical philosophy of education is that it makes normative statements about what education, educators, and the schools should do or not do, about what the aims, content, methods, etc., of education should be or not be.

I

Now consider any such normative philosophy of education, for example, that of Aristotle, Rousseau, Dewey, Whitehead, Russell, Maritain, Brameld, or Phenix. Our problem is to find a scheme for analyzing it, that is,

From *The High School Journal*, 2 (October, 1966) with a section, Part III, added by the author. Reprinted by permission of the author and The University of North Carolina Press.

for understanding it and seeing how it is put together, for taking it apart and putting it together again. One cannot evaluate it in any systematic way until one has analyzed it to see just what it says and what its arguments are.

In general, a normative philosophy of education will include statements of three kinds. (a) It must include normative statements about the aims, principles, methods, etc., of education, as Dewey does when he says that the schools should teach reflective thinking. (b) It will probably include — and it should include — some bits of analysis, for example, definitions of education, teaching, and learning. (c) Almost certainly it will contain some statements of empirical fact, hypotheses about their explanation, psychological theories, experimental findings, predictions, and the like, for example, Russell's statement that a child can be made to feel the importance of learning the dull parts of a subject without the use of compulsion. (d) It may also contain statements of a fourth kind — epistemological, metaphysical, or theological ones such as Phenix's assertion that the meaning of a proposition is defined by the method of validating it or Maritain's doctrine that man is a sinful and wounded creature called to divine life. It is not always easy to tell which kind of a statement is being made in a given sentence, and many sentences in works on the philosophy of education are ambiguous and hard to classify.

To analyze a philosophy of education one must find out what statements of these different kinds it contains and how they are related to one another in the author's reasoning. This is relatively easy to do in the case of some authors, for example, Maritain, harder to do in the case of others, for example, Dewey or Whitehead. What follows is an attempt to provide a guide for doing so.[1]

II

Education is primarily a process in which educators and educated interact, and such a process is called education if and only if it issues or is intended to issue in the formation, in the one being educated, of certain desired or desirable abilities, habits, dispositions, skills, character traits, beliefs, or bodies of knowledge (if it is intended to but does not, it is called *bad* education), for example, the habit of reflective thinking, conscientiousness, the ability to dance, or a knowledge of astonomy. For convenience, I shall refer to all such states as dispositions. Then education is the process of forming or trying to form such dispositions. Note that what I have just done is a rough analysis of the concept of education.

1. For similar attempts on my part, see "Toward a Philosophy of the Philosophy of Education," *Harvard Educational Review, 26,* 1956; *Philosophy of Education,* (New York: Macmillan, 1965), pp. 1–10; *Three Historical Philosophies of Education,* (Chicago: Scott Foresman, 1965), pp. 6–12.

If this is so, then (1) the *main* task of a normative philosophy of education is to list and define a set of dispositions to be fostered by parents, teachers, and schools (and by the pupil himself). That is, it must say what dispositions are desirable and ought to be cultivated. In saying this it will, of course, be making normative statements, but the definitions of the dispositions listed will be bits of analysis. A complete normative theory of education will, however, do two more things. (2) It will give a line of thought to show that the dispositions listed by it are desirable or should be cultivated. Such a line of reasoning may take various forms, but they must all have the same general pattern. They must bring in some basic premises about the aims or values of life or about the principles to be followed in life — about what is desirable or obligatory. These, again, will be normative judgments, the most fundamental ones. Even Dewey brings in such premises, though he often writes as if he does not. In addition, they must show or at least give reasons for thinking that, if we are to live in the way that is desirable or in the way in which we ought to   if we are to live a good or a moral life   then we must acquire the dispositions listed. It is in this part of a philosophy of education that epistemological, ontological, or theological premises most often appear, but they are not logically required. What *is* logically required is, first, some normative premises stating basic goals or principles: for example, Aristotle's premise that the good life is a happy one consisting of intrinsically excellent activities like contemplation, and second, factual claims stating that certain dispositions are conducive to the achievement of those goals or to the following of those principles, for example, Aristotle's further claim that, if we are to achieve the good life as he sees it, we must cultivate such dispositions as moderation, practical wisdom, and a knowledge of mathematics, physics, and philosophy. If we think of basic normative premises as belonging to Box A, the other premises used here, whether they are religious, philosophical, or empirical, as belonging to Box B, and the conclusions as to the dispositions to be fostered as belonging to Box C, then we can represent this part of a philosophy of education as follows:

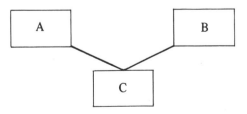

(3) Finally, a complete normative theory of education will tell us what we should do in order to acquire or foster the dispositions recommended by it in Box C, that is, it will make further recommendations about means, methods, curriculum, administration, etc., hopefully accompanying them

with its reasons for making them. This means that it will make normative statements of yet a third kind, and that it will support them by giving empirical evidence (discovered by observation and experiment or borrowed from psychology and other disciplines) to show that the methods and measures it advocates are necessary, helpful, or effective in the formation of the dispositions in its Box C (and that other methods are not). The example cited from Russell earlier will do here; in it he argues that compulsion should not be used, since children can be gotten through even the dull parts of a subject without it. This example also shows that premises from Box A may come in even in this part of a philosophy of education, for Russell is assuming the normative principle that compulsion ought not to be used unless it is necessary. Actually, epistemological premises or other premises from Box B may also appear at this stage; for instance, Cardinal Newman uses his epistemological premise that theology is a body of genuine knowledge in an argument to show that theology should belong to the curriculum of a university. Neglecting such important points, however, we may represent this part of a philosophy of education as follows, taking Box C as giving the dispositions to be fostered, Box D as containing factual statements of the form "Method X is necessary, effective, or at least helpful in the formation of one or more of these dispositions (or the opposite)" and Box E as including recommendations of the form "Method X should (or should not) be used":

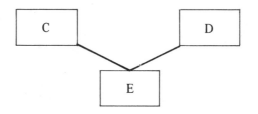

It should be added that bits of analysis may also show up in this part of a theory, for example, in a distinction between indoctrination and teaching or in a definition of compulsion.

III

Since it is often thought that epistemological, metaphysical, or theological beliefs *must* appear among the basic premises of a philosophy of education (in Box B), perhaps it will help if, before going on, I say a little more about the role of such beliefs in educational thought. I shall talk only about epistemological beliefs, but what I shall say will apply also to metaphysical and religious beliefs. To begin with, not all epistemological theories have educational implications by themselves. P. H. Phenix writes,[2]

> The view one takes of the subjective-objective aspects of knowledge has significant bearing on the learning process. If knowledge is completely objective, learning consists in becoming conformed to what is outwardly true. The mind must then be repeatedly impressed with the nature of external things. Drill, memorization of well-established information, careful observation, and constant checking of facts would be some of the means of molding the understanding to agree with what is objectively so.

This sounds plausible. But the conclusion about methods of learning and teaching does not actually follow. Even if knowledge is objective, it does not follow that repetition, drill, memorization, etc., are necessary. Whether such methods are necessary or not depends on whether such methods are in fact needed to bring the mind to the point of conformity with outward fact, whatever that is, and this is an empirical, psychological question, not an epistemological one.

In fact, no epistemological theory can *suffice,* by itself, to provide a basis for drawing a conclusion about what ought to be taught or studied. Such a conclusion requires a normative or value premise as well as an epistemological one. Suppose we hold that music is not knowledge. Does it follow that it should not be taught? Not unless we also accept the normative premise that only knowledge should be taught. Or suppose we believe that mathematics is tautological. Does it follow that it should or should not be taught? That depends on what we take to be the value of such tautological knowledge. I can also make my point by considering an argument used by R. M. Hutchins. He says,[3]

> Education implies teaching. Teaching implies knowledge. Knowledge is truth. The truth is everywhere the same. Hence education should be everywhere the same.

This passage contains four premises, two of them epistemological, but Hutchins's conclusion that the educational curriculum should be everywhere the same cannot possibly be drawn from these four premises without adding the normative premise that the same truths should be taught to everyone (which is precisely the question at issue between Hutchins and his opponents).

2. *Philosophy of Education,* (New York: Henry Holt and Co., 1958), pp. 303–304.
3. *The Higher Learning in America,* (New York: Yale Paperback, 1962), p. 66.

Thus epistemological theories are not *sufficient* to establish a conclusion about education. Are they *necessary* for doing so? Do we, for example, need an epistemological theory to help establish that mathematics should be offered in a liberal arts college? I cannot see that we do. All we need is some nonvocational line of argument to show that an offering in mathematics is desirable, and it is not hard to imagine one which involves no epistemology. For example:

> Knowledge of mathematics is intrinsically good. Intrinsically good kinds of knowledge ought to be taught. Therefore, mathematics ought to be taught.

This argument is, no doubt, oversimplified, but it does show that while a normative or value premise is necessary, an epistemological one is not.

Hence, as Aristotle said, it is ethics and politics that determine what is to be studied, by whom, and to what extent – not epistemology.

If epistemological theories are neither necessary nor sufficient to determine answers to questions about education, two things follow. First, there may be disagreement about education between people who agree in epistemology. Even if their theory of knowledge is the same, they may use different factual or value premises and so come to different educational conclusions. Second, there may be agreement about education between people who disagree in epistemology. For instance, people may agree about the place of mathematics in the curriculum even though they have different views about its nature.

What has been said may suggest that epistemology has *no* relevance to questions about education. But this does not follow. Even though epistemological theories are neither necessary nor sufficient to determine the answers to questions about education, they may still constitute good reasons, or at least relevant considerations, for or against such conclusions. It may still even be that given certain value premises and certain factual assumptions, they are decisive in determining what to teach. For example, if one believes that religious doctrines constitute knowledge (an epistemological theory), then given that all kinds of knowledge should be taught, at least on the elective plan, and that religious knowledge can be acquired by teaching and only by teaching, one may and presumably will conclude that theology should be taught. As was indicated in the previous section, something like this is Cardinal Newman's reasoning in *The Scope and Nature of University Education*. His opponent would probably begin by arguing that theology is not a body of knowledge, being at best a matter of true opinion or faith. Here then epistemology seems clearly to be relevant and even decisive, given certain plausible factual and value premises.

IV

It will now be clear that a full-fledged normative philosophy of education will have two parts, each probably including some bits of analysis; one part falling into the ABC pattern given above and the other into the CDE pattern. In its actual presentation, however, the two parts are often mingled and the patterns are often left unclear, for instance, in Whitehead's essays on education. Of the two parts, the first is the more properly philosophical, and the second is the more practical. Combining the two parts, we may represent a complete normative philosophy of education as follows:

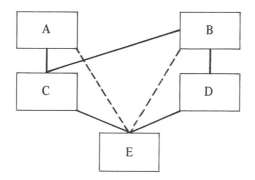

Here the dotted lines are intended to take care of the fact, noted earlier, that premises from Boxes A and B may be used in arriving at the recommendations made in Box E.

It will also be clear that there may be three kinds of normative philosophy of education: (a) one that is complete in the way just indicated; (b) one that does only what was described as the first part of the complete task, giving us only what falls into the ABC pattern, that is, one that provides us only with a list of dispositions to be fostered together with a rationale showing us that they should be fostered and why, leaving the task of implementation to educational scientists, administrators, and teachers; and (c) one that simply begins with a list of dispositions to be cultivated and goes on to give us what falls into the CDE pattern or into what was referred to as the second part of the complete task, telling us what we should do to foster the dispositions listed most effectively and giving us the evidence and arguments to show why we should adopt those methods and procedures. A writer who does the third kind of thing might take his list of dispositions from some more philosophical work; or he might be eclectic, picking up the dispositions on his list from various sources; or he might simply take them to be the dispositions regarded as desirable by society, parents, the state, the church, school boards, or even the pupils themselves — remember how Bianca complains to her would-be educators in *The Taming of the Shrew:*

> Why, gentlemen, you do me double wrong,
> To strive for that which resteth in my choice:
> I am no breeching scholar in the schools;
> I'll not be tied to hours nor 'pointed times,
> But learn my lessons as I please myself.

We can also now see just what one must do in order to understand any complete normative philosophy of education that is placed before one (an analytical philosophy of education is another matter). If one knows this, one will also be able to analyze any less complete normative philosophy of education.

(1) One must first look to see what dispositions it says education should foster (Box C).
(2) Next, one must try to determine the rationale given to show that education should foster those dispositions. To do this one must:
   (a) See what its basic normative premises are — its basic values, principles, or ends (Box A).
   (b) See what factual premises are brought in (implicitly or explicitly), empirical, theological, or philosophical (Box B).
   (c) See how these go together to make a line of argument of the ABC pattern to show that the dispositions listed should be cultivated.
(3) Then one should look for recommendations about ways and means of teaching, administering, etc. (Box E).
(4) Fourthly, one must seek to discover the rationales for these recommendations. To do this one must:
   (a) See what factual statements based on observation and experience are brought in (possibly borrowed from psychology, etc.) (Box D).
   (b) See if any premises from Boxes A or B are used here.
   (c) See how these go together to make a line of argument (or a battery of separate arguments) to show that the ways and means recommended should be used in the cultivation of the dispositions listed (Pattern CDE).
(5) All along, of course, one should notice any definitions or bits of analysis that occur and see how they fit into the discussion.

Finally, it can also be seen from the above analysis of a normative philosophy of education what is involved in "building" one of one's own. However, this should now be so obvious that it need not be spelled out.

JUSTIFYING CURRICULUM DECISIONS

Israel Scheffler

Decisions that confront educators are notoriously varied, complex, and far-reaching in importance, but none outweighs in difficulty or significance those decisions governing selection of content. In view of recent talk of "teaching children rather than subject matter," it is perhaps worth recalling that teaching is a triadic relation, describable by the form *"A teaches B to C,"* where *"B"* names some content, disposition, skill, or subject. If it is true that no one teaches anything unless he teaches it to someone, it is no less true that no one teaches anybody unless he teaches him something.

We do not, moreover, consider it a matter of indifference or whim just what the educator chooses to teach. Some selections we judge better than others; some we deem positively intolerable. Nor are we content to discuss issues of selection as if they hinged on personal taste alone. We try to convince others; we present ordered arguments; we appeal to custom and principle; we point to relevant consequences and implicit commitments. In short, we consider decisions on educational content to be responsible or justifiable acts with public significance.

If these decisions are at once inescapable, important, and subject to rational critique, it is of interest to try to clarify the process of such critique, to state the rules we take to govern the justifying of curricular decisions. Such clarification is not to be confused with an attempt to justify this or that decision; rather, the aim is to make the grounds of decision explicit. Furthermore, clarification cannot be accomplished once and for all time but is rather to be seen as a continuing accompaniment to educational practice.

It is the task of clarification that I shall consider here. I shall offer an analysis of the process of justification along with suggestions for justifying decisions on curriculum.

What is subject to justification? A child may be asked to justify his

Reprinted from *The School Review, LXVI* (1958), pp. 461‒472 by permission of the University of Chicago Press and the author. Copyright 1958 by the University of Chicago. The discussion of justification in this article is based on the author's article "On Justification and Commitment," which appeared in the *Journal of Philosophy,* March 1954.

tardiness, but he would never be asked to justify his cephalic index. Fiscal policies and choices of career are subject to justification, but typhoons and mountain ranges are not. Justifiability applies, it seems, only to controllable acts, or *moves,* as they will henceforth be called.

In this respect, justifiability is paralleled by the notion of responsibility, with which indeed it is intimately related. If I am held responsible for violating a traffic regulation, I expect to be subject to the demand that I justify my violation. Conversely, the child who is called on to justify his late arrival for dinner is being held responsible for his tardiness. The child may escape the need to justify his lateness by denying his responsibility for it. He can deny his responsibility by denying that his lateness was a move at all, by claiming that it could not be helped, was not deliberate or subject to his control.

Now that I have asserted that only moves are justifiable, I must immediately add one qualification. In ordinary discourse, we do not limit justifiability to moves. A city-planning group may debate the justifiability of a projected highway. However, the issue here can ultimately be construed as the justification of moves calculated to produce the highway in question. In general, ostensible reference to the justifiability of nonmoves may be construed as a shorthand reference to the justifiability of moves appropriately related to nonmoves. Where such moves are lacking, the justification of nonmoves fails to arise as an issue. Thus, while we may speak of highways and courses of study as justifiable, we do not inquire into the justification of comets or rainbows. Justifiability may, then, be taken as a universal property of moves; and those that are, in fact, justified comprise a subclass of moves with a certain authority in our conduct.

How are moves justified? If the justified moves represent a subclass of all moves, then to justify a particular move requires that we show it to be a member of this subclass. If no further specification of this subclass is given, we have a relative sense of justification.

Consider chess: we have a board and the standard pieces. We understand what constitutes a move, and we have rules that permit only certain moves. These rules, in effect, define a subclass of all moves. For a player to justify his move as a chess move requires that he show that it belongs to the chess subclass. Such justification is strictly limited, for it depends clearly on the set of rules that define chess. There are an indefinite number of other rule-sets singling out alternative subclasses of moves. A move justified for chess may not be justified for checkers and vice versa. A chess player justifying his move is not implying that chess is superior to checkers. He is only showing that his move conforms to the rules of chess. Hence we cannot speak, strictly, of a move on the board as justified in general or in the abstract; we have to specify also the operative rules.

Some processes of justification resemble the justification of moves in chess and in other formal games. These processes have a well-specified set of rules defining appropriate moves. Justification consists of showing that a move conforms to these rules, that is, belongs to the subclass singled out by them. There is no thought of justifying the set itself as against alternatives. Though it may not be explicitly stated, it is evident that moves are being justified only relative to this set. These conditions seem to apply when, for example, we consider Smith's driving on the right side of the road (in Massachusetts) to be justified. Driving on the right conforms to Massachusetts traffic rules. We are by no means claiming that these rules are unique or superior to alternative rules, for example, rules of countries where driving on the left is prescribed. What is involved here is relative justification. Traffic regulations are, in an important sense, like chess rules or games in general. For one reason or another, we may be interested for the moment in playing a certain game or in seeing what the game demands in a particular case. But the existence of alternative games fails to upset us, nor is the comparative justification of the games as such in question.

Relative justification is not limited to such clear cases as traffic control. Much of our conduct falls within the range of less well-defined rules, or social practices and traditions. Much of the time, we justify this conduct simply by appeal to conformity with established practice. Nor should it be supposed that such justification is always as uncomplicated as that of our traffic illustration. Often a move is justified by appeal to a rule, and that rule by appeal to another. For example, Smith's right-hand driving may be justified by a demonstration of its conformity with Massachusetts law and this particular law by conformity with traditional legal practice throughout the United States. Though various levels are distinguishable, it is still true that the justification as a whole is here carried out in relation to American practice. That is, such practice sanctions a class of certain subclasses of moves, one subclass of which includes the move in question. In effect, one "game" is justified by showing its imbeddedness in another, larger "game."

The relative sense of justification is, however, not exhaustive of the types of justification that one uses and, in itself, is hardly satisfactory for many purposes since every move is both justified and unjustified, in relation to appropriately chosen sets of rules. If I am not, as in a game, asking what move I ought to make in order to comply with some particular set of rules, but am asking what move I ought to make at all, the relative sense of justification will be of no help whatever. At best, it can lead me to another query of the same sort on a new level and leave me equally undecided there. The nonrelative, or general, request for justification is, furthermore, one we often make or imply, and in the most important departments of life — belief, social relations, individual choices.

When we decide broad educational issues, we are often asking not merely what jibes with American practice, past or present, but what is generally justified, whether or not it is sanctioned by practice. The desire to evade this general question is understandable because it is difficult. But this evasion, I think, is responsible for much of the inadequacy of value discussions in education. Two tendencies seem to develop. A move is defended on grounds of its conformity with American practice, and the question of the justification of this practice itself is not considered at all. Or it is flatly asserted that it is the duty of the teacher to conform to the educational practices of his society, an assertion which, besides calling on a non-relative notion of duty that is itself uncriticized, seems to many schoolmen to be far from obvious.

Both the nature of this general request for justification of acts or moves and the possibilities for dealing with it may be illuminated by comparison with belief. To know that a belief is justified in relation to certain evidence does not provide general justification unless we have confidence in the evidence to begin with. With this initial confidence or credibility, we can proceed to provide ground for our belief. Roughly speaking, what we seem to do is to justify beliefs that not only hang together logically but also, as a family, preserve this initial credibility to the highest degree. We judge belief in question by its general impact on all other beliefs we have some confidence in. No matter how confident we are of a particular belief, we may decide to give it up if it conflicts with enough other beliefs in which we have a higher degree of confidence.

In practical situations, of course, we do not actually take all our beliefs into account. We concern ourselves, rather, with a limited domain of beliefs that we feel are interdependent. Furthermore, we do not make piecemeal estimates of the impact of each belief on the credibility of the mass of our beliefs in this domain. Instead, we use summary rules of varying generality. These rules are quite different from the rules of chess, however. They are not simply chosen at will but mirror, in a systematic and manageable form, our confidence in particular beliefs, classes of beliefs, and combinations of beliefs. Theoretically, there is no control (except perhaps that of the demand for consistency) over the design of games, no external requirements they need meet. The rules we use in general justification of belief are subject to the requirement that they be true to our credibilities on the whole. If a rule conflicts with our credibilities, it will be scrapped. We may say that rules are justified if they adequately reflect our credibilities by selecting those groups of beliefs that rank highest in this regard. A particular belief, then, is justified by its conformity with rules so justified. In effect, it is justified if it hangs together with that family of beliefs that as a whole commands our highest degree of confidence.

Formal logic as a code of valid inference provides an instructive example. People judged good and bad arguments long before the Aristotelian code. The latter was intended to systematize individual judgments and derives its authority from its adequacy as a systematization. When we now refer the justification of a particular inference to the ruling of Aristotle, our procedure depends on our confidence in this adequacy. It is a shorthand way of seeing whether or not the inference belongs with the mass of inferences we find most acceptable. Theoretically, no element in our procedure is free from future reappraisal. If, at some future time, we find that the existing code demands the abandonment of an inference that we value or the acceptance of an inference that we detest, we may alter the code. If an inference we are attached to conflicts with our code, we may give up the inference. There is a mutual adjustment of rules and instances toward selection of that family of instances that, as a whole, has the highest claim on our acceptance. An instance or rule that interferes with such selection is subject to rejection.

Codes of deductive or inductive logic may be construed as definitions of valid inference, not in the sense in which definitions may be used to introduce coined terms, but rather in the sense in which we set about defining a term already in common use, where this use controls our definition. The man who invented Scrabble was defining the game in the first sense by laying down rules that were labeled "Scrabble Rules." On the other hand, if a man from Mars were to arrive in the midst of a Scrabble tournament, without benefit of prior study of the official rules, and were asked after some hours to define the game, his task would be considerably different from that of the inventor. He would have to observe, guess, and test, to determine whether his proposed list of defining rules actually squared with the moves of the players. He would be attempting a definition in the second sense.

Even this task would be simpler than that of defining valid inference or, indeed, of defining any term in general use. For our man from Mars could always, as a final resort, check his definition against the official rule book. But for valid inference, as for other notions in general use, there is no official rule book at all. We start by proposing a definition that will serve as a simplified guide to usage but continue to check our proposal against actual use. We justify a particular use of a term by appeal, not just to any definition, but to one that we feel is itself justified by adequate codification of usage. In effect, we justify a particular use by checking it, through adequate definitions, against all our other uses.

These examples illustrate what we may expect and what we may hope to accomplish in the general justification of moves. Justification in relation to a given set of rules is useless unless the latter are themselves justified. But further relative justification by reference to other sets of rules is fruitless. Somewhere there must be control of rule-sets by initial commitments to moves themselves. The rules we appeal to in justifying social moves are rules that we hope are themselves adequate codifications of our initial commitments. The rules we appeal to select those families of moves that, as wholes, command our acceptance to the highest degree. Without initial commitments there can be no general justification, any more than there can be real or controlled definition without initial usage. But the fact that we are attached to a particular move does not mean that we cannot check it against all others we are committed to (by way of rules), any more than our attachment to a particular locution means that we cannot check it against others we hold proper (by way of controlled definitions). Our legal and moral rules serve, indeed, to guide the making of particular moves, but their guidance depends on their presumed adequacy in codifying our initial commitments to moves, on the whole.

In accordance with the two senses of justification just discussed, we may distinguish two levels of justification of educational decisions. On one level, justification involves conformity with a set of rules, reference to which may be implicitly understood. Here the issue is relative. We ask, "Is such and such decision justified according to rule-set S?" For many purposes, the question is legitimate and important, but the answer is often far from simple, even when the rules are fairly well defined. Relative justification is often a highly complicated, intellectually engaging business. To appreciate this fact, one need only recall that there is a whole profession (law) devoted to solving just such questions as the conformity of cases to rule. In education, such justification seems to relate not to specific laws but to broad social practices and traditions, the formulation of which has to be abstracted from our history and is itself a difficult job. Still, such traditions are often cited and used as a lever for changing laws as well as individual decisions.

Yet, legitimate as relative questions are, they do not exhaust our queries in educational contexts. We are not always interested merely in knowing that an educational move conforms to some code. We want to press the issue of deciding among codes. We ask that our moves be justified in terms of some justified code. If our previous analysis is correct, we are seeking justification by rules themselves controlled by the mass of our initial commitments. Of the two levels of justification in educational contexts, the relative type is familiar. The practical issues here may be complicated, and one factor often adds to the complexity: ostensible questions of relative conformity to a given rule may be decided, partly at least, on independent moral grounds. Yet, many of these issues seem familiar in outline. The understanding of general justification presents a more formidable task, since the formulation of relevant rules is of the difficult variety illustrated by the attempt of the man from Mars to codify the rules of a game by watching the play. We need to do something of this sort, but far more complex, since the activity involved is our own and touches on our fundamental commitments.

What rules do we appeal to in general justification of educational decisions on content? The answer to this question consists of a set of rules, not assertions, but the process of compiling an adequate set of rules is as empirical a task as can be imagined. Definitions are not assertions; but to compile a set of definitions one needs to call on all sorts of information, hypotheses, hunches — and the resulting set is always subject to recall, if not to falsification. It is with such qualifications that I offer my list of rules relating to decisions on curriculum. This list should be construed as a hypothesis, tentatively offered and inviting criticism. If it proves wrong, the process of correcting it will itself help clarify the grounds of our curricular decisions.

To simplify our considerations, let us avoid, at least at the outset, the problem of formulating special, complicated rules for deciding on content to be taught at a particular time and in particular circumstances. Let us consider instead all the content to be learned by a child during his formal schooling. Without worrying, for the moment, about the functions of particular segments of this content, let us ask instead what we expect of the content as a whole. Let us, further, state our rules in terms broad enough to allow for practical judgment in applying them to cases.

The guiding principle underlying the following rules is that educational content is to help the learner attain maximum self-sufficiency as economically as possible.

Presumably, self-sufficiency can be brought about economically or extravagantly; content should be selected that is judged most economical. Three types of economy are relevant. First, content should be economical of teaching effort and resources. Second, content should be economical of learners' effort. If a very strenuous way and a very easy way of learning something are otherwise equal, this rule would have us select the easier course. Some such principle seems to figure often in educational discussion. For example, the linking of subject matter to children's interests is often defended on grounds that this technique facilitates learning, and even opponents of this aproach do not argue that these grounds are irrelevant. It is important, however, to specify that our rules all contain a tacit clause: "other things being equal." It may be argued, for example, that the strenuous course makes for perseverance and other desirable habits, as the easy course does not. Here, however, other things are not equal, and the present rule fails to apply. Criticism of extremism in progressive education, for instance, may be interpreted as insisting that the "interest" principle never stands alone but is always qualified by the clause "other things being equal." Once qualified, the rule stands, in my opinion. There is no positive virtue in unnecessarily taxing the learner; his energy may better be saved for other tasks.

Finally, we must consider economy of subject matter; content should have maximum generalizability or transfer value. The notion of generalizability is, however, ambiguous. Accordingly, two types of subject-matter economy need to be distinguished. First, is there an empirically ascertainable tendency for the learning of some content to facilitate other learning? Presumably, this sort of question was at issue in the controversy over classics, and it was discussed in terms of empirical studies. Second, is the content sufficiently central logically to apply to a wide range of problems? This is not a psychological question but one that concerns the structure of available knowledge. Nevertheless, it is through some such principle of economy, in the logical sense, that we decide to teach physics rather than meteorology, for instance, where other considerations are balanced.

The most economical of content in all the aspects described must still meet the requirements of facilitating maximum self-sufficiency. It should be obvious that we do not necessarily, or ever, apply first the rules of economy and then the rules of self-sufficiency. These rules represent, rather, various requirements put on content, and we may apply them in various orders or simultaneously. We turn now to the rules of self-sufficiency.

Content should enable the learner to make responsible personal and moral decisions. Self-awareness, imaginative weighing of alternative courses of action, understanding of other people's choices and ways of life, decisiveness without rigidity, emancipation from stereotyped ways of thinking and perceiving — all these are bound up with the goal of personal and moral self-sufficiency. The problem of relating school subjects to such traits is an empirical one, but I think it extremely unlikely that a solution is to be found in the mechanical correlation of each subject to some one desired trait. Rather, the individual potentialities of each subject are likely to embrace many desired habits of mind. The use of literature to develop empathy is often noted. But to suppose that this function is restricted to literature is to impoverish our view of the potentialities of other subjects. Anthropology, history, and the other human sciences also offer opportunities to empathize. But even the natural sciences and mathematics may be seen not merely as technical equipment but as rich fields for the exercise of imagination, intuition, criticism, and independent judgment.

The making of responsible personal and moral decisions requires certain traits of character and habits of mind, but such decision making also requires reliable knowledge, embodied in several areas of study. Psychology, anthropology, and other human studies illumine personal choice; history, political science, economics, sociology and related areas illumine the social background of choices of career and ideology.

We have spoken of personal and moral self-sufficiency, but this is not enough. Since personal and moral decisions are not made in a vacuum, their execution requires technical skills of various sorts. Content should thus provide students with the technical or instrumental prerequisites for carrying out their decisions. What this goal may require in practice will vary from situation to situation; but, speaking generally, mathematics, languages, and the sciences are, I believe, indispensable subjects, while critical ability, personal security, and independent power of judgment in the light of evidence are traits of instrumental value in the pursuit of any ends. In creating curriculums, the notion of technical or instrumental self-sufficiency provides a counterbalance to emphases on the child's interest. For subjects unsupported by student interest may yet have high instrumental value for the students themselves. To avoid teaching them such subjects is, in the long run, to hamper their own future self-sufficiency, no matter what their future aims may be. Thus, it is misleading to label as an imposition of adult values the teaching of instrumentally valuable subjects.

Finally, beyond the power to make and to carry out decisions, self-sufficiency requires intellectual power. Content, that is, should provide theoretical sophistication to whatever degree possible. Here we may distinguish between logical, linguistic, and critical proficiency — the ability to formulate and appraise arguments in various domains, on the one hand, and acquaintance with basic information as well as with different modes of experience and perception, on the other. The danger here, a serious risk of general education programs, is that of superficiality. But ignorance is also a danger. How to avoid both ignorance and superficiality is the basic practical problem. I should hazard the opinion that the solution lies not in rapid survey courses but in the intensive cultivation of a small but significant variety of areas.

BEHAVIORAL OBJECTIVES IN CURRICULUM DESIGN: A CAUTIONARY NOTE

J. Myron Atkin

In certain influential circles, anyone who confesses to reservations about the use of behaviorally stated objectives for curriculum planning runs the risk of being labeled as the type of individual who would attack the virtues of motherhood. Bumper stickers have appeared at my own institution, and probably at yours, reading, STAMP OUT NONBEHAVIORAL OBJECTIVES. I trust that the person who prepared the stickers had humor as his primary aim; nevertheless the crusade for specificity of educational outcome has become intense and evangelical. The worthiness of this particular approach has come to be accepted as self-evident by ardent proponents, proponents who sometimes sound like the true believers who cluster about a new social or religious movement.

Behavioral objectives enthusiasts are warmly endorsed and embraced by the systems and operations analysis advocates, most educational technologists, and cost-benefit economists, the planning-programming budgeting system stylists, and many others. In fact, the behavioral objectives people are now near the center of curriculum decision making. Make no mistake; they have replaced the academicians and the general curriculum theorists — especially in the new electronically based education industries and in governmental planning agencies. The engineering model for educational research and development represents a forceful tide today. Those who have a few doubts about the effects of the tide had better be prepared to be considered uninitiated and naive, if not slightly addlepated and antiquarian.

To utilize the techniques for long-term planning and rational decision making that have been developed with such apparent success in the Department of Defense, and that are now being applied to a range of domestic and civilian problems, it is essential that hard data be secured. Otherwise these modes for developmental work and planning are severely

From *The Science Teacher, 35* (May, 1968), pp. 27–30. Reprinted by permission of the author and *The Science Teacher*.
NOTE: This paper was delivered at the annual meeting of the American Educational Research Association in Chicago on February 9, 1968. The author would like to acknowledge the assistance of Robert E. Stake, Associate Director, Center for Instructional Research and Curriculum Evaluation, University of Illinois, with whom several of the points developed in the paper were first discussed.

limited. Fuzzy and tentative statements of possible achievement and questions of conflict with respect to underlying values are not compatible with the new instructional systems management approaches – at least not with the present state of the art. In fact, delineating instructional objectives in terms of identifiable pupil behaviors or performances seems essential in 1968 for assessing the output of the educational system. Currently accepted wisdom does not seem to admit an alternative.

There are overwhelmingly useful purposes served by attempting to identify educational goals in nonambiguous terms. To plan rationally for a growing educational system, and to continue to justify relatively high public expenditures for education, it seems that we do need a firmer basis for making assessments and decisions than now exists. Current attention to specification of curriculum objectives in terms of pupil performance represents an attempt to provide direction for collection of data that will result in more informed choice among competing alternatives.

Efforts to identify educational outcomes in behavioral terms also provide a fertile ground for coping with interesting research problems and challenging technical puzzles. A world of educational research opens to the investigator when he has reliable measures of educational output (even when their validity for educational purposes is low). Pressures from researchers are difficult to resist since they do carry influence in the educational community, particularly in academic settings and in educational development laboratories.

Hence I am not unmindful of some of the possible benefits to be derived from attempts to rationalize our decision making processes through the use of behaviorally stated objectives. Schools need a basis for informed choice. And the care and feeding of educational researchers is a central part of my job. . . . However, many of the enthusiasts have given insufficient attention to underlying assumptions and broad questions of educational policy. I intend in this brief paper to highlight a few of these issues in the hope that the exercise might be productive of further and deeper discussion.

Several reservations about the use of behaviorally stated objectives for curriculum design will be catalogued here. But perhaps the fundamental problem, as I see it, lies in the easy assumption that we either know or can readily identify the educational objectives for which we strive, and thereafter the educational outcomes that result from our programs. One contention basic to my argument is that we presently are making progress toward thousands of goals in any existing educational program, progress of which we are perhaps dimly aware, can articulate only with great difficulty, and that contribute toward goals which are incompletely stated (or unrecognized), but which are often worthy.

For example, a child who is learning about mealworm behavior by blowing against the animal through a straw is probably learning much more than how this insect responds to a gentle stream of warm air. Let's assume for the moment that we can specify "behaviorally" all that he might learn about mealworm *behavior* (an arduous and never-ending task). In addition, in this "simple" activity, he is probably finding out something about interaction of objects, forces, humane treatment of animals, his own ability to manipulate the environment, structural characteristics of the larval form of certain insects, equilibrium, the results of doing an experiment at the suggestion of the teacher, the rewards of independent experimentation, the judgment of the curriculum developers in suggesting that children engage in such an exercise, possible uses of a plastic straw, and the length of time for which one individual might be engaged in a learning activity and still display a high degree of interest. I am sure there are many additional learnings, literally too numerous to mention in fewer than eight or ten pages. When any piece of curriculum is used with real people, there are important learning outcomes that cannot have been anticipated when the objectives were formulated. And of the relatively few outcomes that can be identified at all, a smaller number still are translatable readily in terms of student behavior. There is a possibility the cumulative side effects are at least as important as the intended main effects.

Multiply learning outcomes from the mealworm activity by all the various curriculum elements we attempt to build into a school day. Then multiply this by the number of days in a school year, and you have some indication of the oversimplification that *always* occurs when curriculum intents or outcomes are articulated in any form that is considered manageable.

If my argument has validity to this point, the possible implications are potentially dangerous. If identification of all worthwhile outcomes in behavioral terms comes to be commonly accepted and expected, then it is inevitable that, over time, the curriculum will tend to emphasize those elements which have been thus identified. Important outcomes which are detected only with great difficulty and which are translated only rarely into behavioral terms tend to atrophy. They disappear from the curriculum because we spend all the time allotted to us in teaching explicitly for the more readily specifiable learnings to which we have been directed.

We have a rough analogy in the use of tests. Prestigious examinations that are widely accepted and broadly used, such as the New York State Regents examinations, tend over time to determine the curriculum. Whether or not these examinations indeed measure all outcomes that are worth achieving, the curriculum regresses toward the objectives reflected by the test items. Delineation of lists of behavioral objectives, like broadly used testing programs, may admirably serve the educational researcher because it gives him indices of gross achievement as well as detail of particular achievement; it may also provide input for cost-benefit analysts and governmental planners at all levels because it gives them hard data with which to work; but the program in the schools may be affected detrimentally by the gradual disappearance of worthwhile learning activities for which we have not succeeded in establishing a one-to-one correspondence between curriculum elements and rather difficult to measure educational results.

Among the learning activities most readily lost are those that are long term and private in effect and those for which a single course provides only a small increment. If even that increment cannot be identified, it tends to lose out in the teacher's priority scheme because it is competing with other objectives which have been elaborately stated and to which he has been alerted. But I will get to the question of priority of objectives a bit later.

The second point I would like to develop relates to the effect of demands for behavioral specification on innovation. My claim here is that certain types of innovation, highly desirable ones, are hampered and frustrated by early demands for behavioral statements of objectives.

Let's focus on the curriculum reform movement of the past 15 years, the movement initiated by Max Beberman in 1952 when he began to design a mathematics program in order that the high school curriculum would reflect concepts central to modern mathematics. We have now seen curriculum development efforts, with this basic flavor, in many science fields, the social sciences, English, esthetics, etc. When one talks with the initiators of such projects, particularly at the beginning of their efforts, one finds that they do not begin by talking about the manner in which they would like to change pupils' behavior. Rather they are dissatisfied with existing curricula in their respective subject fields, and they want to build something new. If pressed, they might indicate that existing programs stress concepts considered trivial by those who practice the discipline. They might also say that the curriculum poorly reflects styles of intellectual inquiry in the various fields. Press them further and they might say that they want to build a new program that more accurately displays the "essence" of history, or physics, or economics, or whatever. Or a program that better transmits a comprehension of the elaborate and elegant interconnections among various concepts within the discipline.

If they are asked at an early stage just how they want pupils to behave differently, they are likely to look quite blank. Academicians in the various cognate fields do not speak the language of short-term or long-term behavioral change, as do many psychologists. In fact, if a hard-driving behaviorist attempts to force the issue and succeeds, one finds that the disciplinarians can come up with a list of behavioral goals that looks like a caricature of the subject field in question. (Witness the AAAS elementary school science program directed toward teaching "process.")

Further, early articulation of behavioral objectives by the curriculum developer inevitably tends to limit the range of his exploration. He becomes committed to designing programs that achieve these goals. Thus if specific objectives in behavioral terms are identified early, there tends to be a limiting element built into the new curriculum. The innovator is less alert to potentially productive tangents.

The effective curriculum developer typically begins with *general* objectives. He then refines the program through a series of successive approximations. He doesn't start with a blueprint, and he isn't in much of a hurry to get his ideas represented by a blueprint.

A situation is created in the newer curriculum design procedures based on behaviorally stated objectives in which scholars who do not talk a behavioral-change language are expected to describe their goals at a time when the intricate intellectual subtleties of their work may not be clear, even in the disciplinary language with which they are familiar. At the other end, the educational evaluator, the behavioral specifier, typically has very little understanding of the curriculum that is being designed — understanding with respect to the new view of the subject field that it affords. It is too much to expect that the behavioral analyst, or anyone else, recognize the shadings of meaning in various evolving economic theories, the complex applications of the intricacies of wave motion, or the richness of nuance reflected in a Stravinsky composition.

Yet despite this two-culture problem — finding a match between the behavioral analysts and the disciplinary scholars — we still find that an expectation is being created for early behavioral identification of essential outcomes.

(Individuals who are concerned with producing hard data reflecting educational outputs would run less risk of dampening innovation if they were to enter the curriculum development scene in a more unobtrusive fashion — and later — than is sometimes the case. The curriculum developer goes into the classroom with only a poorly articulated view of the changes he wants to make. Then he begins working with children to see what he can do. He revises. He develops new ideas. He continually modifies as he develops. *After* he has produced a program that seems pleasing, it might then be a productive exercise for the behavioral analyst to attempt with the curriculum developer to identify *some* of the ways in which children seem to be behaving differently. If this approach is taken I would caution, however, that observers be alert for long-term as well as short-term effects; subtle as well as obvious inputs.)

A third basic point to be emphasized relates to the question of instructional priorities, mentioned earlier. I think I have indicated that there is a vast library of goals that represent possible outcomes for any instructional program. A key educational task, and a task that is well handled by the effective teacher, is that of relating educational goals to the situation at hand — as well as relating the situation at hand to educational goals. It is impractical to pursue all goals thoroughly. And it does make a difference *when* you try to teach something. Considerable educational potential is lost when certain concepts are taught didactically. Let's assume that some third grade teacher considers it important to develop concepts related to sportsmanship. It would be a rather naive teacher who decided that she would undertake this task at 1:40 PM on Friday of next week. The experienced teacher has always realized that learnings related to such an area must be stressed in an appropriate context, and the context often cannot be planned.

Perhaps there is no problem in accepting this view with respect to a concept like sportsmanship, but I submit that a similar case can be made for a range of crucial cognitive outcomes that are basic to various subject matter fields. I use science for my examples because I know more about this field than about others. But equilibrium, successive approximation, symmetry, entropy, and conservation are pervasive ideas with a broad range of application. These ideas are taught with the richest meaning only when they are emphasized repeatedly in appropriate and varied contexts. Many of these contexts arise in classroom situations that are unplanned, but that have powerful potential. It is detrimental to learning not to capitalize on the opportune moments for effectively teaching one idea or another. Riveting the teacher's attention to a few behavioral goals provides him with blinders that may limit his range. Directing him to hundreds of goals leads to confusing, mechanical pedagogic style and loss of spontaneity.

A final point to be made in this paper relates to values, and it deals with a primary flaw in the consumption of much educational research. It is difficult to resist the assumption that those attributes which we can measure are the elements which we consider most important. This point relates to my first, but I feel that it is essential to emphasize the problem. The behavioral analyst seems to assume that for an objective to be worthwhile, we must have methods of observing progress. But worthwhile goals come first, not our methods for assessing progress toward these goals. Goals are derived from our needs and from our philosophies. They are not and should not be derived primarily from our measures. It borders on the irresponsible for those who exhort us to state objectives in behavioral terms to avoid the issue of determining worth. Inevitably there is an implication of worth behind any act of measurement. What the educational community poorly realizes at the moment is that behavioral goals may or may not be worthwhile. They are articulated from among the vast library of goals because they are stated relatively easily. Again, let's not assume that what we can presently measure necessarily represents our most important activity.

I hope that in this paper I have increased rather than decreased the possibilities for constructive discourse about the use of behavioral objectives for curriculum design. The issues here represent a few of the basic questions that seem crucial enough to be examined in an open forum that admits the possibility of fresh perspectives. Too much of the debate related to the use of behavioral objectives has been conducted in an argumentative style that characterizes discussions of fundamental religious views among adherents who are poorly informed. A constructive effort might be centered on identification of those issues which seem to be amenable to resolution by empirical means and those which do not. At any rate, I feel confident that efforts of the next few years will better inform us about the positive as well as negative potential inherent in a view of curriculum design that places the identification of behavioral objectives at the core.

THE STUDY OF "POLITICS" IN A UNIVERSITY
An Essay in Appropriateness

Michael Oakeshott

The shape of the education offered in a university, like everything else, is subject to change. Those changes which have been engendered within a university by the emergence of some branch of study claiming to be in a condition to take its place beside the others already being pursued by undergraduates have usually been well enough managed. Of course, mistakes have been made, and changes which were distortions have been allowed to take place, but no great damage has been suffered from this cause. The sponsors of a new "subject" of undergraduate study (and I am not here concerned with anything else) have usually not mistaken the sort of qualities they must claim on its behalf if they were to expect to launch it successfully; and in the early stages of its voyage they have been content to heave the lead every inch of the way. It was in this manner that schools of natural science, of modern history, of modern languages, of English literature, and of economics made their appearance in English universities, and studies such as international law and genetics established themselves. Their inception was sometimes eased by the benevolence of a patron content to endow what had been approved; but on every occasion what was admitted to the undergraduate curriculum was something which had already been pursued as an academic study for a generation or more before the proposal was made.

In recent times, however, the shape of university education has been modified by changes springing from a different source. Benefactors with favourite projects of their own, a persuasive and energetic body of evangelists with a patron in their pockets, a profession set upon winning the status of a university study for its *mystique,* or even a government, have made proposals designed to modify this shape. And though some of these proposals have turned out to be less disastrous than might have been forecast, they have not, on the whole, been so well managed. Greed, or the desire to appear abreast of the times, have often supervened to destroy both judgment and proper inquiry, and the shape of a university education has suffered some ill-considered and some destructive changes.

"Politics" found its way into English university education in a somewhat tortuous manner, quite unlike the simple and naive manner in which it entered American university education. Proper consideration was not altogether lacking; there seemed to be something in existing arrangements to which it could appropriately be attached; generous and opinionated benefactors were not absent; persuasive and energetic evangelists often played their part. It was supported by distinguished and sometimes scholarly sponsors; ancient (though, alas, irrelevant) precedent and continental practice (not very closely observed) was cited in its favor; the disposition of the times flattered it. The entry was effected unobtrusively and under a number of different names, which made it appear eligible for whatever interpretation its professors and teachers might be disposed to put upon it. And in these unusual circumstances it is not surprising that, alongside the engagement to teach "politics" to undergraduates, there should be (rather late in the day) an inquiry about what is to be taught. Confidence has not been lacking, but it has often been an irrelevant confidence in political opinions or in the existence of a suitable body of information to be imparted. And the inquiry itself has not always been well directed; it has been too easily silenced whenever a likely formula has been devised. "Politics," we have been told, is "the study of political behaviour," or "the study of power in society," or "the study of political institutions and political theory"; but there has been an ominous silence about the manner in which this study is to be conducted.

This condition of things I find to be unsatisfactory, and I propose to reopen this inquiry and to set it going in a somewhat different direction. The question I propose to consider is: What study under the plausible name of "Politics" is an appropriate component of a university education? And I propose to explore this theme by considering first the character of a university education in general.

I

We have a small stock of ideas at our disposal on this topic. We know that university education is after-school education; and we talk of it as "advanced" or "further" or "higher" or "specialized" education, education for adults, and so on. But these are all vague ideas, and if they were all we had we might have to confess that "university" education is not very different from any other sort of education. This, indeed, is what some people believe to be the case. They are content with the distinction between *elementary* and *advanced*, they think that advanced studies are characterized by greater detail and the requirement of more developed mental powers, and that consequently a 6th Form in a school begins to approximate to a university, and that a technical college is something like a university.

I do not, myself, believe any of this to be the case. I believe that university education is a specific sort of education, in some ways distinguished by its *elementary* character; and that although it is not the only sort of education and cannot take the place of any other sort, it is both important and unique. And I believe, consequently, that every component of a university education is properly a component in virtue of having a certain character or propensity.

Education I will take to be the process of learning, in circumstances of direction and restraint, how to recognize and make something of ourselves. Unavoidably, it is a two-fold process in which we enjoy an initiation into what for want of a better word I will call a "civilization," and in doing so discover our own talents and aptitudes in relation to that civilization and begin to cultivate and to use them. Learning to make something of ourselves in no context in particular is an impossibility; and the context appears not only in what is learned but also in the conditions of direction and restraint which belong to any education.

Some people think of a civilization as a stock of things like books, pictures, musical instruments and compositions, buildings, cities, landscapes, inventions, devices, machines and so on — in short, as the results of mankind having impressed itself upon a "natural" world. But this is an unduly restricted (indeed, an exceedingly primitive) understanding of that "second nature" (as Hegel called it) which is the context of our activity. The world into which we are initiated is composed, rather, of a stock of emotions, beliefs, images, ideas, manners of thinking, languages, skills, practices, and manners of activity out of which these "things" are generated. And consequently it is appropriate to think of it not as a stock but as a capital; that is, something known and enjoyed only in use. For none of these is fixed and finished; each is at once an achievement and a promise. This capital has been accumulated over hundreds of years. And in use it earns an interest, part of which is consumed in a current manner of living and part reinvested.

From another point of view, however, a civilization (and particularly ours) may be regarded as a conversation being carried on between a variety of human activities, each speaking with a voice, or in a language of its own; the activities (for example) represented in moral and practical endeavour, religious faith, philosophic reflection, artistic contemplation, and historical or scientific inquiry and explanation. And I call the manifold which these different manners of thinking and speaking compose a conversation, because the relations between them are not those of assertion and denial but the conversational relationships of acknowledgment and accommodation.

If, then, we recognize education as an initiation into a civilization, we may regard it as beginning to learn our way about a material, emotional, moral, and intellectual inheritance, and as learning to recognize the varieties of human utterance and to participate in the conversation they compose. And if we consider education as a process in which we discover and begin to cultivate ourselves, we may regard it as learning to recognize ourselves in the mirror of this civilization.

I do not claim universality for this image of education; it is merely the image (or part of it) which belongs to our civilization. But it is impossible to escape this sort of contingency, and we must take it as the context of our inquiry if anything relevant to our situation is to be said.

This education begins in the nursery where, for the most part, a child is learning to become at home in the natural-artificial world into which it was born. Here it is learning to use and to rely upon its senses and its limbs, to control its voice, to recognize its emotions, to suffer and overcome frustrations and to accommodate itself to others. It learns to speak, to play with words and at the same time to use and to understand the symbolic language of practical life. Here everything, or almost everything, is play. The product is insignificant; it is the activity it entails that matters. What is learned is all invested in the child itself; though, of course, being a child is having the command of a capital of pleasure and pain which earns an interest in the family life. And here, also, education has no specific orientation; it is not yet significantly concerned with individual talents and aptitudes, though these may show themselves early.

During school days this sort of nursery education continues. To begin with, reading is from books designed to teach the recognition of words; writing is an exercise in caligraphy rather than a significant composition; there is the endless repetition of playing scales and pieces designed to improve dexterity; foreign languages appear merely as saying the same things only in other words; arithmetic is an exercise in handling figures.

But gradually and imperceptibly a transformation takes place, or begins to take place; a transformation for which story-telling, singing, drawing, dancing, and social intercourse (that is, activities which unavoidably have some significant product, however transitory) have paved the way. *What* is read begins to be significant and to afford an entrance into literature; instrumental music becomes less a thing of the hand and eye than of the ear; and even foreign languages begin to appear as organizations of thoughts incapable of literal translation. In short, the intellectual capital of a civilization begins to be enjoyed and even used while the dexterities by which it is known and recognized are still imperfectly acquired. Or, perhaps, we have no more than a glimpse of how it might be enjoyed or used.

However, there is so much information to be gathered from so many different sources that, in school days, the intellectual inheritance appears much more like a stock of ideas, beliefs, perceptions, images, and so on, than a capital. We acquire much that we do not know how to use, and much that we never think of in terms of use, that is, of investment to generate something valuable on its own account. Learning here is borrowing raw material the possible uses of which remain concealed. Or, to put it another way, most of what is learned is immediately and automatically reinvested in the ability to learn so that it appears to have no specific communicable or shareable product.

School education, then, is not merely early education or simple education; it has a specific character. It is learning to speak before one has anything significant to say; and what is taught must have the qualities of being able to be learned without necessarily being understood, and of not being positively hurtful or nonsensical when learned in this way. Or, it may be said, what is taught must be capable of being learned without any previous recognition of ignorance: we do not begin to learn the multiplication tables because it suddenly dawns upon us we do not know the sum of nine 8s, nor the dates of the Kings of England because we know we do not know when Edward I came to the throne: we learn these things at school because we are told to learn them. And further, school education is without specific orientation; it is not yet concerned with individual talents and aptitudes, and if these show themselves (as they may) the design in school education is not to allow them to take charge. At school we are, quite properly, not permitted to follow our own inclinations.

But our "school days" are now a longer period than they used to be; never less than ten years and for some fourteen and fifteen years. And before they come to an end, features of "specialization" (as it is called) have begun to make their appearance in education. This I believe to be a mistake. But one can perceive the illusion of those who have imposed this mistake upon school education, and one can discern the misapplied pressures which have encouraged it. What it entails, however, is that the area of delusive overlap between this level of education and other levels has been increased and what belongs properly to school days is unfortunately curtailed in favour of a kind of "specialization" which belongs neither to a vocational education nor to a university education and which stands in the way of both; namely, a "specialization" in which the range of study is arbitrarily restricted without either an increase in depth or any specific orientation. Or, if there is an orientation, giving this school specialization a turn in a "vocational" direction, then it conflicts with the commendable English tradition that professional education should be seriously undertaken from its beginning and should not be preceded by a sort of pantomime: to learn a profession is to learn how to *do* something and the best preparation for this is not to learn how to act as if you were doing it.

Leaving school is, then, a momentous occasion. It is the signal for the appearance of a new attitude towards the capital we have inherited. Nevertheless, education continues, and it is apt to branch out in two different directions – which I shall call "vocational" education and "university" education. And these represent two different and to some extent complementary attitudes towards the capital which composes a civilization. They are two different kinds of education.

From one point of view, a civilization may be regarded as a collection of skills which together make possible and define a current manner of living. Learning one of these skills — that of a lawyer, a doctor, an accountant, an electrician, a farmer, a motor-mechanic or a commercial traveller — is borrowing an appropriate quantum of the total capital and learning to use it in such a manner that it earns an interest — an interest which, in principle, may be either expended in current consumption or reinvested to produce improvements in the skill itself. Each of these skills has an intellectual content, and many have a component of physical dexterity. A purely physical dexterity (pushing a barrow in Covent Garden comes near to this) is not a skill; it entails a negligible call upon the capital which composes a civilization, and the interest it earns (which is minimal) is all dispersed in current consumption. On the other hand, a skill with a large intellectual content is one which makes a considerable call upon capital (an emblem of which is the length of time required to learn it), and it is capable of earning a large unconsumed interest.

"Vocational" education is that in which these skills are acquired; and in this sort of education a civilization has the naive appearance of the things known and the skills practised which are entailed in a current manner of living. This manner of living is never, of course, fixed and finished; but it has some sort of general direction of contemporary movement depending upon these skills and others which may spring from them. Nor is it ever absolutely coherent: it is composed of skills which are on their way out and those which are on their way in: with us, heraldry and the handloom lie side by side with animal genetics and the computer.

Now, in respect of what is taught and learned in this "vocational" kind of education, some observations may be made. For most people it is an education in *one* skill. The skill may be complicated and may have a considerable intellectual content, or it may be simple and easily learned. But it is, essentially, a highly specialized education, and not only on account of its concentration upon a single skill. For, learning here means acquiring a specific body of knowledge and being able to move about within it with ease and confidence and to use it. The sort of familiarity which a carpenter or a builder may have with his tools and his materials often goes far beyond anything that is achieved, with *his* tools and materials, by a historian of the Papacy or a classical scholar; but there is a reason for this, namely, that his is a strictly circumscribed body of knowledge which does not significantly look outside itself. The design of a "vocational" education is to be concerned with current practice and always with what is believed to be known. How it came to be known, what errors and imperfections it has left behind, are no more significant than the practices of a sixteenth century printer are to a twentieth century linotype operator. The significant principle of specialization in this sort of education derives not only from the fact that most learners are concerned to acquire only one skill, but from its being concerned to impart to the learner what may be called the current achievement of a civilization in respect of a skill or practice needed in the contemporary world. In short, a "vocational" education, while it does not absolutely forbid it, is not concerned with that level of learning at which what is learned is capable of earning an unconsumed interest: it makes no provision for teaching people how to be ignorant; knowledge here is never the recognition of something absent.

And here I want to introduce a distinction which I propose to use later on: the distinction between a "language" (by which I mean a manner of thinking) and a "literature" or a "text" (by which I mean what has been said from time to time in a "language"). It is the distinction, for example, between the "language" of poetic imagination and a poem or a novel; or between the "language" or manner of thinking of a scientist and a textbook of geology or what may be called the current state of our geological knowledge.

Now, what is being studied in a "vocational" education is a "literature" or a "text" and not a "language." What is being acquired is a knowledge of what has been authoritatively said and not a familiarity with the manner of thinking which has generated what has been said. For example, in this sort of education what is learned is not how to think in a scientific manner, how to recognize a scientific problem or proposition, or how to use the "language" of science, but how to use those products of scientific thought which contribute to our current manner of living. Or, if this distinction seems to be too rigid, then it may be said that in a "vocational" education what is learnt is not a "living" language with a view to being able to speak it and say new things in it, but a "dead" language; and it is learnt merely for the purpose of reading a "literature" or a "text" in order to acquire the information it contains. The skill acquired is the skill of using the information, not of speaking the "language."

Further, "vocational" education is learning one of the skills of current life. Generally speaking only those skills which are currently practised are taught. This, where the skill is an ancient skill, sometimes entails drawing upon long accumulated capital; but in most cases it means drawing only upon capital accumulated in the last hundred years, or fifty, or even twenty: for the electrical engineer the world began the day before yesterday. In other words, a "vocational" education is education to fit a man to fill a specific place in a current manner of living, or to satisfy a current demand. And consequently, it is not utterly far-fetched (as it would be in the case of school education and, as we shall see, of a university education) to attempt to determine the number of persons who are needed to be trained in any particular skill if a current manner of living is to be sustained.

Now, as I understand it, university education is something entirely

different from both school and "vocational" education. It differs in respect
of what is taught (and the criterion for determining what is appropriate to be
taught), and in respect of how it is taught; and where it is a specialized
education (which it need not be, but a "vocational" education must be), the
principle of specialization is different from that which is characteristic of
"vocational" education. Or, if that seems too dogmatic, then I may say that I
think that there *is* a sort of education which is clearly different from both
school and "vocational" education, and I think it is the sort which for
centuries has been the concern of what we have hitherto called universities.
And, to put it briefly, a university education is unlike either a school or a
"vocational" education because it is an education in "languages" rather than
"literatures," and because it is concerned with the use and management of
explanatory languages (or modes of thought) and not prescriptive languages.
While a schoolboy may be a passionate reader and may acquire from some
books a store of information and from others a knowledge of himself and of
how to behave, at a university he will be invited to seek something different
from, perhaps, these same books. And he will come to understand that some
books whose information is out of date or whose prescriptive utterances (if
any) are unreliable – Gibbon or Stubbs, Dicey, Bagehot, Clark-Maxwell,
Adam Smith – and are therefore worthless in a "vocational" education,
nevertheless have something to offer appropriate to a university education.

First, a university is an association of persons, locally situated, engaged
in caring for and attending to the whole intellectual capital which composes a
civilization. It is concerned not merely to keep an intellectual inheritance
intact, but to be continuously recovering what has been lost, restoring what
has been neglected, collecting together what has been dissipated, repairing
what has been corrupted, reconsidering, reshaping, reorganizing, making more
intelligible, reissuing, and reinvesting. In principle, it works undistracted by
practical concerns; its current directions of interest are not determined by
any but academic considerations; the interest it earns is all reinvested.

This engagement is not, of course, confined to universities; many who
are not members of one of these associations take part in it. But nowhere else
is it undertaken in the manner I have described (that is, continuously and
exhaustively) except in a university. And when universities have been
negligent of this engagement, there has been nothing comparable to take their
place. For the essence is that it is a cooperative enterprise in which different
minds, critical of one another, are engaged; and that it concerns not merely
that part of our intellectual capital which has been accumulated in the last
fifty or a hundred years, and not merely those items which have some
immediate and practical contemporary relevance. And consequently, in a
society (such as ours) which has a high standard of practical relevance,
universities have often to be defended. And the usual defense is either to
show that they also contribute (as least obliquely) to the prosecution of

current undertakings, or to claim for them the status of an "amenity" — that is, a piece of costly nonsense protected by our sentimental attachment from designed and immediate destruction but not so well protected against the imposition upon them of alien directions of activity.

Secondly, in a university this intellectual capital appears not as an accumulated result, an authoritative doctrine, a reliable collection of information, or a current condition of knowledge, but as a variety of modes of thinking or directions of intellectual activity, each speaking with a voice, or in a "language" of its own, and related to one another conversationally — that is, not as assertion or denial, but as oblique recognition and accommodation. Science, for example, in a university, is not an encyclopaedia of information or the present state of our "physical" knowledge: it is a current activity, an explanatory manner of thinking and speaking being explored. And the same is true of mathematics, of philosophy, and of history: each is an idiom of thought, a "language" neither dead nor used simply to convey results, but in constant process of being explored and used. Doctrines, ideas, theories, which are used elsewhere to yield practical profits or to keep going a practical manner of living (like the Mendelian theory of biological inheritance, the molecular structure of matter, or Parkinson's law), in a university are recognized as temporary achievements whose value is their reinvestment value, and reinvestment here is being used in the exploration of the "language," the explanatory manner of thinking and speaking, to which they properly belong.

Thirdly, a university is a place, not merely of learning and research, but of education. And what distinguishes the education it offers is, first of all, the character of the place itself. To study in a university is not like studying under a learned private scholar, not is it like being taken on the grand tour by a lively and well-informed tutor. Each of these would be an education, but neither is a university education. Nor again, is it like being given the run of a first-class library. University education is the sort of education that may be enjoyed by having the run of a place where the activities I have described are going on and are going on in the manner I have described. And this distinguishes it, at once, from any other kind of education — school education, the education available in a place of specialized "vocational" training, in a polytechnic where a variety of skills are taught, in a specialized research institute which offers a few places for pupils, and that provided by a private scholar, engaged in one of these activities, who takes a pupil, as Döllinger took the young Acton. To be no more than a recognized spectator is to enjoy the opportunity of a kind of education which a different sort of place does not and cannot give, and which universities have offered in varying degrees ever since medieval times when they were places of "chivalric" disputation between Masters and Doctors and undergraduates were spectator-learners of a mystery. In short, there appears in a university what cannot (or cannot so easily) appear elsewhere, the image of a civilization as a manifold of different intellectual activities, a conversation between different modes of thinking; and this determines the character of the education it offers.

Finally, a university is an association of persons engaged in formal teaching. In this respect it is distinguished by the engagements of the teachers. As teachers, they may be either better or worse than those elsewhere; but they are different because they are themselves learners engaged in learning something other than what they undertake to teach. They are not people with a set of conclusions, facts, truths, dogmas, etc., ready to impart or with a well-tried doctrine to hand out; nor are they people who make it their main business to be familiar with what may be called "the current state of knowledge" in their department of study: each is a person engaged in the activity of exploring a particular mode of thought in particular connections.

Nevertheless, *what* they teach is not what they themselves are in process of learning, nor is it what they may have learned or discovered yesterday. As scholars they may live on what are called the "frontiers of knowledge," but as teachers they must be something other than frontiersmen. Nor, again, is what they teach exactly the activity in which they are themselves engaged: their pupils are not exactly apprentices to an activity. A scientist, an historian, or a philosopher does not teach his pupils to be scientists, historians, or philosophers. That is to say, his engagement as a teacher is not merely to educate possible successors to himself — though some of his pupils may turn out to be this. What a university teacher has, and what (because he is not distracted by considerations of immediate usefulness or contemporary appropriateness) he may impart, is familiarity with the modes of thought, the "languages" which, from one point of view, compose the whole intellectual capital of a civilization. What a university has to offer is not information but practice in thinking; and not practice in thinking in no manner in particular but in specific manners each capable of reaching its own characteristic kind of conclusions. And what undergraduates may get at a university, and nowhere else in such favourable circumstances, is some understanding of what it is to think historically, mathematically, scientifically, or philosophically, and some understanding of these not as "subjects" but as living "languages," and of those who explore and speak them as being engaged in explanatory enterprises of different sorts.

Going further, a university may be recognized as an association of teachers of this sort whose activity reflects some beliefs about how this sort of teaching may best be carried on. And the most important of these beliefs (now, alas, somewhat eroded) is that the proper way to impart a mode of thinking (that is, a "language") is in conjunction with the study of an appropriate "literature" or "text": the belief that learning to think scientifically is best achieved by studying, not some so-called "scientific method," but some particular branch of science; and learning to think historically is to be achieved, not by studying something called "the historical method," but by observing and following an historian at work upon a particular piece or aspect of the past. This (but only to the unwary) may suggest an approximation of university to "vocational" education, but that this is an illusion is revealed when we observe that in a university education a "text" is understood, not as an organization of information but as the paradigm of a "language." Consequently, with the recognition in a university that "languages" may be most appropriately studied in conjunction with "literatures" goes the recognition that some "literatures" (that is, some branches of scientific study, some periods or passages of history, some legal systems, some philosophical writers) are in a more appropriate condition to be studied, or offer a clearer paradigm of the "language" concerned, and that it is these "literatures" or "texts," and for these reasons, that the undergraduate is encouraged to read: chemistry rather than solar physics; the history of medieval England rather than of contemporary Java; Roman Law rather than Hittite or Celtic; Aristotle, Hume, or Kant rather than Democritus, Leibnitz, Rickert, or Bergson. And this is a convenient and appropriate way of determining what is to be studied because it leaves room for change and it indicates a criterion by which a branch of learning is to be judged in respect of undergraduate study – a criterion which is purely paedagogic and has nothing whatever to do with vocational or other extraneous considerations, such as the current academic interest of scholars, which may be in an entirely unsuitable condition for undergraduate pursuit.

From this enterprise of teaching undergraduates something about the intellectual capital of our civilization there has emerged, in general, two marginally different manners of setting it out for undergraduate study. Two sorts of "specialized" study have established themselves. In the one (perhaps best represented by "Greats"), a variety of modes of thinking – e.g. historical, philosophical, poetic, legal, and perhaps scientific – are studied, but in connection with "literatures" or "texts" in the Greek and Latin tongues or having place in the world of classical antiquity. In the other (represented by Schools of Modern History, of Mathematics, of Natural Science, etc.), a single "language," or mode of thought, is studied in connection with whatever "literatures" or "texts" there may be available in a suitable condition from time to time – e.g., the Constitutional History of Medieval England, Chemistry, Physics, Geology, etc., the English Law of Property, the poetry of sixteenth century England, and so on. What determines the choice of these "literatures" rather than others is their appropriateness to represent modes of thought; and this is recognized to depend upon their current condition, and (of course) their appropriateness for study by undergraduates who had received a certain sort of school education.

This, then, is what I understand by university education. It is not something nebulous or indistinct, but something clear, unmistakable and distinct from every other sort of education. To be an undergraduate is to enjoy the "leisure" which is denoted by thinking without having to think in the pragmatic terms of action and talking without having to speak in terms of prescription or practical advice – the "leisure," in short, which distinguishes the peculiar academic engagement of explanation. And the belief that it is valuable, even for those who are to pass their lives in practical occupations of one sort or another and for whom (in that connection) a "vocational" education may also be appropriate, to spend three years in which attention (so far as their studies are concerned) is expressly abstracted from prescriptive manners of thinking in order to concentrate it, not merely upon explanations, but upon the understanding of explanatory enterprises, is the belief in which the whole specific character of a university education is abridged. And anyone who wishes to impose a different character upon university education will not only be transforming the character of universities but will also have taken a decisive step in a direction which points to the removal from the scene of this kind of education.

II

Now, it may be supposed that, under the name of "politics" (or some equivalent word), there is something appropriate to be taught and learned in each of the three kinds or levels of education I have mentioned – school, "vocational," and university education. Politics, in fact, is talked and written about, studied and taught in a variety of manners which readily distinguish themselves from one another. We may, indeed, find that our present circumstances are not free from confusion, "politics" being taught (for example) in universities in a manner more appropriate to some other kind of education; but (with this sketch of the respective characters of these sorts of education before us) it should not be impossible to discern the kind of political study appropriate to each.

In respect of school-education there is, I think, little difficulty in determining what in general is appropriate to be taught in this connection. It is, in the first place, something suitable to be learned by everybody, for one of the principles of school education is that it is without significant orientation. And further, it is something that may be learned without the point of learning it being evident to the learner, and something that if learned in this way is not positively harmful or nonsensical. In the thoughts of the teacher it may be either a propaedeutic (like Greek grammar to the reading of Greek poetry) or it may compose a stock of information considered to have some general usefulness on its own account; but in the thoughts of the learner it need not have any more attachment to a specific usefulness than geometry, algebra, or physical geography. In short, what is appropriate is something which offers an introduction to an aspect of a civilization (the civilization which is the pupils' inheritance) understood as a stock of ideas, beliefs, images, practices, etc., rather than as a capital. And this, surely, was the character of "civics" as it used to be taught in schools and is the character of its successor in our school education, namely, "current affairs": an introduction to the current activities of governments and to the relevant structures and practices with some attention to the beliefs and opinions which may be held to illuminate them. Note, perhaps, a very inspiring study, and in its more desiccated passages (e.g., the duties of a town clerk, the House of Commons at work, and the pronouncements of a Kennedy, a Khrushchev, or a Castro) unlike Greek irregular verbs in holding out no evident promise of better things to come. Nevertheless, it is capable of defence as part of a school education on the ground that, with us, politics is everybody's business; and because this sort of study is no more misleading than many other school studies (like economics and history) are bound to be. At least it is something to modify the mystery of the world as it appears in the newspapers, and it entails nothing to prohibit a more profound interest in public affairs such as occasionally (along with county cricket, space travel and church brasses) makes its appearance among schoolboys. The interest it serves is an interest in public affairs.

Nor, I think, is there any greater difficulty in determining the character of what may be called a professional or "vocational" education in politics, that is, an education designed specifically for those who are called upon or who wish to engage in political activity. A "vocational" education (in the sense in which I am using the expression) may appear when three general conditions are satisfied, and it is apt to appear, in some form or other, whenever these conditions are satisfied. First, there must be a specific skill generally recognized to be entailed in a current manner of living; secondly, there must be something in connection with this skill which is capable of being taught, although it may also require practice which cannot formally be taught before the skill itself can be effectively exercised; and thirdly, there must be people who desire to exercise this skill and therefore desire to be educated in it. And it may plausibly be supposed that all these conditions are satisfied in respect of what we recognize as political activity – that is, activity concerned with governing and the instruments of government. Politics is unmistakably one of the skills entailed in our current manner of living. And not only are there people who engage in it professionally (politicians, party managers, agents, and their assistants), but, as in respect of other professional skills (only more so), there are occasional participants or the servants of participants (like government or Trade Union officials) to whom the knowledge which is the stock-in-trade of the professional is also relevant.

Indeed, the particular style of politics which has now imposed itself upon the world calls for and accommodates large numbers of these occasional participants, to say nothing of the political commentators and entertainers who have become a feature of our life and who require this information in their daily business. In these circumstances a "vocational" education in politics has to be recognized as appropriate to a larger, more miscellaneous, and consequently less precisely determined set of students than is the case in some (but not in all) other avocations. And if we hesitate to follow those who find it to be an appropriate "vocational" education for every citizen in a "democracy," or for a sufficient number to leaven the whole, then it may perhaps be recognized as a "vocational" education appropriate to those who are, or who wish to be, politically self-conscious. But this does not entail any modification of its character as a "vocational" education which here, as elsewhere, is an education designed to impart a body of reliable knowledge necessary in the successful exercise of a more or less particularized practical activity. And if the knowledge imparted here is used by some continuously and by others intermittently, by some professionally and by others incidentally, this does not distinguish it from (for example) the knowledge imparted in a professional legal education which is a necessary part of the equipment not only of those who practise the law as a profession but also of many who are engaged in many other businesses and occupations. And lastly, whatever doubts we may have about its extent, reliability and coherence (and whatever else we may think it desirable for a participator in politics to know), it would be absurdly captious to take the view that, in connection with politics, there is no information about current practices and current manners of thinking and speaking such as is the characteristic knowledge imparted in a "vocational" education, or that this knowledge is incapable of being taught. Indeed, there is a vast quantity of this information, and much of it is so obscurely situated that it requires the persistence of a beaver to discover it and the mind of a chancery barrister to put it in order. On the face of it there is no reason why one should not undertake to teach politics as one might undertake to teach plumbing, homemaking, librarianship, farming or how to run a bassoon factory; and this teaching is, in fact, undertaken.

And, to confirm this view, there already exists an extensive political literature (both books and periodicals), not devoid of general interest and capable of answering the curiosity of the unengaged, but satisfying the specification of a literature appropriate to a "vocational" education. It is concerned with current practice; it is designed to convey the sort of information about the conduct of public affairs (what to do and how to do it) which anyone called upon or volunteering to participate needs to know; and the authors of it (by reason of their skill and knowledge) are frequently invited to perform the services of political architects or to act as consultants in the conduct of administration or of foreign affairs.

In this unsophisticated literature the properties of political and administrative devices such as federalism, second chambers, committees of inquiry, public corporations, taxes on capital, sumptuary laws, concentrations of power, etc., are dispassionately examined; the behaviour of voters is studied; the organization and propensities of different political parties are investigated; pressure groups, "establishments," and *élites* are detected; policies are scrutinized in respect of their formation and consequences; the relative efficiency of different administrative areas and of the various methods of communication in current use are considered; and a vast array of information about the current politics of other countries is collected and marshalled ready for those who have to take (or who want to take) decisions or make judgments about the conduct of foreign affairs. And at a somewhat lower level, there are handbooks designed for the guidance and instruction of the inferior ranks of administrators. Of course, all this outdistances in intellectual content (and sometimes in unengaged general interest) the technical literature concerned, for example, with building houses or growing tomatoes; but the disproportion is not overwhelming, and in design and purport all these technical literatures are indistinguishable from one another.

Moreover, technical literatures, even those in the highest class (like those of law or medicine), are apt to have their popular counterparts; and there seems little to stand in the way of the appearance of a vulgar counterpart to this literature of political inquiry and instruction. A little book on *How to Restore old Cottages* may be flanked on the bookstalls by one on *How to Restore old Monarchies*; an article on "A face-lift for the kitchen: new and exciting materials" in a *Do It Yourself* magazine will be followed by others on "Dos and Don'ts in making a Revolution," "How to win an Election," and "What you should know about Public Corporations." Indeed, writings of this kind (with perhaps less obvious titles) have been available for more than a century.

Now, the contemplation of all these investigations has generated the vision of a modern "science" of government and administration, a growing body of what is believed to be well-tested information, daily becoming more comprehensive, about the operation and reliability of the various processes, projects, policies, materials and devices available in current political and administrative activity "to solve the political and governmental problems which confront mankind."

The descriptions we have of this so-called "master science"[1] do not present it as an enterprise in which events are understood in terms of the operation of general laws, but (more modestly) as "a systematic, organized, teachable body of knowledge" springing from the study of political ideas, of

1. W. A. Robson, *The University Teaching of the Social Sciences – Political Science,* UNESCO, 1954; H. J. Blackham, *Political Discipline in a Free Society.*

the constitutions and processes of governments, of the structure and operation of political parties and groups, of the generation of public policy and public opinion and of the relations between states.[2] From this knowledge it is designed to elicit a "body of rational principles" concerning political activity and the administration of public affairs. And when we consider what we are told about "the hopes and expectations reposed in this master science," the design in collecting together this body of knowledge and the design in teaching it, we are left in no doubt that it is intended to be the material of an education in political and administrative activity. The "authentic aims" of this science are: "to study the moral problems of mankind in order to establish the principles of collective morality"; to formulate "the principles which should inspire political organization and action"; "to throw light on political ideas and political action in order that the government of man may be improved"; "to throw some light on the great problems of our time: such as the problem of avoiding war, of increasing international peace and security, of extending freedom, of assisting the development of backward countries, of preventing the exploitation of native races, of using government as a means of raising living standards and promoting prosperity, of banishing ignorance, squalor, destitution, and disease through the social services, of increasing welfare, happiness and the dignity of mankind"; "to solve the political and governmental problems which confront mankind"; "to assuage the maladies and struggles and conflicts of men in society"; "to show the nations how to achieve peace and security." And the design in teaching this science is to equip the student "to comprehend the important political issues of the day"; "to participate effectively in political discussion, to grasp the important questions of policy, to withstand the flattery of the demagogue, to resist the lies of the dictator or the promises of the imposter, to distinguish between propaganda and truth, to bring informed criticism to bear on public authorities, or to appreciate the criteria by which government action can be appraised"; and "to give the voter an intelligent interest in the government of his country" without which "democracy cannot work effectively." In short, what is described here is unmistakably a "vocational" education in politics; not a training appropriate only to a would-be official (though there is much here which is specially appropriate to those who engage professionally in politics or administration), but an education designed for participants in one of the skills which sustain our current manner of living, designed to improve the quality of their participation, and defended on account of "the burning practical importance" of the problems with which this skill is concerned. It is an education with the same sort of design as that of a farmer or a medical practitioner, but (it is alleged) of unmistakably greater importance.

2. This is sometimes generalized as the study of the manifestations, processes, scope, results and moral basis of power in society.

But avoiding flights of fancy, exaggerated expectations, and a certain incoherence between what is set for study and the conclusions designed to be reached, it is difficult to disagree with the proposition that the serious inquiries I have mentioned, whose virtue is to investigate current political ideas and practices in a manner relevant to their use in political and administrative activity, intimate a body of knowledge capable of being taught and appropriate to be taught in a "vocational" education in politics. The current state of our knowledge about voting habits, about the organization of the Conservative Party, about the President of the U. S. A., about the propensities of Trade Unions, and about the structure, control and administration of Public Corporations are as tangible pieces of information as the current state of our knowledge about the properties of the materials and devices used in domestic plumbing. And why should a voter, a political entertainer, a politician, a political agent, or a local government official know less about his business than a doctor, a solicitor, or a librarian?

Moreover, the other main aspect of political activity is, on the evidence, not less susceptible of similar treatment. Politics has always been three-quarters talk, and not to know how to use the current vocabulary of politics is a serious hindrance to anyone who, either as an amateur or as a professional, wishes to participate in the activity. The language of politics is the language of desire and aversion, of preference and choice, of approval and disapproval, of praise and blame, of persuasion, injunction, accusation, and threat. It is the language in which we make promises, ask for support, recommend beliefs and actions, devise and commend administrative expedients, and organize the beliefs and opinions of others in such a manner that policy may be effectively and economically executed: in short, it is the language of everyday, practical life. But men engaged in political activity (like others engaged in business or in the promotion of a religion), in order to make their opinions and actions more attractive, are apt to recommend them in the idiom of general ideas; and in order to make the opinions and actions of others less attractive are apt to denigrate them in terms of general ideas. In this manner (and often by appropriating words and expressions originally designed for a wholly different use) the current vocabulary of politics has made its appearance. It contains such words and expressions as these: democratic, liberal, equal, natural, human, social, arbitrary, constitutional, planned, integrated, communist, provocative, feudal, conservative, progressive, capitalist, national, reactionary, revolutionary, fascist, privileged, private, public, socialist; open, closed, acquisitive, affluent, responsible and irresponsible societies; the international order, party, faction, welfare, and amenity. It is a complicated vocabulary, and to teach its use is clearly appropriate to a "vocational" education in politics. And here, also, there is a literature whose virtue (if not design) is to teach the use of this vocabulary. Books are produced every day which are concerned to teach us how to think politically and to provide an education for those whose business or pleasure it is to speak the current language of politics. Indeed, an expression has been invented (or seconded) to specify this literature; it is the so-called literature of 'political theory'; and 'political theories' (in this usage) are appropriately qualified by adjectives such as 'democratic', 'socialist', 'conservative', 'liberal', 'progressive' — that is, by adjectives which themselves belong to the current vocabulary of politics and are designed to indicate the political colour of the theories.

A "vocational" education in politics, then, is not a merely imagined possibility; the skills it is designed to impart are among the most frequently (and most unskilfully) practised in our current manner of living, and the words and ideas it is designed to familiarize us with are those most frequently used in public discussion: there is unmistakably appropriate material for composing a curriculum for such an education. And whatever the limitations of the "science" of government to be imparted in this education, I am not among those who believe that it must be nugatory because it lacks the imposing generalizations of some other sciences. It can without difficulty sustain its character as a compendium of reliable information useful for those engaged in political activity.[3] And when we consider the relative complexity of this skill, the mixture of amateurism and professionalism which political and administrative activity among us provokes, and the absence of settled professional standards, it is not at all surprising, either that the curriculum of such an education should still lack authoritative definition, or that the institutions offering such an education should (outside the U. S. A., Russia and China) remain comparatively few.

But there is another reason why the appearance of the possibility of a "vocational" education in politics provoked, in this country, no great efflorescence of educational institutions to exploit it. For when, at long last, observation and reflection on current political activity had generated a body of information about government and administration, and when professional political skill ceased to be the exclusive business of Kings and hereditary ruling classes, when (in short) government ceased to be a mystery, and after a suitable interval had elapsed, politics *eo nomine* began to be taught in our universities; and the manner in which it was taught was that which is appropriate to a "vocational" education. Unsuspecting undergraduates, most of whom had no thought of becoming professional politicians or administrators, but in a few of whom there was perhaps a vague desire to be politically self-conscious coupled with an inability to do it for themselves, found imposed upon them a curriculum of study of unimaginable dreariness in which they learned the structures of the current constitutions of the world

---

3. This, however, is the most that can be said for it. The larger claims made on behalf of this "master science" rest either upon the moral prejudices of those who make them (and which we cannot all be expected to share), or upon a naive ethical naturalism.

and whose anatomical studies were enlivened only by some idle political gossip and some tendentious speculation about current policy. As a "vocational" education in politics it was, of course, worthless; and yet the information it offered, and the manner in which it was offered, could have no conceivable interest to anyone except those whose heads were full of the enterprise of participating in political activity or to persons with the insatiable curiosity of a concierge. It merely provided a spurious academic focus for whatever political interest there might be about, and it was saved from manifest academic disgrace by the intrusion of a little genuine historical study. Together with this went the study of some notable books (like Plato's *Republic,* Hobbes's *Leviathan,* Rousseau's *du Contrat Social,* Mill's essay on *Liberty,* and Bosanquet's *Philosophical Theory of the State*) and some less notable tracts, believed to be in some sense "about politics" and therefore assumed to have a political "ideal," or programme, or policy, or device to recommend. And the manner in which they were studied was designed to elicit and criticize this programme: they were recognized, in short, as books of "political theory."[4] Indeed, I can describe the manner in which these books were read only as a mixture between the manner in which one might read an out-of-date textbook on naval architecture and the manner in which one might study a current election manifesto. The result was that we were alive only to the political quaintness (or enormity) of these books, and our attention was narrowed down to listening either for the political *faux pas* or for the echos of political modernity.

Some, of course, escaped. There were individuals who never surrendered to it; those universities in which "politics" had long had its place as an occasion for historical or philosophical study were in some degree fortified against it; and, in any case, English universities are far less deeply compromised than those in America. But this regrettable disposition — regrettable because it conflicted with the most deeply rooted traditions of university education — set a course for "politics" in those universities in which it established itself as an independent "subject" of undergraduate study, a course from which divergence has been difficult even where it has been desired.

It was, no doubt, long ago agreed that this was a manner of studying politics (now perhaps to be found only in American textbooks) not entirely appropriate in a university; and many improvements have been made. But these improvements have, for the most part, been directed not to doing something else more appropriate in a university education, but to doing better what had been ill done before. We have added the study of operation

---

4. And we had commentaries, like Hobhouse's *Metaphysical Theory of the State* (and later Crossman on *Plato Today* and Popper on *The Open Society and its Enemies*), to encourage us in this recognition.

to the study of structure; we have added political parties, pressure groups, civil services, local authorities and public corporations to the study of the constitutions of governments; we have uncovered obscure passages in political organization; we have heard the call of political sociology; we have explored what can only be called the curiosities of politics; and we have tried to elicit information of more general interest by comparing one set of structures with another. In short, we have been neither idle nor unadventurous; but, in the main, we have continued to work at the same level of information as the pioneers of political study in universities — a level appropriate only to a "vocational" education. And in respect of these classics of political reflection, our pupils are still encouraged to read them in order to discover the injunctions about political conduct they are believed to contain in order to reflect upon the appropriateness to us of these injunctions; and they are still written about in this manner. The search for anything in the present teaching of "politics" in our universities (wherever that teaching has firmly established itself) which separates it decisively and unmistakably from what is appropriate to what I have called a "vocational" education in politics, anything which carries us beyond the study of "literatures" as repositories of information to the study of a "language" or a manner of thinking, is not very rewarding. Indeed, the most comprehensive recent description of the teaching of "politics" in universities (from which I have already quoted) accepts without misgiving or apology this "vocational" or participatory study as appropriate to a university education. No doubt there is a certain amount of confusion, but there is little inclination to look in any other direction.

Now, I may be told I have overlooked two directions of movement both of which point to a manner of study which, it may be alleged, has gone some way to emancipate the teaching of "politics" in a university from this "vocational" disposition and to give it what is somewhat naively called a "liberal" character. First, it will be said, we are no longer content to observe and to impart the miscellaneous results of our observation; we have outgrown political anatomy. Instead, we analyse (blessed word) and teach the art of analysis, we compare (no less blessed word) and teach the science of making comparisons, we make ideal models, we construct hypotheses, we formulate the problems of the future and seek solutions. And this (or some of it) may, no doubt, be counted to us as merit: nobody can say we are simple-minded in our study of politics. But none of it has served (or is even designed) to set us on to some other questions than the essentially "vocational" questions: How does it work? How can it be improved? Is it democratic? and so on. And much of it (because it has come to be concerned with imaginary "systems" and "processes," "powers," "establishments" and *élites*, stereotypes of one sort or another) diverts our attention from the often irregular character of political organizations and events, and thus makes our "vocational" education less good than it might be. In short, and in spite of these complexities and subtleties which have given to our original naivety a touch of sophistication, we are still disposed to teach "politics" in universities as a kind of staff-duties course in politics.

But secondly, it will be said, in spite of our rather lamentable tendency to urge our pupils to acquaint themselves with the patterns and structures of current politics (that is, with the contents of political "texts") and to provide for their needs by engaging experts on an ever increasing number of these "texts," experts in the political "systems" of India and Iraq, of Ghana and Indonesia, we do make a notable attempt to teach them how to use a "language," namely, the language of politics. The difference between ourselves and the pioneers of "politics" in universities, it will be said, is that for us the study of the dull and doubtful detail of political structures and operations is designed as a means of teaching our pupils how to think politically. In short we have begun to recognize that "politics" in a university is appropriately concerned with the study of "language" and with "literatures" only as paradigms of this "language." Yet, when we consider the efforts made to persuade our pupils to acquaint themselves with as large as possible a number of these "texts," our disposition to recognize the "authority" of those who are themselves engaged in political activity (or who have retired from it) and our recognition that there is a problem of "bias" in teaching "politics" in a university (all of which can relate only to a "vocational" political education), we may perhaps doubt the truth of this claim. But, even assuming this difference between ourselves and the pioneers is well observed, something else is needed to distinguish our enterprise from that of a "vocational" education in politics. All that is being alleged here is that we offer a "vocational" education superior to that which used to be offered.

To be brief, the difference lies in the nature of the "languages" concerned. To teach the language of current politics is an essential part of a "vocational" education in politics, because skill in using this language, and being familiar with the manners of thinking it represents, is an essential part of political activity. But this is not a language of the same kind as the "languages" which I have suggested it is the distinctive feature of a university education to put before undergraduates. These "languages" – the "languages" of history, of philosophy, of science and of mathematics – are all of them *explanatory* languages; each of them represents a specific mode of explanation. But the language of politics is not a language of explanation, any more than the languages of poetry or moral conduct are languages of explanation. There is no specifically "political" explanation of anything: the word 'politics' stands for holding certain kinds of beliefs and opinions, making certain kinds of judgments, performing certain kinds of actions, and thinking in terms of certain practical, not explanatory, considerabilities. If there is a manner of thinking and speaking that can properly be called 'political', the appropriate business of a university in respect of it is not to use it, or to teach the use of it, but to explain it — that is, to bring to bear upon it one or more of the recognized modes of explanation. If the expression 'political activity' stands for something which plausibly offers itself to be understood and to be explained, the questions a teacher of "politics" in a university should ask himself are: In what manner do I design to explain it? Into what explanatory "language" or "languages" should I translate it? What "languages" of explanation may an undergraduate find himself learning to use and to manage in connection with politics?

Now, I believe that, if we put behind us the alluring but inappropriate "vocational" enterprise of teaching the use and management of the language of politics, the study of "politics" at a university may afford an undergraduate the opportunity of acquainting himself with two different manners of understanding, two modes of thought, two explanatory "languages," namely, the "languages" of history and of philosophy. What falls outside these is, I think, one or other of these manners of thinking disguised in some not very elegant fancy dress. Each of these manners of thinking is a genuine mode of explanation: each operates with clear criteria of relevance; each is capable of reaching conclusions appropriate to itself; in each it may be said that this or that is an error, but also (and more significantly) that this or that is out of character; and statements made in these "languages" do not pretend to have injunctive force. Thus, the appropriate engagement of an undergraduate student of "politics" at a university will be to be taught and to learn something about the modes of thought and manners of speaking of an historian and a philosopher, and to do this in connection with politics, while others (in other Schools) are doing it in other connections. While one undergraduate may acquire some insight into the manner in which an historian thinks and speaks and understands and explains in connection with the English wool trade in the fifteenth century, or in connection with the Papacy in the sixteenth century (these being the chosen "texts"), another, in a School of "Politics," may do the same thing in connection with a political party, the House of Commons, Machiavelli's *Prince* or the Haldane Report. And while an undergraduate in a School of Philosophy may study Kant's *Critique of Pure Reason* (and if he does so in a university manner it is not merely to acquaint himself with Kant's conclusions but to understand Kant's problems and to acquire the connoisseurship which can recognize a philosophical argument), so an undergraduate in a School of "Politics" may read Hobbes's *Leviathan* or Hegel's *Philosophy of Right* and hope to learn from his study something about the philosophical mode of thinking. And if it should turn out that politics is an appropriate occasion for acquiring a familiarity with other authentic languages of explanation, then the opportunity may properly be taken.[5] But it is only in this manner that a study of "politics" unmistakably distinguished from a "vocational" study, and one that can sustain a place in a specifically university kind of education, can appear.

The main hindrance to its doing so is the "vocational" disposition with which "politics" has come to establish itself in a university education and which it has never succeeded in throwing off. I do not think this disposition among university teachers of "politics" is commonly the result of profound reflection, although some are held to it with a passionate attachment which they have tried their hands at defending. It springs, rather, from their being themselves primarily interested in politics in the vulgar sense and in the problems of administration, from their being impressed with the information about political and administrative activity believed to be available, and from an inability to understand why this information should not be imparted as a university education to undergraduates, or, indeed, what else there is plausibly to teach under the head of "politics." Their mistaken disposition, as university teachers, does not spring from the direction in which their own studies have taken them, but from their desire to teach undergraduates what they themselves are interested in, regardless of its inappropriateness.[6] They understand their problem as university teachers to be the problem of raising the study of politics above the level of "current affairs" and to give it a respectable intellectual content. But they rarely understand that this can be

5. It is true that for more than a century the possibility of a genuinely explanatory "science" of politics has been explored. But since nobody is likely to claim that anything in a condition even remotely suitable to be put before an undergraduate as an occasion for his acquiring a familiarity with a scientific mode of thinking has appeared, I have not thought it necessary to consider what our situation would be if this enterpriise had been more fruitful. Nor (except perhaps in America) has anyone attempted to teach such a science to undergraduates.

6. It will, of course, be understood that I am not objecting to dons being concerned with politics. It is long since academics began to take an interest in the activity of governing and the instruments of government, and among the circumstances which in England (and perhaps also in America) have, in recent times, promoted this sort of interest is the fact that many academics, seconded during two wars to government offices, have found there a virgin (but not unsuspected) world and have felt the impulse to explore it. Moreover, the study of politics is not a novelty in European and American universities: it is said that the earliest European professorship in politics, founded at Uppsala in the seventeenth century, was the Chair of "Statesmanship and Eloquence" (doing and talking, the inseparable components of political activity); and something called "political science," constructed on various analogies and offering conclusions of various degrees of abstraction, has been pursued for more than a century. But if every don were to teach undergraduates what he himself is interested in, and if every professorial chair were held to entail or to authorize a counterpart to itself in undergraduate education, there would be little in these days to distinguish a university from a mad-house. And if the contention is that undergraduates in significant numbers want to devote a large part of their university days learning what (it is alleged) will prepare them for a more intelligent participation in politics, the answer is that (except for the few who mistake a university for a place of "vocational" education and who want to "go in" for politics or to become administrators) this is not true; and in any case it is irrelevant.

done only by recognizing that the word "politics" in a university education signifies, not a "subject" of study, but a library of "texts" which, in this kind of education, is merely the occasion for learning how to handle and manage some of the "languages" of explanation.

And if it is said that the manner in which "politics" is taught in universities has not forbidden a connection with history and philosophy, the reply must be that the connection is often resented as a diversion from the proper concerns of "political science," and that wherever it has been made it has been apt to be corrupting rather than emancipating. "History" appears, not as a mode of explanation, but merely as some conclusions of allegedly "historical" writers believed to account for the present structure or to forecast the future prospects of (for example) a political party, or to provide evidence relating to the origin or the efficiency of an administrative device. History is patronizingly admitted so long as it remains in the "background" (whatever that may mean). And "philosophy" appears, not as a manner of thinking but as a misused word to identify what is believed to be a certain kind of interest in politics. Merely to extend our studies backwards a little way into the past in order to account for a piece of political conduct is not "doing" history; it is indulging in a piece of retrospective politics which makes certain that the historical mode of thinking never properly appears. And when in the writings of Plato or Hobbes or Rousseau or Hegel or Mill what is being looked for is the political disposition of these writers, when expressions like 'natural law', 'general will', 'freedom', 'the rule of law', 'justice', or 'sovereignty', which, philosophically speaking, are explanatory concepts, whose explanatory value might have been explored, are turned (as the politician turns everything he touches) into prescriptive concepts, and when what is reflected upon is merely their injunctive force, all chance is lost of learning something about the philosophical mode of thought. When, in this manner, a philosophical argument is turned into a so-called political theory, and it is thought appropriate to give it a political label, calling it 'democratic', 'conservative', 'liberal', 'progressive', or 'reactionary', a "vocational" education in politics may be seen to have reimposed itself; and the opportunity has been lost of understanding that a philosopher is never concerned with a condition of things but only with a manner of explanation, and of recognizing that the only thing that matters in a philosophical argument is its coherence, its intelligibility, its power to illuminate, and its fertility. And when we ask our pupils to display their attainments by discussing such questions as Was Mill a democrat? or, Has the House of Lords outlived its usefulness? or, Would not Ghana do better with a Presidential system of government than a Parliamentary? or, Is Great Britain heading for a One-Party State? we may suspect that a not very high class "vocational" education in politics is at work.

We have far to go; and having got off on the wrong foot, progress towards a proper university education connected with politics is not likely to be very rapid. But there are two precepts which, if followed, would take us in what I believe to be the proper direction.

First, in a School of "Politics" we should never use the language of politics; we should use only the explanatory "languages" of academic study. Of course, the words which compose our vocabulary of politics may be uttered, but only in order to inquire into their use and meaning, in order to take them to pieces and write them out in the long-hand of historical or philosophical explanation. They should never be given the appearance of being themselves explanatory words and expressions. And we should recognize that this so-called "political theory" is itself a form of political activity, and therefore not itself to be taught, but to be explained, historically or philosophically.

And secondly, since in a university we should regard ourselves as supervising, not the study of "texts" understood as organizations of information, but the study of the use of explanatory "languages" in connection with appropriate "texts," these "texts" should be chosen with care and for the relevant (paedagogic) reasons. As things are at present, any but the proper criteria are applied. A part of the world has only to be often in the newspapers, a state has only to be new or powerful, an administrative device has only to be considered interesting or administratively important by the pundits, and its claim to be chosen as a "text" for undergraduate study in a university is believed to be irrefutable. But these, instead of being the best reasons for choosing it, are the worst; they are political, not paedagogic reasons. For example, it appears to me that the place which the politics of contemporary Russia has come to occupy in undergraduate study is indefensible except in the irrelevant terms of a "vocational" political education. We know incomparably less about what goes on in Russian politics than in the politics of any other country in the world, bar perhaps China. Even in a "vocational" political education this "text" would be suspect: to set it for study would be inviting superficial and useless learning – systems instead of realities, mechanical models in place of concrete behaviour – and it would be justified only on account of the power and political importance of the Russian state and therefore the desirability of teaching something about it, however inadequate. But in a university education these are not significant considerations; what matters there is that the material should be in a suitable condition for the enterprise of teaching undergraduates how to think historically. And this, unquestionably, is not the condition of current Russian politics. Why should a school of politics go out of its way to choose for undergraduate study particularly obscure and corrupt "texts," "texts" suitable only for the most skilful emandators, when well-edited "texts," like the politics of France, or Sweden, or the U. S. A., or Spain (to say nothing of Great Britain), are available?

An academic study appears only when an activity is isolated and when it is in a fit condition to be an occasion for explanatory modes of thought. There are large tracts of the human past — arts and literatures, laws and customs, happenings in the world, the thoughts that men have entertained, their inventions and devices — which are eligible for this kind of study. Physical and chemical operations wherever they take place, the properties of numbers, the habits and customs of remote peoples, the structure and composition of the earth, and our own moral ideas, may be disengaged from our approval and disapproval and may be studied from some other standpoint than that of usefulness in the pursuit of our own practical enterprises. Even the study of the scarce opportunities the world offers for satisfying our wants may be detached from considerations of public or private policy. Each, it is true, contains an invitation other than the invitation to explain; but it is an invitation we may easily decline. In respect of current politics (our own or that of neighbouring peoples), however, this is more difficult; it is not unmistakably promising material for the enterprise of explanation. It is too difficult for most people to turn their backs upon the enterprise of participating and of thinking in the "vocational" idiom of participation; it is too easy to confuse injunction and explanation; it is too attractive to neglect philosophy for finding reasons for holding favourite political opinions, and to avoid doing history for ourselves in favour of making use of the convenient conclusions of historians. Politics offers the most difficult of all "literatures," the most difficult of all collections of "texts," in connection with which to learn to handle and manage the languages of explanation: the idiom of the material to be studied is ever ready to impose itself upon the manner in which it is studied. Nevertheless, if we recognize what we should be doing at a university, the difficulty may itself be an attraction; if we recognize that our proper business is not with politics at all but with teaching, in connection with politics, how to manage the "languages" of history and philosophy and how to distinguish them and their different sorts of utterance.

THE DISCIPLINES AND THE CURRICULUM

Jane R. Martin

I would like to inquire here into the relationship between the disciplines and the school curriculum. In particular, I would like to examine a prevalent view of this relationship, one which gives the disciplines the ruling hand in what is and what is not to be taught. It will be necessary to clarify this view and to place it in context. I will then criticize it for I believe it not only to be mistaken but to be quite objectionable. I will propose in conclusion that educational considerations should take precedence where the choice of school subjects and subject matter is concerned, and I will attempt to sketch in briefly some implications of this revised view of the nature of the relationship between the disciplines and the curriculum.

The Principle "Teach the Disciplines"

One dominant theme of curriculum theorizing today is that the disciplines should be taught. On the face of it this is unexceptionable. Who would ever dream of denying that they should be taught? We must distinguish, however, between the moderate claim "Disciplines, among other things, should be taught," and the claim that *only* the disciplines should be taught. The latter is anything but moderate. It is this latter sort of claim about the disciplines that I believe to be implicit in a good deal of the current thinking about curriculum and it is just this sort of claim that I believe to be misguided. I will consider the proposal "Teach the disciplines" to be equivalent to "Only the disciplines should be taught."

Now I suppose no one would hold that in vocational or professional or some other sort of special education only the disciplines should be taught. I will take the claim, therefore, to apply to nontechnical, or what is frequently called general education. Perhaps I should make it clear, however, that I am less concerned with whether or not anyone today really makes this claim than I am with the validity of the claim; that I am less concerned with the way it

From *Educational Philosophy and Theory, I* (1969). Reprinted by permission of *Educational Philosophy and Theory*.

has in fact been formulated and hedged around with qualifications than I am with exploring its consequences when it is construed as being quite general. For this reason I will discuss the view that the disciplines should be taught quite apart from any particular person's writings on the topic.[1]

When we are advised to teach the disciplines (granted that this advice tells us to teach only the disciplines), we are being advised to do one of two things. On the one hand we are being advised to select our school subjects from among the disciplines and only from among them; on the other hand we are being advised to select our school subject matter from the disciplines and only from among them. That is to say, "Teach the disciplines" may be interpreted as a principle governing school subject selection or as a principle governing school subject matter selection. Let us call the principle when interpreted in the former way Discipline Principle S, and let us call the principle when interpreted in the latter way Discipline Principle SM.[2]

Consider first Discipline Principle S. It does not by itself determine what specific subjects will be included in a school curriculum. Rather, it demarks the class of legitimate candidates for school subject. "Teach the disciplines" on this interpretation in effect requires that for every school subject there must be a corresponding discipline, but it does not require that for every discipline there must be a corresponding school subject. Unless unprincipled selection from within the class of legitimate candidates for school subject is sanctioned, other principles of subject selection besides Discipline Principle S would have to be invoked. Various principles have been singled out in this regard, although I am not sure that any has received general acceptance. Sometimes we are advised to choose the most advanced or disciplined of the disciplines. Frequently the disciplines are grouped in

1. I should point out, however, that the view of the relationship between the disciplines and the curriculum to be discussed here is widely held. For explicit formulations of it I refer the reader to, among others, Philip Phenix, *Realms of Meaning* (New York: McGraw-Hill, 1964); Arthur R. King, Jr. and John A. Brownell, *The Curriculum and the Disciplines of Knowledge* (New York: John Wiley, 1966); Paul H. Hirst, "Liberal Education and the Nature of Knowledge" in Reginald D. Archambault, *Philosophical Analysis and Education* (London: Routledge & Kegan Paul, 1965). [The Hirst article is reprinted in Part III]. This view is implicit, moreover, in Jerome S. Bruner's *The Process of Education* (Cambridge, Mass.: Harvard University Press, 1961), surely the most influential book of the last decade in curriculum circles. King and Brownell provide us with an example of the sort of hedging I am referring to; see p. 120 where they allow the school a "nondiscipline curriculum" as a sort of minor and somewhat disreputable adjunct to the liberal (i.e., discipline) curriculum which is its main business. Note also that of the authors cited here only Hirst is talking solely about higher education.

2. This distinction between principles presupposes a distinction between the notion of a school subject and the notion of school subject matter. Very roughly, a school subject consists of subject matter — some might prefer to use the term 'content' — organized in some way. To say what subject matter should be taught is not in itself to say how it should be organized, hence it is not to say what the school subject should be. And to select school subjects is not in itself to say what subject matter should be taught, since different selections of subject matter can be consistent with a given school subject.

families and we are advised to choose one from each family, perhaps the most representative.[3] But whatever principles are held to govern selection of disciplines, their status is subordinate to Discipline Principle S: the overriding consideration is that each school subject be a discipline.

Discipline Principle SM is weaker than Discipline Principle S. For when "Teach the disciplines" is construed as governing the selection of subject matter rather than subjects, we are being told that all the subject matter we teach must come from the disciplines but not that our subjects must. The disciplines, rather than being the source of our school subjects and hence of our school subject matter, are here viewed simply as the source of our school subject matter. How the subject matter being taught is to be organized into school subjects is not at issue. Thus, whereas on Discipline Principle S for every school subject there must be a corresponding discipline, on Discipline Principle SM there need not be. A school subject could be interdisciplinary in that it drew its subject matter from more than one discipline — something Discipline Principle S rules out.[4]

Now we must not overlook the fact that in current curriculum theorizing the Discipline Principle functions together with other principles, in particular with the Principles of Structure and Inquiry. Thus we are not merely advised to teach the disciplines; we are advised to teach structure and to teach inquiry. When the Discipline Principle is taken together with the principles "Teach structure" and "Teach inquiry" we may be said to be advised to teach the structure of the disciplines as inquiry. It is worth noting that there is no necessary connection between the Discipline Principle and the principles of Structure and Inquiry. One could teach the disciplines without viewing them as inquiry: one could, for example, view them as social phenomena or as bodies of knowledge. And one could teach the disciplines without teaching their structure: one could, for example, teach isolated and relatively unimportant bits of information. Conversely, one could teach inquiry without teaching the disciplines: one could, for example, teach students to inquire into social problems — presumably something quite different from teaching one or more of the disciplines.[5] One also could teach

3. E.g., Phenix, *op. cit.*, distinguishes what he calls realms of meaning, classifies the disciplines under these realms, and asks us to choose from the different realms; Hirst, *op. cit.*, suggests (but does not require) that "paradigm" examples of the various forms of knowledge (the disciplines) be selected.

4. Of the authors cited in note 1, Phenix quite clearly advocates Discipline Principle SM, rather than Discipline Principle S, *op. cit.*, p. 319; Hirst is committed only to Discipline Principle SM, *op. cit.*, p. 136ff; King and Brownell seem to be committed to Discipline Principle S, *op. cit.*, p. 120. Bruner would seem to be committed only to Discipline Principle SM; in this connection see his "Man: A Course of Study," *Toward a Theory of Instruction* (Cambridge, Mass.: Harvard University Press, 1966).

5. For an approach to social studies education which rejects the Discipline Principle and the Structure Principle but not the Inquiry Principle see Donald W. Oliver and James P. Shaver, *Teaching Public Issues in the High School* (Boston: Houghton Mifflin, 1966).

structure without teaching the disciplines: one could, for example, teach students the structure of an argument — again something quite different from teaching the structure of a discipline. Yet as a matter of fact the Discipline Principle has been closely connected with the principles of Structure and Inquiry and we will therefore discuss it in this context.[6]

Our course will be to evaluate the Discipline Principle on the two interpretations discussed here by considering what the consequences of following it would be. The gap between curriculum theorizing and actual school practice is a notable one. That there is a gap between curriculum theorizing and those recommendations for curriculum that are not quite theory yet not actual practice may not be as notable but ought not to be ignored. Advocates of the Discipline Principle do not always recommend courses or school subjects which accord with that principle. Our concern is not with these lapses — which may from the standpoint of educational practice be a godsend — but with the implications of the principle when it is taken seriously and as applying quite generally.

When curriculum theorists say "Teach the disciplines," they seem to have in mind what have been called the theoretical disciplines rather than the practical disciplines, that is to say disciplines like physics and economics and geology rather than disciplines like sculpture, the dance, and teaching.[7] Thus they speak of the disciplines of *knowledge,* they want the modes of *inquiry* of various disciplines to be taught, they conceive of disciplines as having basic *concepts,* as making *discoveries,* as formulating *laws* and *theories.* This sort of talk is quite out of place where the practical disciplines are concerned but very much to the point in connection with the theoretical disciplines.

Now the proper definition of a theoretical discipline is a matter of controversy.[8] But this does not mean that we do not know a good deal about theoretical disciplines or that we cannot recognize clear cases, e.g., physics, and clear noncases, e.g., chairs, when we meet them. We know, for example, that a theoretical discipline has some realm of study and tries to give a

6. See Phenix, *op. cit.* Chaps. 26, 27; King and Brownell, *op. cit.,* Chap. III where they characterize a discipline in terms of a mode of inquiry and a conceptual structure; Hirst *op. cit.,* p. 132ff.

7. See Kingsley Price, "Discipline in Teaching, In Its Study and Its Theory," Israel Scheffler, "Is Education a Discipline?," Max Black, "Education as Art and Discipline," in Scheffler, *Philosophy and Education,* 2nd Ed. (Boston: Allyn and Bacon, 1966), for discussions of practical disciplines, theoretical disciplines, and the disciplinary value of disciplines and other things.

8. For a thoughtful analysis of the notion of a theoretical discipline see Israel Scheffler, "Is Education a Discipline?" However, see King and Brownell, *op. cit.,* Chap. III and Phenix, *op. cit.,* Chap. 25, for rather different accounts of the notion. Fred M. Newmann has an interesting discussion of the problem of the definition of the term "discipline" in the course of a criticism of the theory of curriculum under examination here as it applies to social studies education in his "Questioning the Place of Social Science Disciplines in Education," *The Record-Teachers College, 69* (October 1967), pp. 69-74.

systematic account of it; that it has some vocabulary in which this account is expressed; and that it has some methods.[9] This characterization falls short of a definition of a theoretical discipline but it nonetheless gives an idea of the sort of thing advocates of the Discipline Principle are talking about. To be sure, in their concrete proposals these curriculum theorists sometimes forget that they have been construing disciplines in this way and they assign to the rank of school subject a variety of things which, if they are disciplines at all, would come under the heading of practical disciplines. But as I have already noted these lapses should not lead us astray. The sort of thing the Discipline Principle legitimizes as a school subject or the source of school subject matter is a theoretical discipline, where this is to be contrasted both with a practical discipline and also with a whole host of things that do not warrant the label 'discipline' at all — things such as chairs, the Far East, Shakespeare's tragedies.

There is a temptation nowadays to call everything a discipline. This must be guarded against. Some things are not, never were, and never will be disciplines, and some things are not now disciplines although they might conceivably one day become disciplines. Thus to apply the term 'discipline' indiscriminately is at the very least to depart from our ordinary conceptions, and to do so without warning where a curriculum principle is concerned is to mislead. But an unduly generous application of the label 'discipline' does more than mislead. If everything is considered a discipline, then the Discipline Principle gives no guidance and we may as well dispense with it. For a principle to function as it is supposed to, for it to have any practical value, it must not embrace everything; it must rule out certain things. A principle of subject or subject matter selection that legitimizes everything as a school subject or as a source of school subject matter is vacuous.

There is another temptation and that is to call everything that one values (although not everything at all) a discipline. But if succumbing to this temptation does not make the Discipline Principle vacuous, it nonetheless undermines it. The Discipline Principle as well as the other principles I mentioned have, or at least are intended to have, normative force; that is to say, they tell us what we *ought* to select or not select. In effect, the Discipline Principle tells us that certain things are worthy of being selected because they are disciplines or because they come from disciplines, and that certain things are not worthy of being selected because they are not disciplines or do not come from disciplines. If, however, 'discipline' becomes an honorific term, the Discipline Principle is turned on its head. Instead of something being worthy of being selected because it is a discipline or is a part of a discipline, something is a discipline because it or some part of it is worthy of being selected. But if being a discipline is not what makes something worthy of

9. Note that in saying this I am leaving open the question of whether each discipline has a *unique* method, a *unique* vocabulary, etc.

being selected — and on this view it is not — what *does* make a thing worthy of being selected? Unless we know this, the Discipline Principle is useless for we cannot apply it to new cases. And if we do know this, there is no need to use the Discipline Principle for we will be able to decide new cases without it.

Apart from the fact that misuse of the term 'discipline' tends to vitiate the Discipline Principle, when the term is misused we lose sight of the whole point of the curriculum theory to which the Discipline Principle belongs. Curriculum theorists who hold that the disciplines and only the disciplines should be taught believe that the methods, key concepts, and theories of fields like physics, biology, mathematics, and economics have great value; that one who masters these will understand and be able to do a great deal more on his own than one who does not. They justify the Discipline Principle by an appeal to certain characteristics of the standard theoretical disciplines and to the values which they think accrue from studying them. If 'discipline' now refers to things which do not share these characteristics and do not yield these values when studied, the whole reason for advocating the Discipline Principle disappears.

Let us grant, then, that the Discipline Principle has to do with theoretical disciplines and that this notion is to be construed in such a way that it accords with ordinary usage. There are then two very basic criticisms that can be made of it. Both criticisms amount in the final analysis to the same thing: the Discipline Principle rules out of the curriculum subjects or subject matter which ought not to be ruled out. They are best viewed as distinct, however, because two rather different sorts of argument are involved. Even supposing that the first argument could because of changes in the disciplines one day be met, the second would still hold.

The Argument from Relevance

Whatever the proper definition of a theoretical discipline, there is no doubt that each theoretical discipline involves *some* methods of inquiry and *some* vocabulary in which it formulates *some* laws, theories, principles, or the like. It is just these things — the mode or method of inquiry of a discipline, the key terms or concepts of a discipline, and the most important laws or theories or principles — that the theory of curriculum to which the Discipline Principle belongs singles out for attention. The notion of structure is by no means clear, but those who want the structure of the disciplines to be taught seem to be recommending that the basic ideas of a discipline be taught, that is, the basic concepts of a discipline and the relationships among them.[10] Sometimes the methods of a discipline are considered part of its structure.[11]

10. See Jerome S. Bruner, *The Process of Education* (Cambridge, Mass.: Harvard University Press, 1960).

11. Joseph J. Schwab seems to take this tack when he distinguishes between the substantive and the syntactic structures of the disciplines. See, for example, his essay

Even if they are not, when the principle "Teach inquiry" is combined with the principle "Teach the disciplines," the methods of a discipline are put on a par, educationally speaking, with the basic ideas of that discipline. For the two principles together tell us to view the disciplines as fields of inquiry, and methods are surely central to inquiry even if inquiry is not reducible to method.

The fact that the notions of *discipline* and *structure* and *inquiry* themselves are in need of clarification does not stand in the way, then, of evaluating the Discipline Principle. For in the context of the Structure of the Disciplines as Inquiry theory of curriculum it is clear that Discipline Principle S rules out of the curriculum many things which have long been part of it — some of which, at least, ought not to be ruled out. It rules out as school subjects such things as music, art, and the dance; reading, writing, and literature; French, German, and Spanish; physical education, carpentry, and typing; the Far East and problems of democracy. No doubt advocates of the Principle want to rule out some of these; but that anyone wants to rule out all is doubtful. In any case all ought not to be ruled out.

Now I can imagine an advocate of Discipline Principle S objecting to this criticism of it. He might argue that the things I say are ruled out by the Principle are in fact disciplines, hence are not ruled out. But if the Principle is to retain its normative force and be neither vacuous nor trivial, this objection cannot be sustained. On no significant interpretation of 'discipline' is French or the Far East a discipline of any sort; some of the other things listed here might be able to qualify as practical disciplines, but they certainly would not qualify as theoretical disciplines. But, the objection will continue, are there not basic concepts of music, e.g., harmony? Of literature, e.g., metaphor? Of language, e.g., noun? Are not the concepts belonging to each one of these related in significant ways, as in the case of harmony and melody? Do not these fields consist of principles, theories, laws? Are they not theoretical disciplines after all?

There is such a thing as theory of music, there is such a thing as grammar, there is such a thing as literary criticism, and all of these may, perhaps, qualify as theoretical disciplines. But theory of music is not music; grammar, even French grammar, is not French; and literary criticism is not literature.[12] It is true that courses in theory of music are listed in school catalogs under music, that French courses all too frequently turn out to be grammar courses, and that courses in literary criticism fall under literature.

"Problems, Topics and Issues" in Stanley Elam, *Education and the Structure of Knowledge* (Chicago: Rand McNally, 1964). King and Brownell, *op. cit.,* p. 77, follow Schwab in this.

12. To be sure, by its very nature literary criticism, or at least some of it, qualifies as literature in a way that music theory does not qualify as music and French grammar does not qualify as French. Yet insofar as literary criticism constitutes a theoretical discipline it does so not because it itself is literature but because it provides an account of literature.

But at most this indicates that the school subject *music* encompasses theory, that the school subject *French* encompasses grammar, and that the school subject *literature* encompasses literary criticism. To argue that music, French, and literature are theoretical disciplines and therefore do qualify as potential school subjects according to Discipline Principle S because music theory, grammar, and literary criticism are theoretical disciplines, as our imaginary objector is in effect doing, is either to commit the fallacy of composition or to deny the facts of the case. That is to say, it is either to argue invalidly from a characteristic of one part of a whole to a characteristic of the whole itself, or it is to deny that there is more to music than its theory, more to French that its grammar, more to literature than criticisms of it.

At this point our objector may suggest a compromise: he will grant that some parts or aspects of things like music, French, and literature are excluded from the pool of potential school subjects by Discipline Principle S provided we grant that some parts or aspects of things like music, French, and literature do fall in the pool on that Principle. We may accept this compromise without giving up our initial criticism of Discipline Principle S. For even if some parts or aspects of things like music, French, and literature can qualify as school subjects according to the Principle, other parts or aspects of these things cannot. Yet surely they ought to qualify as such. As long as 'music', 'French', and 'literature' are retained as labels of school subjects by advocates of Discipline Principle S, the compromise has its dangers. For it is all too easy to forget that on this principle the school subjects called music, French, and literature consist respectively in theorizing *about* music, *about* French, *about* literature, and that other sorts of study – study *in* music, French and literature as opposed to study *about* these – are ruled out.

In general, when we view the disciplines as sets of theories, laws, principles, and the like arrived at through inquiry, we take them to be asserting things *about* something, be it music, language, literature, falling bodies, living organisms, or abnormal behavior. Now it may as a matter of fact be the case that music theory has something significant to say about music and that literary criticism has something significant to say about literature. There is no guarantee, however, that the theoretical disciplines have something significant to say about all those things which on independent grounds can be shown to be the things our students ought to learn about. How much light can the disciplines shed, for example, on war and peace, marriage and divorce, violence and poverty, love and friendship? Nor is there any reason to think that everything worth teaching must *say* something *about* something. Music, apart from music theory, does not say or assert things about things – at least not in any literal interpretation of 'say' or 'assert' – yet it has great educational significance. A great deal may be said *in* French about things, yet French itself does not say or assert things.

The educational importance of things which do not say something about something will be discussed in the next section. For now let us consider the question of whether the disciplines do have something to say about the things we believe our students should learn about. In the face of the criticism of nonrelevance an advocate of Discipline Principle S can take one of two tacks: He can argue that the disciplines do in fact have something significant to say about important things, e.g., war and peace, violence and poverty, which on independent grounds can be shown to be of educational significance; or he can argue that those things the disciplines do not in fact shed light on are not concerns of education, at least nor formal education, which is, after all, the realm in which the Discipline Principle is intended to apply.[13]

This latter tack, it seems to me, is a desperate one. In order to save the Discipline Principle we are, in effect, asked to relinquish our responsibilities as educators. Given a world which does not cooperate with the disciplines or, perhaps, disciplines which do not keep up with the world, our Discipline Principle advocate is saying, "So much the worse for the world," whereas he should be saying, "So much the worse for the disciplines." I can imagine holding on to Discipline Principle S given that the disciplines did not illuminate the sorts of things I have mentioned only if there were good reason to think that nothing else illuminated them either. If there were nothing outside the disciplines for our students to learn about things like these — things which vitally affect their lives and their times — then, I suppose, the failure of the disciplines to speak to these issues would not count against Discipline Principle S. I doubt very much, however, that there is nothing outside the disciplines worth teaching and learning about things of this sort. In any case, to show that there is nothing is a difficult, if not impossible, task; one which Discipline Principle advocates have not to my knowledge undertaken.

Perhaps a more promising tack is to argue that the disciplines do in fact have something to say about those things educators believe students ought to learn about. A sophisticated advocate of Discipline Principle S would, I think, grant that the disciplines do not in all cases talk *directly* about these things; that 'marriage' and 'divorce' are not terms belonging to physics or biology or even to psychology or sociology; that statements such as "One out of every four marriages ends in divorce" do not belong to any discipline. He would grant this but maintain that the disciplines speak *indirectly* about these things; that they are relevant or applicable to our everyday concerns, although their own vocabularies are technical and their theoretical statements

13. I suppose there is a third possibility. He can acknowledge the educational significance of the sorts of things under discussion here, admit that the disciplines do not shed light on them, yet refuse to recognize that this has any bearing on the Discipline Principle. We are assuming, however, that our Discipline Principle advocate is rational.

are in many instances quite abstract and are perhaps not obviously related to these concerns. He might also argue that two disciplines, namely history and philosophy, do talk directly about these things.[14]

Now in principle this is certainly true: the theoretical disciplines can speak to concrete, everyday affairs even if they do not speak directly about them. There are no laws or theories of cracking automobile radiators, yet supposing that an automobile radiator has cracked during a cold night certain laws of physics will apply to this event and will figure prominently in an explanation of it.[15] History, moreover, does talk directly about war and peace, and philosophy talks about the good life and the good society. It is an open question, however, if at the present time the theoretical disciplines do in fact have significant things to say to those common, ordinary, everyday, but important things our students ought to learn about. No doubt some disciplines do speak right now to some of the vital issues with which education should be concerned; that all of them do, or that all the things that from the educational point of view need to be illuminated are illuminated by the disciplines, seems to me to be quite problematic. It is also an open question if at the present time history and philosophy talk directly about all the things our students should learn about.

It is one thing to say that the disciplines can in principle apply to the important things in life and it is another thing to say that they do as a matter of fact apply. To say that we recognize exactly what their relevance is for these things, given that they are in fact relevant, is something else again. There is no reason to suppose that a discipline as a whole is relevant to some particular problem or issue; on the contrary, we must expect that some parts of the discipline will be relevant and that other parts will not be. But then it is necessary to decide which parts of a discipline shed light on which problems or issues. This may at times be determined quite easily, but it must be remembered that laws and theories and principles wear no badges of relevance and that the task of determining what is relevant to what is itself a task of inquiry with success by no means guaranteed.

Suppose now that the disciplines, or at least some of them, are relevant to those things which our students should learn about and that the respects in which they are relevant are known. Their relevance will not normally be obvious to the student, but will have to be made obvious to him in the course

14. Although advocates of the Discipline Principle invariably consider history to be a theoretical discipline it is not at all obvious that it is in fact one nor that it meets the criteria these writers themselves set up for a discipline. For example, they conceive of a discipline as having some central concepts peculiar to it and it is questionable that history meets this condition.

15. The cracked radiator example is taken from Carl G. Hempel's essay "The Function of General Laws in History," *Journal of Philosophy,* XXXIX, 1942. Reprinted in Hempel, *Aspects of Scientific Explanation* (New York: The Free Press, 1965). Hempel uses it for a different purpose. See Scheffler, "Is Education a Discipline?" section VI, for a discussion of the relevance of the disciplines to everyday affairs.

of his education. Granted that the cracking of a radiator can be explained in terms of some laws of physics, it does not follow that a student who has learned the relevant laws will automatically see their relevance to the case at hand. If the disciplines are to shed light *for him* on the problems and issues in question, they must be taught in such a way that their relevance for these problems and issues becomes clear. No doubt it is possible to do this: physics and the other theoretical disciplines can be taught so that their applicability to such things as war and peace, violence, and poverty can be grasped by the student. The question we must ask, however, is if the curriculum theory to which the Discipline Principle belongs sanctions teaching the disciplines in this way.

When the Discipline Principle is conjoined with the Structure Principle and the Inquiry Principle there is no doubt about the way in which the disciplines are to be viewed for purposes of education: they are to be viewed in the way in which practitioners of the discipline themselves view it. To be sure, the three principles when taken together do not require that the student actually engage in inquiry; they do not demand that he learn to be an inquirer or even learn how to inquire. Teaching the structure of the disciplines as inquiry is compatible with simply teaching and learning *about* inquiry.[16] But whether the student learns to inquire or simply learns about inquiry, the intent of the theory is that he see the disciplines from the "inside." He is not merely to become acquainted in one way or another with the methods of the practitioner of a discipline – with his conceptual apparatus, with his findings, with his aspirations and general orientation – but to view them from the standpoint of that practitioner.[17]

Now the practitioner – certainly the practitioner advocates of this theory have in mind – typically is not concerned *qua* practitioner with the question of the practical relevance of his work.[18] One mark of a theoretical discipline is its theoretical orientation and its remoteness from practical, everyday concerns. To teach a discipline in such a way that the relevance of its various parts or aspects to particular everyday issues and problems became clear would, I should think, subvert the whole point of the curriculum theory at issue. Quite simply, to teach the disciplines as relevant to practical concerns is not to teach them as inquiry. This is not to say that their methods

16. What is at stake is that the disciplines be shown as fields of inquiry and that students come to see them as such. This can be accomplished in a number of ways. I do not want to suggest that advocates of these principles do not also advocate that students engage in inquiry, indeed that students learn to be inquirers. My point is simply that the three principles under discussion do not by themselves necessitate this.

17. One could study the methods of the practitioner of a discipline without looking at that discipline from the "inside," e.g., one could become acquainted with the methods of physics through a study of philosophy of science.

18. I have said that the task of determining exactly which parts or aspects of a discipline are relevant to any given thing outside the discipline is itself a task of inquiry. Inquiry into the relevance of a discipline for our practical, everyday affairs must, however, be distinguished from the inquiry carried on within that discipline.

of inquiry may not be one of the things about them having relevance for practical concerns. Nor is it to say that there is anything intrinsically wrong with viewing them in this way. Rather it is to say that to focus on their relevance for such concerns is in effect to view them from the "outside," hence in a way which is not sanctioned by the Structure of the Disciplines as Inquiry theory of curriculum.[19]

History and philosophy are in much the same boat as the other disciplines: even if they do not talk directly *about* the things we have in mind, they may speak *to* them. To the extent that this is the case, however, the points just made apply to history and philosophy as well as to the other disciplines. Moreover, on the theory of curriculum under consideration, even when history and philosophy talk directly about important, everyday things, what they have to say about some particular topic is considered to be of much less importance than their methods, their key concepts, and the like. We must also take into account the possibility that neither history nor philosophy illuminates important things in the proper way. The concerns of philosophy are very, very general, and there is a real question as to the illumination that philosophy can give directly to particular questions and issues. History, on the other hand, is concerned with particular problems and issues, and it would seem, therefore, to be able to illuminate well the things it does talk directly about. One wonders, however, if historians in talking about topics such as war and peace do in fact single out for attention the things our students ought to know about these topics. History is notable for its discussions of rulers and generals and politicians, and for its lack of attention to the life and point of view of the ordinary man.

Whatever the fate of history and philosophy on this theory of curriculum, I would not be surprised if at this point in our discussion an advocate of the Discipline Principle retreated from Discipline Principle S to Discipline Principle SM. Surely, he will say, the latter principle gets over this argument from relevance even if the former principle does not. For Discipline Principle SM requires only that our school subject matter come from the disciplines; it allows for the organization of subject matter around topics which do not themselves belong to some discipline. Thus those things which educators hold on independent grounds to be worth learning about can on Discipline Principle SM be learned about even if Discipline Principle S does in

---

19. Arno A. Bellack in his discussions of the curriculum has invoked a distinction similar to the inside-outside distinction I am introducing here, namely the distinction between a participant's language and an onlooker's language; see, for example, Bellack's "What Knowledge Is of Most Worth?" in William M. Alexander, *The Changing Secondary School Curriculum* (New York: Holt, Rinehart and Winston, 1967). If I understand him correctly, Bellack wants students to learn both sorts of languages; in effect, then, he advocates their viewing the disciplines from the outside as well as the inside. He is, moreover, concerned about some of the problems with the Discipline Principle I am raising here.

fact rule them out of the curriculum. For example, Discipline Principle SM allows as school subjects the Far East, poverty, and war and peace. What is required is that the subject matter to be learned come from the disciplines. But the issue of relevance is in a sense taken care of: elements from the various disciplines relevant to the topic at hand are incorporated into the one interdisciplinary subject. Thus in the case of the Far East, for example, the subject matter may include findings from history, geography, economics, and so on insofar as they have to do with the Far East.

Without doubt Discipline Principle SM is to be preferred to Discipline Principle S: it allows disciplines to be school subjects but makes it possible for other things to qualify as well. Yet Discipline Principle SM does not satisfactorily get over the objection raised here initially in relation to Discipline Principle S. Discipline Principle SM does not function in isolation. The principles of Structure and Inquiry do not lose their force when Discipline Principle SM is substituted for Discipline Principle S. It is still the case that the disciplines are to be viewed from the inside; their structure and methods are still the primary focus.

The main concern of the Structure of the Disciplines as Inquiry theory of curriculum is that the student come to understand the disciplines — understand them by getting "inside" them. The disciplines can be understood from the "outside" — by looking around them rather than looking into them, e.g., by seeing how they came to be the way they are or by seeing how they function in society as a whole. But the theory at issue does not place value on this sort of understanding. Thus, in an important sense it makes no difference whether the Discipline Principle is given a strong or a weak interpretation. For whether the disciplines constitute our school subjects or our school subject matter, the educator must focus on certain internal features of the disciplines. Subject matter from various disciplines may be organized around some topic to which these disciplines are applicable, but interest nonetheless must be on the methods and basic ideas of these disciplines. So long as it is possible to stress these and at the same time illuminate some topic outside the disciplines, our objection amounts to very little. But the Discipline Principle in the context of this theory does not allow for illumination of things, no matter how important, to which the disciplines are not relevant, nor does it allow us to focus on a topic if in doing so the structural and methodological aspects of the disciplines are slighted. Given a conflict of interests — to illuminate some vital everyday sort of topic or to illuminate the methods and structure of the disciplines — the outcome is never in doubt: the methods and structure of the disciplines have priority.[20]

I have been discussing up to this point the relevance of the disciplines, and in particular their relevance as they are conceived by the Structure of the

20. Hirst, *op. cit.,* pp. 136-137, for one, makes this crystal clear.

Disciplines as Inquiry theory of curriculum, for learning about all sorts of important things. We must not forget, however, that the Discipline Principle as we are interpreting it here holds not merely that the disciplines should be taught but that *only* the disciplines should be taught. In evaluating the principle we must not forget then that it rules out subject matter that does not belong to any discipline. Yet there is no guarantee that such subject matter might not be very illuminating. If we are willing to grant, as I think we must, that topics such as war and peace, poverty and violence, love and friendship are educationally important, then we ignore at our peril subject matter which does not belong to the disciplines. Literature and art — and I am not speaking here about literary criticism or aesthetics — are not theoretical disciplines, yet they may illuminate these topics. Commonsense knowledge may be quite relevant. Practical wisdom is not to be sneered at, especially when theoretical wisdom is scarce. The Discipline Principle would have us believe that nondisciplinary knowledge is not worth having. Yet surely nondisciplinary knowledge of a thing is in some cases at least better than no knowledge of that thing; moreover, it is difficult to imagine our disciplinary knowledge ever bearing fruit in everyday life if it were not supplemented with nondisciplinary knowledge.[21]

The Argument from Verstehen

There is more to education than advocates of the Discipline Principle seem ever to have dreamed of. Thus far we have simply questioned the adequacy of this principle in relation to one educational objective, namely that our students *learn about* those things we consider important enough to be learned about. But education is not and ought not to be limited to learning about: there are skills to be acquired, techniques to be mastered, activities to be learned, works of art to be appreciated; there are emotions to be fostered, attitudes to be developed, convictions to be encouraged, ways of acting to be promoted. The Discipline Principle and, indeed, the curriculum theory to which it belongs, must be condemned for ignoring all these things — that is to say, ignoring them except as they enter into one particular context.

When we are told to teach the disciplines and only the disciplines, one human context is given special status insofar as education is concerned. Whether students are taught to inquire in the manner of the practitioner of the discipline or simply taught *about* this mode of inquiry, the activity of one who engages in a discipline is to be studied in a way that no other activity is

21. For an interesting discussion of commonsense knowledge and its relation to disciplinary knowledge see L. R. Perry, "Commonsense Thought, Knowledge and Judgement and Their Importance For Education," *British Journal of Educational Studies,* XIII, May 1965, pp. 125-138. [Reprinted in Part III.]

to be studied, namely from the standpoint of the actor. Whether students learn the skills and techniques which enter into disciplinary inquiry and acquire the attitudes and convictions of an inquirer or whether they simply learn about these things and learn to appreciate them, the disciplines are seen from the "inside." Other human activities or contexts, if they are studied at all, are studied through the study of one or another discipline. But to the extent that the disciplines illuminate human conduct they do so from the "outside": they take the standpoint of a spectator toward the activity in question, not the standpoint of an actor. Thus, for example, the activities and practices of the consumer and the manufacturer may be studied in the course of studying the discipline of economics. But if they are, they are studied not from the standpoint of an actual consumer or manufacturer but from the standpoint of an economist looking at a consumer or manufacturer. If the economist is interested at all in seeing the world as the consumer or manufacturer does, he is interested only to the extent that it aids his theorizing about their activities and practices.

Philosophers and historians have sometimes maintained that the historian must explain and understand human behavior in a special way. They have argued that because we are human we must put ourselves in the position of the people we are studying: we must look at things through their eyes, think their thoughts, feel their feelings. William Dray, one of the most influential contemporary advocates of this position, argues that where actions are concerned the historian's task is to take the actor's standpoint and to set forth his reasons for acting as he did.[22] If this account of history is correct, then perhaps the present criticism of the Discipline Principle loses part of its force. For on this view of history, to take the point of view of the practitioner of history – the historian – would in turn require that one look at the actions of historical figures from the standpoint of the actor. History could then be taught in the way advocates of the Discipline Principle want, namely as a field of inquiry, and at the same time students would see things other than the disciplines from the "inside."

For reasons that will become apparent shortly, even if this account of history is correct, much if not all of the force of the criticism I am making of the Discipline Principle remains. I myself am very skeptical of this doctrine, sometimes called the Doctrine of *Verstehen,* as it is usually presented.[23] But whatever its claims as an account of history, I do think there is an important moral to be drawn from it for education. It may not be the case that because we are human we must put ourselves in the actor's position if we are to explain and understand what he has done, but it surely is the case that we

22. *Laws and Explanation in History* (London: Oxford University Press, 1957), Chap. V.
23. See my "Another Look at the Doctrine of Verstehen," *British Journal for the Philosophy of Science, 20,* 1969.

must put ourselves in the actor's position if we are to learn to act as he does and if we are to come to see the world as he does. The Doctrine of *Verstehen* has educational force, then, independent of any logical or methodological force it may have in history and the social sciences.[24]

There are human contexts and activities over and above that of the disciplines which our students should study from the "inside." I do not for a moment mean to suggest that inquiry as it is carried on in the disciplines ought not to be studied from the standpoint of the inquirer himself; on the contrary, I think there are very good reasons for holding that it should be so studied. What is objectionable about the Structure of the Disciplines as Inquiry theory of curriculum is not that it tells us to teach inquiry from this standpoint but that it prevents us from teaching other activities from this standpoint. No matter how much value one places on the disciplines and their modes of inquiry, they are not the whole of life nor ought they to be the whole of education. Artistic practice and appreciation may contain elements of inquiry within them, but neither one is reducible to inquiry any more than is professional practice, such as of medicine or law. Political, social, and individual moral problems can be inquired into, but right political and social action is no more reducible to inquiry than is moral behavior. Yet these things, along with many, many others – child rearing, family living, community action, to name just a few – ought at the very least to be candidates for study from within.

In maintaining that the Doctrine of *Verstehen* has educational force I do not want to be misunderstood. I am not suggesting that every human context, that every human activity, that all human behavior, ought to be studied from the actor's standpoint. I am not advocating that we teach pickpocketing and lynching, sadism and character assassination. My point is not that education should embrace the teaching of anything at all but simply that the Discipline Principle and its accompanying theory rule out much too much. It is by no means easy to say in any general sort of way which activities, which human contexts ought to be looked at from the "inside" in the course of a person's education. We may point without too much difficulty to particular cases that seem quite obviously to belong in the curriculum, or at least in the pool of potential subjects or subject matter, and others which seem just as obviously not to belong in it. But a general principle that would function as the Discipline Principle is intended to function – that is to say, a principle that although it would not by itself determine what is to be our school subjects or at least our school subject matter, would differentiate between those things which ought not to enter into the curriculum in these ways and those which may – is not easily found. Fortunately for us it is not necessary to come up with an alternative to the Discipline Principle in order to show that principle to be inadequate.

24. Dray, *op. cit.*, argues against the view that the Doctrine has methodological force only and for the view that it has logical force.

One alternative to the Discipline Principle which seems peculiarly relevant to the present discussion may be abstracted from the writings of R. S. Peters. Peters's account of education merits closer examination than we can possibly give it here, yet we would be remiss if we did not consider a portion of it at least briefly for Peters appears to take seriously the very argument we have just been leveling against the Discipline Principle. Peters proposes that we view education as initiation into worthwhile activities and modes of conduct and I think we may fairly construe him as offering an alternative to the Discipline Principle, which we will call the Worthwhile Activities Principle.[25] Now in one respect the principle "Teach worthwhile activities and modes of conduct" is clearly superior to the Discipline Principle: it allows for activities besides the disciplines and their attendant modes of inquiry to be in the curriculum for study from within. Thus Peters mentions as a worthwhile activity literary appreciation as well as science, philosophy, and history. Yet in another respect the Worthwhile Activities Principle, at least when taken in the context of Peters's Initiation Theory, is unduly restrictive. Students are to be initiated into worthwhile activities — that is to say they are to learn them by studying them from the "inside."[26] While this allows them (as the Discipline Principle does not) to take the actor's point of view and to engage in activities other than inquiry, it does not allow them to study *about* objects of educational significance unless such study is, as it were, accidentally accomplished while they are being initiated into the various worthwhile activities. Yet as I have already argued, there are any number of things students ought to learn about, and there is no more guarantee that they will learn about them given this principle than that they will learn about them given the Discipline Principle.

There is, however, a more important point to be brought out in connection with Peters's Initiation Theory. When Peters talks about getting inside worthwhile activities, he is concerned that the student become committed to them and in some sense or other make them his own. In claiming that the Doctrine of *Verstehen* has pedagogical force, that is, in arguing that students ought in the course of their education to get "inside" human activities and contexts other than the disciplines and their modes of inquiry, I have not been saying that they must necessarily stay inside; that they must necessarily adopt these activities and contexts or make them their own. When the historian is told to look at things from the point of view of the actor, be it because it will help him to explain and understand human

25. See "Education as Initiation" in Reginald D. Archambault, *Philosophical Analysis and Education* (London: Routledge & Kegan Paul, 1965); also *Ethics and Education* (Chicago: Scott, Foresman, 1967), Chap. 4. It should be noted that Peters himself speaks throughout of education, not teaching.

26. Thus Peters says that the teacher's task is to "try to get others on the inside of a public form of life that he shares and considers to be worthwhile"; the teacher, having been initiated, is already on the inside according to Peters; see "Education as Initiation," pp. 104, 107.

actions or because he must do so to explain and understand them, he is surely not being told to turn into or become that sort of actor. Nor must the student in the course of his education become the sort of person whose point of view he is made to see or whose activity he is gotten to participate in.

There surely are a number of activities and contexts the student ought to get "inside" of with a view toward making them his own in the course of his education. Presumably these will be worthwhile activities. But there is a place in the curriculum for activities and modes of conduct that are not worthwhile: activities and modes of conduct that the student views from the "inside" in order to reject, in order to improve upon, in order to do away with, in order to learn to cope with. Racial discrimination is not a worthwhile activity; neither is living in poverty and despair in a ghetto. Yet there may be good reason for having students take the actor's point of view in cases of this sort. It may be true that education ought to "pass on" worthwhile activities only, but even if it is, it does not follow that the *only* thing it ought to do is pass things on.

A curriculum is needed which introduces the student to a wide range of human activities and human contexts — wider than either the Discipline Principle or the Worthwhile Activities Principle demarks — and allows him to study such activities and contexts from a variety of points of view including that of the actor. This is not to say that every sort of human conduct ought to be studied or that any sort at all ought to be studied. Nor is it to say that every sort that should be and is studied ought to be viewed from the "inside." To reject the Discipline Principle and even the Worthwhile Activities Principle as too restrictive is not necessarily to advocate anarchy. The moral to be drawn from our discussion is not that anything goes where curriculum is concerned, but rather that educational considerations ought not to be lost sight of. Indeed I want to urge that they take precedence and that where they conflict with some general rule or principle, then the rule or principle — not the educational considerations — must give way.

Had we taken the Discipline Principle to be making the moderate claim "Teach the disciplines among other things" I would not have objected to it. As a matter of fact the disciplines constitute one very important sort of human activity, one which I have no doubt should at some point in the course of nontechnical education be studied from the "inside" — although not *only* from the inside. But nontechnical or general education surely ought to be viewed in a broader framework than that provided by the Discipline Principle. Some have suggested that we conceive of the curriculum in terms of "the forms of knowledge," and perhaps this does provide a broader base than does the Discipline Principle.[27] Yet much the same arguments can be adduced

27. Hirst, *op. cit.,* speaks in this way. He seems, however, to have in mind the distinct disciplines. Phenix, *op. cit.,* speaks of ways of knowing but again seems to be talking about the disciplines.

against the Forms of Knowledge Principle "Teach only the forms of knowledge" as have been directed here at the Discipline Principle. If the forms of knowledge include other things besides the disciplines, they still do not include enough; that is, they do not unless the notion of a form of knowledge is made so weak that anything — or else anything one wishes — counts as such — in which case the Forms of Knowledge Principle loses its force.[28]

When the curriculum is conceived of in terms of the disciplines or, for that matter, in terms of the "forms of knowledge," the disciplines loom large: they take up all or almost all "curriculum space." Surely there are advantages to this. When they are spread out across the whole curriculum it is possible to dwell on the special characteristics of each discipline, or at least of each group or family of disciplines. Each one, or each group, is seen as unique; studying history from the "inside" is as far removed as one can possibly imagine from studying physics or mathematics from the "inside."[29] It will be argued that if the disciplines are allotted a relatively modest part of the curriculum space, justice cannot be done them.

It is true that the tendency to dwell on the special characteristics of each distinct discipline may have to be curtailed if curriculum space is redistributed. There is not possibly time to teach the disciplines or forms of knowledge in the way advocates of the relevant principles want them taught if those disciplines or forms of knowledge are given what seems to me to be their fair share, but no more than their fair share, of room in the curriculum.[30] But it must not be forgotten that the separate disciplines, although without doubt distinct and in some respects unique, do have common characteristics. Were the common elements rather than the noncommon elements stressed, justice could be done the disciplines, although probably not the sort of justice many advocates of the Discipline Principle have in mind.

Compare a curriculum whose school subjects are history, physics, economics, and the like, with one whose school subjects are the humanities, the natural sciences, the social sciences.[31] A curriculum of the first sort enables the student to study distinct disciplines in detail and to luxuriate, if

28. Hirst may well have left himself open to this criticism when he allowed the arts to qualify as forms of knowledge, *op. cit.,* p. 130.

29. Advocates of the Discipline Principle invariably stress the distinctive features of each discipline.

30. One wonders if there is even time to do what advocates of the Discipline Principle want to do when the disciplines are given all the space in the curriculum. Consider: "What is being sought is, first, sufficient immersion in the concepts, logic and criteria of the discipline for a person to come to know the distinctive way in which it 'works' and then sufficient generalization of these over the whole range of the discipline so that his experience begins to be widely structured in this distinctive manner." Hirst, *op. cit.,* p. 132.

31. See Bellack, *op. cit.,* for a "broad groupings of knowledge" approach to curriculum planning.

he or his teachers wish, in those aspects of a discipline that separate it from all the others. A curriculum of the second sort need not do away with all study of the separate disciplines as such, but it must surely dwell on family resemblances, (else why group certain disciplines with certain others for study?) and must just as surely overlook much of the rich detail that goes into making each discipline appear unique. In effect, the scale to which the different disciplines are drawn shifts as the school subject shifts. Given the school subject *history,* the discipline history can be drawn to a large scale; given the school subject *the humanities* (or would it be the *social sciences?*) the discipline history must necessarily be drawn to a smaller scale with many of the characteristics missing that were so prominent in the large-scale drawing.

Consider now a curriculum conceived as embracing a wide and varied range of human activities and conduct, as encompassing forms of living or activity and not just forms of knowledge. Such a curriculum would have to give ample space to the arts, to the professions, to various sorts of work, and to all sorts of other practical activities; it would also have to leave room for a variety of social activities and roles – not just the role of inquirer and the one-time favorite role of citizen – and it would not be able to ignore things in what for want of a better designation I will call the personal realm, things such as character development. A curriculum so conceived might well have space for neither distinct disciplines nor families of such disciplines as separate school subjects but might only have space for the theoretical disciplines as a *single* school subject. Here, not merely family resemblances but resemblances holding across families would be brought into focus. Details about families – indeed details about distinct disciplines – might not be totally ignored, but elements common to the various disciplines would surely be singled out for attention. The scale to which any one particular discipline was drawn would be small; indeed, the separate disciplines might not be portrayed at all. It would be possible, of course, to present one particular discipline to the student as a sort of paradigm of a discipline. But in this case the special characteristics of the particular discipline would be sacrificed to the paradigmatic aspects of it. We would in effect have a large-scale drawing of the disciplines as a group, presented by means of a particular example, rather than a large-scale drawing of the particular discipline.

There are, indeed, many ways in which the school subject *the disciplines* could be taught. It is not my purpose to list them, let alone settle on any one here; I merely wish to point out that when the disciplines are assigned a limited place in the curriculum, as I think they should be, it may be necessary to think more than we have been thinking about the things that make them alike and less about the things that make each one so special. I have no doubt that there are real dangers in approaching the disciplines en masse rather than individually. One obvious danger is that students will be misled and will come away from their study of the disciplines thinking that one discipline is no different from another. But this need not happen any more than it need happen that a student of music comes away thinking that all music sounds alike. Another danger is that the substantive matter of the disciplines – the key concepts and basic ideas and their relationships – will be lost to view. How can even the most important findings of the disciplines be taught if all the disciplines are relegated to a single school subject? There is nothing, however, in the present view of the place of the disciplines in the curriculum which prevents the findings of the various separate disciplines from entering into any or all the subjects of the curriculum as subject matter to be taught and learned. Where various social roles are studied, the findings of sociology, psychology, anthropology, and history could all come into play. And the substantive content of the natural sciences, or at least some of it, would surely find its proper home as well.

The smaller the curriculum space allotted the disciplines, the more room there will be in the curriculum for all the other human contexts worthy of study from within and without. There is one grave difficulty with the present attempt to put the disciplines in educational perspective, however. If we grant that students ought to see the disciplines from the standpoint of the actor, we must wonder how this can be accomplished if individual disciplines are not taught as such. There are no practitioners of the disciplines in general in the way that there are practitioners of history and physics and economics. Now I do not want to hold that it therefore makes no sense to talk about taking the actor's point of view, for we might be able to give sufficient content to the construct "practitioner of the disciplines in general" to allow us to talk intelligently about his point of view and about putting oneself in his position. But if we want our students to get "inside" *actual* human contexts – to engage in actual disciplinary activity or simply to get the feel of what it is like – they must engage in or get the feel of some *particular* discipline.

Let the student get "inside" at least one particular discipline, by all means; let him gain the know-how of the practitioner; let him feel at firsthand the pull of inquiry into some particular set of questions asked within a particular conceptual framework. But let us not suppose that he must get inside each discipline now fighting for a position in the curriculum in the course of his general education. I see no more reason to suppose that he should do this than to suppose that he must get inside each art. To be sure a myth has developed among educators that one cannot understand a particular discipline or art unless one has some competence in that discipline or art. There are any number of ways to understand any given thing, and although it may be the case that an artist can understand art in a way that a nonartist cannot, it does not follow that a nonartist cannot understand art at all. Similarly with the disciplines. There may be good educational reasons for including in a curriculum that assigns limited space to the disciplines the study of some discipline from within with the hope that the student will gain some competence in it, but we need not worry that those disciplines which are not studied from the "inside" cannot be understood.[32]

If we acknowledge that the disciplines constitute one way of life or form of human activity among many, and that the many deserve a place in the educational scheme of things, we will have to look for ways to do educational justice by the disciplines both from the "inside" and from the "outside" without doing injustice to everything else. Advocates of the Discipline Principle are of course in part reacting against what they consider to have been the utter disregard or misunderstanding of the disciplines by educators. The very thing I advocated above — namely, bringing in disciplinary findings insofar as they relate to important topics — is the very thing they have found to be horrifying. Mathematics, they will remind us, simply cannot be learned in the way it should be learned by bringing it into a unit on mining. I hope I will not be construed as recommending a return to the pre-Structure of the Disciplines days where subject matter from the disciplines was (or at least is said to have been) diluted and distorted, and schooling in general was (or at least is said to have been) soft-headed. I do not think that the disciplines must have a ruling hand over what goes into the curriculum in order for educational justice to be done them. What is important, it seems to me, is that at some point in the curriculum they are taken as important objects to be learned about and as important human contexts to be studied and entered into. Over and above this, it is important that they serve, along with other things, as sources of subject matter insofar as they bear on whatever is being studied. I fully agree with advocates of the Discipline Principle that education ought not to misunderstand or distort the disciplines; my purpose here has been simply to urge that advocates of the disciplines ought not be allowed to misunderstand or distort education.

32. I would hope that there would be a wide choice of disciplines to be studied from within, for it is no more reasonable to suppose that all students will profit from getting "inside" some particular discipline than that all will from getting "inside" art or music or the dance.

Part II

AIMS AND OBJECTIVES

Introduction

    R. S. Peters gives us an extended analysis of the concept of mental health, an analysis that includes within it a discussion of the notions of human nature, basic needs, and growth or self-actualization in his essay "'Mental Health' as an Educational Aim." On the basis of this analysis he concludes that mental health is not suited to the role so often assigned it of unifying educational ideal. Talk of mental health, he says, after examining Marie Jahoda's six criteria of mental health, is necessarily negative. It stipulates that there be a degree of regulation and absence of conflict for any system of wants to be satisfied and lays down necessary conditions for this, but it does not tell us what wants are worth satisfying. It is, then, relevant and important for education to the extent that warped and stunted children may result from foolish teaching methods; but it cannot provide education with positive ideals. On Peters's view the task of education is to hand on worthwhile traditions, skills, and activities in such a way that the ideals and principles immanent in them are also handed on. Education is concerned, then, with the maintenance and extension of rationality in a way that goes far beyond the minimal requirements of mental health. It is in no sense a remedial business, and mental health talk in relation to educational ideals besides its other inadequacies is to be condemned for likening the teacher to a special sort of doctor.

    Peters is concerned with the inability of the concept of mental health to function as a unifying educational ideal. In "Learning with Understanding" Hugh G. Petrie is concerned with something much less exalted than a unifying ideal; something, indeed, which those who argue over unifying ideals may take for granted as an educational aim. Petrie neither advocates nor rejects the view that what is learned must be learned with understanding. Instead he devotes his attention to the question of what it is to learn with understanding. He asks first what it is to learn a fact with understanding. He proposes three necessary conditions for this, conditions very much like but not identical with the traditional conditions of knowledge. In the course of elaborating on them he brings to light a number of important decisions involved in curriculum development. He argues, for example, that the notion of having good reasons is essentially open-ended and that there can be, therefore, any number of levels of understanding. But if this is so, the curriculum designer has a major job: he must identify the relevant contexts and the relevant kinds of understanding to be aimed at. Petrie asks next what it is to learn a subject matter or discipline with understanding. This question leads to an examination of the notion of structure and of the view that the structure of a discipline should be taught. He concludes that learning a discipline with understanding involves learning facts and a methodology and the essay ends with an account of the nature of methodological principles and what it is to learn a methodology with understanding.

The discovery approach to teaching and learning is opposed in the minds of many to rote learning and linked instead with learning with understanding. Petrie has some interesting things to say about this approach and its connection with learning with understanding. J. P. White's essay "Creativity and Education: A Philosophical Analysis" sheds further light — some direct, some indirect — on discovery and its place in education. White examines the notion of creativity and discusses the place of creativity in education. He argues that 'creative', when used in relation to Dostoevsky as novelist or Einstein as scientist, is an evaluative term, whereas when it is applied to the child who thinks up as many uses for a brick as he can, or the child who has to discover a mathematical rule for himself, it is not. When, therefore, we call children who do things of this sort 'creative' we must recognize that their creativity is not the creativity of the scientist or novelist. White discusses the possibility that there is an empirical connection between educational cases of creativity and creativity of the Einstein variety. He does not rule it out any more than he rules out the possibility that creative activities are effective in producing learning, but he points up some important differences between the two sorts of creativity. Now all this may be granted yet it may be maintained that at least the girl in infant school who crayons what she likes is creative in just the same sense that an artist is. White discusses this view and the issues in aesthetics lying behind it at length and ends by raising the question of whether teachers ought to try to make pupils creative in the value sense of 'creative.'

White denies that the boy who thinks up uses for a brick is being creative in the sense that the really creative people throughout history have been creative, but he does not deny that the boy's enterprise is an imaginative one. Yet what is it to say that an enterprise is imaginative or that someone is using his imagination? And what is the place of imagination in education? K. Charlton in "Imagination and Education" explores the notion of imagination and deplores its neglect in education. He argues that to encourage imagination is not to encourage escape from reality, as is sometimes supposed, but is rather to encourage an important means of apprehending reality. He points out that imagination enters into science and history as well as into poetry and art and argues that curriculum proposals which are based on the assumption that imaginative and logical thinking are fostered through very different types of content are misguided. Charlton approaches the notion of imagination through an investigation of the uses to which the term 'imagination' and its cognates are put. He concludes that imagination is not to be thought of as a nuclear faculty; it is not a distinctive kind or type of thinking which is exercised in one way regardless of context. To see things in the mind's eye is an exercise of imagination, but so is growling like a bear or getting inside the mind of a crusader or, for that matter, the mind of one's fellow man.

Each essay in this section contributes to our understanding of some educational aim or objective — or at least of some purported aim or objective. Whether understanding an aim or objective breeds advocacy or contempt is another matter as these essays testify. Each essay in this section also brings to light some general and quite basic problem about educational aims or objectives. The Peters essay raises what is perhaps the most basic question of all, namely whether talk of aims in relation to education is legitimate, and, if it is, in what contexts it is. We cannot here do justice to Peters's question, but in view of the fact that any number of essays in this volume discuss aims and objectives without qualms, we would do well to emphasize that Peters is talking about education *as a whole*. It is one thing to object to the view that education as a whole must have an aim beyond itself and quite another thing to maintain that aims or objectives do not enter into education *at any point*. The parts of a whole need not share the characteristics of that whole. Thus, even if Peters is right in maintaining that education ought not be viewed as a means toward something else, it does not follow that talk of aims and objectives has no place in discussions of curriculum. Actually, Peters seems to be objecting not only to the view that education as a whole has some aim outside itself, but also to the view that certain parts of education — the study of science, history, literature, carpentry, for example — have aims of this sort. But the distinction just drawn applies at this level too. Thus, supposing he is right that the subjects studied ought not to be viewed as having aims beyond themselves, it still does not follow that talk of aims and objectives has no place in discussions of curriculum.

Peters's essay makes clear the importance of specifying what an aim is *of.* White's essay reveals the need for this also, for his discussion of creativity and education reminds us that at least some things can function as an aim in one context and as a means in another. Thus, for example, if making a person creative in the value sense were a legitimate objective of, say, mathematics education, and "creative activities" such as figuring out a mathematical rule on one's own did in fact foster such creativity, then creative activities would be a means to achieving the aim of creativity. Yet a teacher might have to bring effort to bear to get a student to engage in creative activities so that a unit or lesson might have some creative activity — itself a means to a larger goal — as *its* goal. Indeed, even if the goal of creativity in the value sense were rejected, there might be other goals in relation to which creative activities functioned as means and, if there were, these activities might again appear as goals in some educational context.

The Peters and White essays bring out the context-bound character of aims or objectives. Petrie's essay touches on the question of the relation between aims and the means for achieving them. He claims that his analysis of learning with understanding shows the logical requirements that *any* instructional technique must meet if it is to bring about learning with understanding, but that empirical research is needed to show how best to meet these requirements. He claims, that is to say, that the aim or objective of learning with understanding does not require or dictate some particular instructional technique, although it may rule some instructional techniques out. Presumably this point holds not only for the aim in which he is interested but for other aims as well. Now Petrie's discussion of the discovery and lecture methods of teaching makes it clear that the empirical research he calls for will only bear fruit if alternatives are recognized and tested. One would expect this point too to hold quite generally. And if it does, then the problem of how best to meet the logical requirements placed by some aim or objective on any instructional technique becomes in part the problem of envisioning techniques that deserve to be tested. As Petrie's essay demonstrates, philosophical analysis can be of help in this task.

Insofar as Petrie's essay touches on the problem of the relation of aims and the means of achieving them, it does so through a discussion of instructional techniques or what might be called methods of teaching. Charlton's essay touches on the same problem from a different point of view. In his discussion of imagination and education he attacks the view that one particular sort of content must be used if a certain kind of thinking is to be fostered. His position in regard to aims and content is, then, parallel in important respects to Petrie's position in regard to aims and instructional techniques. It is interesting to compare Charlton's position on aims and content with the stand taken by Scheffler in his essay in Part I of this book. Scheffler takes subjects as given, so to speak. He casts doubt on the view that each subject has the potentiality to develop one desired trait and he takes the position that each subject embraces many such traits. Charlton starts from the other end. He takes the desired traits as given and casts doubt on the view that only one subject has the potentiality to foster any given trait. The two positions are independent for it would be possible to deny that for each subject there is only one trait yet hold that for each trait there is only one subject, and it would be possible to deny that for each trait there is only one subject yet hold that for each subject there is only one trait. If both positions are adopted, however, the picture we get of aims and content is not nearly so tidy a one as we might wish. It is an open and flexible picture, however, and we may in the long run be grateful for it.

"MENTAL HEALTH" AS AN EDUCATIONAL AIM

R. S. Peters

Introduction

In England we are developing a highly differentiated society and we are often warned that we shall soon have not merely two nations but a league of nations without a common culture and shared ideals. This should not surprise us; for where are such unifying ideals to be fostered? The study of literature, history, and the classics has had to be cut down to make room for the vast expansion in scientific education without which our society cannot survive, and the Church is rapidly losing the authority it once had as the source of unifying ideals. We tend to treat the doctor who looks after our bodies and the psychiatrist who looks after our minds with more respect than we treat the priest who advises us about our souls — if we still think we have one. For they are scientists; and it is scientists who are now coming to be thought of as repositories of wisdom about the mysteries of life.

This general trend explains why the educationist sometimes inclines his ear towards a new expert, the psychologist, when he is at loss to find new unifying educational ideals to replace the old religious ones. There is thus much talk in educational circles of "the mental health of the child," "wholeness," "integration," "adjustment," and all that sort of thing.[1] We no longer talk of turning out Christian gentlemen; we talk of letting people develop mental health or mature personalities. In America, so we are told, Freud's priestly role is much more explicitly acknowledged. Philip Rieff, for instance, in his recent book called *Freud, the Mind of the Moralist*,[2] sees Freud as the prophet of "psychological man," the final product of the quarrel

From T. H. B. Hollins (Ed.) *Aims in Education* (Manchester, England: Manchester University Press, 1964) and *Studies in Philosophy and Education*, Vol. III, No. 2, pp. 185–200. Reprinted by permission of the author, Manchester University Press, and Studies in Philosophy and Education, Incorporated.

NOTE: This article, which is based on a talk given on the B. B. C. Third Programme, was read as a paper to the Philosophy of Education Society at Harvard in March 1961. The author wishes to express his thanks to those participants in the discussion whose comments led to minor alterations and additions to the paper. It was first presented in embryonic form at the Department of Education in Manchester in 1960.

1. See, for instance, W. Allinsmith and G. Goethals, *The Role of the School in Mental Health,* (New York: Basic Books, 1960).

2. I. P. Rieff, *Freud, the Mind of the Moralist,* (New York: Viking Press, 1955).

of Western man with his own spirit. The classical legacy of political man, he declares, is an archaism; the Christian legacy of religious man has been repudiated; and experience has revealed the emptiness of the optimistic liberal picture of economic man. Freud heralded the advent of psychological man, the egoist trained in cautious prudence.

This estimation of Freud's role as a moralist may bear witness to the great influence of Freud on American intellectuals; to an Englishman it sounds somewhat quaint — rather like regarding Marx as the prophet of the health services. Nevertheless the general trend is with us, as is shown in the frequent references to psychological notions such as "mental health" in discussion about educational ideas.

The Concept of "Human Nature"

What, then, is the nature of such ideals and how far can the psychologist take us in justifying them? It might first of all be pointed out, of course, that "mental health" as an ideal is obviously a normative notion and that moral philosophers have demonstrated conclusively the illegitimacy of passing from facts about man's nature to normative ideals. This is obvious and banal; the more interesting question is *how far* psychological considerations can take us in establishing such ideals. The psychologist would, presumably, have to start from generalizations about human nature. But his initial difficulty is to give much in the way of content to the concept of a general human nature. There is an obvious and important sense, of course, in which he must, like Aristotle, assume such a general human nature. Men, he could say, have wants, but reason about them; they deliberate and choose and impose rules on them; they adopt plans and schedules. They are not just drawn towards goals like moths towards a light.

Now such a formal account is, as a matter of fact, very important if we are concerned with bringing out what is distinctively human; and, as will be seen later, it is indispensable to the notion of "mental health." Nevertheless, from the point of view of an empirical psychologist it is deficient because it lacks content; it merely articulates the sort of concepts that are necessary for describing typically human actions and activities.

The content of the scheme is filled in by reference to the standards of particular societies. That which a man wants, that for the sake of which he acts, his end, is something that has been picked out and named as a result of a particular social life which has reached the level of describing, explaining, and justifying what a man does. Dogs can only be said to wait for their dinner by analogy with men; for it is the framework of rules and standards that converts a substance into "food" and which makes it part of our "dinner"; and it is by reference to ends like "eating dinner," "getting married," and "getting promotion" that we give content to our explanatory schemes. What we call "human nature" will therefore vary from society to society; and there is not much future in trying to erect any universal standards of what is good for man on that basis, unless we have in mind an ideal such as "adjustment." But a man could be perfectly "adjusted" if he conformed to the standards of a Nazi society; and few psychologists would want to hold up the Nazi mentality as an ideal of mental health or of the good for man.

But must accounts of human nature to which a psychologist would appeal in justifying an ideal such as that of "mental health" be as culture-bound as this? Is there nothing in terms of the contents of human nature which could provide counsels which escape the local autonomy of differing cultural standards? Could not, for instance, the followers of Freud make a case for wants which are varied in their manifestations but universal in their insistence — like those for food, sex, and safety? Any man ignores these at his peril in spite of the fact that what counts as appropriate objects for such wants will vary from culture to culture.

Basic Needs and Mental Health

When we come to a level like this, which is the level of basic needs, we have indeed come to a point where the psychologist may be able to give advice which is not altogether culture-bound; but it is important to be clear about the sort of advice it is and how essentially limited it is. For the notion of "needs," to which the doctrine appeals, really presupposes the notion of "wants." What a man needs is that which it would be injurious for him not to have. But the standard of what constitutes injury depends on what a man wants. We speak of a man's need for money. But what is money necessary for? Presumably for things like his dinner, which is something that he wants. And if we say that any man needs food, that is because it is necessary for keeping alive which, presumably, everyone wants to do. But to be alive, unless we are merely talking about keeping our hearts beating, involves the satisfaction of a variety of wants. Thus, although the manner of being alive, the wants that are thought to be worth satisfying, will vary according to personal and cultural preferences, there are, it could be argued, at least some things, like food, water and oxygen, which are necessary conditions for the satisfaction of any other wants, whatever these wants may be.

The psychologist, however, speaks of love and safety as needs, not just of water, food and oxygen. What are these more intangible things necessary for? The answer is that the psychologists have shown them to be necessary for the realistic development and effective *regulation* of wants within a system, whatever the system may be. The miser, for instance, has a style of life which is witness to the need for safety being satisfied in a way which disregards the need for love and to love. A man may come to see money not as what it is — a means of satisfying other wants — but as something valuable in itself. And this irrational want may spread like a cancer until a man's whole outlook becomes distorted and warped. Similarly a paranoid's estimation of every situation is constantly distorted by the all-intrusive thought that people are plotting against him.

And so we return, after a detour, to the rather formal notion of what is essentially human from which we started — the rationality of man as exhibited in his realistic appraisal of himself and his environment and in the regulation of his wants. And, in spite of its formal character, this conception of man as essentially rational not only provides a standard for psychological counsel which is not culture-bound but also includes most of the conceptions of "mental health" which are current in the literature on the subject. To establish this latter point I propose to consider the six approaches to a concept of "mental health" which Marie Jahoda distinguishes in her acute and commendably short work on the subject.[3]

Jahoda's Six Criteria of Mental Health

Jahoda, after an exhaustive examination of different psychological conceptions of mental health, thinks that they all fall under one or more of the following six criteria:

(1) Self-awareness and self-acceptance.
(2) Growth and self-actualization.
(3) Integration.
(4) Autonomy.
(5) Perception of reality.
(6) Environmental mastery.

I wish to show that all these notions except one can either be subsumed under the more general notion of "rationality" or be shown to be one of the "needs" already distinguished whose satisfaction is a necessary condition of such rationality.

Of the above six criteria Jahoda herself explicitly links the last three with the individual's relation to reality. Her fifth criterion of "perception of reality" is the clearest case of this. This may be manifest, first of all, in perception that is free from need-distortion, which is the reverse of that of the psychotic. Situations, of course, can be appraised in terms of a variety of objective criteria on the basis of which what is really so can be distinguished from how it may appear to a particular percipient. To be rational implies, amongst other things, to be disposed to assess situations in terms of such objective criteria; to be irrational is to see them under the aspect of what is

3. M. Jahoda, *Current Concepts of Positive Mental Health,* (New York: Basic Books, 1958).

needed or wished for. A "mentally healthy" or rational person, on this view, will seek evidence to distinguish between what he wishes a situation to be and what it really is, even if his finding goes against his wishes. "One lacking in mental health will not seek evidence, or will reject it, if it is presented to him and does not suit him" (p. 52). This freedom from distortion is also sometimes stressed in the context of knowledge of others, where additional sensitivity is required in order to perceive situations from the other person's standpoint and thus to anticipate and predict his behaviour. This is surely a capacity for objectivity in a context where such objectivity is notoriously difficult.

The sixth criterion of "environmental mastery" includes a rather ill-assorted rag-bag. The ability to love, for instance, is often stressed; but on my view this features as a basic need, as a necessary condition for rational behaviour and hence for "mental health" as well as an exemplification of it, where "love" may refer either to a capacity for affection or to the more specialized neo-Freudian notion of "genitality" as the "potential capacity to develop orgastic potency in relation to a loved partner of the opposite sex" (p. 55). Similarly, "adequacy in personal relationship," which is another quality falling under this criterion, is a combination of realistic appraisal of others and of not being stunted by an inability to care for them. Others stress adequacy in work and play or a more general ability to master the environment, or to adapt efficiently to it, which is exemplified in the carrying out of tasks and roles. Such notions surely fall under the general requirement of practical rationality, the effective imposition of plans and rules on wants. Jahoda makes this explicit in her own requirement for mental health in which emphasis is laid on efficiency in problem-solving behaviour (pp. 62-64). There may well also be some basic need for mastery or achievement underlying such behaviour which is on the same psychological level as the need for love and security already dealt with in my account of basic needs. White's notion of "competence" would cover the sort of thing which I have in mind.[4]

"Autonomy," Jahoda's fourth criterion of mental health, is clearly related to rationality in that there is a long-standing tradition which equates rationality with self-determination in the sense of acting on thought-out principles. Thus Jahoda's last three criteria are clearly related to the concept of reality in so far as this includes the capacity for forming rational beliefs, for taking efficient and socially appropriate means to ends, and for acting on thought-out principles.

There is, however, another notion often associated with rationality which is that of *regulation* of wants in relation to each other by foreseeing the consequences of satisfying them and imposing schedules on them in terms

4. R. White, "Competence and the Psycho-sexual Stages of Development" in *Nebraska Symposium on Motivation,* 1960.

of practicality, compatibility and compossibility, so that the individual is not involved in perpetual frustrations and conflicts. And this notion takes care of Jahoda's third criterion, which is the much vaunted "integration of the personality" — a notion as old as the Greek one of the harmony of the soul. This "balance of psychic forces in the individual" (pp. 36-39) implies, in Freudian terms, the accommodation by the Ego of the Id and Superego without eliminating or denying their demands. This is made possible, in part, on the view of psychologists such as Allport, by the adoption of some "world view" which unifies an individual's outlook, especially by the singling out of long-range goals. It would indeed be impossible to impose such schedules on wants and to make decisions about priorities without general rules and the distinction between long-term and short-term interests. Whether much more than this is involved in a "world view" is difficult to say. The notion of a world view, like that of "commitment," has emotional overtones to it which convey different things to different people. Certainly little more than a basis on which decisions about priorities can be made is required for "integration." Those who are able to regulate their wants in this way are often spoken of as having "frustration tolerance" or as being able to "delay gratification." Tension does not put them into a panic. (p. 42).

Jahoda's first criterion of realistic awareness and acceptance of oneself is easy enough, too, to include in the unifying notion of the rationality of man. For ever since Socrates those who have believed in developing man's rationality have stressed the importance of self-knowledge and self-acceptance. Allport stresses what he calls

> self-objectification, that peculiar detachment of the mature person when he surveys his own pretentions in relation to his abilities, his present objectives in relation to possible objectives for himself, his own equipment in comparison with the equipment of others, and his opinion of himself in relation to the opinion others hold of him. (p. 26).

This does not imply undue preoccupation with oneself, but a realistic estimate of oneself when such an estimate is appropriate. This, of course, is a particular case of the criterion of realistic belief. Fromm makes this explicit when he describes mental health as characterized by "the grasp of reality inside and outside of ourselves, that is, by the development of objectivity and reason" (p. 27).

I come now to the only one of Jahoda's criteria which it is difficult to incorporate in this analysis — the second one of growth or self-actualization. And there is a good reason for this; for, in my view, it goes beyond both a limited notion of rationality and beyond that of "mental health." And that, as I shall hope to show, is why it is the special concern of the educator rather than that of the psychiatrist. It will be worthwhile, therefore, to consider this second criterion more carefully.

Self-actualization and Civilization

To date, the analysis of "mental health" has dealt only with the development and regulation of wants in a manner which is realistic, undistorted, and comparatively free from conflict. Nothing has been said about which wants are worth satisfying. What has been stressed, however, is that a man can develop undistorted wants and regulate his wants effectively only if his basic needs are not grossly thwarted. This effective regulation of a system of wants is often referred to as the "integration of personality" or "mental health." The psychologist has laid bare some of the conditions which militate against its development. He is thus in a position to prescribe certain things which men need above the level of food, water, and oxygen. For unless we satisfy our needs for love and safety we shall be forever at sixes and sevens with ourselves, not satisfying a variety of wants properly because of conflict and indecision, or suffering from strange fears and distorted wants which cloud our perceptions and warp our judgment. But advice about mental health and what is necessary for it is negative, limiting sort of advice. It does not tell us what wants are worth satisfying; it stipulates merely that there must be a degree of regulation and absence of conflict for any system of wants to be effectively satisfied, and lays down certain necessary conditions for this.

Advocates of "growth" or "self-actualization," however, explicitly go beyond the requirement of the satisfaction of basic needs and the limited, rather formal, requirements involved in the notion of rationality or "mental health" so far outlined; and they write these additional recommendations into their account of "mental health." Maslow, for instance, distinguishes "deficiency motivation" from "growth motivation." The former covers what I have called basic needs — biological needs together with those for love, security, etc. — which he regards as forms of "tension reduction." These are to be contrasted with "self-actualization of potential capacities and talents, to devotion to a mission in life or a vocation, to activity rather than rest or resignation. A self-actualizing person experiences the maintenance of tension in these areas as pleasurable; he cannot be understood as being motivated here by the need for tension reduction. The greater the amount of growth motivation, the healthier a person is" (p. 33). Allport too maintains that "by growth motives we refer to the hold that ideals gain upon the process of development." It is connected with the extension of the self, with "investment in living" and with growth and direction towards goals higher than the mere satisfaction of basic needs. Presumably, then, on this showing, a peasant living just above the subsistence level would be mentally unhealthy. He would have some practical shrewdness, perhaps, and some traditional system of values which would give him principles by reference to which he could regulate his wants. He would thus satisfy the third criterion of "integration." He would not, however, be "self-actualizing" because I am postulating that he has no goals which are higher than the mere satisfaction of basic needs.

Now it is admirable enough to hold up such self-actualization as an ideal; though its justification is a difficult matter;[5] but it is odd to build it into a concept of "mental health." And does it not differ radically, in emphasis at any rate, from the criteria of the Freudian school, to mention only the classical exponents of the notion of "mental health"? For, it might be argued, does not the Freudian take us farther than telling us what we must have if we are to satisfy and regulate any system of wants? Does he not also intimate a more positive policy by suggesting that some wants are natural, whereas others are artificial, derivative, and hence unimportant in comparison with the natural ones? Sex, eating, drinking, he would hold, are fundamental to man in a way in which art and arithmetic are not. Wants, in other words, can be arranged in tiers, with the bottom level nearest to nature.

Whatever is meant by 'nature' in this account, it is really of little help, even to a Freudian, in deciding which wants are worth pursuing. For on this view scientific investigation itself, to whose ideals Freud himself was resolutely committed, is an "unnatural activity" — a sublimation of infantile sexual curiosity or a method of reassuring himself against insecurity. Nevertheless he has to make judgments in which the time he is to give to science must be weighed against the rival attractions of food, sex, and the pursuit of power. The explanation which he gives of such activities may influence his judgment. A Freudian, for instance, would be unlikely to discount the claims of sex in the ways in which an artist or religious man might. But such a view of human nature would do little more than limit his judgments about what was worth doing. It would not provide positive counsels for his own life or for the education of his children.

In this respect a Freudian is in the same kind of boat as the rest of us. For, without going into any special theories, we can easily see how psychological considerations of this sort do little more than limit the range of our judgments. A man might have plenty of food, sex, drink, and security — a pastoral life surrounded by the joys of the countryside. But when we spoke to him of the delicacies of human relationships, of art, of the excitement of discovery, he might spit and say that we needed our brains tested. From a psychological point of view he might be mentally healthy, integrated, adjusted — all of these things — but at the level of what Plato called "the necessary appetites." The Freudian can do little more than tell us that we neglect these at our peril; for he sees mental illness and neurosis as brought about by the ways in which such basic needs are thwarted or stunted. But his ideal of mental health is a negative one, to be defined against the absence of

5. See R. S. Peters and A. P. Griffiths, "The Autonomy of Prudence," *Mind,* April 1962.

such deviations, distortions and conflicts. It is tantamount to the requirement that man should try to preserve his essential nature as a rational animal.

Those, however, who speak of "growth" and "self-actualization" explicitly go beyond these minimal requirements in their account of "mental health." And this is not very conducive to clarity; for though people may be missing a lot that they might find satisfying if they don't devote themselves to art, music, and good causes, it is odd to describe them as mentally ill. It may, perhaps, be the case that in a highly complex and competitive society men may become mentally ill if they don't get absorbed in something or other above the level of the necessary appetites – even if it be in football or sailing rather than in the campaign for nuclear disarmament. But a condition necessary for mental health under certain social and economic circumstances should not be written into the meaning of "mental health."

The Role of the Educator

We have indeed reached the limit above which counsels about mental health cease to have much application. For we have come to the point where Mill posed the contrast between the pig satisfied and Socrates dissatisfied. We have also, surely, come to the point where the psychologist leaves off and the educator takes over. For civilization is the constant endeavour of man to impose artifice on nature, to rise above the level of the necessary appetites. It involves the perpetuation of a whole mass of complicated activities that are worth doing for their own sake and that are not merely fuel for the glowing fire of our natural needs. The teacher is at the key point in this constant endeavour of man to hand on these activities and the critical attitude necessary for their continuance and development. To hand on these activities properly is also to hand on the ideals and principles which are, as it were, immanent in them. To teach science *as* science, philosophy *as* philosophy, or history *as* history is to pass on respect for truth, argument, and evidence; it is not simply to hand over a lot of information. These disciplines make explicit criteria by reference to which various forms of belief can be rationally assessed. The educator is therefore concerned in a positive manner with the maintenance and extension of rationality in fields which go far beyond beliefs which are necessary for the satisfaction of the necessary appetites. For the beliefs with which he is concerned are part and parcel of a quite different form of life.

But there are foolish and wise ways of handing on this thin crust of civilization, just as there are imaginative and dull ways of doing it. The psychologist cannot, *qua* psychologist, provide a justification of civilized activities, although his theorizing and practice as a psychologist is a preeminent example of a civilized activity; but what he can do is to warn teachers about foolish ways of passing on such activities. There are levels of development in childhood, and damage can be done if even the basic skills of reading, writing and arithmetic are passed on too early; there are ways, too, of teaching skills which may be damaging. And the importance of such skills can be emphasized with complete disregard for basic needs like those for love and security. Warped and stunted children may result from foolish methods of teaching. This is where talk of mental health, of integration, and of wholeness is relevant as a negative counsel of great importance. It is something that educators should never neglect while they educate people. But I have never been able to grasp how it could be thought that such counsels could ever provide positive ideals. For education is not a remedial business, unless one views life as something merely to be endured like an illness. The objection to talking of mental health as a unifying ideal for education is not simply, then, that it can at best be only a rather limited and negative counsel; it is also that it confuses the function of the educator in society with that of the doctor. The main function of the teacher is to train and instruct; it is not to help and cure.

While the educator is engaged in handing on the traditions, skills and activities which distinguish civilized life from that of the savages he must also be concerned with the development of rationality in a sense which is more basic than the development of critical standards by means of which highly sophisticated systems of belief can be assessed. He must be concerned with preserving the nature of man as a rational animal as covered by at least four of Jahoda's criteria of "mental health." Such an intelligent concern for the pupil as well as for the traditions of thought, the rules and the skills to be handed on has traditionally been referred to as the training of character and of the emotions. The former is concerned with rationality in the sense of helping children to impose plans and rules on their wants; the latter is concerned mainly with the development of objective standards of appraisal so that the child will come to view himself and the situations in which he is placed under aspects other than that of threat or what is wished for. The educator may also address himself to the task implicit in Jahoda's fourth criterion – the development of autonomy in the child, though little is known about how best this is done.[6] To speak of the teacher as being concerned with these things as well as with the transmission of knowledge and skills is a salutary corrective to a one-sided approach to children. But it is much better to speak of these things in traditional terms than to speak of mental health. For that confuses the image of the teacher's function in society. It is unnecessary and misleading to saddle the teacher with a remedial function by saying that "mental health" should be one of his aims when what is covered by this term can be referred to in more traditional ways which do not carry the

6. See R. S. Peters, "Freud's Theory of Moral Development in Relation to that of Piaget," *Brit. J. Educ. Psychol.,* Vol. XXX, Part III, Nov. 1960.

implication that the teacher is a special sort of doctor. This is not, of course, to say that there should not be experts readily available to whom the teacher can refer cases of breakdown; there are school doctors after all, and school dentists, so why not school psychiatrists? It is only to say that "mental health" should not be regarded as an aim of an educator.

The cynic, of course, might reply that schools for many adolescents are in such a sorry state that there is little more that can be done than to have policemen in to stop riots, caretakers to keep the place clean, doctors and dentists to look after physical health and psychiatrically trained "teachers" to care for the "mental health" of the inmates. For the conditions of schooling and the attitudes of the inmates make any talk of "education" as out of place as a fashion parade would be on a dung hill. But the cynic here concedes the main point which I am trying to make; and it is questionable whether his counsel of despair is justified in the light of examples of what can be done by imaginative teachers with the most unlikely material in appalling circumstances. Education is so much a matter of confidence, of imagination, and of enthusiasm; and it has not got to take the form of initiating farm-workers into a love for Shakespeare and symphony concerts. The emphasis on mental health reflects, amongst other things, a failure of nerve on the part of educators, a retreat from the positive.

Furthermore the reference to "mental health" as an educational aim is yet another way of perpetuating the obnoxious view that education must have some aim beyond itself, that it must have some practical use in "the outside world" or that it must be some sort of "investment" which it is worthwhile for a community to spend money on. Presumably "the outside world" refers to activities like business, government or running a home, which are "life" in some sense in which devoting oneself to photography, philosophy or painting are not. Education, on this view, is all right if it helps a man to make money, to get on with his neighbours or with his wife; if it can't it must be an ivory-tower eccentricity advocated by egg-heads. Now though activities such as science may contribute to practical ends it is treason to civilization to see them only under such an aspect. For education is not just a *preparation* for "living" in this sense; it is an initiation into a distinctive form of live. For an educated man is one who has an understanding of his own past, of literature and scientific discovery, and other practically "useless" activities, which distinguish him from rats and savages. Such a man would agree that material things have to be produced, houses built, wars fought perhaps, and governmental tasks efficiently and fairly carried out. For these practical concerns are necessary for perpetuating those truly civilized activities which distinguish civilized men from savages. Indeed much of the study of history, literature and philosophy is concerned with the evaluation, criticism and suggested improvement of ways of living. One of the diseases of contemporary thought about education is its preoccupation with the practical, with the mechanics of life, to the exclusion of concern about what sort of life is worth living.

It can be argued that such disciplines of thought and feeling have a practical function in so far as they constitute some general requirements for citizenship in a democracy. For such a society is a formal façade unless it is peopled by men and women who understand their own past and who can think critically and with understanding about current problems. There is some truth in this; but it has to be stated more cautiously. In the first place the democratic way of life, in so far as it embodies principles like equality, justice and liberty, is an articulation in a social context of "rationality" in some of the senses already distinguished.[7] And this way of life, in so far as it can approximate under modern conditions to the Athenian polis, might be regarded as valuable in itself. But it might also be regarded as instrumentally valuable in that it is necessary, in so far as it provides conditions of security and noninterference, for other pursuits that are worth while in themselves. This was Spinoza's defence of democracy. This point can be illustrated by the story of the philosopher who was upbraided by the Marxist for only being concerned to understand the world and not to change it. The philosopher asked the Marxist what people were going to do when the classless society had been attained. To the admission by the Marxist that people might then get round to more theoretical pursuits like philosophy, the philosopher replied, "Maybe I am ahead of my time, then."

In the second place disciplines like history and literature are debased and distorted if they are used consciously to inculcate "critical thinking" and sensitivity. Such habits of mind may in fact develop if people enter imaginatively into philosophy, history and literature and come to appreciate what they are from the inside. They must care about the problems there presented and must come to appreciate things like the cogency of arguments, the elegance of proofs, the inevitability of events. But they can only do this from the inside. Without this initiation into the activity, "critical thinking," sensitivity, and so on become superficial secondhand things, a gloss which enables people to talk at parties, not structures built deeply into their minds. And the disciplines themselves become distorted and mangled. Indeed the classics may come to appear only in books of "Readings"!

Whether an activity is practical or not depends on the aspect under which it is viewed. Both science and carpentry can be viewed as instrumental to something else or they can be valued for what they are, for the extent to which they come up to their own intrinsic standards of excellence. For many people the delights of history, science and literature are difficult to appreciate. But there are civilized delights in simpler skills which are

7. See S. I. Benn and R. S. Peters, *Social Principles and the Democratic State,* (London: Geo. Allen & Unwin, Ltd., 1960), *passim.*

attainable by most men. The question is whether things are done mainly because they contribute to extrinsic ends such as money or prestige or whether they are delighted in for their own sake. And, of course, many activities are and must be regarded under both aspects. The preoccupation with the practical is the tendency to look on activities only under a means-end aspect.

In the struggle to develop a civilized form of life many have become mentally ill, and many of the great advances in civilization have been made by men who were patently mentally ill. So what? Does this detract from the value of their efforts? Surely not. It shows however that what is called "self-actualization" is often pursued at a cost. And if some enthusiastic educators, who really understand what education is about, sometimes push their pupils too hard and forget that they have emotions to control, a love life to lead, and a "living" to be earned, it may be salutary to remind them of this from time to time. But this is better done by speaking of this in terms of vocational training, of the training of the emotions and of character. For such old-fashioned ideals did at least not confuse the task of the educator with that of the doctor. They did at least imply that children were to be treated as responsible agents worthy to carry on the activities of a civilized community; they did not imply, as does the stress on mental health, that children are to be treated as patients who have to be weaned in a kindly way to nibble at the raw meat of the modern world.

LEARNING WITH UNDERSTANDING

Hugh G. Petrie

Even a casual glance at current literature on curriculum is sufficient to impress one with the wide diversity of interests and problems. One hears of curriculum theory, planning, implementation, and evaluation. Distinctions are made among the curriculum as a whole, the curriculum of any given area or subject matter over the period of schooling, and the curriculum contained in an individual course or unit. And yet there is a cluster of constantly recurring problems which seem to exercise people working in the area of curriculum more than any other. This cluster of problems is illustrated by the contrasts: subject centered — child centered, content — problem solving, discipline — whole child, education for knowledge — education for life.

And yet for all the smoke, there seems to be one point of mutual agreement between these camps. Whatever is learned must be learned with understanding. So rather than take sides in this issue, I simply want to ask the prior questions, What is learning with understanding? What is it to learn a subject matter with understanding? What is it to learn a fact with understanding? What is it to learn a methodology with understanding? What are the relations, if any, among these prima facie different kinds of learning with understanding?

To answer these questions I will first explicate learning an individual fact with understanding. Then using the notions developed there I shall turn my attention to learning a subject matter or discipline with understanding. Finally I shall consider what it is like to learn with understanding how to

This selection is published here for the first time.

NOTE: The reader familiar with current work of an analytic nature in the philosophy of education will note many parallels in this work and Israel Scheffler's *Conditions of Knowledge* (Chicago: Scott, Foresman and Co., 1965). Although I am deeply indebted to Scheffler for the direction given my thoughts by his earlier book, *The Language of Education* (Springfield, Ill.: Charles C. Thomas, 1960), the present essay is largely based on my own doctoral dissertation, "Rote Learning and Learning with Understanding" (Stanford University, 1965), which was written independently of any knowledge of Scheffler's *Conditions of Knowledge*. That such a parallel of ideas and arguments should have arisen independently at the same time may hopefully be some confirmation of their cogency. The slightly different twist I have given to the classical analysis of knowledge in applying it to learning with understanding will, I hope, justify repeating some of the lines of argument already familiar to the reader of *Conditions of Knowledge*. Of course, any errors that remain are my responsibility alone.

solve problems in a subject matter, i.e., the methodology of the discipline. On the way I shall comment on the notions of "structure" and "discovery" as these are commonly used in the educational literature. Perhaps through a clearer picture of just what 'learning with understanding' means in these different areas, curriculum workers will more readily be able to see just what it is they are trying to do.

Learning an Individual Fact with Understanding

"John has learned with understanding that the earth revolves around the sun." "Sue has learned with understanding that the factors of X^2-X-6 are $X+2$ and $X-3$." "Bill has learned with understanding that people in mobs behave much differently than they do individually." Sentences such as these refer to examples of what I call learning an individual fact with understanding. The general formula is *"X has learned with understanding that p,"* where p is what logicians call an atomic proposition or the negation of an atomic proposition. Specifically, p is *not* a conjunction or disjunction or other truth-functional compound of simple sentences although it may be the negation of a simple sentence, e.g., "Sally has learned with understanding that the earth is not flat."

I propose the following as necessary conditions of *"X has learned with understanding that p."*

(1) X has come to believe through experience that p
(2) p
(3) X has good (justifying) reasons for believing that p.

Interpreted as they are below, I think that these three conditions also constitute a jointly sufficient condition for X's having learned with understanding that p.

It will be noticed that these conditions are closely connected with the classical analysis of knowledge as justified true belief, and since it seems obvious that knowledge and learning with understanding are intimately connected, the proposed analysis is at least initially plausible.

Let me now turn to a somewhat schematic defense of each of these conditions.[1] It might be urged that quite often students learn things which they do not really believe and even learn them with understanding. This sort of situation arises most often in advanced classes where the student is somewhat skeptical of what the teacher is presenting. But a moment's reflection should show that in such cases if the professor urges a particular proposition, p, which the student does not come to believe, then the student

1. This defense is spelled out in more detail in the author's "Rote Learning and Learning with Understanding," unpublished Ph.D. dissertation, Stanford University.

has not learned that p, but rather he has learned that the teacher *believes* that or *says* that p. In such cases the student also often learns that if he wants a good grade he should *say* or *write p* on a test in this course. But none of this shows that believing p is not a necessary condition of learning with understanding that p.

A more interesting problem arises when it is noted that belief is "intensional."[2] That is, roughly, what a person will come to believe depends not so much on the truth or falsity of what is believed or on the actual "state of affairs" represented by that belief, but rather on how the person "looks" at the "state of affairs." An illuminating example in the field of education concerns the oft-voiced student complaint, "I didn't know that was what was wanted." To give a somewhat trivial example, suppose a student has learned with understanding that the sum of the squares of the legs of a right triangle is equal to the square of the hypotenuse. Then he is faced with the question on a test to state and prove the Pythagorean theorem. But suppose further that for some reason the student has not learned that (and hence does not believe that) the Pythagorean theorem is identical with the one he has learned. He will not be able to answer the question despite the fact that he has learned the theorem.

Such examples can, obviously, be multiplied and made more sophisticated. What these examples point up for the curriculum worker and test constructor is that curricula and tests must introduce and test material in ways which the student can relate to his existing conceptual scheme of belief and knowledge. This also points to the importance, not merely pragmatic, of knowing what stage of cognitive development a student has reached at a particular point and introducing material to him which he can make a part of his conceptual apparatus. For the student's way of "looking" at the world is at least in part constituted by his already existing beliefs, and because of the intensionality of belief, material, if it is to be assimilated, must not merely be in a form which is true but must also be couched in concepts already grasped by the student. Or if new concepts are introduced, this must be done by relating them to the student's already existing conceptual scheme. This notion has long been recognized by educational psychologists. But what I am arguing here is that this is not merely a contingent fact, but a conceptual truth related to the notions of belief and understanding. A close examination of the psychological literature on this point will, I am confident, show that the "experiments" proving the necessity of relating new concepts to old in the learning process logically could not have yielded different results.

As concerns the truth condition, I cannot here enter into any detailed discussion of various theories of truth. I think it will be sufficient to note that

2. See, for example, W. V. O. Quine, *Word and Object* (New York: The Technology Press of the Massachusetts Institute of Technology, and John Wiley and Sons, Inc., 1960) for an excellent discussion of the intensionality of belief.

my analysis seems absolutely independent of any *particular* definition of truth which might be offered. Even a pragmatic conception of truth,[3] which I do not think is defensible, could only at best, it seems to me, collapse the truth condition into a consideration of the evidence condition. To put it another way, I am not concerned with giving an analysis of *knowing* that we have learned with understanding, but only of what it *is* to have learned something with understanding.

As far as the evidence condition is concerned, it should be obvious that this condition is necessary for understanding in almost any sense of that extremely vague and ambiguous term. To paraphrase Plato's famous example, a jury may have learned that the defendant in a trial is innocent in the sense that the jurymen have come to believe it and it is in fact, true; but if they have been persuaded of this through the defense attorney's rhetoric and not through sound argument, then they would not have learned *with understanding* that the defendant is innocent and would also not *know* that he is innocent. The general problem of just what it is to have a good reason is, however, extremely important and I shall return to it below.

It will be noticed that my analysis of having learned a fact with understanding differs from the classical analysis of knowledge in that in my analysis the belief must have been acquired through experience. The reason for this restriction is obvious enough. Knowledge of facts is, or at least may be, broader than the learning of facts. There may be some sort of innate knowledge or other kinds of direct knowledge which we would not want to say was learned. My phrase "through experience" is simply meant to rule out those kinds of knowledge if they exist. Furthermore, many of the problems connected with these conditions as an analysis of knowledge simply do not arise when they are considered as an analysis of learning with understanding. In particular it is sometimes claimed that to have reasons good enough to justify a knowledge claim, one must *know* the reasons and thus one is open to a charge of circularity if one is analyzing knowledge. Obviously such a charge will not apply to this condition as a part of an analysis of learning.

Secondly, in order to stop the infinite regress of having to have reasons for reasons for . . . , many philosophers have tried to isolate some special kind of knowledge which does not require reasons. Prime candidates for the objects of such knowledge are our own perceptions, sensations, thoughts, memories, and undertakings. The myriad problems surrounding such "directly evident" knowledge simply need not concern me, since it seems obvious enough that we do not learn (with understanding or otherwise) that we have a pain, for example. We simply know it, or so the argument runs. We may indeed learn how to identify our pains, but this is more like the acquiring of a procedure or skill than the acquiring of a fact. We may even learn with

3. See Israel Scheffler, *Conditions of Knowledge* (Chicago: Scott, Foresman and Co., 1965) for a detailed discussion of the truth condition to which I generally subscribe.

understanding that such directly evident knowledge (if it exists at all) is related to inferential knowledge in certain ways, but that is on an entirely different level from learning with understanding that we have a pain.

Finally, I want to allow a derivative sense of learning with understanding, which is just like the one I have explicated except that it lacks the truth condition. Such a conception seems to take care of the following two cases: (1) Consider the student of Ptolemaic astronomy who, on the basis of the evidence he then possessed, believed he knew that the sun revolved around the earth. Such a student could be said to have learned with understanding in this derivative sense that the sun revolved around the earth. (2) Consider the historian attempting to say what it would be like *given what was then known* to have claimed to know that the sun revolved around the earth. This historian may be said in the derivative sense to have learned with understanding that the sun revolved around the earth. Such a distinction between the primary and derivative senses of learning with understanding enables us, I believe, to grasp more clearly the difference between an internal critique of a position (i.e., a critique based on what was reasonable on the basis of the evidence known at the particular time) and an external critique of the position (i.e., a critique based on the total evidence). In any event, the most important part of the analysis for the purposes of education – the evidence condition – is the same in both primary and derivative senses and it is to this condition that I now turn.

What is it to have good reasons for a belief? It seems to me that the various answers given to this question constitute almost the whole of the history of epistemology. Classically the sources of such reasons have been given as perception, memory, self-awareness, and reason. Each of these sources provides us with reasons prima facie good enough for knowledge. But occasionally these reasons conflict. For example, until the recent development of satellites, perception provided only reasons for believing that the sun revolves around the earth. After all, it certainly *looks* as if it does. Of course, reason or theory gave us other reasons for supposing that we can explain these "looks" in virtue of the earth's rotation. Admittedly, this is oversimplified, but perhaps not a very great oversimplification of the situation that obtained at the time of the Copernican revolution, with the added feature that the Ptolemaic system could also "explain" the then observed facts quite as adequately, although perhaps not as simply, as the Copernican theory.

But what are we then to say when our prima facie good enough reasons conflict? It seems as if we must weigh up the reasons for and against in some way and come to a kind of rational *decision* as to which to make primary and which to explain away. But if we do this, we are left with a kind of paradox. For originally at least a part of our purpose in explicating good reasons was to reach some sort of criterion of what it is rational or justifiable to believe. But in carrying out this explication we seem to be left with the problem of at least occasionally making a rational decision about the very criteria of rationality.

On the other hand it has been argued by such as Hanson[4] and Kuhn[5] that the very material which serves as the "facts" to be accounted for by our theories, is itself theoretically dependent. That is, for example, the sun will only look as if it revolves around the earth if we are already committed to a Ptolemaic kind of astronomy. If, however, we believe in a Copernican astronomy, the situation will be that it looks to us as if the earth's horizon is falling away from the sun, i.e., that the earth is rotating. But even under this conception, the conclusion which is important for my purposes is the same, viz. that the criteria of having justifiable reasons for a fact and hence for having learned it with understanding are dependent on an interplay between experience and the criteria for the intelligibility of that experience.

It is considerations such as these which lead me to claim that the notion of having good reasons is essentially open-ended. If this is so, then a complete specification of what it is ultimately to understand anything is not possible. For particular inquiries, at particular times, and for particular people, the conditions for understanding are more or less fixed, and it is within each of these particular contexts that we can determine whether or not someone has learned something with understanding.

To say the above is not to imply that there are *no* constraints on rationality. Of course there are. Our theories and reasons should be as simple as possible; they should have maximum explanatory and predictive power. They must square with experience even though there may be no unique way of so squaring. Rather I am suggesting that there is a constant interplay, never to be entirely eliminated, between our canons of evidence and those particular reasons that we decide are good enough at particular times in particular contexts.

Even if there are some immutable general restraints on rationality and intelligibility — even, that is, if we can appeal to some standard of justification to decide if the Hanson-Kuhn type of argument is justified or unjustified — nevertheless it remains true that in the more limited area of traditional school subjects, the criteria of understanding them is open-ended in the way in which I have sketched above.

If the thrust of the preceding discussion is in the main correct, then there seems to be the implication that there can be any number of different levels of understanding possible. This is so because we must specify and decide for particular contexts what will count as "good enough" reasons. But

4. Hanson, N. R., *Patterns of Discovery* (Cambridge, Eng.: Cambridge University Press, 1958).
5. Kuhn, Thomas S., *The Structure of Scientific Revolutions* (Chicago: University of Chicago Press, 1962).

if we add to this the entirely plausible notion that a businessman need not and should not have the same kind of understanding of arithmetical truths as a mathematician, then a major job of the curriculum designer is immediately apparent: He must identify the relevant contexts and the relevant levels of understanding to be aimed at and tested for among the various kinds of students who will be schooled under his curriculum. And equally clearly, such decisions will be at least in part value decisions.

These are old conclusions, to be sure, but hopefully the considerations leading up to these claims will give added weight to them. Note too that the considerations thus far advanced do not depend on individual differences in the student's basic intellectual and emotional makeup, but rather on differences in kinds of understanding deemed desirable by value consideration of the roles the fully educated student is expected to fulfill.

Let me now turn to the problems of curriculum concerned with the individual differences of the students themselves. It seems to me that such problems can be most illuminatingly approached through a consideration, not of what it is to *be* a good reason, but rather of what it is to *have* a good reason. It is obvious enough that at least a necessary condition of having a reason for a proposition is that one believe the reason. But as already noted in my discussion of the belief condition and the intensionality of belief, this means once again that reasons must be presented in language and concepts which the student can grasp. It does no good simply to get a student to parrot a teacher's reasons if these are cast in terms the meaning of which is unknown to the student. For if the student does not grasp the meaning — and meaning here is to be interpreted in a narrow linguistic sense — of the terms employed by the teacher, he cannot, logically cannot, believe the reasons being offered and a fortiori cannot have the reasons which are necessary to his understanding.

But of even more importance is the fact that mere belief in reasons is insufficient to guarantee understanding. Two simple examples will help to make this clear. A student may believe the axioms and rules of proof of geometry, but unless he can also put them together in just the right way, he does not *have* good reasons for believing a particular theorem of geometry, although logically the axioms and rules of proof *are* good reasons. Or consider the case of the detective story in which at a particular point the reader is informed that he has all the clues that the detective had and is invited to try his hand at determining who did it. Clearly, we very often do not have the clues in such a situation in a strong enough sense to guarantee our having learned with understanding who did it.

What these examples show is, roughly, that to 'have' reasons in a strong enough sense to guarantee understanding it is not sufficient merely to believe them. We must also see the point of the reasons as reasons. We must be able to fit them into a whole structure of explanation and inference. And to be able to foster this as educators requires that we know and take into account the various individually different ways in which such structures are conceived and worked out by different individuals. Individual differences must be taken into account in a consideration of having good reasons. Obviously, different socioeconomic backgrounds can also influence the conceptual scheme of the student, thus showing the necessity of taking this factor into account in curriculum planning.

The foregoing discussion gives, I think, the theoretical support necessary to see the importance of the recent work by Piaget, Bruner, and others in mapping the cognitive apparatus of students at various stages in their development and the various strategies they use for seeing the point of different sorts of reasons. Without such work we have only common sense notions to guide us in constructing curricula which the students can understand.

On the other hand, there is no reason to assume, as some apparently have, that so-called "discovery" methods of teaching are inherently better than traditional lecture methods, for example. In the absence of detailed knowledge of a student's cognitive development and problem solving techniques, it may be more reasonable to expect that he will be able to fit new material into his conceptual scheme and thus really have reasons for his beliefs if he is allowed to discover the reasons for himself. However, a lecture carefully planned and structured with the knowledge of what the student's conceptual scheme is at the time may be much more effective and lead to just as great an understanding. What my arguments show is what any instructional method must take into account if it is to aid in learning with understanding. I have been concerned with the logical requirements of learning with understanding and not with evaluating particular pedagogical techniques.

Learning a Subject Matter or Discipline with Understanding

Given the foregoing brief sketch of what it is to learn some particular proposition with understanding, I want now to try to apply the ideas developed there to the notion of learning a subject matter with understanding. It might be supposed in learning a subject matter that there is first of all a more or less definite set of what might be called the facts of the subject, i.e., $P_1, P_2, P_3, \ldots$. It might be further supposed that in order to learn a subject one must learn a certain subset of these facts. Presumably this subset contains the basic or most important facts of the subject, but the criteria for marking out this subset are, unfortunately, never specified. Then what could be more natural, it might be urged, than to say that to learn a subject with understanding is simply to have learned with understanding most of the items of the subset of the important facts of the subject. Such a move would tie in very nicely with the preceding analysis of learning a particular fact with understanding. Furthermore, it might be urged that with the new emphasis on the structure of a discipline, one might even be able to begin to spell out that subset of facts of the subject which are basic. They are, simply, those facts which represent the structure of the subject.

I shall return to this notion of structure below, but independently of this notion it seems that the model sketched above is highly oversimplified because it does not take into account other than mere factual learning, even though the factual learning may be learning with understanding. As one example of this omission, let me consider briefly the notion of learning how to do something. That this sort of learning is not generally to be assimilated to learning with understanding is, I think, quite clearly shown by the following considerations: It is obvious enough that in many different sorts of learning situations one may have learned that in order to do such and such, one must do thus and so, and even have learned this with understanding, and yet not be able to do thus and so because one has not learned how to do it. One must learn techniques and procedures as well as facts. The most obvious examples are in skills such as swimming or skiing where one often learns that such and such are the principles that must be followed but has not yet learned how to do this. Conversely, many people have learned how to swim or ski without having the foggiest idea of what the principles are which describe their performance.

This point can be easily generalized. If there are any techniques or procedures in a subject matter which must be mastered in addition to factual learning, and almost all subject matters seem to have at least a few, then the above model, which speaks only of learning facts, will not be sufficient to account for learning a subject matter with understanding.[6] It is surely one of the most important tasks of the curriculum planner to isolate these other kinds of learning and see that they too are given their appropriate emphasis if the subject matter is to be learned with understanding.

However it can be objected, and rightly so I think, that in most if not all of the usual academic subjects learning the facts of the subject is crucial to understanding the subject. Furthermore, in recent times the emphasis on learning with understanding those facts which express the "structure" of the subject seems to provide a way of specifying just what facts must be learned if the subject is to be understood.[7] It is to this notion I shall now turn.

6. See Gilbert Ryle, *The Concept of Mind* (New York: Barnes and Noble, 1949) for the classic statement of the argument against reducing the learning and knowledge of skills to the learning and knowledge of facts. See also, Israel Scheffler, *Conditions of Knowledge* (Chicago: Scott, Foresman and Co., 1965) for a more detailed argument in this vein as applied directly to problems of education.

7. See Jerome Bruner, *The Process of Education* (New York: Vintage books, a division of Random House, 1960) for the classic source of the current discussion of "structure."

As I understand the current talk in this area, the structure of a subject seems to mean the principles of the subject; that is, the general statements, axioms, laws, and definitions which compose what can be called the theory of the subject. These are the statements which enable one to relate the particular facts of the subject into a meaningful whole. The structure of any scientific discipline seems fairly well defined. It is that empirically interpreted axiom system which together with empirical boundary conditions enables one to explain the facts in the field of the particular science. The structure of the more humanistic subjects such as history and literature is not so easily identified, but the feeling seems to be that it is that part of these areas which enables one to see the area as a meaningful related whole. Vague as this is, it already indicates major problems for the curriculum worker concerned with how to fit various subjects together into the total educational program. For if structure is to give any sort of guide to curriculum workers in this area, it would seem that there would have to be a structure of knowledge as a whole to guide such comprehensive efforts. But such a comprehensive structure, if it exists at all (and I have given reasons above for thinking that it does not exist), is clearly not anywhere in sight at the present. So structure at best can only be a guide to someone working with the curriculum of a particular subject. It is of no help whatsoever to the curriculum worker concerned with the total school program.

But even here the notion of structure seems to be more of a catchy slogan than any real sort of guide. To begin with, "the structure of a subject" is a false definite description. That is, it is not at all clear that even the exact sciences have a unique structure, let alone the humanistic studies. In fact it might be plausibly urged that a student does not understand a subject until he sees this divergence of ways of looking at "the" structure of his discipline. For example, there is no clear agreement in psychology as to whether "the" structure of psychology is to be viewed as a search for merely descriptive generalizations connecting stimulus and response, or whether a more complete theoretical framework is ultimately to be gained. To take another example from logic, there is still quite a bit of controversy as to whether the set-theoretical, truth-functional approach or the constructive, intuitionistic approach is the proper way to view "the" structure of logic. The situation is, of course, even worse in the humanistic studies. Thus for a curriculum worker to speak of "the" structure of a subject would imply that he has made some sort of value decision as to which of various structures is to receive the honorific title of "the structure." This is not to say that the curriculum worker should not make such a decision, but only to suggest that if he is not aware of this decision, a deep understanding of the subject in the sense of understanding various structures runs the risk of being ruled out of court at the outset. And notice that this sort of deep understanding is totally different from the notion of a deeper understanding gained by "spiralling" back on an already presupposed unique structure.

Secondly, as has been pointed out since Dewey, there is the danger of simply assuming that the logical structure of any subject, understood as above, automatically points the way to the pedagogical structure. The classical method of teaching geometry in terms of axioms and theorems to be derived shows most explicitly this sort of unwarranted conflation of logical structure with pedagogical structure. And by pedagogical structure I simply mean that way of presenting the material in order to lead most efficiently to an understanding of the logical structure or structures. The distinction is familiar enough so I shall not belabor the point.

In passing, however, one must note that there is an equal danger on the other side. Most of the newer inductive or discovery approaches to the teaching of the exact studies recognize very well the above distinction between logical structure and pedagogical structure. However, many of the advocates of such discovery teaching seem to argue that since pedagogical structure *need* not be identical with logical structure, therefore pedagogical structure *cannot* be identical with logical structure — a clearly invalid inference. The confusion seems to lie in treating a logical point as if it were a psychological one. The logical point is this: If at least a part of learning a subject with understanding is to learn with understanding that *p,* where *p* expresses a basic principle of the subject; and if the learning of particular propositions with understanding involves coming to have good reasons in a strong sense; then a necessary condition of learning a subject with understanding is that the materials can be tied into the existing conceptual scheme of the student in the rather complex way I have sketched. But then, noting work by such as Piaget that indicates children at certain stages have little grasp of formal relations, the psychological conclusion is drawn that formal subjects must be taught inductively. This may be true, but it cannot be derived from the logical point alone. It could be derived only if additional premises were available stating something to the effect that methods teaching formal relations as such, starting from what the student does already know, are uniformly less successful than the inductive methods. But no such evidence is available and the effort required to get it would be staggering. Add to this the possibility of changing a student's state of development at a given time by different prior instruction and the enormity of the empirical task at least begins to become apparent.

An exactly parallel conflation arises when discovery teaching is compared with lecture methods. The advocates of discovery teaching seem to have got hold of the logical point that if understanding is to occur, the material must be in such a form that the student can believe it and *have* it as reasons. From this alone it is concluded that letting the student discover principles for himself is bound to be better than lecturing him. This may be true given the present style of lecturing, but once the logical point is noticed and the lecturer makes use of the knowledge he can glean about the students' state of development in preparing his lecture, it is not at all obvious that the lecture will be inferior in any way. In fact, I think everyone is already aware that occasionally a lecture, perhaps by luck, just happens to "hit" the students, and such a lecture would almost surely be a more efficient way of learning the material than the usual trial and error methods of discovery learning. What my analysis does, I think, is to show the logical requirements that any instructional technique must meet if it is to be successful. How best to meet these requirements clearly calls for much more empirical research.

These considerations lead directly into yet another problem with the notion of structure. Again supposing that at least a part of learning a subject with understanding is to learn with understanding that *p*, where *p* is a principle of the subject, and where this last logically involves coming to have good reasons in accordance with my analysis, it should be obvious that the notion of structure does not dictate the *level* or *kinds* of reasons which may be held. I have already argued that one can learn with understanding that *p*, with a great number of different levels of reasons. I further argued that no one level could claim any kind of priority without a decision or value judgment as to what will count as good enough in the given context. But if this is so, then the curriculum worker is not freed from his task of making value judgments as to the level of understanding required of any particular student. And furthermore, it is only if the value judgment is *explicitly* made that one could begin to evaluate the relative success of various programs in promoting the desired level of understanding.

Thus I see no reason to say that a high school student in a physics class, a college student taking physics, a graduate student in physics, and a professor in physics could not all have learned with understanding that $e = mc^2$. What differentiates them is the *kinds* of reasons each may have for his belief; whereas, understanding, it seems to me, can be most profitably viewed as the ability to fit a proposition into one's conceptual scheme at any of the different levels of reasons. I am not, of course, wedded to these particular words but rather to the two different distinctions of different kinds of reasons on the one hand, and the success or failure of being able to fit a fact (on any level) into one's conceptual scheme on the other.

Thus the notion of a "spiral curriculum" in which the (a?) structure is assumed and then the work spirals back upon this structure with ever increasing depth, or as I would prefer to say, with different kinds of understanding, is a notion which I can easily accept. But even though such a conception may be of some use to the curriculum worker, it cannot free him from the necessity of deciding at what places in the spiral different kinds of students should enter and leave. He must still decide what kind of understanding a mathematician should have of quadratic equations, vs. what an engineer should have, vs. what a fine arts major should have.

In summary, then, learning a subject matter with understanding is a complex matter. It includes, but is not exhausted by, learning with understanding that the principles which express the structure of the subject are the case. Depending on the subject it may also include many other kinds of learning besides the learning of facts, even with understanding. And most important of all it is open-ended in that the kind or level of understanding required must be decided on with reference to the particular student's needs, desires, and goals.

Learning a Methodology with Understanding

In general, learning the methodology of a particular field of inquiry or of inquiry generally is a matter of learning how to solve problems in the field, to carry on investigations, or to conduct inquiry in general. I have already urged that learning *how* cannot in general be reduced to learning *that*. From this it would certainly be plausible to maintain that one need not learn methodology in the sense of learning that one should do such and such at all. Rather the distinction must be noted, and the peculiar nature of learning how to do something in the sense of becoming proficient in performing in the appropriate way be emphasized. Such procedures as practice in the skill or technique would then seem to be the appropriate ways of learning a methodology. Thus the acquisition of skills and procedures can occur independently of the acquisition of rules describing the skills; e.g., people can learn how to ski without learning the precepts contained in a skiing instruction manual. Moreover, as is also evident, one may learn the precepts of skiing without learning how to ski. Thus learning a methodology with understanding is not to be assimilated in any straightforward way to learning facts with understanding.

Nevertheless there is a certain sense in which learning a methodology, if the methodology is made explicit, can be construed as learning facts on the "learning that" model. That is, if certain methodological principles can be extracted from the successful practice of the methodology then one might learn that *p*, where *p* is one of these principles, and even perhaps learn it with understanding. On the other hand it still remains true that one could learn the principles of methodology without becoming a good methodologist; that is, without learning how.

There are, however, several other problems associated with making a methodology explicit in terms of principles and then learning that these principles are the case. These problems seem to stem from the general form in which these principles are usually expressed: if one wants to do such and such, then one does thus and so. The problem in methodology seems to be that the hypothetical does not express a logical or even a universal contingent relationship. Methodological principles are usually heuristic only — they provide neither necessary nor sufficient conditions for reaching the desired result. To see this, let me adapt some language from logic. I shall call a methodological procedure "decidable" if and only if by following the procedure one is guaranteed of finding the correct solution if one exists. Thus a principle for spelling 'cat' would specify a decidable procedure for me since, if we follow it, we are guaranteed of success. It might run: To spell 'cat', leave a letter-wide space, then write 'C', then leaving no letter-wide space, write 'A' .... In the case of decidable methodological procedures it would seem as if the methodology could be learned with understanding in a strong sense. That is, all that might be lacking in assuring success would be practice in performing the particular actions. In my example one would merely have to learn how to write 'C', etc. On the other hand very few decidable methodological procedures seem to exist for more complex areas. In mathematics the nonexistence of a decidable procedure for applying 'is mathematically true' in systems strong enough to generate arithmetic has been rigorously demonstrated.

That most methodological principles are only heuristic — that they merely may provide aids in reaching solutions — can easily be shown. To see that such principles do not generally provide sufficient conditions for reaching a solution, one need only consider the investigator who follows the principle and yet fails to come up with an answer, e.g., the scientist who tries to find an explanation for some event in the accepted theory but fails, the mathematician who tries to construct a proof for a given proposition but fails. That the principle does not supply necessary conditions for a solution is also easy to see in the case of the scientist who makes a good intuitive guess as to an hypothesis without following any methodological principle at all.

But the fact the methodological principles are generally only heuristic is often obscured when these principles are made explicit. Too often does one become a slave to methodology. By the very fact that there is an explicitly formulated methodology, one can too easily slip into thinking that the procedures are decidable and not merely heuristic. And so we run the risks of not accepting some solution to a problem simply because it was not arrived at by the methodologically sanctioned principles and of stifling creativity by explicitly formulating a methodology which too often gives the impression that no answer exists if following the methodological principles does not lead one to it. It seems that it is then an empirical question as to whether or not teaching a methodology explicitly in a form designed to foster 'learning that' will aid or hinder intuitive kinds of thought. It should be noted, however, that if the methodological principles are learned with understanding, then the reasons for believing them should include not only inductive evidence that they do aid in the solution of problems, but also reasons for believing that they are, after all, only heuristic.

The upshot of this discussion seems to be that although it may be possible to learn with understanding that p, where p expresses a methodological principle, it is not in general necessary or sufficient for learning how to discover new truths in a subject matter or in general. Learning methodology in the full-blown sense of coming to be able to carry on one's investigations in a rational way is learning how to do certain things. However, even though 'learning how' is not reducible to 'learning that', it is not plausible to say that 'learning how' entails no 'learning that' statements. In particular, it seems that if someone has learned how to carry on investigations in a certain area, he must have learned that certain facts of the subject are the case. For example, it does not seem conceivable that one could have learned how to add long columns of figures without having learned that $1 + 1 = 2, 1 + 2 = 3$, and so on.

It seems that this point can be generalized to situations in which one has learned how to carry on original investigations leading to new knowledge. Roughly, the facts that must be learned in order to learn how to be a good methodologist are those pervasive facts that are such that any methodological procedure which depended for its success on the falsity of one of these facts would be automatically vitiated. Thus any procedure of adding long columns of figures that did not accord with the facts of arithmetic could not be successful. If this is so then it is a necessary condition of learning how to solve new problems that one has learned that certain facts are the case although there may be no general way of determining uniquely what these facts are. Learning a methodology cannot — logically cannot — be separated from learning subject matter.[8]

Furthermore, I can now give a sense in which learning a methodology with understanding depends upon learning facts with understanding. The person who wishes to learn a methodology with understanding needs to learn at least some of the pervasive known facts of the subject matter with understanding, and of even more importance he needs to learn with understanding that certain of the facts of his subject matter have methodological implications — vitiating some procedures and allowing others. Of course learning a methodology with understanding also requires that one acquire the requisite skills and procedures as well as the facts of the subject matter as well as the fact that there are logical relations between these facts and certain investigative procedures.

Summary

Several points have emerged from the discussion. First, I have argued for the inevitability of making value judgments in work in curriculum. These value judgments emerge in several places: in the kinds of reasons to be required for understanding, in where and when to enter and leave a spiral curriculum for different kinds of students, and in deciding how to present

8. See my "The Strategy Sense of 'Methodology'," *Philosophy of Science,* Vol. 35, No. 3, September, 1968, for a more detailed discussion of these points.

methodology. No doubt there are many other places as well. Furthermore, I have tried to clarify certain logical features of learning with understanding in a variety of situations and point to places where empirical work needs to be undertaken. Both the logical clarification and the empirical work should help curriculum workers make these value judgments in a more rational way.

Then I have argued for the necessity of spelling out as precisely as possible the different kinds of learning required in learning a subject with understanding. One must also see the proper "mix" of these various kinds of learning, as the mix will clearly vary from subject to subject.

And I have tried to show just what might be meant by learning the 'structure' of a subject, 'discovery' learning, and the 'spiral curriculum'. Properly understood these are valuable concepts, but they do not provide any sort of panacea for curriculum workers. I have urged that logical structure not be identified with pedagogical structure and, conversely, that a too facile separation of these two kinds of structure could easily obscure the vast amount of empirical work yet needed to help determine the best pedagogical structure or structures.

Finally, and perhaps most importantly, I have argued for the inadequacy of mere factual learning, even if it is learning with understanding, in accounting for learning a subject with understanding. I have indicated that learning techniques and procedures as well as other kinds of learning are also necessary. On the other hand, I have urged that one cannot learn how to solve problems in an area, or in general, without learning that certain facts are the case. A curriculum if it is to be coherent cannot choose between subject matter and methodology, between content and problem solving. Each has its place and each is connected in various ways with the others, but the exact connection is not always obvious and some supposed connections do not exist. Hopefully, the foregoing has begun to clear up these myriad relations.

CREATIVITY AND EDUCATION:
A PHILOSOPHICAL ANALYSIS

J. P. White

The appearance of yet another article on creativity and education needs a preliminary apology. So much has been written on creativity in the last ten years, from technical articles on the validation of creativity tests to books like *The Goldmine between Your Ears,* and so widely has the cult of creativity been adopted by teachers in Colleges of Education and elsewhere, that it is profitable perhaps to stop for a moment and look critically at some of the assumptions lying behind the various ideas which are being currently propagated. For, as I shall try to show, many of these ideas are radically confused; and it is in the desire to prevent such conceptual confusion from diverting teachers, especially in primary schools, from educational to non-educational or even anti-educational purposes, that I have written this article.

I. Four Cases of Creativity

In this section and the next I want to say something in general about the notion of creativity; later I shall go on to talk about creativity in education.

Let me begin by considering four cases:

(1) A girl at an infant school is given a pad of newsprint and a box of crayons. She is left alone to draw what she likes instead of having to fill in a colouring book with fixed outlines.

(2) A boy of twelve is asked to write down as many uses as he can think of for a brick. He produces a great number of unusual uses (as a bedwarmer, paperweight, bookend, etc.).

(3) A primary school child, learning mathematics, is given certain data and has to discover on his own a rule which explains them, instead of being told the rule by the teacher.

(4) Dostoevsky as a novelist or Einstein as a scientist.

From *British Journal of Educational Studies, Vol. XVI,* No. 2, (June, 1968), pp. 123–137. Reprinted by permission of the author and the *British Journal of Educational Studies.*

Each of the persons mentioned in these examples, might be called by some "creative." What, if anything, have they in common?

(a) An answer frequently found in educational writings runs as follows. In each of these four people the "creative process" is at work. How it functions is mysterious: all one knows is that it is the product of some innately given power related in some intimate but obscure way to our unconscious mind. It is a power which thrives on exercise but withers away if checked. All children are born with creative powers, perhaps in varying degrees. Only in a few children do these powers develop to such an extent that as adults they can become Dostoevskys or Einsteins. Most children's creative growth is checked by parents' and teachers' rigid insistence on following rules in which the children are explicitly instructed. Creative growth in one direction, say in mathematics, can be checked by too great insistence on following explicit rules in other areas, e.g., art. Teachers who move away from such insistence on rules and allow children more spontaneity, as in (1) and (3), are developing, not stunting, these creative powers.

On this account, the three children in (1)-(3) differ only in degree from Dostoevsky or Einstein in their creative thinking. Great artists and scientists, reporting on their processes of thought, commonly stress the importance of being free from conventional rules: creative thinking is a matter of letting the mind play round a topic, of "incubating" ideas, and leaving the unconscious to make those connexions between them which give rise to "inspiration." The children in the first three examples are playing freely with ideas in a similar, though less developed way.

(b) I want to argue that the account just given is a fairy story. What the four cases have in common is the application to each of them of a *word;* 'creativity'. But the meaning of this word is not a mysterious inner process. In fact, it has no one meaning in these different examples, but a number of meanings, with just enough in common between them to make it plausible, though confusing, to apply the same word to all four cases.

One source of confusion here goes back to educationists' traditional adherence to some sort of faculty psychology. Teachers have long since been encouraged to believe that their task consists in training some faculty of the mind, e.g., in strengthening the Will or the Memory. Plenty of practice of character-building or retentive tasks has been thought useful in toughening up these "mental muscles." Although such faculty psychology is today largely outmoded, there still seems today to be much support for the notion of a *creative* faculty, which for its development requires practice of a different sort: not practice in storing ideas, as with the Memory, but practice in letting ideas *flow* from their sources in the Unconscious.

Now faculty psychology, as Ryle emphasizes in the *Concept of Mind,* rests on a pictorial model of the mind as some sort of ghostly machine with different parts which carry out different functions: willing, remembering, etc. It is particularly easy to resort to such pictorial models, because of the natural but dangerous tendency we have to construe all substantival expressions as if they stand for things in the world in the way that 'chair' stands for actual chairs. In using an expression like 'training the Will' we naturally incline to think that there are parts of our mind called 'wills' which are trainable in some such way as horses or sheepdogs are trained. But in fact, as Ryle and other recent writers have shown, the logic of mental words is more complicated than this simple 'name-thing' theory of meaning would allow.

In the next section I shall examine the logic of 'creative' as used in the fourth example, to refer to such figures as Dostoevsky and Einstein: it will become clear, I hope, why in these cases 'creativity' is not to be seen as labelling a faculty. Later, in Sections III and IV I shall turn to the other three cases, which are of more direct educational interest.

II. The Logic of Creativity

I shall begin the analysis of 'creative' in the case (4) sense by looking at a typical example of its use. The following passage is from the back cover of D. F. Pears' recent book on Bertrand Russell:

He [Pears] traces the development of Russell's metaphysics and theory of knowledge during his great creative period from 1905 to 1919. In these fifteen years a considerable part of the history of philosophy was the history of the development of his ideas.

There are two ways in which this quotation is helpful in bringing out the logic of 'creative':

To uncover the meaning of a word it is often useful to ask what it is being contrasted with. Here the contrast is between the sort of work Russell did from 1905 to 1919 and what he did before and after this time. It is clear that what the writer has in mind in making this contrast is the *value* or *importance* of Russell's work in metaphysics and theory of knowledge from 1905 to 1919 as compared with what went before and after. In a similar way we might contrast Dostoevsky as a 'highly creative writer' with a writer of hack detective stories, who we might deny was 'creative' at all: again it is the value – in this case the aesthetic value – of the works of the two novelists which is at issue. As with artists, so with scientists: how far are we prepared to call them 'creative' seems to vary according to the value of their discoveries as assessed by the intrinsic standards of their discipline.

The second point has already partly emerged and is indeed logically connected with it. It is that 'creative', like 'free', is not a term that has any application on its own, unqualified. We cannot call a man 'free' unless we make it clear, explicitly or implicitly, what he is free *from*, i.e., unless we specify some constraint on something he wants to do. Similarly, to say that a person is 'highly creative' is not very informative unless it is clear in what area of activity he is creative, that is, has produced valuable work. It is clear from that quotation about Russell that the specific area to which his 'creative period' refers is metaphysics and theory of knowledge. This point about the necessary specificity of 'creative' is logically connected with the point about its connexion with 'value', because the criteria of what is valuable in a certain sphere of activity differ from activity to activity: a physical theory, a symphony, a hypothesis about the rise of the gentry in Tudor England – all these may be valuable within their respective domains; but why they are valuable would involve a very different explanation in each case, which would take one far into the disciplines of physics, music and history.

The claim that 'creative' is a term which cannot be used without specification may perhaps be challenged by reference to such a genius as Leonardo da Vinci whose creativity, it may be said, found expression in everything he turned his hand to. Is he not an example of a person who is generally creative *tout court*?

The answer is that Leonardo was indeed 'generally creative' in one way, but not *tout court*. For in this context to say that he was generally creative is reducible to saying that he produced valuable works not in one area but in several. The implicit specificity of the word is still there, but in this case, unlike other cases, more than one area of activity is referred to. 'Creative' still, even in this case, picks out not something about a person's inner processes, but about what he publicly produces.

This last point prompts me to a remark about taking 'creative' as a psychological term, rather than as an evaluative term as I have done above. If 'creative' were a psychological term, describing inner faculties and processes, we could not properly apply the term to Shakespeare, Newton, etc., without knowing what sorts of things went on in their minds as they worked out their masterpieces. But we do know that Shakespeare, for instance, was a creative genius without knowing anything about what processes he underwent. He may have undergone all sorts of things, for all we know. 'Creative thinking', therefore, is not a peculiar type of thinking that has different, nonpublicly observable, features from other types of thinking. A creative thinker is one whose thinking leads to a result which conforms to criteria of value in one domain or another. 'Creative' is a medal which we pin on public products, not the name of private processes. Of course, it may be the case that the thought processes of those whom we call 'creative' may be of a very peculiar sort. But if so – and here I am not claiming that there is any evidence for this – that would be a coincidence: it is not in virtue of that that we call them 'creative' but in virtue of their achievements.

III. Creativity in Education: Creativity Tests and Discovery Methods

In this section and the next I shall try to see how far the children in cases (1), (2) and (3) of the first section, who are said to be 'creative', are so in anything like the same sense as a creative worker in (4) is 'creative'. I shall also be concerned, as well as with these logical points, with the evaluative question of how useful it is to promote in schools the sorts of creativity picked out in these first three examples. Because most of the arguments in these matters centres round the sort of creativity manifested by the girl crayoning in the first example, I shall postpone my full discussion of this case, devoting to it the whole of the section after this. I shall deal now with cases (2) and (3).

Case (2) What has the boy thinking out different uses for a brick in common with creative artists or scientists in (4)? He appears to have more in common with them than the child crayoning in (1) who is doing what she likes. For his achievement presupposes two things:

(A) that he knows what a brick is and what its usual uses are, and
(B) that in his supposition of what a brick might be used for he is guided in his thinking by certain *rules*. It is presumably not open to him to put down *anything* as a use of a brick. There has to be some intelligible connexion between the use proposed and the brick itself: the use has to be compatible with the properties of the brick. It would not do, for instance, to say that a brick could be used as a trumpet (unless some way is found of making this intelligible). Therefore, the boy's thinking must be guided by the rule that the use must conform to the brick's properties.

In (A) and (B) the boy is unlike the girl in the first example. She did not have to know anything in particular; he does. She could do what she liked; he has to follow certain procedures. In (A) and (B), however, the boy is like a creative artist or scientist. For there are certain things — scientific theories, traditional procedures, properties of materials, etc. — which the creative worker has to know and (B) artistic or scientific creativeness involves an imaginative leap to a new perspective. This imaginative enterprise is guided by certain rules which differ from discipline to discipline: the scientist searches for a hypothesis, but not of any sort, but one which is likely to *fit the facts* he is concerned with (just as the boy with the brick had to think up uses fitting the fact that bricks have such and such properties); the poet searches for images, rhymes, etc., which will help to make an aesthetically valuable poem.

Where examples (2) and (4) diverge, i.e., when the boy is unlike a creative worker, is in the *point* of their activity. We call good artists and scientists 'creative' because they have produced something aesthetically or intellectually valuable. But there does not seem to be any value – if we discount extrinsic value, e.g., in helping one to get high marks in a creativity test – in producing ingenious uses for a brick. If so, the boy in example (2) is not 'creative' in the sense of example (4). He may have certain things in common with creative workers, but he lacks precisely that feature in virtue of which we call them 'creative'.

'Creativity' as in example (2) is educationally relevant in (at least) two different contexts. It may appear in the context of what is taught: teachers may think it desirable to promote such "imaginative activity," by teaching children how to write stories or poems, and giving high praise to a child who uses his imagination in the way the boy with the brick did. Or it may appear – as indeed the "use of a brick" example does – in tests of creativity. If it is believed in either of these cases that the children called 'creative' are creative in the same sense as creative artists etc. in (4) are creative, then this belief is just false, unless what the case (2) children produce can be shown to be intellectually or aesthetically valuable. It may be held, on the other hand, especially as far as creativity testing is concerned, that although creativity in case (2) is not *identical in meaning* with creativity in case (4), there is an *empirical* connexion between the two cases, in that a child scoring high in a creativity test is more likely to produce creative work in the case (4) sense, than a child who scores low. The final test of this claim is, as I say, empirical – provided that one can give more specific content to the general notion of "producing creative work." The hypothesis seems a far more plausible one if, when specified, it claims that a boy who can think up two hundred uses for a brick is, say, a good bet as a potential advertising copywriter, than if it claims he is likely to make advances in nuclear physics. This is because undergoing the "brick" test and writing advertising copy both involve setting one's sights on what is unfamiliar and likely to surprise. Doing research in physics involves setting one's sights on the pursuit of truth in a particular area, with all the supreme difficulties that this brings with it. In other words, doing physics and thinking out the uses of a brick have very little in common: one could imagine many children enjoying the fantasy of the "brick" test who shied at the rigours of physics. There *might* be an empirical connexion between the two cases: as a philosopher I cannot rule it out by logic; but just as it is in the last analysis an empirical question whether or not children getting toy typewriters on their ninth birthday tend to take up sedentary occupations, in neither case does there seem to be any reason why the hypothesis is likely to be true.

The previous paragraph is about creativity testing. But many of its points are relevant to the question: how far is it educationally desirable to get children to be creative (in the present sense) in the poems and stories they write in English lessons? If it could be shown that there is an empirical connexion between their being creative in *this* sense, and their being creative in the example (4) sense, such that the first tends to promote the second, there might be something to be said for it. But, just as in the previous argument about doing physics, there is a gap between being imaginative, where this connotes aesthetic value, and being imaginative like the boy with the brick. Prima facie, one would doubt an empirical connexion for this reason: there may be one; but as far as I know, this has not been proved.[1]

Case (3) What has the child "discovering" a mathematical rule in common with a 'creative' mathematician in example (4)? He has not discovered a mathematical rule unknown to mathematicians. So he is clearly not 'creative' in the example (4) sense. But, one might argue, the first man who did discover the mathematical rule was 'creative' in this sense, and the child is in one way in a similar position to this early genius: *for him* it is as valuable a discovery as it was for the first discovered: both have broken new ground.

But this will not do. The argument involves a shift from the notion of "valuable within mathematics," for which specific criteria can be laid down, to the obscurer notion of "valuable for him." Not only is this obscure, but it is unclear that learning the rule in the so-called "non-creative" way, i.e., by being told what it is by the teacher, could not be in some sense "valuable for him." If so, the argument blurs the distinction which it was intended to clarify.

A different argument might be that the child is 'creative' because he is thinking in the same sort of way as a creative mathematician does. But (1) once again, if this means that his private thought processes are like those of the creative mathematician, we meet the objections that we do not usually know what these are in the case of creative mathematicians, and that we call the latter 'creative' in virtue of the importance of what they discover, and (2) if one means that he follows the same sort of procedures as the creative mathematician, then this is false. For the boy and the mathematician are in different situations. In the case of the boy, his teacher has structured the situation in such a way, by e.g. providing clues to guide the child close to the desired goal, that the child takes it for granted that there is a rule to be discovered, that the teacher knows what it is, and that by following the teacher's direction he can come to find out what it is as well. None of these conditions holds for the creative mathematician, who therefore could not have made his discovery in the same way as the child.

It seems, therefore, that we cannot call the child 'creative' because he is in any way like a creative mathematician. If we are to hold to the notion of

---

1. It might be held that children producing imaginative stories, etc., in the "boy-with-the-brick" sense of 'imaginative', *are* writing imaginatively in the "aesthetically valuable" sense. Some of the grounds for claiming this may rest on arguments which I discuss in Section IV below.

'creative' to distinguish a child learning by discovery methods from one learning by being instructed, the only meaning which 'creative' seems to have is that the child is not told what the answer is. But even this is not crystal clear. For if a teacher gives a great number of clues, so that almost any one could work out the answer, but the teacher does not actually say what the answer is, on the account so far given, children discovering the answer should be called 'creative' — but in fact the term tends only to be applied when very few clues are supplied and the child has to deduce a good deal on his own. So if we want to, we can say that a child is 'creative' when he finds out a rule without being told and without many clues; but (1) the criteria for the application of the term are still not clear, as one needs to know — roughly, at any rate — how many clues he can have without losing the title, and also what counts as a clue; no indication is given of how these matters are to be settled, and (2) there is the familiar point that the rationale for using the word 'creative' is not clear, and that there is the danger of confusing its use in this context with its use in others.

With regard to the educational value of 'discovery' methods, there is not much to say. Assuming one can produce acceptable criteria for distinguishing these methods from others, it is an empirical question to decide how far they are more likely than other methods to produce learning. One might well hypothesize that methods placing more stress on the child's initiative and curiosity were motivationally more recommendable than more 'formal' methods in certain circumstances; but whether this is so depends, as I say, on empirical tests.

IV. Creativity in Education: Aesthetic Subjects

We still have not dealt with the case of the girl at the infant school crayoning what she likes on her pad of newsprint (case (1)). What, if anything, has she in common with the creative artist of example (4)? One is immediately tempted to reply: not very much. They both make marks on paper, true, but beyond that there is this important and obvious difference between them: the artist is making his marks with a particular intention in mind, to produce an aesthetically satisfying picture, and he makes use of all sorts of professional techniques to make his marks conform to this end; neither of these things can be said of the little girl. To say that *she* is 'creative' is to say nothing more than that she is drawing what she wants, with no one telling her what to do. What educational value there is in this is difficult to see.

This is one answer. But a different answer — one which is currently, not to say perennially, influential in educational circles — runs quite otherwise. According to this answer, to say that a child producing paintings in art lessons (or poems and stories in English lessons) is being 'creative', is to use this word in precisely the same sense as one uses it of well-known artists and writers: that is, a creative child is one who produces something of aesthetic value, not merely one who does what he wants. The aesthetic value of children's art may be less than that of artists' work, or, as Herbert Read believes, it may be impossible to compare the two in respect of aesthetic value;[2] but in either case, there is no denying that at least some children's work is aesthetically valuable (and so creative).

There are a number of different ways in which such a conclusion is commonly supported. In what follows I shall outline and discuss some of these arguments. The matter is somewhat complicated by the facts (1) that some proponents of children's creativity would argue that *all* children are creative in the sense under discussion, and others that only *some* are, and (2) that some are especially concerned with literature and others with visual art. Some of the arguments which follow are restricted to a claim about some but not all, children or about one art-form in particular, others may be taken in a less restricted sense. I shall try to make clear the scope of the arguments as I go.

(1) The first argument is that (all or some) children's free art (visual or literary) has a certain *originality*: this is what makes it of aesthetic value.

There are two problems here: (a) what is meant by calling a child's product 'original'? and (b) how far is originality a criterion of aesthetic value?

(a) Let us take the case of the little girl crayoning (a child writing a story would do as well). Some might claim that *whatever* the child produced under free conditions would be original. Now, clearly, part at least of the meaning of 'original' here is 'different, in some way, from previous products';[3] but the problem is, different in what way? Suppose the child used her freedom to produce a conventional picture of a house with smoke curling from the chimney-pots and a curved front path. Would this count as being original? If not – on the grounds that the picture is not different from conventional expectations – the argument that all children's free work is original falls to the ground, for children *do* produce conventional work. One might try to defend it by arguing that even though the drawing is conventional the way in which it is drawn with these particular colours and proportions, is something of the child's own. It is the details of the execution which make it original. But this sort of argument is self-defeating; for if one allows in this way any perceptible difference in the way a picture is drawn to signify originality, then even colouring in fixed outlines might well lead to an

2. Herbert Read, *Education Through Art* (London: Faber and Faber, 1943), pp. 210-212.

3. One must also rule out sheer *coincidence* as a ground for denying originality, as one does with well-known artists: if a masterpiece happened to be very similar in some respects to an earlier work, we would not deny its originality if the artist could not possibly have known the earlier work. Thus, too, with the child.

original work (it would indeed be surprising if it did not). But since it is part of the thesis under discussion that originality is a result of free conditions only and that fixed outline colouring stultifies its development, the argument contains a contradiction.

We are still not clear what might usefully be meant by 'originality'. Suppose we examine the more restricted thesis, that only some free work is original, that is, only that work which does not conform to conventional expectations in the way that the conventional drawing of the house did. Let us admit — without worrying too much over the criteria for conforming to conventional expectations — that many young children's drawings are original in this sense. Let us take, for example, drawings which do not appear to represent anything recognizable, like plates 1a, 1b, and 2 in Read's *Education through Art.*

In some ways such drawings resemble "abstract" paintings produced by adult artists: if one went only by what one saw without knowing who the artist was, one might conceivably even mistake a child's drawing in some cases for an adult's. But there is an important difference between the two artists here. To say that both are producing something which is "different from conventional expectations" obscures the fact that the adult artist is *reacting against* conventional standards, while the child clearly is not. Originality in the case of the adult has written into it this intention — to produce something different — which in its turn implies a knowledge of what the conventional standards are. Unconventional children's drawings, like the ones in Read's book, are not original in this sense, since the children who draw them have neither this intention nor this knowledge.

(b) But even if young children's work were original in this sense — and with older children the predicate may in certain cases be applicable — originality is not a sufficient condition of aesthetic value.[4] For if an adult artist, say, decides to break out of the tradition in which he has been trained and succeeds in this, it does not follow that his work will be of aesthetic merit: his work may be merely bizarre, incapable of providing any aesthetic experience. Sometimes, it is true, we use the term 'original' in a more restricted sense than this, only calling a work original if it is different from previous work in such a way that it is a vehicle of a hitherto unfelt aesthetic experience. But this is to include in the concept of originality the concept of aesthetic value. If in the thesis under discussion — that all or some children's work is aesthetically valuable insofar as it is original — 'original' is to be understood as a value term, the thesis becomes trivially true by definition.

The overall conclusion on argument (1), therefore, is that it is either true by definition or invalid if interpreted in the other senses already

4. This is to omit the further question whether originality is even a *necessary* condition of aesthetic value. On this, see S. Hook, (Ed.), *Art and Philosophy* (New York: New York University Press, 1966), p. 24, ff., p. 29 ff.

mentioned. This is not to deny that some children may sometimes produce work which is original (where this implies aesthetic value). Being able to tell when they do so depends on what criteria there are of aesthetic value. I turn to this problem in the following section.

(2) A second argument supporting the thesis that children's art (all or some; visual or literary) is aesthetically valuable may rest on the presumed subjectivity of judgements of aesthetic value. One might follow Ayer[5] in arguing that to say, "That painting is good" is simply to express the feelings of approval the painting evokes in one, just as in a moral context to say, "He is a good man" is simply to express the feelings of approval which his actions evoke in one. On this theory, provided that a person looking at a child's drawing or poem approves of it, that is sufficient to make it aesthetically valuable (for him). Since children's art products often do meet with others' approval, it follows that much, if not all, of children's art is aesthetically valuable.

Now there is much that has been written about such an 'emotive' theory of aesthetic judgement,[6] and in an article of this length I shall restrict myself to two observations: (a) Ayer's theory tries to account for the widespread variation in aesthetic standards from age to age, culture to culture and individual to individual. But the existence of such variation is not incompatible with the existence of objective standards. For the disputants might agree on the existence of certain very general aesthetic canons — formal harmony, for instance, or expressive power — but disagree either about more specific canons (about the importance of the classical unities in drama, say) or about the weight that should be put on the general canons (some tending to favour formal qualities, say, others expressive). (b) Seeing that both aesthetic and moral judgements can be reduced to expressions of (dis)approval, what distinguishes a moral from an aesthetic judgement? How does one know that an admirer of a painting is showing *aesthetic* rather than moral approval of it? If there exists a domain of the aesthetic as well as a domain of the moral, then how is this domain delimited? If it is not delimited in any way, it is not distinguishable from the moral; but if it is delimited there must be some sort of criteria for delimiting it. Therefore not anything that people like looking at could count as aesthetically valuable. So if people just like looking at a child's painting this in itself does not show that it is of any *aesthetic* merit. There are all sorts of reasons why people might like looking: they might be proud of the progress that the child — if he were their child — was making in his control of the pencil; they might be delighted at seeing the picture as of *aesthetic* interest? As I said, there must be *some* criteria here. The difficulty of spelling out these criteria in words should not be taken to show that such criteria do not exist. If we are to talk in aesthetic terms at all, they *must* exist.

5. A. J. Ayer, *Language, Truth and Logic* (2nd ed.) (London: Gollancz, 1946), Chap. 6.
6. Cf. M. Beardsley, *Aesthetics* (N. Y.: Harcourt Brace, 1958) Chap. X.

(3) A third argument to show that some children's work is aesthetically valuable might run as follows: "You have been writing about the 'aesthetically valuable' as if this is a term only applicable to acknowledged works of art. But just because children's art is not aesthetically valuable according to the criteria applicable to a Rembrandt or a Matisse, it does not follow that it is not aesthetically valuable. For, as Herbert Read shows, many children's drawings possess the 'specific aesthetic quality' of 'naivety' – indicating, as he says, 'a certain "vision" of things which is peculiar to children and perhaps to certain rare adults who retain this childlike faculty.' "[7]

Part of this thesis I accept. A work does not have to be of the first rank to be aesthetically valuable. Paintings displayed at local amateur exhibitions may be of aesthetic merit (even though, compared with those in the Tate, they may not be rated so highly). So it is not impossible that children's work can be seen as aesthetically valuable if one does not pitch one's requirements too high. It is true also that if their work is aesthetically valuable there must be *some* criteria here to which they conform. But talk of "naivety" as a specific aesthetic quality makes little sense; for to be an aesthetic quality, naivety must be something publicly observable, like harmony or grace. But in the quotation from Read it picks out something in the private world of the mind – a certain unsophisticated way of looking at things; there is no guarantee that someone with such an outlook will produce anything aesthetically valuable even in a limited way. I leave open the question whether there are other *sui generis* aesthetic qualities to be found in children's art. There may be: one would have to deal with further claims as they arise.

Before I leave the three arguments (1)–(3) there is a last, but most important point to make about them. Suppose that by these or other arguments it could be shown decisively that all, or at least some children's unguided work is aesthetically valuable. Would this in itself justify the exclusive use of unguided activity *educationally*? Surely not: for there would still be forms of aesthetic experience which the child could not enjoy without being initiated into literary or artistic traditions; the longer he is left on his own producing his (admittedly aesthetic valuable) drawings and stories, the more he is being deprived of opportunities to extend his aesthetic sensibility in other directions.

The three arguments just discussed are both intended to support the thesis that (some or all) children's work is aesthetically valuable. Another argument supports a somewhat different thesis, one restricted to children's "creative writing." This is that many if not all children are capable, in certain free conditions, of writing *literature*. This is what Britton argues in a recent paper on the teaching of English.[8] He claims that when a child becomes a spectator of his own past experience and writes about this for its own sake,

7. Read, *op. cit.,* p. 212.
8. J. Britton, "Literature" in *The Arts and Current Tendencies in Education* (London: University of London Institute of Education, 1963) p. 42.

he is doing something which falls in the same category as what adult poets and novelists do. There is only a difference of degree between them: both are writing 'literature'. Now if one defines literature as retrospective description of the sort mentioned, then it may well be the case that most children can write literature in certain "free conditions." But this definition of literature says nothing about aesthetic value. The daily journal of a dull Victorian lady might be devoid of aesthetic value: yet on this definition it might well be a piece of literature. Now to call a piece of work 'literature' is usually to imply that it is aesthetically valuable in some way. There is no harm in redefining the word, as long as it is clear what it is taken to mean; but the question now is: given that children are capable of writing literature in the redefined sense, what is the point of encouraging them to do so? It may be educationally valuable to get children to write something of *aesthetic* interest, for at least this achievement is some indication that they are coming to understand what the realm of the aesthetic involves, and I take it as axiomatic here that such an understanding is a necessary part of a proper education. But to show that it is educationally valuable to write down one's retrospections requires further argument.

This leads me into a more general discussion of the educational value of creative activities in the present sense, that is, those in which the teacher plays a minimal role, merely providing materials and possibly also topics about which the children can draw or write what they want. I have tried to show that these activities cannot be justified on the grounds that what the children produce is creative in the sense of aesthetically valuable. But it may be claimed that there is an *empirical* connexion between these activities and being creative in the "value" sense.

There are two theses here, one broader, one narrower. (1) The broader thesis, espoused by, for instance, Lowenfield and Read, is that free activity in art lessons is an efficient way of promoting creativity in the value sense in *any* discipline, and conversely, that to disallow such free activity is to dam up the child's creative forces and make him less likely to produce valuable work in physics, history, etc., *as well as* in art. Read, quoting Jaensch, observes, "Once the creative powers are freed in one direction... once the shackles of school passivity are broken at one point, a kind of inner liberation, the awakening of a higher activity generally sets in. Above all, to the eidetic sphere of development, as well as to the mentality of the artist, there belongs a peculiar structure of the mental powers, particularly of thinking; and the arousing and vivifying of these powers benefit all the subjects taught, even the most rigorously logical."[9] Read argues, therefore, that education should be "through art," that is, intellectual education should have a solid bedrock of art education.

9. Read, *op. cit.,* p. 59.

Now this thesis seems to be based on a conception of creativity (in the value sense) as some sort of inner source of mental energy which can be dammed up or, alternatively, set free to flow into different channels of intellectual or aesthetic activity. I hope my argument in the second section is sufficient to dispose of this claim: 'creative' is a term applying to public products rather than private processes.

As well as this, the thesis also ignores differences in what counts as being creative in different areas. It may or may not be likely that a child with plenty of experience of free activity in art lessons will later go on to produce something aesthetically valuable in visual art. But it is hard to see how such experience will help him to produce something, say, mathematically or scientifically valuable. It is certainly not sufficient: the mathematical or scientific understanding which this presupposes requires a rigorous initiation into these disciplines. Such initiation is not only helpful but necessary to the production of something valuable in these areas. This is a logical truth. But what grounds there are for the present thesis — that free activity in art is also helpful — are not made clear. Plato in the *Republic* puts education in the arts as the bedrock of his curriculum, with mathematics and dialectic emerging from it; but he at least provides a rationale for this in terms of his theory of knowledge and psychology. But assuming, for reasons too long to go into here, that *this* sort of rationale will not do, what sort of rationale is given us? There is no such *logical* connexion between free activity in art and creativity in mathematics, etc. (as there is between the latter and learning mathematics); but neither does the thesis rest on any validated *empirical* connexion. (2) The narrower thesis is that free activity in art (or English) lessons is an efficient way of promoting creativity in the value sense *in art or literature.* But how plausible this thesis is depends on precisely what is being claimed. Let us look at art, by way of example. If the point of letting very young children play freely with paints, paper, clay, etc., is to familiarize them with (some of) the properties of these materials, then this is clearly a rational technique for starting children off on the road to producing aesthetically interesting pictures. But in itself it will not take them very far: in addition, all sorts of techniques will have to be learned — of colour mixing, drawing, etc. — and, most important, the children will have to be initiated into the domain of the aesthetic. Similar points could be made about 'creative writing' in the present sense of the term. That free writing might be a useful device in certain specific situations will be generally accepted: it might provide practice for a child learning handwriting, or it might be useful remedially for a child who has a "block" about writing. But in order to write something of literary value, all sorts of further techniques are necessary — as well as ideas worth expressing. In view of these requirements in the creation of something valuable both in art and in literature, it would seem that in both cases the longer one leaves the child to his own devices — except for the specific purposes mentioned – the *harder* it becomes for him, not less, to get inside the relevant discipline.

In all this I am stressing the need for teachers of creative activities in the present sense to be critical of the more grandiose claims that are made for them and to ask themselves what – discounting these – are their *aims* in encouraging free activity and whether free activity is an adequate means to these ends. I am not denying that there are such aims which are both realizable and worthwhile. Some of these, as I indicated in the previous paragraph – like teaching properties of materials or handwriting – are clearly *educationally* worthwhile. (No doubt there are other such aims besides the ones I mentioned.) But there are at least two other ways, not necessarily connected with education, in which free activities may be valuable.

(1) They may be *therapeutically* valuable. Just as some disturbed adults find relief from their anxieties in dabbling in paint or scribbling down their thoughts, this may also be true for certain disturbed children. As long as one does not make the mistake of seeing all children as requiring to be cured – a mistake connected with the belief that education is largely a matter of promoting mental health[10] – activities which are 'creative' in the sense that one just does what one wants may have a limited therapeutic use.

(2) They may be worth making some provision for simply because, given that they are in no way immoral, children enjoy them. For the child is not merely to be seen as a recipient of education; there is also his own world, his own interests and strivings, to be taken into account. Just as we provide adventure playgrounds, so we have good grounds for providing the paint and the ink and the paper, etc., for other sorts of pastimes.

I said above that (1) and (2) are not necessarily connected with education. I mean by this that they could be, and sometimes are, pursued in institutions other than schools – whose job, I take it, is essentially that of educating. It happens in many cases that these purposes, especially (2), are pursued at school. Where they are, teachers of creative activities may have these further purposes in mind. What is important, however, is to be clear on the distinctions I have mentioned: has the work an educational purpose, or is it not necessarily connected with education – and within these categories, what is it precisely aiming at?

V. Conclusion

I have devoted this article to teasing out some of the problems to do with the meaning of 'creativity' and its place in education. Instead of

10. Cf. R. S. Peters, "Mental Health as an Educational Aim," in T. H. B. Hollins, (Ed.) *Aims in Education* (Manchester, Eng.: Manchester University Press, 1964). Reprinted above.

summarizing, I will finish by raising, but not solving, a further problem. On the whole I have been somewhat sceptical of the educational value of creative activities in some of the senses of this term. But I have not discussed the pros and cons of the teacher's aiming at making his pupils 'creative' in the value sense of the term; that is, at getting them to produce something of value in history, physics, literature, etc. I have taken it as axiomatic here that if creative activities in some sense or other *did* lead to this result, this would be enough to show their educational value. But would it? Is it any part of the educator's task to teach people to be creative? This raises very large questions about the nature of education in general and — for this is again, I think, where the main problems are — about the nature of aesthetic education in particular. I hope to go into these problems at another time.

IMAGINATION AND EDUCATION

K. Charlton

I

It is a commonplace, which few I think would deny, that if we were to ask the question "What do you count as thinking?" most people would, at the very least, start by mentioning rational and conceptual thought. Some would even stop there, citing as evidence the ways in which people reason, and pointing to the way in which a person's thought develops through concrete thought to reversible and divergent thought.

To do this, however, would be to ignore a large area of human experience of which mystical thought is one part, dreaming another and certainly imagination another. Where would you place imagination in the picture of your own or your pupil's thinking? And would you be able to resist the temptation to equate it with day-dreaming and then to go on to compare it adversely with rational thought?

You will notice that I have rather cagily entitled this lecture "Imagination and Education." A more forthcoming title might have been "The Education of the Imagination" or "Education for Imaginative Thinking." I have deliberately chosen the first, however, because it seems to me that the other two put the cart before the horse, or at the very least imply that we all know what imagination is. They imply that the important problem is how to devise efficient means for educating imagination; or, to differentiate a little, to find out whether the imaginative powers of the child are stronger or weaker than those of an adult; or to identify which material would best evoke or stimulate imaginative thought in a child. These you will notice are all empirical questions, questions whose answers can be found by going out into the field, setting up an inquiry, and measuring the results.

But before this can be done in any valid way, the researcher has to be quite clear in his mind just what it is he is measuring, and whether what is in his mind is, in fact, a complete description or definition of what imagination is. All too often, and usually without making this clear in the introduction to

Professor Charlton's inaugural lecture in the Chair of Philosophy and History of Education at the University of Birmingham, England, March 2, 1967. Published in *Educational Review*, 20 (November, 1967), pp. 3–18. Reprinted by permission of the author and the *Educational Review*.

the report of his research, the researcher is measuring only one part of the universe called imagination. We need, therefore, to ask some prior questions. What are we trying to measure? What do we count as imaginative thinking?

I wish first of all, then, to remind you of the variety of uses to which we put the word 'imagination', and in the light of this to ask why the concept has been neglected in the past, at both school and university level, and then, finally to examine the current moves towards its rehabilitation.

It is when we apply the word 'imagination' and its cognates to particular activities, that is, apply them in different contexts, that we begin to see the complexities.[1]

Let us first of all, then, clear away a simple descriptive usage. I have in mind here those occasions when the word is used to report at first hand the occurence of images; for example when we say, standing in front of a block of stone, "I am imagining what it will be like when it is finished." Here the reporter is talking about his own imaging, and obviously such an activity can be reported only in the first person singular, for this kind of mental activity is necessarily private and not susceptible to public observation. There may, of course, be outward signs of some mental activity, but these are not a necessary part of the activity. A person's face, for example, may be quite immobile, quite inexpressive, when such imaging is taking place; and if there are signs we cannot legitimately infer that a particular mental activity called 'imaging' is taking place. We have to rely on a firsthand report.

A more common usage occurs when we ask our pupils, for example, to "imagine that you are working in a nineteenth-century cotton factory" or "imagine that you are visiting an African cocoa plantation"; or as we say more colloquially, "Conjure up in your mind's eye..." or "Can you visualise the scene...?" What we are asking our pupils to do here is to "see in their mind's eye," to "see *in* their imagination."

Several points arise from this. First of all, we usually help our pupils visualise in this way by providing prior descriptions of cotton factories, cocoa plantations, and so on, and occasionally we even pull out a wall picture or two, show some slides or a film. If the subject matter allows we may make a personal visit. In other words, we provide our pupils with the requisite experience on which to base their visual images, so that they are related, these images, in some degree to reality. We can say that in some degree they are reality based. Occasionally, of course, we fail to prepare our pupils, in this way, and for example, when studying Shakespeare's *Henry V* we ask them, at the very beginning of the play, to pay heed to the Chorus when he bids us:

> Suppose within the girdle of these walls
> Are now confined two mighty monarchies,
> Whose high upreared and abutting fronts

1. Cf. Anis Flew, "Images, Supposing and Imagining," *Philosophy, 28* (1953), pp. 246–54, and E. J. Furlong, *Imagination* (London: George Allen & Unwin., 1961).

> The perilous narrow ocean parts asunder:
> Piece out our imperfections with your thoughts;
> Into a thousand parts divide one man,
> And make imaginary puissance....

Without adequate preparation the result is not far to seek: a host of anachronisms and anachronistic thought on the part of the pupils.

But it is also possible (out of the classroom as well as in it) to "conjure up" all kinds of mental images which are *not* related to reality, and not even immediately stimulated. For example, this takes place when we lie on the beach or sit in an armchair with our eyes closed, and *in* our imagination waft away into a waking dreamland. (Indeed, some children can do this in the classroom with their eyes wide open!) Here our imagination rides on a free rein, and our imagings have no counterpart in the external world; they have a characteristic unreality, an other-worldliness. So, in this context and to emphasise this characteristic, we use words like 'fantastic', 'fanciful', or 'imaginary'.

Now, though we use visual imagery here and talk about "seeing in the mind's eye," this is not to be equated with seeing in its normal usage. For one thing we can only see, in the real sense, when our eyes are open and our surroundings are illuminated, whereas we can see in our mind's eye with our eyes shut and in the dark. In the same way we can choose and discuss at will the pictures in our head, whereas in reality we can only see what is there to be seen.[2]

But there is a further point. Though all this time we have been using examples of *visual* imagery, it is quite possible to indulge in imagery based on our other senses: for example, when we report, "I could almost feel the smoothness of the silk," or "I could almost smell the burning flesh as the martyrs roasted," or "I could hear the bells jangling wildly whilst my teacher read Edgar Allan Poe's poem." Each of these equally well exemplifies our usage *in* imagination, but without recourse to visual imagery.

The remarkable thing, of course, is how dominant visual imagery is in our own culture, how great is our reliance on visual imagery. So much so, that though we have a word like 'visualise' we don't have words like 'auralise' or 'tactualise', or 'olfactorise'.

A final point to be noted here is that though we do 'conjure up', it is fallacious to think that we conjure up 'out of nothing', despite William Blake's affirmation that "Imagination is the Divine Vision, not of the World or of Man, nor Man as he is a Natural Man, but only as he is a Spiritual Man. Imagination has nothing to do with Memory."[3] It may well appear to be the

2. Cf. J. M. Shorter, "Imagination," *Mind,* LXI (1952), pp. 528–42.
3. G. Keynes (Ed.), *The Complete Writings of William Blake* (1966), p. 783.

case, and many scientists, inventors and poets have reported in these terms,[4] but this is usually because, in moments of particularly vivid imagining, we recall to consciousness what until that moment had been in the subconscious inaccessible to conscious awareness. An interesting example of this is Keats' poem "On First Reading Chapman's Homer." Keats read Chapman's translation for the first time one evening in a friend's lodging. He returned to his own rooms after midnight and by breakfast had produced his poem perfectly formed. This has often been cited as an example of spontaneous combustion in a poet, but in fact, to continue the metaphor, there is no smoke without fire, and, as John Middleton Murry has shown,[5] the poem was the culmination of a long period of reflection and preparation. The synthesis which was Keats' poem was new. But the elements synthesised were fragments of the poet's past experience, which had been vibrated in the poet's memory by the reading of the book, although their original context was perhaps forgotten. As John Dryden put it, "The composition of all poems is, or ought to be, of wit; and wit in the poet...is no other than the faculty of imagination, which like a nimble spaniel beats over and ranges through the field of memory till it springs the quarry it hunted after; or, without metaphor, which searches over all the memory for the species or ideas of those things which it designs to represent."[6] In a quite different context John Tyndall was making the same point when he observed, "Newton's passage from the falling apple to the falling moon was an act of the prepared imagination."[7]

There is a third use of our term, however, which we also come across in the classroom, as elsewhere, and to which we usually attach a positive value judgment; that is, when we talk of pupils 'thinking imaginatively', or younger children 'playing imaginatively', or when we applaud a piece of acting as done 'with a great deal of imagination'. In each of these cases, acting or playing or thinking imaginatively, we say the activity is engaged in '*with* imagination'.

The implication here is that this is something a good deal more rational than is possible when we day-dream *in* imagination, and indeed some would go further in their usage, and insist that this third kind of imagining involves what is called creativity. We see this a good deal in the behaviour of young children, as for example when we see them playing at being mothers or nurses

4. Cf. Rosamond E. M. Harding, *An Anatomy of Inspiration* (3rd edition, 1948), Chap. II, and W. I. B. Beveridge, *The Art of Scientific Investigations* (Melbourne: Heinemann, 1950), Chap. V.

5. John Middleton Murry, *Keats,* 4th edition, (New York: Noonday Press, 1955), Chap. IV.

6. Preface to *Annus Mirabilis* in W. P. Ker (ed.), *Essays of John Dryden* (1960), I, p. 14, cited G. G. Watson, "Contributions to a Dictionary of Critical Terms: *Imagination and Fancy,"* *Essays in Criticism,* III (2), 1953, pp. 201⁻14.

7. John Tyndall, *Faraday as a Discoverer* (1868), cited Beveridge, *op. cit.,* p. 50.

or teachers, in which they project themselves into the world of adults. Gilbert Ryle, in *The Concept of Mind,* uses as his example the case of children "playing bears,"[8] and this is a common enough situation in any infant or junior school, when the teacher says, "Imagine you are bears, children" or "Let's pretend we are bears, children."

Now, the assumption in such a situation is that the children have some previous experience of bears, either at firsthand by visiting a zoo, or vicariously when, for example, the teacher shows them how bears behave, or when they have been looking at a film strip or pictures. If they didn't have this experience, their pretending would be characterised as 'imaginary'. Having no counterpart in the external world, it would not be reality based. It would be a fiction, a "figment of their imagination." It would be one *kind* of imagination.

Given this assumption, however, that the children have some previous experience, their subsequent behaviour can be described in one of two ways. Either the child merely imitates or copies the teacher, as we say in a dull or *un*imaginative way, or the child does it well, going some way beyond the particular example of the teacher, not merely imitating or copying but adding something of his own, acting or responding imaginatively, acting or responding *with* imagination. We find both of these uses, don't we, in the medieval geographers' construct, the *Imago Mundi,* in which they made a copy of the world, though at the same time blithely filling in the coastal details of their *Terrae Incognitae.*

This correlative, 'pretending', to return to our children playing at bears, is a deliberate action, simulating or dissimulating with skill, with intention, with conviction.[9] In other words, it is a relatively sophisticated action or performance, and in this context we contrast reproductive thought and productive thought.[10] One kind of response we characterise as 'unimaginative', coping with the reproduction but without any high degree of skill in the imitation. If, on the other hand, there is a good deal of skill in the imitation, we count this as imaginative, we say that it *merits* the adjective 'imaginative'. One needs to point out here, of course, that constant indulgence in making-believe does not necessarily make a child imaginative. If he always makes-believe about the same thing in the same way then we say he *lacks* imagination. 'Imaginative' here implies some degree of originality.

When we talk about imaginative poets or imaginative scientists we are still talking in terms of a value judgment, and we lay even greater emphasis in

8. Gilbert Ryle, *The Concept of Mind* (London: Hutchinson & Co., 1949), Chap. VIII; Cf. E. J. Furlong, "Playing Bears," *Philosophical Quarterly,* VII (1957), pp. 359–63 and Shorter, *loc. cit.,* pp. 531–2.

9. Cf. J. L. Austin and G. E. M. Anscombe, "Pretending," *Proceedings of the Aristotelian Society, Supplementary Volume XXXII* (1958), pp. 261–94.

10. C. A. Mace, "Concerning Imagination," *Proceedings of the Aristotelian Society,* XLIII (1942–3), pp. 21–36.

these contexts on the originality of the product. The essence of imagination here is the seeing of relations which previously have gone unobserved, and this is characterised, particularly, in the poet's use of words, and especially in his metaphorical use of words.[11] Here he uses metaphors as something more than a merely rhetorical device to serve as an ornament to language. Here the poet is involved in perceiving similarities between dissimilars, and thus in a very real sense we can say that it is possible to observe the Eureka syndrome as much in a poet's successful search for a word or an image (in the poet's sense of the term) as in a scientist's or an inventor's search for an explanation or an appropriate mechanism.

Once again, of course, we have to set limits to this particular kind of thinking, and to beware, as Nevil Coghill reminds us,[12] of that "lawlessness" that can overtake our imagination, a lawlessness which is apt to forget the nature of the medium in which it is trying to imagine.

A fourth usage is to be observed when we say, "Let's imagine, for the sake of argument, that such and such is the case." Here, when we are imagining, we are supposing, postulating, or assuming; toying with or entertaining an idea.

It would seem that this hypothesis-forming type of thought is very far removed from the day-dreaming type of mental activity, which, by some people's definition, would not count as thinking. Here we are talking about a tough, powerful wrestling with an idea. As with the metaphor, the hypothesis is a construct of the imagination, and in this sense exercising our imagination is an intellectual exercise in which we make intelligent use of the knowledge available to us.

On the other hand, the most creative type of hypothesis is that bold, audacious one which seems to fly in the face of experience, in the face of conventional, usual, customary experience, and in this sense it can be claimed that a really imaginative scientist is one who would say to himself, "Let's see how far we can go with the hypothesis that . . . ." Here we could say that the thinker was flying in the face of reality, and it is in this context that we find ourselves turning to look to our earlier uses of the word 'imagination', to the sense of 'pretending' (though without fraudulent intent) or 'acting' *as if* such and such were the case. An *un*imaginative thinker is likely to dismiss these "as if" propositions as being so remote from what is the case, from what is already known (in other words so remote from reality), that he will prematurely dismiss the possibility as a hunch not worth following up. The imaginative scientist (or detective) working, as we say, *with* imagination, is

11. John Middleton Murry, *Countries of the Mind: Essays in Literary Criticism* (2nd series, 1931), pp. 1–16; C. Day Lewis, *The Poetic Image* (London: J. Cape, 1947), pp. 17ff.
12. N. Coghill, *Shakespeare's Professional Skills* (Cambridge, Eng: University Press 1964), pp. xii–xiii.

willing to stick his neck out in such a situation. But he does so with the feeling that there might be something in it. It is not just random thought. We would call that blind guessing.

There is a final point to be made about this suppositional kind of imagination, or imagining, and this is that it does not necessarily involve imagery. For some people, exercising their imagination in this particular way, mental images are a recognisable psychological accompaniment. But not more than this; they are not the essence of the activity.[13] For example, mentally working out a simple geometrical problem in the head may involve someone in, say, visualising the necessary diagram. It would be possible however, to solve the problem without recourse to visualising at all. Some people, on the other hand, often combine visualising with actually drawing the diagram, and say that the drawing of the simplest elements of the diagram facilitates the visualising of the rest, thus enabling them to solve the problem more quickly.

There is a final usage which can be dealt with fairly quickly. I refer here to the occasions when we say, "I imagined that I had got over the idea of cabinet responsibility to 5B, but . . .", or "I imagined there would be no difficulty in keeping the class quiet, but . . ." Here we use 'imagine' to get over the idea that we believed such and such would have been the case, but that in fact we were mistaken; e.g., "I imagined it to be so at the time but I now see that I was mistaken." In other words our use of the word 'imagine' here needs the benefit of hindsight when we are talking about ourselves and our own mental activity. There is, of course, a slightly different use when, for example, a senior master, walking along the corridor with the latest recruit to his department, says, "I imagine you will have no difficulty with 3B", leaving unsaid "though I am not sure, and indeed would show no surprise in the event you did have difficulty with 3B." This mental reservation, this indirect factual disclaimer is made explicit when we say of someone known to have an over-fondness for spirituous liquor, "He imagines that he can see a little pink elephant on his shoulder," or when the experienced desert traveller says of a tenderfoot member of his party, "He imagines that he is seeing an oasis (when in fact he is seeing a mirage)." Here we are emphasising not simply the mistakenness, but also the fact that the image has no basis in reality, and so on these occasions we very often say that it was "purely mental" (as contrasted with "actual").

Even so it would be stretching the concept of imagination too far to say that a person suffering from *delirium tremens* or taken in by a mirage is exercising his imagination. He thinks he sees something and reports accordingly, though in reality there is nothing there to see. I, reporting the situation, know him to be mistaken, but he does not know. In the case of the drunkard, the little pink elephant appears quite involuntarily, but I can

13. Cf. Hidé Ishiguro, "Imagination," in B. Williams and A. Montefiore (eds.), *British Analytical Philosophy* (London: Routledge & Kegan Paul, 1966), pp. 153-78.

deliberately see a little pink elephant 'in my mind's eye' without fear of self-deception. If I say to someone, "Imagine that you see a little pink elephant" this means the same as "Visualise a little pink elephant." In other words the use of the imperative here does not correspond with the use of the indicative, and 'imagining' that one sees little pink elephants is a quite different mental activity from visualising such creatures.

As always we are making distinctions, but as always, too, we have to remember that the categories which have been mentioned so far are not incompatible, they are not absolute categories. For example, it is perfectly possible for a child sitting in a classroom in full daylight to conjure up *in* his imagination Columbus sailing the ocean blue, and at the same time to do this *with* imagination. Again, he might conjure up the same situation using his other senses, for example by conjuring up the sound of the waves, the smell of the salt air, the taste of brackish drinking water. Further, though we have taken most of our examples from *thinking* imaginatively, it is perfectly possible to *act* imaginatively and to *feel* imaginatively.

Thus, imagination is not to be thought of as a nuclear faculty (to use Gilbert Ryle's terminology). It is not to be thought of as a distinctive kind or type of thinking, which we can exercise in one way only, irrespective of the context. We can and do think and feel and act imaginatively in different ways and in different contexts, and it is misleading therefore to talk, as the Harvard Report *General Education in a Free Society* does, of distinct modes of thinking, i.e., logical thinking, relational thinking, and imaginative thinking, which can be identified, and fostered through distinctive and, more important, opposed types of content. Not only is imaginative thinking separated off from the other two, but its meaning is stipulated as "whatever is distinctive of the thinking of the poet." The Report goes on, "Logical thinking is straight, as opposed to crooked thinking, and that of the poet may be described as curved thinking."[14] What is meant by the latter, however, is not vouchsafed! In fact seeing things in the mind's eye is an exercise of imagination, growling like a bear is an exercise of imagination, and getting inside the mind of a crusader is an exercise of imagination, and we do great harm to children in their education when we force them to separate reason from imagination, and then go on to make a value judgment detrimental to the latter.

II

Now here is a rich and complex area of experience, one which man alone can achieve, that is the ability to conceive of things and to experiment with situations not present to the senses, an ability which has been crucial to

14. J. B. Conant (ed.), *General Education in a Free Society* (Cambridge, Mass.: Harvard University Press, 1945), p. 67.

the development of man. Why, then, has it been so neglected in education, especially at the secondary and higher levels? And neglected not by apathy or by default, but rather more positively as something not academically respectable. In other words, its neglect has not simply been a matter of thoughtlessness, nor simply of having to leave something out of an overloaded timetable or curriculum. It has been positively rejected.

There would appear to be several reasons for this rejection. In the first place it is the result of the prestige which has been accorded to and has been acquired by scientific method. Francis Bacon set the train in motion: "The imagination being not tied to the laws of matter, may at pleasure join that which nature hath severed, and sever that which nature has joined, and so makes unlawful matches and divorces of things."[15] But the train gathered speed with the growth of Positivism from the mid-nineteenth century onwards. It was than that the methods of science began to make their major impact, insisting especially on objective, verifiable, measurable fact or reality as the only proper object of inquiry. Imagination, in this context, was associated first of all with "conjuring up out of nothing" and secondly with a lack of that essential sense data which could be observed, recorded and measured in an objective way. This was the background against which psychology gave up trying to examine the content of the human mind (and gave up especially the method of introspection, as a highly suspect form of evidence) and instead turned to the study of behaviour, which could be observed and relatively easily measured, and the results verified.

A second reason also has to do with the history of psychology, and this concerns the fall from grace of the notion of faculty psychology, i.e. the dividing up of the mind into various discrete faculties, of which 'the imagination' was one. When faculties went out with the bath water as not scientifically respectable, so also did the baby 'imagination'.

Imagination also suffered at the hands of some misguided followers of the Social Realist school of educational philosophy, who insisted that too much imagination in a child's upbringing led it away from reality, down the slippery slope of day-dreaming, towards illusion, delusion, and hallucination. Too many fairy stories and too much imaginative work would result in unreal expectations in and of the real world, and this was confirmed, it seemed, by the queer personal life of those who dealt in imagination, that is the Romantic poets. Shakespeare, as always, could be called upon to confirm the suspicions of the day:

> The lunatic, the lover and the poet
> Are of imagination all compact.
> The poet's eye, in a fine frenzy rolling,

15. Francis Bacon, *The Advancement of Learning,* Book II, Chap. XIII, in *Works* (1803 edition), I, pp. 89-90.

> Doth glance from heaven to earth, from earth to heaven;
> And as imagination bodies forth
> The form of things unknown, the poet's pen
> Turns them to shapes, and gives to airy nothing
> A local habitation and a name.
> Such tricks hath strong imagination
> That, if it would but apprehend some joy,
> It comprehends some bringer of that joy;
> Or in the night, imagining some fear,
> How easy is a bush suppos'd a bear.
>
> — *Midsummer Night's Dream,* V.i.7-23

Against this background, then, imagination was thought of in terms either of a diseased mind or of a frivolous relaxation. The distrust was based, first of all, on intellectual grounds (it wasn't scientific, it wasn't tough, it wasn't rigorous), and, secondly, on moral grounds (it was associated with Bohemian life).

But we are moving away from both of these extreme positions, especially away from Positivism and its myth of a distinct and preferred kind of thought and inquiry which is objective and impersonal. Nowadays we find historians claiming that theirs is an imaginative study, and geographers devote Presidential Addresses to "The Place of Imagination in Geography," and consider the role of imagination in "The Problem of Geographical Description."[16] Likewise the scientist, who claims that there is something more to being a good scientist than setting up a laboratory experiment and recording the results. It is highly significant, for example, that prefaced to the Nuffield Chemistry Project is a quotation from August Kekulé, the founder of structural theory in chemistry. The quotation that is used runs, "Let us learn to dream, gentlemen, then perhaps we shall find the truth," and the passage from which it comes reads as follows:

I was sitting, writing at my text-book; but the work did not progress; my thoughts were elsewhere. I turned my chair to the fire and dozed. Again the atoms were gambolling before my eyes. This time the smaller groups kept modestly in the background. My mental eye, rendered more acute by repeated visions of the kind, could now distinguish larger structures, of manifold conformation: long rows, sometimes more closely fitted together; all twining and twisting in snake-like motion. But look! What was that? One of the snakes has seized hold of its own tail, and the form whirled mockingly before my eyes. As if by a flash of

16. J. K. Wright, *"Terrae Incognitae:* the place of imagination in geography," *Annals of the Association of American Geographers,* 37 (1947), pp. 1-15; D. Lowenthal, "Geographical Experience and Imagination: towards a geographical epistemology," *ibid.,* 51 (1961), pp. 241-60; and H. C. Darby, "The Problem of Geographical Description," *Transactions and Papers of the Institute of British Geographers* (1962), pp. 1-14.

lightning I awoke; and this time also I spent the rest of the night in working out the consequences of the hypothesis.

Let us learn to dream, gentlemen, [adds Kekulé] then perhaps we shall find the truth . . . but let us beware of publishing our dreams before they have been put to the proof by the waking understanding.[17]

This hypnagogic imagery, as the psychologist calls it,[18] which may have the vividness of the after-image with which we are all familiar, is not to be dismissed as irrelevant and inappropriate. But it needs to be tamed (as Kekulé well realised), tamed of that 'lawlessness' to which I referred earlier, and tamed by a further act of imagination which relates seeming unreality to reality.

Here is imagination founded in reality, as indeed Coleridge meant it to be, a method of apprehending reality. Not imagination in the sense of escaping from life (though for brief spells this may be a useful technique for recharging the batteries), but imagination as a means of developing our awareness of reality. Imagination here does not lie in the play of fantasy, but in getting as close as possible to life. It was for the same reason that Shelley insisted that the exercise of imagination, far from leading a child into a "cloud cuckoo land" of illusion and hallucination, could contribute to his moral development by encouraging him to put himself in someone else's place, and thus to exercise what Bertrand Russell has called "a hypothetical sympathy," which required an imaginative effort of the will as well as of the intellect, to "enter into minds unlike our own."

This last phrase, "enter into minds unlike our own," is from Herbert Butterfield's *Whig Interpretation of History*,[19] which was published in 1931. It was repeated almost verbatim by Professor Trevor-Roper over a quarter of a century later when he stipulated that historical imagination means "not the act of making the past picturesque and remote from ourselves, like a castle pageant, but of making it fully intelligible to us, by enabling us to enter as it were into the minds and passions of people, who in some ways seemed very different from us." Such observations remind us that the historian is intimately concerned to clarify his use of the term imagination. For too long historians had interpreted imagination as "ornament," as Macaulay had, for example, when he claimed that "a perfect historian must possess an imagination sufficiently powerful to make his narrative affecting and

17. Cf. O. T. Benfey, "August Kekulé and the Birth of Structural Theory of Organic Chemistry," *Journal of Chemical Education*, 35 (1958) pp. 21–23, and W. V. and K. R. Farrar, "Faith and Doubt: the Theory of Structure in Organic Chemistry," *Proceedings of the Chemical Society* (1959), pp. 285–90.

18. Cf. Peter McKellar, *Imagination and Thinking* (London: Cohen & West, 1957).

19. H. Butterfield, *The Whig Interpretation of History* (London: G. Bell & Sons 1931), p. 9, and H. R. Trevor-Roper. "Historical Imagination," *The Listener*, 27th Feburary 1958, pp. 357–8.

picturesque,"[20] and hence was only too willing to fill in the gaps with imaginary history. Agnellus, the ninth-century Bishop of Ravenna, compiling biographies of his predecessors, put it this way: "Where I have not found any history of any of these bishops, and where I have not been able by conversation with aged men, or by inspection of the monuments which remain, or from any other authentic source, to obtain information concerning them, in such a case in order that there might not be a break in the series I have composed the life myself, with the help of God and the prayers of the brethren."[21]

Because this was the way history had been written for so long it is not surprising, I suppose, that von Ranke and his followers started to reject imagination, and to search instead for "what actually happened." Even so, just as the landscape painter does not merely make a faithful copy of nature, but selects, simplifies, leaves out what he considers unimportant, and includes only what he considers to be essential, so too the historian. It is the artist and historian, not nature or history, who are responsible for what appears in the picture or in the history book, and in this sense both artist and historian are inevitably "pictured within" (if we might be allowed to extract Elgar's phrase from another medium).[22] We may smile, in our superior way, at Agnellus' naive frankness, but in fact the historian attempts to fill in "the breaks in the series" with every inference he makes. "The historian's picture of his subject [to quote R. G. Collingwood], whether that subject be a sequence of events or a past state of things, thus appears as a web of imaginative reconstruction, stretched between certain fixed points provided by the statements of his authorities; and if these points are frequent enough and the threads spun from each to the next are constructed with due care, always by the *a priori* imagination and never by merely arbitrary fancy, the whole picture is constantly verified by appeal to these data, and runs little risk of losing touch with the reality which it represents."[23] It is important to note in addition, of course, that these "fixed points" are not simply the data of the authorities untouched, uncriticised by the historian. They should be the end-product of constructively sceptical scrutiny of this data or evidence. The points are not given, are not given ready made, they are achieved by critical thinking on the part of the historian about his data. He, the historian, is responsible for them. Even the eye-witness account does not absolve the historian (or the detective) from checking its validity, from relating it to other available evidence.

20. Macaulay, *Essays on History,* in *Works* (ed. Lady Trevelyan), 1875, V, p. 122.

21. Cited H. J. Muller, *The Uses of the Past* (New York: Mentor Books, Mentor Edition, 1954), p. 232.

22. Cf. Margaret Macdonald, "Art and Imagination," *Proceedings of the Aristotelian Society,* LIII (1952–3), pp. 205–26.

23. R. G. Collingwood, *The Idea of History* (Oxford, Eng: Clarendon Press, 1946), p. 242.

The historian, then, is engaged in an act of recreation. Like the art critic and the literary critic he acts at least one remove from reality. Historians of philosophy or of sculpture, for example, are concerned with books and pieces of sculpture not in so far as these exist materially, but in so far as they have a meaning, and equally obviously this meaning can only be apprehended by reproducing, and thereby quite literally realising, the thoughts that are expressed in the books of philosophy, or the artistic concepts that manifest themselves in the pieces of sculpture. The historian reconstitutes his material by means of an imaginative recreation, but in so doing uses his imaginative capacity in a way which is not necessarily the same as that used by the artist, the poet and the scientist, though each is aiming in his way at apprehending reality.

We also have to make clear how and where (at what stage in his work) an historian uses imagination. He obviously needs to use it in the preliminary stage of hypothesis-forming, in the recombining of his data, and in the exercise of "hypothetical sympathy," and yet also (without betraying his craft) at the stage of writing, in his recounting with imagination the fruits of his historical study. Thus, an historian lacking in imagination in the preliminary stages would be considered a poor historian. Lacking it at the stage of writing he would be considered a dull historian. And the best historian must surely be well-equipped at both stages.

Any discussion of historical imagination is still further complicated if we extend the inquiry to cover historical fiction, and to the way in which the historical novelist approaches the past.[24] If we insist on considering fiction (of any kind) in terms of truth and falsity, then of course we have now entered the realm of falsity. But within this realm we can still distinguish between the literally false and the misleadingly false. Historical fiction is obviously not of the latter kind, but must nevertheless avoid running the risk of a complete break with reality. In other words, the historical novelist must, in his writing, pay attention to the limits of credibility unless he wishes to revert to the Gothic tale of the eighteenth century. He shares with the historian the problem of seeing a former age in all its concrete detail, on its own terms and in its own proper setting. He shares, too, the need to "unload his mind of all remembrance of after-events." But whereas the historical novelist has only to construct a picture of the past which is coherent, one that makes sense logically and psychologically, the historian's product has also to be true, in the sense that it has to stand or fall in relation to the available evidence.

Even so, the historical novelist can remind the historian of the dangers of his becoming a chronicler, an antiquarian, a dry-as-dust (if erudite) compiler. And the historical novelist can do this reminding best, precisely

24. A. H. Hannay, "Is the Imagination Creative?" *Proceedings of the Aristotelian Society*, XXVI (1935‒6), pp. 109‒30.

because he introduces imagination into the reckoning: not the imagination which invents the imaginary, but the imagination which helps us to penetrate into the minds of the people of the past, to search for their unspoken premises, to remember their relative incapacity to think and feel as we do or rather to remember our own relative incapacity to think and feel as they did.

. . .May I summarise what I have said by a reminder against thinking of imagination in terms of a global faculty, homogeneous in its functioning, and restricted to a particular nonrational area of experience and knowledge; against equating it, necessarily, with an imaginary, unreal, dreamlike and irrational world, which is put in direct contrast with the world of reason and conceptualisation; against equating it, necessarily, with seeing in the mind's eye; against insisting, indeed, on its necessary association with mental imagery at all.

But these reminders, though necessary, are all negative, and I must end on a positive note. If we are to pay attention in the reform of our curriculum — for example, to the structure of the subjects of study which go to make it up, rather than thinking of them as bodies of knowledge — we must remember that we never just imagine. We are always exercising a mathematical or historical or pictorial or poetic imagination, and that within these categories we exercise imagination in different ways with different results. The activities themselves vary widely according to the media.

The common factor in all these activities, however, which justifies their classification as imagination, is that they mark a point where we are aware of leaving a given sensation or perception in order to gain an awareness of, a consciousness of, a knowledge of something that isn't given. In exercising imagination (to quote Arthur Koestler) we engage in "an act of wrenching away an object or a concept from its habitual associative context, and seeing it in a new context. It is an act both of destruction and of creation, for it demands the breaking up of a mental habit, the melting down with the blow lamp of Cartesian doubt, of the frozen structure of accepted theory to enable the new fusion to take place."[25] And it seems to me that these notions can be applied to the study of education as much as to the education of children and undergraduates. Of course, no one person excels in every kind of imagining. A person who has imaginative powers in one direction may be totally lacking in another. As educators we have to decide whether "lacking" is to be interpreted as "has not and never will, by some innate defect," or "has not and therefore ought to be given remedial attention." Even then we have to decide on a prior premise, "that we ought to develop all kinds of imaginative thinking in all of our pupils." But that is another story.

25. Arthur Koestler, *The Sleep Walkers* (Baltimore: Penguin Books, 1964), p. 519.

Part III

THE NATURE OF KNOWLEDGE

Introduction

In his essay "Liberal Education and the Nature of Knowledge" Paul H. Hirst reconstructs and examines critically two historically important conceptions of liberal education — the Greek, and the modern as formulated in the Harvard Committee Report *General Education in a Free Society*. He finds the Greek conception of liberal education in terms of the pursuit of knowledge, although rooted in some highly questionable philosophical doctrines, to be sounder than the modern conception in terms of the qualities of mind it ought to produce. Hirst sets out, therefore, to formulate a modern equivalent of the Greek notion: a conception worked out fully in terms of the forms of knowledge but unencumbered by metaphysical and epistemological speculation. Having done this, he discusses the implications of this reinterpretation of liberal education for the practical conduct of education. This latter discussion, of interest in its own right, touches on a number of topics of the utmost importance for curriculum.

May Brodbeck's essay "Toward a Fabric of Knowledge — Common Elements Among Fields of Learning" is an interesting companion piece to Hirst's. Hirst, in reinterpreting the notion of liberal education, recommends that the various forms of knowledge be taught. These forms — the disciplines — have on his view a number of distinctive characteristics and it is on these that he focuses attention. Brodbeck, on the other hand, is concerned to show us the similarities among the fields of teaching and learning. She recognizes that there are some very real differences among them but argues that the similarities, not the differences, are of first importance for understanding and teaching them. To make her point she takes us on a brief tour of what Hirst has called the forms of knowledge. We are shown elements common to the physical and biological sciences; we are shown elements common to both of these, that is to say the natural sciences and the social sciences; and we are shown ways in which literature in particular and the arts in general relate to the social sciences.

Hirst and Brodbeck may be said to give us different tours of the same terrain. L. R. Perry, in his essay "Commonsense Thought, Knowledge and Judgement and Their Importance for Education," is concerned to show us a different terrain. Hirst's forms of knowledge and Brodbeck's fields of learning would seem, at least for the most part, to fall under what Perry calls specialized or expert knowledge, in contrast to commonsense knowledge. It is this latter which interests Perry. Perry argues that, contrary to the belief of many, commonsense knowledge cannot be superseded by specialized knowledge. This is not to say that it is infallible, but rather that it supplements specialized knowledge. Its task is to relate specialized knowledge to ordinary commonsense situations. Commonsense, for example, must decide which varieties of specialized knowledge are relevant to a given situation, how much of each variety is relevant and how these relevant but unrelated varieties of specialized knowledge are to be related. Some might suppose that Perry, in view of his conclusions about commonsense knowledge, would advocate an educational program quite unlike the one proposed by Hirst. But Perry sees the basic job of the school as the teaching of the various types of specialized knowledge and thus concludes his essay by suggesting points in such an education at which training in commonsense thought might be appropriate.

Each of the essays in this section has important things to say about knowledge. Each is, in effect, an essay in epistemology as well as an essay in philosophy of curriculum. But if the essays when taken singly reveal something of the nature of knowledge, when taken together they raise the question of the relationship between analyses of knowledge and curriculum decisions. It is often supposed that there is a one-way street between the curriculum planner or developer and the epistemologist down which the epistemologist sends a description of whatever knowledge the curriculum person happens to be interested in. If the Hirst and Brodbeck and Perry essays teach us nothing else, they teach us that this view of the matter is too simple. Descriptions are necessarily selective. Supposing an account of the nature of knowledge to be correct, then, we must remember that a choice or decision is implicit in it: certain aspects of the knowledge in question will have been selected, others will not have been. And we must realize that a different description of the same variety of knowledge could be given. But if alternative descriptions can be given, on which one ought the curriculum decision be based? We can not appeal to epistemology for an answer to this question. In effect we are asking which of alternative true descriptions of knowledge is better *for our purpose* and our purpose, of course, is educational.

We must choose the account of knowledge which is suited to our educational purpose. In an important sense, then, it is a mistake to say, as some do, that what we teach will depend on our view of knowledge. Of course we don't want to lie to our students about the nature of knowledge; we don't want to tell them things about it that are not true. Yet given these qualifications, it is as accurate to say that our view of knowledge will depend on what we want to teach as it is to say that what we want to teach will depend on our view of knowledge. Epistemology is relevant to problems of curriculum but, and this is what is too often forgotten, the street between curriculum planner or developer and epistemologist is two-way.

It is important to distinguish between analyses of knowledge like those of Hirst, Brodbeck, and Perry, and analyses of knowing — or, if you wish, what it is for someone to *have* knowledge. The essay in this volume that comes closest to dealing with this latter question is not in this section but in the preceding one. That essay, on learning with understanding (Petrie), is as much an essay in epistemology as is any of the three essays to follow, but it is directed to rather different issues. Suppose a curriculum planner has an accurate and appropriate account of the nature of, say, scientific knowledge. This account will not answer the question of what conditions a person must meet if he is to be said to understand science or to know that such and such a scientific statement is true. The nature of scientific knowledge will, to be sure, have some bearing on the further question but independent philosophical analysis, of the sort provided above by Petrie, will be necessary to answer it.

Accounts of learning with understanding and knowing will not in themselves, however, solve our curriculum problems. Given that we know what conditions a person must meet if he is to be said to understand or know something, we must still decide whether or not we want our students to understand or know and what we want them to understand or know. Hirst takes the position that we do want them to understand and talks briefly in his paper about what understanding the various forms of knowledge consists in. We must distinguish, however, between understanding a form of knowledge and understanding something by means of or in that form of knowledge: for example, understanding the discipline of science as opposed to scientific understanding of some phenomenon or understanding the historical enterprise as opposed to historical understanding of some enterprise. Hirst seems to be advocating both, but it is well to remember that the two things are distinct. One can understand things with the help of some form of knowledge without understanding that form of knowledge, and one can understand some form of knowledge without understanding things with the help of that form of knowledge.

LIBERAL EDUCATION AND
THE NATURE OF KNOWLEDGE

Paul H. Hirst

The phrase 'liberal education' has today become something of a slogan which takes on different meanings according to its immediate context. It usually labels a form of education of which the author approves, but beyond that its meaning is often entirely negatively derived. Whatever else a liberal education is, it is *not* a vocational education, *not* an exclusively scientific education, or *not* a specialist education in any sense. The frequency with which the term is employed in this way certainly highlights the inadequacies of these other concepts and the need for a wider and, in the long run, more worthwhile form of education. But as long as the concept is merely negative in what it intimates, it has little more than debating value. Only when it is given explicit positive content can it be of use in the serious business of educational planning. It is my contention in this paper that whatever vagaries there have been in the use of the term, it is the appropriate label for a positive concept, that of an education based fairly and squarely on the nature of knowledge itself, a concept central to the discussion of education at any level.

The Greek Notion of Liberal Education

The fully developed Greek notion of liberal education was rooted in a number of related philosophical doctrines; first about the significance of knowledge for the mind, and secondly about the relationship between knowledge and reality. In the first category there was the doctrine that it is the peculiar and distinctive activity of the mind, because of its very nature, to pursue knowledge. The achievement of knowledge satisfies and fulfills the mind which thereby attains its own appropriate end. The pursuit of knowledge is thus the pursuit of the good of the mind and, therefore, an essential element in the good life. In addition, it was held that the achievement of knowledge is not only the attainment of the good of the mind

From Reginald D. Archambault (Ed.) *Philosophical Analysis and Education* (London: Routledge & Kegan Paul Ltd., and New York: Humanities Press Inc.),1965. Reprinted by permission of the author, Routledge & Kegan Paul Ltd., and Humanities Press Inc.

itself, but also the chief means whereby the good life as a whole is to be found. Man is more than pure mind, yet mind is his essential distinguishing characteristic, and it is in terms of knowledge that his whole life is rightly directed.

That knowledge is equal to its task was guaranteed by the second group of doctrines. These asserted that the mind, in the right use of reason, comes to know the essential nature of things and can apprehend what is ultimately real and immutable. Consequently, man no longer needs to live in terms of deceptive appearances and doubtful opinions and beliefs. All his experiences, life and thought can be given shape and perspective by what is finally true, by knowledge that corresponds to what is ultimately real. Further, the particular way in which reason is here represented as attaining knowledge, results in a view of the whole of man's understanding as hierarchically structured in various levels. From the knowledge of mere particulars to that of pure being, all knowledge has its place in a comprehensive and harmonious scheme, the pattern of which is formed as knowledge is developed in apprehending reality in its many different manifestations.

From these doctrines there emerged the idea of liberal education as a process concerned simply and directly with the pursuit of knowledge. But the doctrines give to this general idea particular meaning and significance; for they lead to a clear definition of its scope and content, and to a clear justification for education in these terms. The definition is clear, because education is determined objectively in range, in structure and in content by the forms of knowledge itself and their harmonious, hierarchical interrelations. There is here no thought of defining education in terms of knowledge and skills that may be useful, or in terms of moral virtues and qualities of mind that may be considered desirable. The definition is stated strictly in terms of man's knowledge of what is the case. The development of the mind to which it leads, be it in skills, virtues or other characteristics, is thought to be necessarily its greatest good.

The justification that the doctrines lend to this concept of education is threefold. First, such an education is based on what is true and not on uncertain opinions and beliefs or temporary values. It therefore has a finality which no other form of education has. Secondly, knowledge itself being a distinctive human virtue, liberal education has a value for the person as the fulfillment of the mind, a value which has nothing to do with utilitarian or vocational considerations. Thirdly, because of the significance of knowledge in the determination of the good life as a whole, liberal education is essential to man's understanding of how he ought to live, both individually and socially.

Here, then, the Greeks attained the concept of an education that was "liberal" not simply because it was the education of free men rather than slaves, but also because they saw it as freeing the mind to function according to its true nature, freeing reason from error and illusion and freeing man's conduct from wrong. And ever since Greek times this idea of education has had its place. Sometimes it has been modified or extended in detail to accommodate within its scheme new forms of knowledge: for instance Christian doctrines and the various branches of modern science. Sometimes the concept has been misinterpreted: as in Renaissance humanism when classical learning was equated with liberal education. Sometimes it has been strongly opposed on philosophical grounds: as by Dewey and the pragmatists. Yet at crucial points in the history of education the concept has constantly reappeared. It is not hard to understand why this should be so.

Education, being a deliberate, purposeful activity directed to the development of individuals, necessarily involves considerations of value. Where are these values to be found? What is to be their content? How are they to be justified? They can be, and often are, values that reflect the interests of a minority group in the society. They may be religious, political or utilitarian in character. They are always open to debate and detailed criticism, and are always in need of particular justification. Is there not perhaps a more ultimate basis for the values that should determine education, some more objective ground? That final ground has, ever since the Greeks, been repeatedly located in man's conception of the diverse forms of knowledge he has achieved. And there has thus arisen the demand for an education whose definition and justification are based on the nature and significance of knowledge itself, and not on the predilections of pupils, the demands of society, or the whims of politicians. Precisely this demand was behind the development by the Greeks of an education in the seven liberal arts, an introduction to and a pursuit of the forms of knowledge as they were then conceived. It was precisely this demand that prompted Newman and Arnold in the nineteenth century to call for an education that aimed at the cultivation and development of the mind in the full range of man's understanding. It is the same demand that today motivates such classical realists as Maritain and R. M. Hutchins.

A Typical Modern Statement: The Harvard Report

It may well be asked, however, whether those who do not hold the doctrines of metaphysical and epistemological realism can legitimately subscribe to a concept of education of this kind. Historically it seems to have had positive force only when presented in this particular philosophical framework. But historical association must be distinguished from logical connection and it is not by any means obvious that all the characteristic features of the concept are dependent on such philosophical realism. If the doctrines about mind, knowledge and reality mentioned at the beginning of this paper are regarded as at best too speculative a basis for educational planning, as well they may be, the possibility of an education defined and justified entirely in terms of the scope and character of knowledge needs re-examination. The significance of the concept originally came directly from the place the basic doctrines give to knowledge in a unified picture of the mind and its relation to reality. Knowledge is achieved when the mind attains its own satisfaction or good by corresponding to objective reality. A liberal education in the pursuit of knowledge is, therefore, seeking the development of the mind according to what is quite external to it, the structure and pattern of reality. But if once there is any serious questioning of this relationship between mind, knowledge and reality, the whole harmonious structure is liable to disintegrate. First there arise inevitably problems of definition. A liberal education defined in terms of knowledge alone is acceptable as long as knowledge is thought to be necessarily developing the mind in desirable ways, and hence promoting the good life. But if doubt is cast on these functions of knowledge, must not liberal education be redefined stating explicitly the qualities of mind and the moral virtues to which it is directed? And if knowledge is no longer seen as the understanding of reality but merely as the understanding of experience, what is to replace the harmonious, hierarchical scheme of knowledge that gave pattern and order to the education? Secondly there are equally serious problems of justification. For if knowledge is no longer thought to be rooted in some reality, or if its significance for the mind and the good life is questioned, what can be the justification for an education defined in terms of knowledge alone?

Difficulties of both kinds, but particularly those of definition, can be seen in the well-known Harvard Committee Report: *General Education in a Free Society*.[1] (In the Committee's terminology the aims of a "liberal' and a "general" education are identical.) Though certain of the doctrines that originally supported the concept of a liberal education are implicit in this work, the classical view of the significance of knowledge for the mind is considerably weakened, and the belief that in metaphysics man has knowledge of ultimate reality is ignored, if not rejected. The result is an ambiguous and unsatisfactory treatment of the problem of definition and a limited and debatable treatment of the question of justification. Some examination of the Report on both these scores, particularly the former, will serve to show that adequate definition and justification are not only not dependent on the classical doctrines, but can in fact be based directly on an explication of the concepts of "mind" and "knowledge" and their relationship.

The Report attempts the definition of a liberal education in two distinct ways: in terms of the qualities of mind it ought to produce and the

1. *General Education in a Free Society:* Report of the Harvard Committee (London: Oxford University Press, 1946).

forms of knowledge with which it ought to be concerned. What the precise relationship is between these two is not clear. It is asserted that they are "images of each other," yet that there is no escape from "describing general education at one time looking to the good man in society and at another time as dictated by the nature of knowledge itself."[2] Which of the forms of description is to be given pride of place soon emerges, however. First, three areas of knowledge are distinguished, primarily by their distinctive methods: the natural sciences, the humanities and social studies. But it is made plain that "the cultivation of certain aptitudes and attitudes of mind" is being aimed at, the elements of knowledge being the means for developing these. Liberal education is therefore best understood in terms of the characteristics of mind to which it leads. "By characteristics we mean aims so important as to prescribe how general education should be carried out and which abilities ought to be sought above all others in every part of it. These abilities in our opinion are: to think effectively, to communicate thought, to make relevant judgments, to discriminate among values."[3] The meaning of each of these four is elaborated at some length. Amongst the many things detailed of "effective thinking" it is first said to be logical thinking of a kind that is applicable to such practical matters as deciding who to vote for and what wife to choose: it is the ability to extract universal truths from particular cases and to infer particulars from general laws: it is the ability to analyse a problem and to recombine the elements by the use of imagination. This thinking goes further than mere logic, however. It includes the relational thinking of everyday life, the ability to think at a level appropriate to a problem whatever its character. It includes too the imaginative thinking of the poet, the inventor, and the revolutionary. "Communication," though "obviously inseparable from effective thinking," is said to involve another group of skills, those of speaking and listening, writing and reading. It includes certain moral qualities such as candour, it covers certain vital aspects of social and political life and even the high art of conversation. "The making of relevant value judgments" involves "the ability of the student to bring to bear the whole range of ideas upon the area of experience," it is the art of effectively relating theory to practice, of abstractions to facts, of thought to action. Finally there is "discrimination among values." This includes the distinction of various kinds of value and their relative importance, an awareness of the values of character like fair play and self-control, intellectual values like the love of truth and aesthetic values like good taste, and, in addition, a commitment to such values in the conduct of life.[4]

As to how exactly these abilities come to be those developed by the three types of knowledge, little is said. It is noted that "the three phases of

2. *Ibid.*, p. 58.
3. *Ibid.*, pp. 64–65.
4. *Ibid.*, pp. 65–73.

effective thinking, logical, relational, and imaginative, correspond roughly to
the three divisions of learning, the natural sciences, the social studies, and the
humanities, respectively."[5] The difficult connection between education in
the making of value judgments and the formation of moral character is noted.
Otherwise the remarks are of a general nature, emphasizing that these abilities
must be consciously developed in all studies and generalized as far as possible.

    This double, if one-sided, characterization of liberal education seems to
me unsatisfactory and seriously misleading if what is said of the four abilities
is examined more closely. In the first place, the notion that a liberal
education can be directly characterized in terms of mental abilities and
independently of fully specifying the forms of knowledge involved, is I think
false. It is the result of a misunderstanding of the way in which mental abilities are in fact distinguishable. From what is said of "effective thinking," it is
perfectly plain that the phrase is being used as a label for mental activity
which results in an achievement of some sort, an achievement that is, at least
in principle, both publicly describable and publicly testable – the solving of a
mathematical problem, responsibly deciding who to vote for, satisfactorily
analysing a work of art. Indeed there can be effective thinking only when the
outcome of mental activity can be recognised and judged by those who have
the appropriate skills and knowledge, for otherwise the phrase has no
significant application. Thus although the phrase labels a form of mental
activity, and such mental processes may well be directly accessible only to the
person whose processes they are, its description and evaluation must be in
public terms occurring in public language. Terms which, like 'effective
thinking,' describe activities involving achievements of some sort, must have
public criteria to mark them. But in that case, none of the four abilities can in
fact be delineated except by means of their detailed public features. Such
characterisation is in fact forced on the Committee when they come to
amplify what they mean. But their approach is simply illustrative, as if the
abilities are directly intelligible in themselves, and the items and features of
knowledge they give merely examples of areas where the abilities can be seen.
If the public terms and criteria are logically necessary to specifying what
the abilities are, however, then no adequate account of liberal education in
terms of these can be given without a full account in terms of the public
features of the forms of knowledge with which it is concerned. Indeed the
latter is logically prior and the former secondary and derivative.

    In the second place, the use of broad, general terms for these abilities
serves in fact to unify misleadingly quite disparate achievements. For the
public criteria whereby the exercise of any one of these abilities is to be
judged are not all of a piece. Those that under the banner of "effective thinking" are appropriate in, say, aesthetic appreciation are, apart from certain

5. *Ibid.*, p. 67.

very general considerations, inappropriate in, say, mathematical thinking. In each case the criteria are peculiar to the particular area of knowledge concerned. Similarly, for instance, "communication" in the sciences has only certain very basic features in common with communication in poetic terms. It is only when the abilities are fully divided out, as it were, into the various domains and we see what they refer to in public terms that it is at all clear what is involved in developing them. To talk of developing "effective thinking" is like talking of developing "successful games playing." Plainly that unifying label is thoroughly misleading when what constitutes playing cricket has practically nothing in common with what constitutes playing tiddly-winks. The implications of the term are not at all appreciated until what is wanted is given detailed specification. It is vitally important to realize the very real objective differences that there are in forms of knowledge, and therefore in our understanding of mental processes that are related to these. Maybe this unfortunate desire to use unifying concepts is a relic of the time when all forms of knowledge were thought to be similar, if not identical in logical structure and that the "laws of logic" reflected the precise psychological operations involved in valid thinking. Be that as it may, the general terms used in the Report are liable both to blur essential distinctions and to direct the attention of educational planners into unprofitable descriptions of what they are after.

Thirdly, in spite of any protestations to the contrary, the impression is created by this terminology that it is possible to develop general unitary abilities of the stated kind. The extent to which this is true is a matter for empirical investigation into the transfer of training. Nevertheless such abilities must necessarily be characterised in terms of the public features of knowledge, and whatever general abilities there may be, the particular criteria for their application in diverse fields are vital to their significance for liberal education. But to think in these terms is to be in danger of looking for transfer of skills where none is discernible. We must not assume that skill at tiddly-winks will get us very far at cricket, or that if the skills have much in common, as in say squash and tennis, then the rules for one activity will do as the rules for the other.

Failure to appreciate these points leads all too readily to programmes of education for which quite unwarranted claims are made. It is sometimes said, for instance, that the study of one major science can in itself provide the elements of a liberal education — that it can lead to the development of such abilities as effective thinking, communication, the making of relevant judgments, and even to some extent, discrimination among values. But this facile view is seen to be quite untenable if it is once understood how these abilities are defined, and how any one form of knowledge is related to them. Much more plausible and much more common is the attempt to relate directly the study of particular subjects to the development of particular unitary abilities. The Harvard Committee do this with subdivisions of effective thinking when they suggest that, roughly speaking, logical thinking is developed by the sciences, relational thinking by social studies, and imaginative thinking by the humanities. This, of course, could be said to be true by definition if logical thinking were taken to be just that kind of thinking that is developed by the study of the sciences. But such a straight and limited connection is not at all what is indicated in the Report. The forms of thinking there are much more generalised. It follows then that logical, relational and imaginative thinking must be independently defined. Because of the vagueness of the terms it might appear that this would be simple enough. But in fact this very vagueness makes the task almost impossible, for any one of the three terms might, with considerable justice, be applied to almost any example of thinking. (And the appropriateness of using such a term as 'imaginative' to describe a distinct type of thinking rather than its manner or style is very debatable). Even if this most serious difficulty were overcome somehow, there would remain the problem of establishing empirical evidence, for asserting both the existence of such an ability, and that a particular study leads to its development. Generally speaking there is little such evidence. What there is on transfer of training suggests that it occurs only where there is marked logical similarity in the elements studied.[6]

Finally the characterisation of a liberal education in these terms is misleading owing to the tendency for the concept to be broadened so that it is concerned not only with the development of the mind that results from the pursuit of knowledge, but also with other aspects of personal development, particularly emotional and moral, that may or may not be judged desirable. This tendency can be clearly seen in the Report's comments on the abilities of communication, making relevant judgments and discriminating among values. Stretching the edges of the concept in these ways leads to a much wider, more generalised notion of education. It then ceases to be one defined directly in terms of the pursuit of knowledge as liberal education originally was, and thus cannot be justified by justifying that pursuit. But this is surely to give up the concept in favour of another one that needs independent justification. The analysis of such a concept is beyond our present concern.

A Reassertion and a Reinterpretation

On logical grounds, then, it would seem that a consistent concept of liberal education must be worked out fully in terms of the forms of

6. Precisely the same criticisms might be made of some remarks by Professor P. H. Nowell-Smith in his inaugural lecture, *Education in a University* (Leicester: Leicester University Press, 1958), pp. 6–11. In these he suggests that the prime purpose of the study of literature, history and philosophy is that each develops one of the central powers of the mind – creative imagination, practical wisdom, and logical thought. Once

knowledge. By these is meant, of course, not collections of information, but the complex ways of understanding experience which man has achieved, which are publicly specifiable and which are gained through learning. An education in these terms does indeed develop its related abilities and qualities of mind, for the mind will be characterised to a greater or less degree by the features of the understanding it seeks. Each form of knowledge, if it is to be acquired beyond a general and superficial level, involves the development of creative imagination, judgment, thinking, communicative skills, etc., in ways that are peculiar to itself as a way of understanding experience. To list these elements, picking them out, as it were, across the forms of knowledge of which they are part and in each of which they have a different stamp, draws attention to many features that a liberal education must of course include. But it draws attention to them at the expense of the differences among them as they occur in the different areas. And of itself such listing contributes nothing to the basic determination of what a liberal education is. To be told that it is the development of effective thinking is of no value until this is explicated in terms of the forms of knowledge which give it meaning: for example in terms of the solving of problems in Euclidean geometry or coming to understand the poems of John Donne. To be told instead that it is concerned with certain specified forms of knowledge, the essential character-istics of which are then detailed explicitly as far as possible, is to be given a clear understanding of the concept and one which is unambiguous as to the forms of thinking, judgment, imagination, and communication it involves.

In his Gulbenkian Foundation Report: *Arts and Science Sides in the Sixth Form,* Mr. A. D. C. Peterson comes considerably nearer than the Harvard Committee to the definition of a liberal education (once more termed here a "general education") by proceeding in just this fashion. Being concerned that this should not be worked out in terms of information, he shies away from any direct use of the term 'knowledge' and defines the concept modestly as one that "develops the intellect in as many as possible of the main modes of thinking."[7] These are then listed as the logical, the empirical, the moral, and the aesthetic. The phrase 'modes of thinking', it is true, refers directly to forms of mental activity, and Mr. Peterson's alternatives for it, 'modes of human experience', 'categories of mental experience', and (elsewhere) 'types of judgment', all look in the same direction. Yet the "modes" are not different aspects of mind that cut across the forms that human knowledge takes, as the Harvard Report's "abilities" are. They are, rather, four parallel forms of mental development. To complete this treatment so that there is no ambiguity, however, it must be made clear

---

more we are up against the question of the definition of these "powers" and if that problem can be solved, the question of sheer evidence for them and the way they can be developed.

7. *Arts and Science Sides in the Sixth Form:* Gulbenkian Foundation Report (Oxford University Department of Education, 1960), p. 15.

in a way that Mr. Peterson does not make it clear, that the four forms can only be distinguished, in the last analysis, in terms of the public features that demarcate the areas of knowledge on which they stand. Logical, empirical, moral, and aesthetic forms of understanding are distinguishable from each other only by their distinctive concepts and expressions and their criteria for distinguishing the true from the false, the good from the bad. If Mr. Peterson's "modes" are strictly explicated on the basis of these features of knowledge, then his concept of education becomes one concerned with the development of the mind as that is determined by certain forms of knowledge. This is to be in sight of a modern equivalent of the traditional conception of liberal education.

But the reassertion of this concept implies that there is once more the acceptance of some kind of "harmony" between knowledge and the mind. This is, however, not now being maintained on metaphysical grounds. What is being suggested, rather, is that the "harmony" is a matter of the logical relationship between the concept of 'mind' and the concept of 'knowledge', from which it follows the achievement of knowledge is necessarily the development of mind – that is, the self-conscious, rational mind of man – in its most fundamental aspect.

Whatever else is implied in the phrase, to have "a rational mind" certainly implies experience structured under some form of conceptual scheme. The various manifestations of consciousness, in, for instance, different sense perceptions, different emotions, or different elements of intellectual understanding, are intelligible only by virtue of the conceptual apparatus by which they are articulated. Further, whatever private forms of awareness there may be, it is by means of symbols, particularly in language, that conceptual articulation becomes objectified, for the symbols give public embodiment to the concepts. The result of this is that men are able to come to understand both the external world and their own private states of mind in common ways, sharing the same conceptual schema by learning to use symbols in the same manner. The objectification of understanding is possible because commonly accepted criteria for using the terms are recognised even if these are never explicitly expressed. But further as the symbols derived from experience can be used to examine subsequent experience, assertions are possible which are testable as true or false, valid or invalid. There are thus also public criteria whereby certain forms of expression are assessable against experience. Whether the "objects" concerned are themselves private to the individual like mental processes, or publicly accessible like temperature readings, there are here tests for the assertions which are themselves publicly agreed and accepted.

It is by the use of such tests that we have come to have the whole domain of knowledge. The formulating and testing of symbolic expressions has enabled man to probe his experience for ever more complex relations and for finer and finer distinctions, these being fixed and held for public sharing in the symbolic systems that have been evolved. But it is important to realise that this progressive attainment of a cognitive framework with public criteria has significance not merely for knowledge itself, for it is by its terms that the life of man in every particular is patterned and ordered. Without its structure all other forms of consciousness, including, for example, emotional experiences, or mental attitudes and beliefs, would seem to be unintelligible. For the analysis of them reveals that they lack independent intelligible structure of themselves. Essentially private though they may be in many or all of their aspects, their characteristic forms are explicable only by means of the publicly rooted conceptual organisations we have achieved. They can be understood only by means of the objective features with which they are associated, round which they come to be organised and built. The forms of knowledge are thus the basic articulations whereby the whole of experience has become intelligible to man, they are the fundamental achievement of mind.

Knowledge, however, must never be thought of merely as vast bodies of tested symbolic expressions. These are only the public aspects of the ways in which human experience has come to have shape. They are significant because they are themselves the objective elements round which the development of mind has taken place. To acquire knowledge is to become aware of experience as structured, organised, and made meaningful in some quite specific way, and the varieties of human knowledge constitute the highly developed forms in which man has found this possible. To acquire knowledge is to learn to see, to experience the world in a way otherwise unknown, and thereby come to have a mind in a fuller sense. It is not that the mind is some kind of organ or muscle with its own inbuilt forms of operation, which if somehow developed, naturally lead to different kinds of knowledge. It is not that the mind has predetermined patterns of functioning. Nor is it that the mind is an entity which suitably directed by knowledge comes to take on the pattern of, is conformed to, some external reality. It is rather that to have a mind basically involves coming to have experience articulated by means of various conceptual schema. It is only because man has over millennia objectified and progressively developed these that he has achieved the forms of human knowledge, and the possibility of the development of mind as we know it is open to us today.

A liberal education is, then, one that, determined in scope and content by knowledge itself, is thereby concerned with the development of mind. The concept is thus once more clearly and objectively defined in precisely the same way as the original concept. It is however no longer supported by epistemological and metaphysical doctrines that result in a hierarchical organisation of the various forms of knowledge. The detailed working out of the education will therefore be markedly different in certain respects. The distinctions between the various forms of knowledge which will principally govern the scheme of education will now be based entirely on analyses of their particular conceptual, logical and methodological features. The comprehensive character of the education will of course remain, since this is essentially part of the definition of the concept, but any question of the harmonious organisation of its various elements will depend on the relationships between them that are revealed by these analyses.

But if the concept is reasserted in these terms, what now of the question of its justification? The justification of a liberal education as supported by the doctrines of classical realism was based on the ultimacy of knowledge as ordered and determined by reality, and the significance of knowledge for the mind and for the good life. Having weakened these doctrines, the Harvard Committee's justification of their concept ignores the question of the relationship between knowledge and reality, and there is a specific rejection of the view that knowledge is in itself the good of the mind. They assert, however, the supreme significance of knowledge in the determination of all human activity, and supplement this, as is certainly necessary because of the extended nature of their concept, by general considerations of the desirability of their suggestions. When once more the concept is strictly confined so as to be determined by the forms of knowledge, the return to a justification of it without reference to what is generally thought desirable on social or similar grounds becomes possible. And such justification for the concept is essential if the education it delineates is to have the ultimate significance that, as was earlier suggested, is part of its raison d'etre. This justification must now however stem from what has already been said of the nature of knowledge as no metaphysical doctrine of the connection between knowledge and reality is any longer being invoked.

If the achievement of knowledge is necessarily the development of mind in its most basic sense, then it can be readily seen that to ask for a justification for the pursuit of knowledge is not at all the same thing as to ask for the justification for, say, teaching all children a foreign language or making them orderly and punctual in their behaviour. It is in fact a peculiar question asking for justification for any development of the rational mind at all. To ask for the justification of any form of activity is significant only if one is in fact committed already to seeking rational knowledge. To ask for a justification of the pursuit of rational knowledge itself therefore presupposes some form of commitment to what one is seeking to justify. Justification is possible only if what is being justified is both intelligible under publicly rooted concepts and is assessable according to accepted criteria. It assumes a commitment to these two principles. But these very principles are in fact fundamental to the pursuit of knowledge in all its forms, be it, for instance, empirical knowledge or understanding in the arts. The forms of knowledge are in a sense simply the working out of these general principles in particular ways. To give justification to any kind of knowledge therefore involves using the principles in one specific form to assess their use in another. Any particular activity can be examined for its rational character, for its adherence to these principles, and thus justified on the assumption of them. Indeed in so far as activities are rational this will be possible. It is commitment to them that characterises any rational activity as such. But the principles themselves have no such assessable status, for justification outside the use of the principles is not logically possible. This does not mean that rational pursuits in the end lack justification, for they could equally well be said to have their justification written into them. Nor is any form of viciously circular justification involved by assuming in the procedure what is being looked for. The situation is that we have here reached the ultimate point where the question of justification ceases to be significantly applicable. The apparent circularity is the result of the interrelation between the concepts of rational justification and the pursuit of knowledge.

Perhaps the finality of these principles can be brought out further by noting a negative form of the same argument. From this point of view, to question the pursuit of any kind of rational knowledge is in the end self-defeating, for the questioning itself depends on accepting the very principles whose use is finally being called in question.

It is because it is based on these ultimate principles that characterize knowledge itself and not merely on lower level forms of justification that a liberal education is in a very real sense the ultimate form of education. In spite of the absence of any metaphysical doctrine about reality this idea of liberal education has a significance parallel to that of the original Greek concept. It is an education concerned directly with the development of the mind in rational knowledge, whatever form that freely takes. This parallels the original concept in that according to the doctrine of function liberal education was the freeing of the mind to achieve its own good in knowledge. In each case it is a form of education knowing no limits other than those necessarily imposed by the nature of rational knowledge and thereby itself developing in man the final court of appeal in all human affairs.

As here reformulated the concept has, again like the original, objectivity, though this is no longer backed by metaphysical realism. For it is a necessary feature of knowledge as such that there be public criteria whereby the true is distinguishable from the false, the good from the bad, the right from the wrong. It is the existence of these criteria which gives objectivity to knowledge; and this in its turn gives objectivity to the concept of liberal education. A parallel to another form of justification thus remains, and the concept continues to warrant its label as that of an education that frees the mind from error and illusion. Further, as the determination of the good life is now considered to be itself the pursuit of a particular form of rational knowledge, that in which what ought to be done is justified by the giving of reasons, this is seen as a necessary part of a liberal education. And as all other forms of knowledge contribute in their way to moral understanding, the concept as a whole is once more given a kind of jusification in its importance for the moral life. But this justification, like that of objectivity, no longer has the distinct significance which it once had, for it is again simply a necessary consequence of what the pursuit of knowledge entails. Nevertheless, liberal education remains basic to the freeing of human conduct from wrong.

Certain Basic Philosophical Considerations

Having attempted a reinstatement of the concept without its original philosophical backing, what of the implications of this for the practical conduct of education? In working these out it is necessary first to try to distinguish the various forms of knowledge and then to relate them in some way to the organisation of the school or college curriculum. The first of these is a strictly philosophical task. The second is a matter of practical planning that involves many considerations other than the purely philosophical, and to this I will return when certain broad distinctions between forms of knowledge have been outlined.

As stated earlier, by a form of knowledge is meant a distinct way in which our experience becomes structured round the use of accepted public symbols. The symbols thus having public meaning, their use is in some way testable against experience and there is the progressive development of series of tested symbolic expressions. In this way experience has been probed further and further by extending and elaborating the use of the symbols and by means of these it has become possible for the personal experience of individuals to become more fully structured, more fully understood. The various forms of knowledge can be seen in low level developments within the common area of our knowledge of the everyday world. From this there branch out the developed forms which, taking certain elements in our common knowledge as a basis, have grown in distinctive ways. In the developed forms of knowledge the following related distinguishing features can be seen.

(1) They each involve certain central concepts that are peculiar in character to the form. For example, those of gravity, acceleration, hydrogen, and photosynthesis characteristic of the sciences; number, integral, and matrix in mathematics; God, sin, and predestination in religion; ought, good, and wrong in moral knowledge.

(2) In a given form of knowledge these and other concepts that denote, if perhaps in a very complex way, certain aspects of experience, form a network of possible relationships in which experience can be understood. As a result the form has a distinctive logical structure. For example, the terms

and statements of mechanics can be meaningfully related in certain strictly limited ways only, and the same is true of historical explanation.

(3) The form, by virtue of its particular terms and logic, has expressions or statements (possibly answering a distinctive type of question) that in some way or other, however indirect it may be, are testable against experience. This is the case in scientific knowledge, moral knowledge, and in the arts, though in the arts no questions are explicit and the criteria for the tests are only partially expressible in words. Each form, then, has distinctive expressions that are testable against experience in accordance with particular criteria that are peculiar to the form.

(4) The forms have developed particular techniques and skills for exploring experience and testing their distinctive expressions, for instance the techniques of the sciences and those of the various literary arts. The result has been the amassing of all the symbolically expressed knowledge that we now have in the arts and the sciences.

Though the various forms of knowledge are distinguishable in these ways it must not be assumed that all there is to them can be made clear and explicit by these means. All knowledge involves the use of symbols and the making of judgments in ways that cannot be expressed in words and can only be learnt in a tradition. The art of scientific investigation and the development of appropriate experimental tests, the forming of an historical explanation and the assessment of its truth, the appreciation of a poem: all of these activities are high arts that are not in themselves communicable simply by words. Acquiring knowledge of any form is therefore to a greater or less extent something that cannot be done simply by solitary study of the symbolic expressions of knowledge, it must be learnt from a master on the job. No doubt it is because the forms require particular training of this kind in distinct worlds of discourse, because they necessitate the development of high critical standards according to complex criteria, because they involve our coming to look at experience in particular ways, that we refer to them as disciplines. They are indeed disciplines that form the mind.

Yet the dividing lines that can be drawn between different disciplines by means of the four suggested distinguishing marks are neither clear enough nor sufficient for demarcating the whole world of modern knowledge as we know it. The central feature to which they point is that the major forms of knowledge, or disciplines, can each be distinguished by their dependence on some particular kind of test against experience for their distinctive expressions. On this ground alone however certain broad divisions are apparent. The sciences depend crucially on empirical experimental and observational tests, mathematics depends on deductive demonstrations from certain sets of axioms. Similarly moral knowledge and the arts involve distinct forms of critical tests though in these cases both what the tests are and the ways in which they are applied are only partially statable. (Some would in fact dispute the status of the arts as forms of knowledge for this very reason.) Because of their particular logical features it seems to me necessary to distinguish also as separate disciplines both historical and religious knowledge, and there is perhaps an equally good case, because of the nature of their empirical concepts, for regarding the human sciences separately from the physical sciences. But within these areas further distinctions must be made. These are usually the result of the groupings of knowledge round a number of related concepts, or round particular skills or techniques. The various sciences and the various arts can be demarcated within the larger units of which they are in varying degrees representative in their structure, by these means.

But three other important classifications of knowledge must in addition be recognised. First there are those organisations which are not themselves disciplines or subdivisions of any discipline. They are formed by building together round specific objects, or phenomena, or practical pursuits, knowledge that is characteristically rooted elsewhere in more than one discipline. It is not just that these organisations make use of several forms of knowledge, for after all the sciences use mathematics, the arts use historical knowledge and so on. Many of the disciplines borrow from each other. But these organisations are not concerned, as the disciplines are, to validate any one logically distinct form of expression. They are not concerned with developing a particular structuring of experience. They are held together simply by their subject matter, drawing on all forms of knowledge that can contribute to them. Geography, as the study of man in relation to his environment, is an example of a theoretical study of this kind, engineering an example of a practical nature. I see no reason why such organisations of knowledge, which I shall refer to as "fields," should not be endlessly constructed according to particular theoretical or practical interests. Secondly, whilst moral knowledge is a distinct form, concerned with answering questions as to what ought to be done in practical affairs, no specialised subdivisions of this have been developed. In practical affairs, moral questions, because of their character, naturally arise alongside questions of fact and technique, so that there have been formed "fields" of practical knowledge that include distinct moral elements within them, rather than the subdivisions of a particular discipline. Political, legal and educational theory are perhaps the clearest examples of fields where moral knowledge of a developed kind is to be found. Thirdly, there are certain second order forms of knowledge which are dependent for their existence on the other primary areas. On the one hand there are the essentially scientific studies of language and symbolism as in grammar and philology. On the other hand there are the logical and philosophical studies of meaning and justification. These would seem to constitute a distinct discipline by virtue of their particular concepts and criteria of judgment.

In summary, then, it is suggested that the forms of knowledge as we have them can be classified as follows:

(1) Distinct disciplines or forms of knowledge (subdivisible): mathematics, physical sciences, human sciences, history, religion, literature and the fine arts, philosophy.

(2) Fields of knowledge: theoretical, practical (these may or may not include elements of moral knowledge).

It is the distinct disciplines that basically constitute the range of unique ways we have of understanding experience if to these is added the category of moral knowledge.

The Planning and Practical Conduct of Liberal Education

Turning now to the bearing of this discussion on the planning and conduct of a liberal education, certain very general comments about its characteristic features can be made though detailed treatment would involve psychological and other considerations that are quite beyond the scope of this paper.

In the first place, as liberal education is concerned with the comprehensive development of the mind in acquiring knowledge, it is aimed at achieving an understanding of experience in many different ways. This means the acquisition by critical training and discipline not only of facts but also of complex conceptual schemes and of the arts and techniques of different types of reasoning and judgment. Syllabuses and curricula cannot therefore be constructed simply in terms of information and isolated skills. They must be constructed so as to introduce pupils as far as possible into the interrelated aspects of each of the basic forms of knowledge, each of the several disciplines. And they must be constructed to cover at least in some measure the range of knowledge as a whole.

In a programme of liberal education that is based directly on the study of the specific disciplines, examples of each of the different areas must of course be chosen. Selection of this kind is not however simply an inevitable practical consequence of the vast growth of knowledge. It is equally in keeping with what a liberal education is aiming at. Though its aim is comprehensive it is not after the acquisition of encyclopaedic information. Nor is it after the specialist knowledge of the person fully trained in all the particular details of a branch of knowledge. Such a specialist can not only accurately employ the concepts, logic, and criteria of a domain but also knows the skills and techniques involved in the pursuit of knowledge quite beyond the immediate areas of common human experience. Nor is liberal education concerned with the technician's knowledge of the detailed application of the disciplines in practical and theoretical fields. What is being sought is, first, sufficient immersion in the concepts, logic and criteria of the discipline for a person to come to know the distinctive way in which it "works" by pursuing these in particular cases; and then sufficient generalisation of these over the whole range of the discipline so that his experience begins to be widely structured in this distinctive manner. It is this coming to look at things in a certain way that is being aimed at, not the ability to work out in minute particulars all the details that can in fact be discerned. It is the ability to recognise empirical assertions or aesthetic judgments for what they are, and to know the kind of considerations on which their validity will depend, that matters. Beyond this an outline of the major achievements in each area provides some grasp of the range and scope of experience that has thus become intelligible. Perhaps this kind of understanding is in fact most readily distinguishable in the literary arts as critical appreciation in contrast to the achievement of the creative writer or the literary hack. But the distinction is surely applicable to other forms of knowledge as well.

This is not to assert that "critical appreciation" in any form of knowledge can be adequately achieved without some development of the understanding of the specialist or technician. Nor is it to imply that this understanding in the sciences, the arts or moral issues can be had without participation in many relevant creative and practical pursuits. The extent to which this is true will vary from discipline to discipline and is in fact in need of much investigation, particularly because of its importance for moral and aesthetic education. But it is to say that the aim of the study of a discipline in liberal education is not that of its study in a specialist or technical course. The first is concerned with developing a person's ways of understanding experience, the others are concerned with mastering the details of knowledge, how it is established, and the use of it in other enterprises, particularly those of a practical nature. It is of course perfectly possible for a course in physics, for example, to be devoted to a double purpose if it is deliberately so designed. It may provide both a specialist knowledge of the subject and at the same time a genuine introduction to the form of scientific knowledge. But the two purposes are quite distinct and there is no reason to suppose that by aiming at one the other can automatically be achieved as well. Yet it would seem to be true that some specialist study within a discipline, if it is at all typical of the discipline, is necessary to understanding the form of knowledge in any developed sense. The study of a discipline as part of liberal education, however, contributes practically nothing directly to any specialist study of it, though it does serve to put the specialism into a much wider context.

A liberal education approached directly in terms of the disciplines will thus be composed of the study of at least paradigm examples of all the various forms of knowledge. This study will be sufficiently detailed and sustained to give genuine insight so that pupils come to think in these terms, using the concepts, logic and criteria accurately in the different domains. It will then include generalisation of the particular examples used so as to show the range of understanding in the various forms. It will also include some indication of the relations between the forms where these overlap and their significance in the major fields of knowledge, particularly the practical fields, that have been developed. This is particularly important for moral education, as moral questions can frequently be solved only by calling on the widest possible range of human understanding. As there is in fact no developed discipline of moral knowledge, education in moral understanding must necessarily be approached in a rather different way. For if it is to cover more than everyday personal matters this has to be by the study of issues that occur in certain particular fields of knowledge. The major difficulty this presents will be referred to briefly later. The important point here is that though moral understanding has to be pursued in contexts where it is not the only dominant interest, the aim of its pursuit is precisely the same as for all other elements in a liberal education, the understanding of experience in a unique way. What is wanted (just as in the study of the disciplines *per se*) is, basically, the use of the appropriate concepts, logic, and criteria, and the appreciation of the range of understanding in this form.

It is perhaps important to stress the fact that this education will be one in the forms of knowledge themselves and not merely a self-conscious philosophical treatment of their characteristics. Scientific and historical knowledge are wanted, not knowledge of the philosophy of science and the philosophy of history as substitutes. A liberal education can only be planned if distinctions in the forms of knowledge are clearly understood, and that is a philosophical matter. But the education itself is only partly in philosophy, and that is only possible when pupils have some grasp of the other disciplines themselves.

Precisely what sections of the various disciplines are best suited to the aims of liberal education cannot be gone into here. It is apparent that on philosophical grounds alone some branches of the sciences, for instance, would seem to be much more satisfactory as paradigms of scientific thinking than others. Many sections of physics are probably more comprehensive and clear in logical character, more typical of the well developed physical sciences than, say, botany. If so, they would, all other things being equal, serve better as an introduction to scientific knowledge. Perhaps in literature and the fine arts the paradigm principle is less easy to apply though probably many would favour a course in literature to any one other. But whatever the discipline, in practice all other things are not in fact equal and decisions about the content of courses cannot be taken without careful regard to the abilities and interests of the students for whom they are designed.

Yet hovering round such decisions and questions of syllabus planning there is frequently found the belief that the inherent logical structure of a discipline, or a branch of a discipline necessarily determines exactly what and exactly how the subject is to be taught and learnt. The small amount of truth and the large amount of error in this belief can only be distinguished by clarifying what the logic of a subject is. It is not a series of intellectual steps that must be climbed in strict order. It is not a specific psychological channel along which the mind must travel if there is to be understanding. This is to confuse logical characteristics with psychological processes. The logic of a form of knowledge shows the meaningful and valid ways in which its terms and criteria are used. It constitutes the publicly accepted framework of knowledge. The psychological activities of the individual when concerned with this knowledge are not in general prescribed in any temporal order and the mind, as it were, plays freely within and around the framework. It is simply that the framework lays down the general formal relations of the concepts if there is to be knowledge. The logic as publicly expressed consists of the general and formal principles to which the terms must conform in knowledge. Coming to understand a form of knowledge involves coming to think in relations that satisfy the public criteria. How the mind plays round and within these is not itself being laid down at all, there is no dragooning of psychological processes, only a marking out of the territory in which the mind can wander more or less at will. Indeed understanding a form of knowledge is far more like coming to know a country than climbing a ladder. Some places in a territory may only be get-at-able by a single specified route and some forms of knowledge may have concepts and relations that cannot be understood without first understanding certain others. But that countries are explorable only in one way is in general false, and even in mathematics, the most strictly sequential form of knowledge we have, many ways of coming to know the territory are possible. The logic of a subject is relevant to what is being taught, for its patterns must be accepted as essential to the form of knowledge. But how those patterns are best discerned is a matter for empirical investigation.

School subjects in the disciplines as we at present have them are in no way sacrosanct on either logical or psychological grounds. They are necessarily selections from the forms of knowledge that we have and may or may not be good as introductions for the purposes of liberal education. In most cases they have developed under a number of diverse influences. The historical growth of the subjects has sometimes dominated the programmes. The usefulness of certain elements, the demands of higher specialist education, certain general "psychological" principles such as progressing from the simple to the complex, from the particular to the general, the concrete to the abstract, all these factors and many others have left their marks. This being so, many well established courses need to be critically reexamined both philosophically and psychologically before they can be accepted as suitable for liberal education. Superficially at least most of them would seem to be quite inappropriate for this purpose.

Though a liberal education is most usually approached directly in the study of various branches of the disciplines, I see no reason to think that this must necessarily be so. It is surely possible to construct programmes that are in the first place organised round certain fields of knowledge either theoretical or practical. The study of aspects of power, natural as well as social and political, might for instance be one element in such a scheme: or a regional study that introduces historical, geographical, industrial, and social considerations: or a practical project of design and building involving the sciences, mathematics and visual arts. In this case, however, it must be recognised that the fields are chosen because together they can be used to develop understanding of all the various forms of knowledge, and explicit steps must be taken to see that this end is achieved. There will necessarily be the strongest tendency for liberal education to be lost sight of and for the fields to be pursued in their own right developing the techniques and skills which they need. These may be valuable and useful in many ways, and perhaps essential in many a person's whole education. (Certainly liberal education as is here being understood is only one part of the education a person ought to have, for it omits quite deliberately for instance specialist education, physical education and character training.) But a course in various fields of knowledge will not in fact be a liberal education unless that aim is kept absolutely clear and every opportunity is taken to lead to a fuller grasp of the disciplines. Again some fields of study will be better for this purpose than others but all will demand the highest skill from the teacher, who must be under no misapprehension as to what the object of the exercise really is. Yet it is difficult to see how this kind of approach can be fully adequate if it does not in the end lead to a certain amount of study of the distinct disciplines themselves. For whatever ground may have been covered indirectly, a satisfactory understanding of the characteristically distinct approaches of the different forms is hardly possible without some direct gathering together of the elements of the disciplines that have been implicit in all that has been done.

Whatever the pattern of a liberal education in its later stages, it must not be forgotten that there is being presupposed a broad basic education in the common area of everyday knowledge where the various disciplines can be seen in embryo and from which they branch out as distinct units. In such a basic primary education, the ever growing range of a child's experience and the increasing use of linguistic and symbolic forms lays the foundation for the various modes of understanding, scientific, historical, religious, moral, and so on. Out of this general pool of knowledge the disciplines have slowly become ever more differentiated and it is this that the student must come to understand, not confusing the forms of knowledge but appreciating them for what they are in themselves, and recognising their necessary limitations.

But is then the outcome of a liberal education to be simply the achievement of a series of discreet ways of understanding experience? In a very real sense yes, but in another sense not entirely. For one thing, we have as yet not begun to understand the complex interrelations of the different forms of knowledge themselves, for they do not only have unique features but common features too, and in addition one discipline often makes extensive use of the achievements of another. But we must also not forget that the various forms are firmly rooted in that common world of persons and things which we all share, and into this they take back in subtle as well as simple ways the understanding they have achieved. The outcome of a liberal education must therefore not be thought of as producing ever greater disintegration of the mind but rather the growth of ever clearer and finer distinctions in our experience. If the result is not some quasi-aesthetic unity of the mind neither is it in any sense chaos. Perhaps the most suggestive picture of the outcome is that used by Professor Michael Oakeshott, though for him it has more literal truth than is here intended. In this the various forms of knowledge are seen as voices in a conversation, a conversation to which they each contribute in a distinctive way. If taken figuratively, his words express more succinctly than mine can precisely what it seems to me a liberal education is and what its outcome will be.

> As civilized human beings, we are the inheritors, neither of an inquiry about ourselves and the world, nor of an accumulating body of information, but of a conversation, begun in the primeval forests and extended and made more articulate in the course of centuries. It is a conversation which goes on both in public and within each of ourselves. Of course there is argument and inquiry and information, but wherever these are profitable they are to be recognized as passages in this conversation, and perhaps they are not the most captivating of the passages. . . . Conversation is not an enterprise designed to yield an extrinsic profit, a contest where a winner gets a prize, nor is it an activity of exegesis; it is an unrehearsed intellectual adventure. . . .
> . . . Education, properly speaking, is an initiation into the skill and partnership of this conversation in which we learn to recognize the voices, to distinguish the proper occasions of utterance, and in which we acquire the intellectual and moral habits appropriate to conversation. And it is this conversation which, in the end, gives place and character to every human activity and utterance.[8]

8. Michael Oakeshott, *Rationalism in Politics and Other Essays* (London: Methuen, 1962), pp. 198–199.

TOWARD A FABRIC OF KNOWLEDGE – COMMON ELEMENTS AMONG FIELDS OF LEARNING

May Brodbeck

On the face of it, there are, of course, many very different fields of organized knowledge. There are things like physics, chemistry, biology, and botany. There are the social studies and history. There are the languages and literature. There is also mathematics. Yet student and teacher alike would be quick to point out that not all these different titles reflect altogether different things. Some can be grouped together into different categories of similar things. Most obviously, of course, there are the physical sciences, the biological sciences, the social disciplines and history, language and literature. Certainly these traditional categories are not without some justification. There are clearly differences between the living and the nonliving, as lizards and plants are different from rocks. This difference is reflected by the distinction between the biological and the physical sciences. Even more clearly, there are differences between men and inanimate things, as well, of course, as differences between men and animals.

All these differences in subject matter seem obvious enough, but then we recall that there is also a rubric called "natural science" that puts physics, chemistry, and biology in the same boat. And if we think of natural science as being concerned with knowledge of inanimate and animate matter, and the social studies with knowledge of man and society, we can be left with only two major categories — one covering the fields yielding knowledge of facts and one covering those, like language and mathematics, concerned with skills. But what of the study and teaching of literature? Does it convey facts, skills, both, or some third element?

Our traditional course titles are more than just an administrative convenience, for they do actually reflect differences in subject matter. These differences in subject matter, in turn, imply differences in techniques — laboratory experiment, field studies, pencil-and-paper work, reflection, and reading. Yet, real as these differences are, they are all relatively superficial. I suggest that it is of the first importance for understanding and for teaching these various fields that the similarities among them, rather than their differences, be seen as fundamental. I shall, first, try to explain why I believe

From *Educational Record,* 43 (1962) pp. 217–222. Reprinted by permission of the author and the American Council on Education.

this to be so with respect to the more patently so-called factual disciplines. I shall then comment upon the relationship between these and the study of literature.

Nowadays very few would object to my grouping the physical and biological sciences together as one large natural science. The reasons for this are that, first, they are all concerned with describing the observable properties of things, animate or inanimate. Second, since they are sciences, rather than activities like collecting and cataloguing, they all want to explain and to predict changes in these properties of things. To do this, they seek laws or generalizations and formulate theories, which are connections among such laws or generalizations. In these respects, physiology and physics are the same. This is what we mean by calling them both sciences. Their concepts, whether of mass or of mitosis, are tied to what we can observe. Their generalizations are formulated on the basis of past experience and are tested by new observations, confirmed or falsified as the case may be. Very few biologists today would hold – note the words "very few" instead of "none" – that such intriguing concepts as "vital force" or "entelechy" are essential to biological explanation. It is true that biologists often use such notions as "function" and "purpose" that do not occur in the physical sciences. But with a little analysis it can be shown that such terms are in principle dispensable in favor of the same notions of "cause," "law," and "necessary and sufficient conditions" that are used in physics. I believe that it is fair to say that this belief is part of the accepted frame of reference of modern biology.

All this, of course, is merely a long-winded way of saying that biology is a natural science, but the long way is worthwhile, partly because it was not always accepted as true. The controversy between the so-called vitalists and mechanists was fierce in the last century. More to the point, the long way helps make explicit what I wish to convey by the overworked phrase 'scientific method.' Frequently it is used merely as a word that means something is good or we like it. I want it to mean something more specific than that. Also it helps us to answer the question about the so-called social disciplines, that is, the social studies of the secondary schools and the social sciences of the colleges and the universities. Are they, too, natural sciences? Surely the differences between man, on the one hand, and both animals and inanimate things, on the other, make a much greater difference. Men share physical properties with sticks and stones; physiological ones with mice and dogs. But men, after all, not only have weight and blood pressure, they not only speak and act, they also love and hope, remember and despair. Moreover, men make choices – in particular, they can choose between good and evil. Do not these differences make a much greater difference? This issue, of course, is still controversial, unlike that between the vitalists and the mechanists, and to discuss it is to probe sensitive tissue, and probing sensitive tissue inevitably causes pain. I can only hope that I shall not cause any unnecessary pain.

The biological and the physical sciences share a common method, in the sense of *principles* of investigation, rather than specific techniques. But they also can be said to share a common subject matter. Their concepts must refer to what can be observed. The scientist seeks to describe and to explain observable phenomena. In order to explain, he looks for causes or, what amounts to the same, for laws or generalizations connecting one or more observable properties of things with others. These generalizations must, in turn, be subject to test by further observation. If they are confirmed, they can be used to explain facts already known or to predict new ones. Explanation in natural science is always by reference to such laws or generalizations. What we explain after it happens could in principle be predicted beforehand. This is the so-called deterministic thesis or frame of reference of modern science, of, indeed, physical science since the time of Galileo. Are all these notions also applicable to the social disciplines? I use the term 'discipline,' of course, so as not to beg the question as to whether or not they are sciences.

There are by now many old and tired arguments in favor of the proposition that the study of man is inherently different from the study of things. There are equally many old and tired rejoinders to these arguments. A detailed rehearsal of all these arguments and rejoinders is neither possible nor necessary, but it may help if I identify, if by little more than name, some of them. The arguments in favor of a difference between the study of man and of things divide into two kinds — those that imply only a difference in degree and those that imply a difference in kind. Of the former, those arguments that imply a difference in degree are mostly from the complexity of human affairs, from the inability to quantify social and psychological attributes, and from the inability to experiment with people. The usual retort to complexity is to refer to handy meteorology. Meteorology is very complex, but we believe it to be a science.

As for quantification, no one at all familiar with modern research in education or economics and the use in these areas of relatively sophisticated statistical techniques will seriously claim that *no* quantification is possible in the social disciplines.

The counter to the argument from experimentation is astronomy. We do not experiment on the motion of the stars. Also, of course, the fact remains that, after all, some experimentation with people is possible.

Another argument, which stands in a class by itself but is essentially an argument for a difference in kind, is the argument arising from uniqueness: the argument that since men are all unique, all very different from each other, no generalizations or laws about them can be formulated. Since scientific description and explanation depend upon laws, a science of man and society is impossible. But this argument is so self-defeating that it supports neither a difference in degree nor in kind. For one thing, it proves too much: as with men, so with stones, no two are entirely alike. On this ground, there could be no physical science either. Moreover, if all men were indeed unique, then there would be no way, scientific or otherwise, to know about man – we could only gaze in awe at his infinite diversity. Although how we would even know, by insight or otherwise, that all these different entities were, nevertheless, all *men* remains a mystery.

Besides uniqueness, I can think of three other arguments in favor of the view that the difference is not merely one of degree but of kind. To speak succinctly, one is the argument from *values,* the other from *freedom,* and the third from *mind.*

With respect to values, it is pointed out that the physical scientist, studying inanimate objects which do not choose their behavior, does not pass moral judgment on the facts he uncovers. He does not blame or praise the atom, not even the hydrogen atom, for acting as it does, though he may, of course, make such judgments about the purposes to which this knowledge is put. The student of man and society, on the other hand, concerned with human behavior, most of it in situations where choice between alternatives is possible, very likely has moral convictions about the behavior he observes. He not only observes, he may also praise and blame. Those who argue for an essential difference between the study of man and the study of things maintain that it is not possible to separate the social scientist's description of human behavior from the moral judgment he passes upon it. The two are so implicated with each other that no objective social science is possible. This view, called "sociological relativism," requires a long analysis of its own. I must give it short shrift here and say only that even in matters where our hearts are engaged, the scientific criteria of evidence can enable us to separate out the evaluative from the factual components of our statements about the world. A prediction that is based on a wish or a hope, instead of the way things are, is subject to test after all, and if things are not the way one wishes or hopes or thinks they ought to be, then the prediction will be falsified.

The argument from freedom or the denial that human actions are lawful or caused is, of course, a very radical argument. It, too, is a very long story, but if it were indeed the case that human decision enters in an essentially unpredictable way into human affairs, then no social *science* would be possible. Of course, no other knowledge of human affairs would be possible either. Yet the argument is unimpressive if only because most people who believe in an uncaused will always concede that *some* human actions are caused, maybe even *most.* This concession is inevitable, since we clearly can and do predict a great deal of behavior. Neither psychotherapy nor vocational counseling nor any other kind of counseling would otherwise be possible. As far as the possibility of a science is concerned, the admission that there is some causality is quite enough to keep the social scientist busy.

The last and most profound argument is that from mind. People obviously have minds as well as bodies. Materialism, or the denial of this obvious fact, is simply absurd. It is also true that we cannot know what is going on in someone else's mind in the same way that we know about his body. Some hold that because of this, the study of man must be intrinsically different from the study of things, for concepts tied to what can be observed are not sufficient for describing and understanding man. The method of explanation used in the natural sciences is, therefore, not applicable to the study of man. Here in the study of man we must use mental concepts referring to people's motives and purposes, and these, of course, are not observable. We obtain knowledge about these unobservable states of other people's minds not by observation, but by that special insight, empathy, or understanding that is available to us as fellow human beings.

I shall comment further about this kind of understanding and its usefulness later. For the present, though, I shall merely point out that it is quite different from scientific explanation. Moreover, there is every good reason to believe that scientific explanation of man is possible. The best available knowledge that we have suggests that mental events do not occur by themselves, so to speak. Rather, whenever there is a mental event, like a thought or a purpose, there is also a corresponding nonmental, publicly observable event, either physiological or behavioral or, most likely, both. Without embracing an absurd materialism, the social scientist can restrict his studies to those observable phenomena that parallel the private mental events. In this way, we may speak of his indirectly rather than directly describing mental events. By thus limiting himself to indirect description, his concepts are tied to what can be observed. Among these observable characteristics, paralleling the mental ones, he may well find generalizations by means of which he can explain why people are as they are and behave as they do. In principle, thus, on fundamentals the social disciplines are no different from the natural sciences.

What is the bearing of this perhaps too abstract philosophical discussion of the similarities among the various disciplines on questions of education? More than might appear. Let me use an analogy which, I think, is more than an analogy. We all know that among the many social problems caused by rapid technological change, one of the most pressing and disturbing is the need for men to become highly adaptable to marked changes in the kinds of jobs they may be called upon to do during their lifetime. Our most progressive engineering schools, for instance, now recognize this prominent feature of our times by giving less and less attention to specific techniques and their accompanying "hardware" and more time to training in fundamental knowledge. For the hardware and techniques rapidly become obsolescent — and unless a man has the basic training that enables him to face novel situations, he, too, rapidly becomes obsolescent.

My analogy is clear, I trust. We cannot really hope — certainly not in the secondary schools and probably not even in the undergraduate college years — to equip a student with very much of the huge body of knowledge accumulated in the various subject fields. There is simply too much of it. Nor does the student generally have either the technical background or the maturity to grasp more than a small fraction of this knowledge. He can and must, of course, learn the fundamentals — the basic principles of the various fields. But even for these to have meaning for him and to serve as a foundation upon which he can later add, he must also understand the general features of any and all sciences. The specific concepts in a field may change, but not the criteria for good concepts. What, then, are the criteria for "good" concepts within science? What precisely do we mean when we say that A causes B, and what constitutes the evidence for such assertions? What is the nature of a scientific law and of a theory? What is the difference between an adequate scientific explanation and a specious one? If a certain course of action is taken now, what kind of knowledge must we have to make justified and not merely plausible predictions about what will happen in the future?

The student who grasps that the answers to these questions are essentially the same whether he is studying stones or mice or men has gained more than abstract knowledge. If he understands that juvenile delinquency or the changes in social mobility patterns are to be explained in the same way as we explain the motion of the stars, he has grasped a good deal about the problems and the potentialities of the social disciplines. He has the kind of flexibility of mind that a period of rapid technological change requires, particularly to anticipate and resolve the social problems to which that change gives rise. He also has other things of value to him personally and as a citizen. Marxism, for instance, calls itself a science, namely, "scientific materialism." How many of our students, no matter how stuffed with the "facts" of physics or sociology, could give an articulate, clear rebuttal of this claim? With the kind of training in what physics and sociology have in common that I am suggesting, it would be child's play to rebut this claim. And this is important.

Suppose, for the sake of the argument, you grant me my thesis that the areas dealing with the inanimate, with life, and with man do have certain fundamental features in common. How are these fields, then, related to language and literature? There is even more to the teaching of language than the transmission of indispensable skills. Much sense and much nonsense have been spoken lately about the role of the schools in training for what is broadly called "good citizenship." Sense — if the criticism (whether justified or unjustified is not the issue now) is to the effect that there is deliberate, direct indoctrination of specific values and goals held by the individual teacher. Nonsense — if the criticism implies that the schools should play no role at all in training for citizenship. It is nonsense because all societies seek to perpetuate their traditions, their beliefs about the nature of the good society, and the duties of its members. Always and everywhere the school has served as a major channel for perpetuating a society's traditions and for fostering in its members those attitudes the society deems valuable. They always have and, in the nature of things, it is safe to say they always will. The issue is not whether it should be done but how to do it.

How most effectively can the broader interests of the nation as a whole, over and beyond party and sectional interests, be served? In an earlier era, this function was very largely served by the study of the classics. Here the young found their heroes, the source of inspiration for the notion of self-sacrifice in a higher interest, for the common good or for country. Today that role has been inherited by the teaching of literature and history. History reveals our heroes to the young and illuminates the causes they have deemed worth fighting and, if need be, dying for. Every work of literature contains implicit moral judgments. This is one difference between literature and, say, sociology. Through the teaching of literature, these implicit moral judgments are transmitted to and absorbed by the student. In literature, too, is depicted the nature of man and of the society in which he lives. The novelist uses the method, if such it can be called, that the social studies must in principle, if not in practice, eschew. The novelist or playwright uses his exceptional empathetic understanding to reveal as much as he can about the human world around us.

To grant and even to insist that the artist uses understanding or empathy is one thing. To claim that such understanding is a special kind of knowledge on a par with, or even superior to, scientific explanation is quite another thing. Rather, the phenomenon of understanding and empathy is itself something to be explained by the methods of science — when we know enough. But when the time comes that we can explain empathy, we can perhaps also dispense with it. Meanwhile, we do not know enough. This means that those fields studying man scientifically and the study of literature must complement each other.

First, the social disciplines are like the other sciences in that they do not make value judgments. Science describes and explains. Among other things, however, the social scientist also describes and explains, or tries to, the implicit and explicit value judgments of our society and how they affect our behavior. If literature articulates and helps form these judgments, as I believe it does, then literature and science need each other in many different ways. From science, both physical and social, we may learn what man and society actually *can* achieve. Certain physical and, even more particularly, social processes aid and abet the realization of our goals and ideals, while others retard and hinder them. The more scientific knowledge we have about these processes, the more we can mold things to fit our heart's desires. The conflict between the way things are and our beliefs about the way they ought to be is one of the great topics of literature. It is also one of the most important areas in which we need more scientific knowledge. Language and literature can thus articulate the values whose effects and methods for realization science investigates.

There is also a second way in which they need each other. The writer's understanding has already been mentioned. Whatever is accessible to it is also, in principle, accessible to scientific explanation. Until it is, the knowledge that understanding yields is very precarious, much too precarious to be the basis of policy or action. But the writer's understanding can suggest hypotheses about man and society to the scientist. If these are then formulated in such a way that they can be tested, we are on firmer ground. Thus the nonscientific fields may suggest what scientific description can confirm. We have a more profound grasp of the nature and potentialities of the social disciplines when we appreciate that they are fundamentally or "in principle," as philosophers like to say, the same as the natural sciences. Because this is so, the social scientists are in a position to describe, explain, and predict the impact on our lives of the values and ideals that guide us. To articulate and to perpetuate these values and ideals is, in large part, the job of the arts, language, and literature.

COMMONSENSE THOUGHT, KNOWLEDGE, AND JUDGEMENT AND THEIR IMPORTANCE FOR EDUCATION

L. R. Perry

I

Commonsense knowledge is often criticized in technical and philosophical writing. The intention of this article is to suggest that some misunderstanding may be found there of the role of commonsense knowledge and its relation to specialized knowledge. People allude to common experience, general knowledge and the like, chiefly when they wish to vindicate the claims of expert knowledge, especially in contemporary philosophical writing. No doubt, in the past, commonsense knowledge has had its defenders, just as it now has its detractors, and perhaps both are overenthusiastic. For my part, I have not found reason to believe either that it is the touchstone of knowledge and the arbiter of reason, or that it is crude, primitive, and finally to be superseded.

The word 'commonsense' normally conveys a choice of meanings to the reader, and the context rarely guides us clearly as to what is meant. I have no intention of offering an exhaustive examination of the ways in which it is used, but wish to mention some meanings which seem to offer guidance as to what role it is playing.

First, we have what may be called the pejorative use of commonsense. Lord Russell talks of "three defects of common beliefs, namely, that they are cocksure, vague and self-contradictory"[1] — one of many instances in his works. Professor O'Connor says, "They [i.e., many medieval philosophers] were fully convinced that men could prove from ordinary commonsense knowledge plus a few so-called 'self-evident' principles a large number of statements about the existence and nature of God . . . "[2] and he goes on to pour scorn on this.

In each case, the writer shows us the limitations of commonsense. It is exhibited to us as a defective way of dealing with experience. We learn from

From *British Journal of Educational Studies XIII* (May, 1965), pp. 125–138. Reprinted by permission of the author and the *British Journal of Educational Studies*.
1. Bertrand Russell, *The Problems of Philosophy* (London, 1927), p. 3.
2. D. J. O'Connor, *Introduction to the Philosophy of Education* (London: Routledge & Kegan Paul, 1957), p. 24.

the context that there is a better way, believed in and recommended by the author. Those who speak of commonsense in this way would not deny, I think, that for the present it has its uses. Rather we are led to believe, more usually by implication, that it is capable of a crude variety of discussion of the subject being dealt with. A satisfactory discussion, however, could only arise from the use of specialized knowledge. Often, as in psychological literature, we find it said that commonsense thinking was formerly the standard means of covering the ground; but now, its duty done, it can go into retirement, to be replaced by keener discussion, knowledge more apt, and greater clarity. Nor is the reader disappointed, for these undertakings are fulfilled. We are invited to conclude, by many instances of this kind, that the first intelligent step to the handling of our experience is to supersede commonsense. But, though we may freely grant that there often is a better way of dealing with matters than by commonsense, we cannot therefore conclude that commonsense can be put aside unless we can show that specialized knowledge has the same aim in handling experience as commonsense, and that they both have the same experience to interpret. Writers who criticize commonsense knowledge do not offer to show this.

Next, there is a use of the word according to which its function is to provide authority for assertions, verification of argument, justification of knowledge adduced, material for illustration of a point, and so on. When many specialized or technical means of presenting something to the reader have been used, it is urged that our own commonsense provides us with convincing further evidence; or we may be told that, with the technical evidence before us, our ordinary judgement may be relied upon to clinch matters. We may find such remarks as "there is no need to labour what is well known to everyone," "readers will know from their own experience that this argument is absurd." Professor O'Connor, for instance, treating of the aims of education, says, "I am saying merely that these aims do as a matter of fact command a wide measure of assent among persons interested in such matters,"[3] and it is clear from the context that this is not an appeal to expert knowledge. Out of all this comes the thought that commonsense is here conceived as a body of knowledge and of the ways of using that knowledge, not set before us in any particular discussion, but needed to make that discussion fully intelligible. Indeed, one suspects that even in a technical discussion of a subject, where no reference to common knowledge and experience is made, there is often to be found an implied reference to such knowledge. This second use of the word appears to link up with the first; for what is left behind when it is emphasized that commonsense is crude and to be left aside, is rejoined when we reach a point of discussion where commonsense is suitably and relevantly appealed to. Where technical or

3. D. J. O'Connor, *op. cit.,* p. 9.

specialized discussion begins, commonsense ends; but whilst the former is having its say the latter is apt to reappear. This leads one to conjecture that specialized discussion is conducted constantly with reference to a similar context of commonsense discussion and perhaps cannot be made perfectly intelligible without it. We may say, then *(a)* commonsense is not adequate for problems requiring specialized treatment; *(b)* it is needed in addition to specialized knowledge in order to make complete sense of the specialized treatment by relating it to general experience.

Thought of as knowledge, then, commonsense is needed to supplement specialized knowledge by setting it in a more general context, and it also appears to play some part in assisting the specialized argument by placing it in this setting. Commonsense knowledge is a large number of generalizations used in daily life and not superseded by specialized knowledge. For example, it is commonsense to put on an overcoat in the depth of winter. When some specialized knowledge is relevant to us, our commonsense knowledge is not jettisoned, it is made more profound and lucid by being brought into relation to a systematic theory. A notable area of such commonsense knowledge is that of human conduct and relations between persons. We have a tremendous knowledge of how people behave, and readily understand what has caused a child to cry or moved a man to show signs of exasperation. The related specialized knowledge is psychology, which has achieved a more complex and subtle explanation of conduct. Our great experience in reading human actions and purposes tends to build a resistance to it of a kind referred to below. And it is this same experience which causes us to associate commonsense knowledge with "practical" knowledge. For much of it occurs in connection with the intention to *do* something.

But there is nothing final and unalterable about these commonsense generalizations, and to find commonsense embattled against attempts to supersede it, because of some supposed quality of infallibility, rightly brings down the criticism of Bradley: "Common Sense, taken (as too often it may be seen) at its worst, is in its essence a one-sidedness, which we must not be afraid to mark as stupid or even, perhaps, to denounce as immoral."[4] Hospers, in a very different philosophical atmosphere, discussing how people assume statements to be true, says: "In ordinary life we are confronted with this every day: a person with deep prejudice will simply assume *a priori* that a certain statement is true, and he will reject any evidence that may turn up against the statement. . . ."[5] This, among others, is the attitude of those who wish to rely upon their commonsense when specialized knowledge is available upon the matter with which they are concerned. Such people are like so many Mrs. Partingtons, attempting to sweep back the sea of thought. This

4. F. H. Bradley, *Collected Essays* (Oxford: Clarendon Press, 1935), p. 639.
5. J. Hospers, *An Introduction to Philosophical Analysis* (London: Routledge & Kegan Paul, 1956), pp. 144–145.

attitude however is more subtle, widespread and enduring than at first sight appears: for example, many diagnose and treat their own ill health, where medical advice is readily available. Perhaps this attitude in part arises from bewilderment as to when and how far to use specialized knowledge; but nevertheless the criticism is justly directed against those who persist in refusing technical advice on a matter that can be decided more effectively by means of that advice.

The allusion above to commonsense knowledge and practical problems is the point at which another aspect of commonsense, distinct from the mass of low level generalizations which we rely on in daily living, may be mentioned. This is the awareness of what knowledge it is necessary to apply to particular problems or situations. If a man fails to see the obvious relevance of a generalization he has to a particular case, he is called "unpractical" or "has no commonsense." This could happen for example in practical problems like buying a house. As well as using the many types of expert knowledge needed, he will lack commonsense if he does not draw on his knowledge of what other people do when they buy houses. So that, as well as having the knowledge, he has to know where it is available for use, or in other words where to *apply* it.

We may up to this point, then, suggest that commonsense knowledge cannot be superseded, and moreover that it utilizes a sense of relevance, of applicability, rather like specialized knowledge. It is with this second sense that this paper is particularly concerned. It is seen, in a commonsense context, most clearly in connection with practical problems, in estimating the relevance of the various kinds of specialized knowledge, though these are of course not the only type of problems with which it deals.[6]

Commonsense discussion, therefore, may legitimately object to being superseded when specialized thinking makes an unjustified claim to deal more effectively with a subject: unjustified, because specialized verdicts have to be modified, as a rule, to be useful in the general field of experience, and it is the task of commonsense to do this, and to judge what weight to assign to the various kinds of relevant specialized knowledge. Because commonsense thought is concerned with experience lying outside the specialized area, it is justified not only in modifying but even on occasion overruling expert knowledge. Thus the politician overrules the general, the businessman the architect, or the teacher the psychologist. None of us sympathize with a commonsense that refuses to be enlightened; but many will agree that commonsense must defend itself against attempts to equate the general field of experience with the specialized one. Whether, then, the teacher is guided exclusively by the psychologist would depend upon whether the teaching situation is regarded as exclusively the purview of psychology. Some writers

6. Cf. F. H. Bradley, *Essays on Truth and Reality* (Oxford: Clarendon Press, 1944), e.g. pp. 99, 101.

imply that they do,[7] but others do not.[8] It is not necessary to produce examples of commonsense thought at work. Whenever we find a matter discussed in a nonspecialized way, where the knowledge and reasoning used do not claim special authority, and where expert knowledge is freely drawn upon and accepted as authoritative, then usually commonsense thought is at work. For example, a political discussion among ordinary people may criticize current policy, an amateur carpenter may plan a piece of furniture, a householder may decide the layout and planning of a garden. It seems feasible to suggest that, in daily life, most people spend most of the time dealing with experience on commonsense lines, leaving this only on occasion in order to take up a specialized viewpoint. It is surely no accident that this is so, for it is incumbent on all individuals to meet a very wide range of experience. It may be argued that we could cope with it better in other ways, and eventually shall. I do not know. But meantime commonsense, that primitive means, is the one available now, because it seeks rather to make all experience coherent than to make a deep investigation of any one type.

In what follows below, my chief concern is to challenge the view that specialized knowledge should entirely supersede commonsense. Before taking up this directly, I will try to clarify matters by discussing the relation between commonsense knowledge and the specialized types.

Specialized knowledge seems to have emerged from commonsense in no systematic way, but as the unceasingly moving interests and problems of the different epochs have brought it about. Over long years a great fund of specialized knowledge has become available. It would not be relevant here to comment on the origin of types of specialized knowledge, or of commonsense knowledge: clearly they have both been present, as distinct varieties, as far back as we can go. However, I have used the word 'emerge' because, in my view, commonsense constitutes the first and most primitive way of dealing with experience, and it is the way we habitually use most; and also because specialized knowledge appears to arise out of a concentrated effort, by many and over a time, on the material originally present to commonsense thought and action. Such an effort has been made in many directions.[9]

In the effort to deal with experience at a more specialized level, we devise methods of proceeding. The circumstance that there are different methods, with different resulting types of knowledge, arises out of our reactions to the nature of experience, and we are guided as to the acceptance, rejection, or modification of our methods by the degree to which experience becomes intelligible. It would be too far from our present purpose to discuss the nature of experience. Suffice it to say, that we have different types of

7. Cf. D. H. Russell, *Children's Thinking* (Waltham, Mass.: Blaisdell, 1956), p. 333 seq.

8. N. Isaacs, *The Foundations of Common Sense* (London: Routledge & Kegan Paul, 1949), e.g. Chap. 1.

9. Cf. J. H. Newman, *A Grammar of Assent* (London: 1887), Chaps. IX, VIII.

specialized knowledge, arising from experience — that is, different commentaries of a technical kind, as well as the commonsense commentary.

These specialized varieties of knowledge are freely available to commonsense, which is the most primitive level of human reaction to experience, the spoken and written content of the inexpert mind, and also of the expert mind when dealing with matters in which it has no special skill. (It is hard to understand why, among the critics of commonsense, the mass of inexpert material resulting is not more closely examined and analysed, to find out what characteristics it in fact has.)[10] Commonsense draws freely on this specialized knowledge, because it needs by turns *all* and not *some* specialized knowledge for the accomplishment of its business.

If this way of looking at commonsense is correct, then we may expect a very free interaction between it and the specialized types of knowledge, so that what is called commonsense at any particular time will be indebted for much of its content and ideas to specialized knowledge. It is also possible that the impetus to investigation leading to the origination or enriching of specialized types of knowledge is not unconnected with the interests and concerns of commonsense knowledge and thought. To those thinking principally of applied science, the practical concerns may seem preeminent, but for the reasons mentioned above one suspects that nonpractical specialized knowledge also owes much of its development to commonsense thinking.

The task of commonsense then will not ever be to act as if it were expert knowledge, but rather to relate all relevant types of expert knowledge to the situation with which it has to deal. Such a task will involve a decision as to when and how far expert knowledge should be utilized. Nor is this a job for the expert, who is disqualified precisely *in his capacity as expert.* The task of commonsense has to be sharply differentiated, therefore, from that of any variety of expert knowledge. It draws on specialized knowledge, certainly, but how far it does so, what types of expert knowledge are called upon, and how far they are related together so as to illuminate the problem before commonsense knowledge, must be the business of commonsense knowledge itself, because it alone is grappling with the whole field of experience covered by the problem before it. For example, in deciding our opinion about a certain piece of government policy, say the expansion of technical education, we may require economic, scientific, historical, and sociological knowledge. But how far we consult these and what weight we give to each, we use our own commonsense knowledge to decide.

What then becomes of any hope of superseding commonsense? It could

10. This problem has of late attracted the attention of psychological investigators: cf. J. S. Bruner, *et. al., A Study of Thinking* (New York: Wiley, 1956), pp. 7, 13, 55: but cf. a remark of J. M. Keynes, *A Treatise on Probability* (London: MacMillan, 1921), p. 17.

presumably be done only if the commonsense method of approach to problems were identical with that of some specialized knowledge, and its field of experience delimited so as to coincide with the field of that specialized knowledge. Since it deals with all methods and with all types of expert knowledge, and its distinctive task appears to be bound up with this, proposals to supersede it by any particular specialized knowledge are based surely upon a failure to understand what commonsense is about.[11]

II

If the above treatment of commonsense is correct, the consequences for school education are important. The school, like the home, contributes its share to commonsense knowledge in the form of a large number of generalizations. But it has no special concern or responsibility for this, which probably can be handed on only partly and incidentally by any formally planned institution. The business of the school is the introduction of the children to the varieties of specialized thought and knowledge. In carrying out this task, however, it loses sight of the great importance of commonsense in the second sense distinguished above. This sense, of what is relevant to situations, *is* compatible with the commitments of formal education. For the urgent thing is that children be shown how to *apply* the knowledge they acquire, not only in the expert area but elsewhere. For years, in fact, school learning has included some idea of application of that learning, but it amounted to little more than the expression of a wish.

An example of this vague idea is provided by the nineteenth century concept of a statesman in Britain.[12] He was thought of fundamentally as an amateur equipped with a type of education enabling him to deal effectively with problems of government and policy. We might say, in the language used here, that he had a superior and well-informed commonsense. Two suppositions appear to be involved here.

(1) If an education comprises varieties of knowledge a, b, c, it will serve to master any situation involving the use of them or of expert knowledge A, B, C, whose rules are to some extent in common with a, b, c.

11. Commonsense has not attracted much attention in philosophical thinking since the classical discussions in which Moore and Bradley disposed of the pragmatist arguments. Oakeshott, in *Experience and Its Modes* (Cambridge, Eng.: University Press, 1933), has a very interesting section on Practical Experience, to which this paper is indebted. I do not, however, share his fears that commonsense will be overwhelmed by scientific techniques (expressed in *The Voice of Poetry in the Conversation of Mankind* [London: Bowes and Bowes, 1959], pp. 14‒15), for it seems rather that commonsense, like the aspen-tree, is effortlessly easy to bend but difficult to break.

12. Cf. T. K. Arnold, *Miscellaneous Works* (London, 1858), p. 360 and J. H. Newman, *Scope and Nature of University Education* (London, 1928 edition), pp. 137, 160, 163, 168.

(2) The same education will also give a lead in mastering knowledges d, e, f, and expert knowledges D, E, F, not dealt with in that education.

An example of (1) is as follows: a man studies say Greek and Latin history and literature and Latin language. He wants to solve a problem of constitutional law of the British empire. He has studied the Greek polis and the Roman empire, which has given him a notion of the structure of empires (knowledge a) and of constitutional law (knowledge b) as they appear in history. These were assumed to be in some way relevant to his problem. He then consults constitutional law, which is expert knowledge B corresponding to b above, and this he is able to understand in virtue of his study of b. His education is thus thought to put him in possession of rules of sufficient generality to span various empires and kindred areas of expert knowledge. But how far are such rules applicable? How general are they in fact? Suppose the structure of the Russian or Ottoman empires were concerned (as they frequently were) or that the constitution of the Manchu empire needed to be understood (as it did). How would the statesman fare then — would his general rules cover such instances? Perhaps the answer is no, but we have now moved to d, e, f, of supposition (2).

Let us suppose this is true — that we have moved from the similar to the dissimilar, even though we do not know how to apply any general rule so as to differentiate the one from the other. Suppose now the problem is one of international trade, involving economics, a dissimilar expert knowledge not previously studied by the statesman. Whence does he get his "lead" in mastering it? From Athenian banking, or the rules of provincial trade under Trajan? One might as well try to deal with a General Staff on the basis of a study of the campaigns of Alexander and Caesar. Either the rule derived is so general that it covers everything, or the statesman must undertake new learning. And if the rule covers everything, it will clearly leave everything to be done in a particular branch of knowledge. It might point to an appropriate attitude — say, "be careful not to make mistakes," or it might be a logical rule such as the law of contradiction. In which case it does not justify the inclusion of any *particular* types of subject matter in the education of statesmen, for any will serve. It looks as if the important point is the obligation of the statesman (then as now, on entering any new Ministry) to undertake new learning, unless he is to "stand aloof in giant ignorance" — a situation not unknown in nineteenth century politics. We conclude that supposition (1) is true of some situations but not all, whilst supposition (2) is either true but trivial or simply false. Perhaps no one ever defended it in this simple form, but state practice appears to have reposed faith in it.[13] Nevertheless, it contains the primitive hope of a transfer of learning on which

13. Cf. E. C. Mack, *Public Schools and British Opinion, I* (London, 1938), pp. 105-6, 291-2 and II (N. Y., 1941), Ch. I and M. Arnold, *Thoughts on Education* (Ed. L. Huxley) (London, 1912), p. 102.

all general educations are founded, and on which any plan for training commonsense thought must finally rest.

This older viewpoint was in part discredited by the application of transfer of training arguments from psychology.[14] Once it became clear that learning subject (*a*) was an advantage to pupils when they came to learn subject (*b*), the question for educationists was how this affected the curriculum. The cry arose, if some subjects gave no such advantage, why learn them? Why learn Latin if it was no advantage in learning "how to think"? It was not sufficiently emphasized, in the early days of discussion, that transfer is not merely of knowledge or thought procedures but also of attitudes; and it was not clearly seen that, in any case, arguments resting upon the "similarity" (a fundamentally vague term) of bodies of knowledge have no immediate relevance to curriculum problems. The curriculum is not primarily concerned with the similarity of the subjects it purveys; it is concerned rather to be anticipatory of adult life insofar as it seeks to furnish pupils with the wherewithal to solve problems. If similarity of subject matter were relevant to its use to solve problems, the teaching of it in a way allowing for this would be vindicated. And so it is, where preparation for certain kinds of profession – e.g., engineering – is concerned. But how about preparation for commonsense problems, with which general education is also concerned to deal? If Latin were an advantage in tackling these, it would have a claim to be considered. It might have transferable elements, other than "learning to think," which were of value. In fact, a good deal of the nineteenth century literature is more concerned with attitudes engendered by the study of Greek and Latin than with the intellectual discipline they provide.

With the transfer of attitudes, however, we are not here concerned, save to point out that it is part of the transferable elements in a general education. We shall not pursue it because we are here concerned with commonsense thought and knowledge rather than with the attitudes accompanying them. The problem raised by consideration of the case of the statesmen was, whether a particular type of general education has particular merits in preparing pupils for problems at a commonsense level. The fact that certain knowledge is similar to other knowledge in a curriculum is not relevant, as we have tried to show.

In a general education, principles of a very general kind are transferred – e.g., work consistently according to rules, avoid irrelevance, try various solutions, verify the work, and so on. Neglecting the attitude component of these, one would observe that both in the education of

14. Cf. R. F. Grose and R. C. Birney (Eds.), *Transfer of Learning* (Princeton: Van Nostrand, 1963), Chaps. I, II, VII, and P. B. Ballard, *The Changing School* (London, 1930), Chap. XIV, and L. W. Webb, "Transfer of Learning" in C. E. Skinner, *Educational Psychology* (New York: Prentice Hall, 1951), J. L. Mursell, *Successful Teaching* (New York: McGraw Hill, 1946), p. 70 seq., and P. Sandiford, *Educational Psychology* (London: Longmans, Green & Co., 1941), p. 290 seq.

statesmen and the transfer of training position the *application* of these principles is largely left to look after itself, whereas what is asserted here is the need for training in how to apply them if effective application is looked for. Practice in the application of these principles is required not only in the problems offered in the original area of learning, but in those mixed problems characteristic of commonsense activity.

School pupils start from a position where they do not conceive of expert knowledge and have no notion of the power to solve problems which it confers. Problems are vaguely conceived and handled ineffectively by them. As the awareness of the nature and procedures of expert knowledge develops, so *pari passu* the pupil is being equipped to deal with the possible field of application of these expert procedures. This is partly restricted to the expert field itself, but in part is effective elsewhere, in all varieties of problem requiring several types of knowledge for their solution. The pupil is thus being furnished with the means to an ever more ample and resourceful commonsense. These means however are not likely to be fully effective without some teaching of the procedures for solving the type of problem concerned.

It will thus be clear why no proposal for altering the curriculum is made here. Assuming that the transfer of principles (and probably of attitudes) is looked after by a large variety of curricular subject matter, the point to emphasize appears rather to be how the application of the principles taught is treated. As to the content of the curriculum, a comment on the types of knowledge it might be expected to contain is offered later.

To determine where training may be effective, let us first consider some of the characteristics of commonsense thought, knowledge and judgement, as they impinge upon school education. First, the content of commonsense activity is provided for by the teaching of specialized knowledge in school subjects, that is, the knowledge it uses is not of some distinctive kind. Expert judgement, however, may be characterized either by the use of one body of knowledge and one method, or, where mixed disciplines like medicine, architecture and education itself are concerned, several knowledges and methods. Both the first and the second kind are expert, for they utilize to the full the knowledges and methods available. But commonsense judgement does not do so. It aims at adequacy for the occasion, not expert levels of thought and knowledge. It is content with less than there is to know and to think. And this in no way invalidates its position (see part I), which arises from the type of problem with which it is concerned.[15]

15. Cf. M. Polanyi, "Problem Solving," in *British Journal Philos. Science,* VIII, No. 30, and some interesting psychological comment by Duncker, and Bloom and Broder, in T. L. Harris and W. E. Schwahn, *The Learning Process* (New York: Oxford University Press, 1961). On mixed disciplines cf. a comment by P. H. Hirst, "Philosophy and Educational Theory," in *British Journal of Educational Studies,* XII, I, Nov. 1963.

The problems with which commonsense is concerned may be called problems of personal policy, as contrasted with those of the expert type, which are here called problems of enquiry. The buying of an article, say, can be looked at aesthetically, economically, from a social status viewpoint. In all of these and still others an expert commentary is available. But it is utilized only to the point where a solution of the problem is attainable. Two features of commonsense problems may be here maintained.

(1) A particular solution is desired, and we work with it in solving the problem;

(2) To grasp the problem involves more than one variety of knowledge.

On the first, in striking contrast to problems of an expert kind, the person and his wishes are in the forefront, and the solutions, like the relevance of expert commentary, are judged in terms of their power to gratify those wishes. A high level of expertise is only accidentally relevant to this type of problem. For instance, a man wants to take his family on holiday: is the car equal to it? He obtains a garage report that it seems all right. He does not get a general "schedule of dilapidations" prepared by an automobile engineer, accompanied by pressure to get rid of the car immediately. (Many owners know they can obtain this, but continue to run the car. The expert commentary is only one factor in their problem!) The solution the man wants is to continue to run the car. He chooses what will authorize this, modifying only on very immediately relevant contrary evidence.

Second, the problem cannot be seen at all as an application of one variety of knowledge. To regard it as an application of expert knowledge is to proceed as if it were an enquiry, like an expert problem, whereas in fact it is a matter of reviewing policy. So, if he wants to know what to think about Picasso, he will dismiss the critic who tells him that Picasso is not an artist at all, and likewise the one who tells him that Picasso is of interest only sociologically, or psychoanalytically. These offerings fail to envisage his problem, which is, what sort of opinion should one hold of Picasso's *art*? For commonsense starts from acceptance of him as an artist come flood or fire. (This example may serve once again incidentally to rebut the view that commonsense is exclusively concerned with problems of what to do: for what to think, what to believe, are quite as much problems of policy.) What is then necessary for a commonsense judgement?[16] We shall want:

(1) Several varieties of knowledge;

(2) a clear notion of the problems, to guide us in what is relevant;

(3) a commentary on the problem from each of the varieties used;

(4) an assessment of the importance we intend to attach to each commentary;

16. This analysis leans heavily upon the reflective approach to problems. Clearly there are other approaches. But thinking especially of commonsense thought and judgement, it seems desirable to concentrate upon the type of problem best illustrating them.

(5) a rough idea of the shape of the conclusion we seek, in terms of its concern to us, in order to assess this relative importance of commentaries.

There is no attempt here, be it noted, to suggest that the *knowledge* used is related to other knowledge, or that the *thought* is related to other thought in some vast continuum. Each type of knowledge is assessed separately in terms of what it achieves for the person using it. And it is assigned an importance in terms of the type of solution desired. No relation occurs, other than directly to the person handling the problem. If, in the buying of an article, the person relinquishes the aesthetically most desirable in order to avoid bankruptcy, he wishes for solvency more than the highest aesthetic appeal. But if not (as sometimes happens) he goes down fighting!

Now there is obviously material for training here in school circumstances. One may suggest:

(1) Teaching upon the distinctive nature of varieties of knowledge (not to be confused with subject division, which takes this for granted);

(2) teaching upon the types of problem which pupils are being trained to solve, and the distinctive type catered for in mixed disciplines and commonsense;

(3) teaching upon the application of learning to mixed disciplines, which, from the point of view of one variety of knowledge, is a question of application of knowledge to another field;

(4) teaching pupils clearly to envisage the type of solution desired, in order that this may play an effective role as suggested above.

Each of these points appears likely to educate the sense of relevance with which we are principally concerned. A complete training in this is not possible in formal circumstances like those of the school. A good deal of it, for example, assessment of importance or "ranking" of relevant generalizations, needs the kind of traditional training referred to by Oakeshott[17] in addition. Yet, although the school in many senses is only a rehearsal of life, it is capable of a type of teaching that will sharpen and enrich the sense of relevance which is so heavily used in adult experience of commonsense situations.

We need to look at how this affects the curriculum. The main curricular pre-occupation is the training it gives in specialized thought and knowledge. Provided that this material is in close touch with the specialized knowledge currently in use among adults, it will furnish some of the material necessary for training a sense of commonsense relevance equal to the demands that will be made upon it. The crux of the matter is how the curriculum is to be used not merely for the teaching of specialized knowledge but for the application of it. Now, it seems that teaching of specialized thought begins by choosing an area of knowledge already established by means of the particular

17. Michael J. Oakeshott, *Rationalism in Politics* (London: Methuen & Co. Ltd., 1962), p. 59 (The Tower of Babel).

specialized procedure, and then showing to pupils the rules by which this knowledge has been attained and by which more similar knowledge can be attained. The application of such knowledge as suggested in this paper, however, has to do with how it is used in areas other than the expert area, which is the case with problems arising in mixed disciplines and in commonsense. In other words, this knowledge is then presented to the pupil in the context of a mixed type of problem, not of an expert problem. The assumption commonly made is that once teaching has attained its goal of showing how expert problems are solved, there will be a carry-over or transfer of this knowledge to other areas where it may be useful *without further educational attention* by the school, and this is the assumption disputed here. If the teaching of expert thought and knowledge has to be in the presence of problems previously solved by this means, how is it to be expected that the application of this to mixed problems does not involve the presentation and examination of mixed problems? Surely only in this way can the sharpening of a sense of commonsense relevance be attained.

The need to do this can, it seems, be easily met in the teaching of school subjects. For they are not pure varieties of knowledge, they are several varieties grouped round a principal one. For example, the teaching of history involves, say, discussion of plastic art and origins of science, or the teaching of biology involves reference to chemistry and physics. The normal teaching procedure is to treat the principal variety of knowledge as the real teaching job and dismiss the others as irrelevant. Whereas, if what is said above is true, two points need stressing. One, that teaching that there *are* different varieties, and what differentia they have, would clarify the specialist task. The other, that pupils are but imperfectly aware of all this and the very notion of expert and nonexpert knowledge is only dawning, and in need of specific and detailed attention for that reason. The notion of expert or specialized knowledge is in fact not complete unless its application is also dealt with in school circumstances. To show types of expert knowledge lying side by side helps to make the nature of a mixed problem or enquiry clearer. In other words, it seems plausible to suggest that the occasions occur naturally in school subjects for showing how the expert knowledge is applied. So that no alteration of content of teaching is implied here, but merely a different way of handling what is thought "irrelevant" to the main purpose.

This leads on to a comment on specialization in education. Few would deny that there is a time to specialize and that this forms a vital part of an educational programme. It is when this is used as a plea for ignoring all uses of specialized knowledge save the expert one that the mischief is done. The manner of teaching can either be directed to the implanting of a notion of types of specialized knowledge as a number of discrete fragments, or it can be directed in addition to suggesting that, though separate, the varieties of specialized knowledge can and do come into use together constantly in commonsense situations. And this latter is clearly in line with the intention of giving a general education. A general education is one designed among other things to make an impact on commonsense problems. The number of these problems is great, their pressure constant, and everyone spends a great part of his life dealing with them. Neglect in training how to apply knowledge and thought, and discriminating where it is relevant, results in the evils of an ignorant hostility to expert findings on the one hand and a servile acceptance of them on the other. And these evils are by no means restricted to the uneducated: they are rife among those who are themselves experts in one field or another.[18] No one would deny that the training of a flexible, sensitive and resourceful commonsense is a formidable undertaking. But with the results of its neglect around us, we can say that it is the training we need, and for which our education is in part designed.

In conclusion, here are some of the main points made. First, by taking some views of commonsense, we saw the possibility of a distinctive 'commonsense' thought and knowledge. With the emphasis on knowledge, we can point to a very large number of loose generalizations currently used and possessed by everyone. The emphasis on thought comes out as a sense of the relevance of this knowledge to situations and problems, in other words, how to apply it. This gave us ground for supposing that commonsense cannot be superseded by expert knowledge, because it has a different function.

Turning to education, we found that the school ought to be concerned with developing this sense of relevance as part of a general education, though there are limits to what can be done in the school. From discussion of more vague earlier views, it was clear that something like this was always hoped for but pupils were left to pick it up for themselves. But we maintained that only with training would the commonsense thought of the pupil reach its maximum resourcefulness and amplitude. Points at which training might be appropriate were then suggested, and it was held that these could arise naturally in the course of the teaching of specialist subjects which is the basic job of the school, whilst pupils are gradually learning the idea of specialized thought and knowledge. Finally, a criticism of one view of specialization was offered, and Thomas Arnold's opinion of the consequences of neglect of general education was quoted to conclude the discussion.

18. T. K. Arnold, "Thus we see everyone ready to give an opinion about politics, or about religion, or about morals, because it is said these are every man's business. And so they are, and if people would learn them as they do their own particular business, all would be well . . . this general ignorance does not make itself felt directly − if it did, it were more likely to be remedied; but the process is long and roundabout; false notions are entertained and acted upon; prejudices and passions multiply; abuses become manifold; difficulty and distress at last press upon the whole community; whilst the same ignorance that produced the mischief now helps to confirm or aggravate it . . . and sets them upon some vain attempt to correct the consequences . . ."

Part IV

SUBJECTS AND SUBJECT MATTER

Introduction

What are the distinctive contributions the study of science can make toward reaching the objectives of a liberal education is the question Ernest Nagel asks in his essay "Science and the Humanities." In the course of answering it, Nagel gives us insight into the nature of scientific method and the knowledge reached by that method. Despite the fact that Nagel is interested in aspects of method which cut across disciplines more than in those which do not, his recommendation that science be taught with a strong emphasis on methodological issues would seem to be in keeping with Hirst's program of liberal education set forth in Part III of this book. Nagel's conception of liberal education, however, is very different from Hirst's. Hirst, it will be recalled, confines liberal education to the forms of knowledge. Nagel does not. Poetry and painting, for example, are not on his view forms of knowledge, yet they do belong in a liberal education. Hirst agrees that they belong there but considers them to be forms of knowledge. This difference between the two men may seem to be on such a theoretical level that it makes no difference in practice. The question of the cognitive status of poetry and painting and also such things as music, religion, and ethics is far from settled, however. Thus, while on the one hand the dispute between Hirst and Nagel over cases is not surprising, it must be recognized on the other hand that the two conceptions of liberal education could, depending on the way these philosophical disputes turn out, result in very different programs.

Frederick A. Olafson in "Philosophy and the Humanities" seems to be asserting the very thing Nagel denies, namely that the humanities yield knowledge. Yet if we read his essay carefully, we see that Olafson is not basing his claim of cognitive status for the humanities on the sort of argument Nagel rejects. On the contrary, he bases it on a careful re-examination of the concept of the humanities. The humanities, Olafson argues, are a special kind of historical study. They are concerned with human beings and a certain class of their cultural achievements. What distinguishes them from other studies with a similar interest is that they do not abstract from the concepts in terms of which people see themselves in the way other studies do; thus concepts such as purpose, value, action, are central to the humanities. This view of the humanities allows Olafson to affirm that the humanities yield a distinctive form of knowledge without embracing a philosophically dubious theory of knowledge. It also leads him to some interesting comments on education in the humanities and to some important suggestions for philosophical research related to such education.

Olafson cites W. B. Gallie's book *Philosophy and the Historical Understanding* as representative of the sort of work in philosophy that contributes substantially to an understanding of the humanities. A chapter entitled "The Uses and Abuses of History" from that book is included here. Gallie's book contains an extended account of historical understanding to which no brief summary can do justice. Fortunately one is not really needed for Gallie's discussion of the values of historical understanding proceeds relatively independently of that account. Gallie is concerned to show that historical understanding can be of use to us, indeed must be used by us, in our everyday life. He argues that especially in relation to the institutional side of life it can teach us what we are or where we stand in the light of where we have come from; it can assist us to meet and cope with difficulties; it can help us to see not only what we can and cannot do, but what we might and might not do. Gallie's justification of the study of history — for his essay may be regarded as just this — is in some ways analogous to Nagel's defense of the study of science. Gallie, like Nagel, argues that his subject has a distinctive contribution to make to something else held to be of value. But there is one crucial difference between Gallie's approach to the study of history and Nagel's approach to the study of science: Nagel is advocating the study of methodology; Gallie is not.

Gallie may not in fact be opposed to the study of historical methodology by nonspecialists. In the present essay, however, he is concerned with the way nonspecialists view certain phenomena — institutions, doctrines, practices, and the like — rather than with the way they view the practices or thought processes of those who investigate these phenomena. Now since the law is part of the institutional side of life and is, then, one of the things Gallie would have us understand historically, it is interesting to compare Paul A. Freund's view of the way the law should be studied with Gallie's discussion of the uses of history. In his essay "The Law and the Schools" Freund deplores the fact that the law is neglected as a subject for appropriate study in general education, and that insofar as it is included in the curriculum, it is viewed from the outside. He argues for vicarious participation in the process of legal thinking – a kind of thinking which, as he analyzes it, involves at least seven modes of thought. We may assume that the vicarious participation he is advocating is something like the immersion Hirst advocates in connection with the forms of knowledge and is in keeping with Oakeshott's view that subjects be studied in the university as languages not texts, although – and this needs to be emphasized – it is not at all clear that the law is an explanatory language or that it is a form of knowledge. The question remains whether Freund is advocating what Gallie is advocating. To a certain extent he may be, for he recommends immersion in the literature of the common law and this may be thought of as historical study. Yet his interest throughout is in legal reasoning rather than in the history or development of that reasoning. One suspects, therefore, that a Galliean study of the law in the schools would be compatible with a Freundian study but would be no substitute for it.

The law as Freund views it for the purposes of general education is a human activity or enterprise or practice. So is art. Presumably, then, we could get a view of art from the inside, a view analogous to the one Freund wants us to get of the law. Walter H. Clark, Jr., in his essay "On the Role of Choice in Aesthetic Education" does not, however, advocate our looking at art from within. It is not that he wants us to study art from the standpoint of, say, a sociologist or psychologist. It is rather that he does not view aesthetic education as a study of the process of creating works of art, but as a study of works of art themselves. He is concerned with the experiencing, not the creating, of art. These are two very different things on his view: creating is primarily a matter of doing; experiencing is primarily a matter of having things happen to one. Choosing, according to Clark (who in his essay gives an illuminating analysis of this notion), is a kind of doing, a kind that enters in crucial ways into the creating of art. One may if one wishes view the education of artists as education for choosing well, Clark says. But he denies most emphatically that the education of experiencers should be conceived in this way. Choice enters into experiencing, but its role there is subsidiary. To focus too sharply on choice in aesthetic education is, he argues, to confuse means with ends.

If the role of choice in aesthetic education is subsidiary, its role in moral education, at least as Nancy Gayer conceives of that education, is of central importance. Mrs. Gayer in her essay "On Making Morality Operational" takes the position that we should be trying to get our pupils to develop into autonomous moral agents. Moral agents are not simply experiencers, nor are they simply thinkers; they are doers of a certain sort. Students ought, therefore, to be encouraged to make choices in the classroom. As Mrs. Gayer sees it, however, actual classroom practice all too often interferes with the making of genuine choices. Her essay is directed toward uncovering some of these practices so that teachers may become aware of the unplanned, unnoticed moral education that their pupils in fact get. Once aware, they will be able to decide if the values they are inculcating are the ones they want to inculcate and will be well on the way to making moral education deliberate and rational. Mrs. Gayer pays special attention to the teacher's language on the grounds that unplanned moral instruction comes about in the very act of speaking. She examines at some length the teacher's misuse of the word 'may' — a misuse which when seen in relation to the mystique of the democratic classroom has important ramifications for moral education.

Like Mrs. Gayer, Joanne Reynolds Bronars is concerned in her essay "Tampering with Nature in Elementary School Science" about the values that are being transmitted in the classroom without anyone's really realizing it. But whereas Mrs. Gayer stresses the connection between the teacher's language and unplanned moral instruction and draws her examples primarily from the sphere of classroom management, Mrs. Bronars focuses on the science program of the elementary school and stresses the connection between the child's learning experiences and unplanned moral instruction. The learning experiences or activities which worry Mrs. Bronars on several counts are those in which children control, distort, or stop the life processes of some kind of living organism in order to learn something about its functioning. She argues that children are not in a position to make decisions involving the control and destruction of any form of life. Childhood is on her view a time for developing a reverence for life and an understanding of man's interrelatedness with nature. She therefore advocates science study focused on observation of living things in their natural habitat rather than on experimentation with living things wrenched from an ecological system.

One assumption underlying the decision to include in the curriculum those classroom activities to which Mrs. Bronars objects is that children learn more easily and thoroughly through firsthand experiences involving direct manipulation of concrete materials. One of the many questions Stephen I. Brown asks in "On Some Bottlenecks in Mathematics Education" is what in fact the impact of such concrete experience is on the student of mathematics, in particular on his sense of intuition. Mathematics and Intuition is one of four topics Brown considers in his essay. The others are Mathematics and Science, Goals of Teaching Mathematics, and Creation of Mathematical Ideas. These are philosophical topics and from them Brown generates all sorts of interesting questions that he thinks ought to be considered by those interested in curriculum development. Some of these, e.g., "What do we mean by an *intuitive understanding*?", call for philosophical analysis, but others, e.g., "What kind of teaching tends to develop one's sense of intuition?" call for empirical investigation. We have, then, a program for curriculum research, one which will keep philosophers, mathematics educators and empirical researchers busy for a long time.

Some of the issues Brown raises in connection with mathematics education are of quite general interest. He asks, for example, whose domain the school curriculum is and wonders if mathematics educators ought to play the role of middleman between the schools and the experts from on high. We would do well to wonder about the relationship of educators to experts and to the schools no matter what the subject or who the expert. Brown suggests that mathematics educators might have something important to say to mathematicians. Recalling our discussion in the Introduction to Part III of this volume of the two-way street between curriculum development and epistemology, we will have to acknowledge that this is very likely the case. The account an expert gives of his subject, like the account a philosopher gives of it, is necessarily selective. But if different accounts can be given of a subject, a choice must be made of the one to be used in curriculum development. This choice is an educational one, not a mathematical or historical or literary one as the case may be, and not one to be decided purely by philosophical analysis. It is then a mistake to view the educator as receiving the word from on high, for the word from on high is in turn determined at least in part by educational considerations.

This point is worth stressing here since the essays in this section might otherwise be considered by some to contain the word from on high on such topics as the nature of science, the nature of the humanities, the nature of law and art and morality. It should be remembered in reading these essays that even if they contain words from on high, they by no means contain *the* word. After all, the topics discussed are all controversial. If our authors may be considered experts, it should nonetheless be recognized that the experts no more agree about the nature of science or law or the humanities than they do about the nature of morality or aesthetic experience. Even if the experts did agree, our authors would not be in a position, qua experts, to pass down *the* word to educators. What the child ought to learn and what the expert takes to be the nature of his field are quite distinct questions.

Our experts, however, may also be considered philosophers of curriculum. We can expect them therefore to move back and forth between issues having to do with a particular field and issues having to do with the teaching or study of that field. As a matter of fact, each essay in this section raises issues in relation to a particular subject or subject matter which have relevance for education in many other subjects or subject matters. For example, the Clark essay points up a distinction between the process or task side of an activity and the product or outcome side; the Freund essay points up a distinction between a view of the process side of an activity from the inside and a view of it from the outside and, given a view from the inside, between just looking and participating. These distinctions surely have relevance far beyond the confines of education in art or the law. And so does the reminder implicit in Mrs. Gayer's essay that whether we want our students to get within an activity and look or get within and participate, a decision must be made about *what* it is they are to look at or participate in.

If the essays included in Part I of this volume suggest that curriculum development is a complex matter, the essays in this section leave no doubt about it. For we may think of theoretical distinctions like the ones just mentioned as revealing points in curriculum development at which decisions must be made, and if we do, we see that a host of curriculum decisions are involved in what is often considered to be the difficult — difficult because on what basis does one decide? — but nonetheless straightforward matter of selecting curriculum content. It should perhaps be pointed out that there are many decisions to be made even where the process or task side of human activities is not at issue. The Olafson essay, for example, reminds us that insofar as we focus on some product or outcome of a human endeavor, we may view it independently of that endeavor or as a result of it. And implicit in Nagel's discussion of the value of scientific knowledge for a rational ordering of life is the assumption that the outcome of some human endeavor may, or may not, be studied with a view to its uses and applications.

The picture becomes even more complicated when the activity at issue in curriculum development is theoretical rather than practical. When, for example, the activity is history or science or literary criticism — that is to say, when it studies some things in the world in order to say things about them, regardless of whether what it says qualifies as a full-fledged theory — it is necessary to distinguish not only between the process and product sides of the activity, but between both of these and the things in the world the activity studies and talks about. Thus, for example, Gallie draws our attention to things in the world — e.g., institutions — and tells us we should understand *them* in a particular way; but someone else might have drawn our attention to history, a study about the world, and might have told us to understand *it* in a particular way. Now it is surely possible to pay considerable attention to the objects under study by a theoretical activity while focusing on that theoretical activity, but it is not necessary to do so. Moreover, if one does want to focus on particular things rather than on some theoretical study of those things, Mrs. Bronars's essay brings out the fact that there is the possibility not only of acquiring understanding of those things but of our acquiring various attitudes toward them.

Whether the thing being considered for inclusion in a curriculum is a theoretical activity, a practical activity, or something else altogether, there is always a decision to be made about whether to keep it "intact," so to speak, or to distribute it around the curriculum. It is a commonplace to find advocates of moral education and citizenship training arguing that these things ought not to be made separate subjects, but ought rather to be distributed around existing subjects, e.g., literature or history. The Gallie essay with its implicit assumption that different sorts of understanding can be had of a given thing — for example, historical and sociological understanding of an institution — suggests that history and other theoretical activities can also be distributed around the curriculum. The subjects studied might for example be institutions, doctrines, practices, places, flora and fauna, with the various theoretical activities introduced into these insofar as they shed light on the objects in question. But of course it is possible to keep the theoretical activities intact, so to speak, by making them the subjects studied and to distribute objects around the curriculum so that, for example, war is studied in history, economics, and literature; and politics in philosophy and sociology.

There are far more decision points in curriculum development than the essays in this section reveal even granting that these essays reveal more decision points than have been made explicit here. If the picture is one of complexity, it is also one of untold possibilities. For even if one's vision is limited to the decision points implicit in these and the other essays in this volume, one gets a glimpse of the great variety of curricula that can be generated. There are, of course, all manner of practical constraints on curriculum development, constraints which for the most part are ignored by the essays in this volume but which cannot be ignored by curriculum practitioners. Yet when all is said and done about time, money, overcrowding, and the many other realities of life and of education, we need only reflect on the many decision points and on the many alternatives at each one which are relatively unaffected by these practical constraints to realize that there is a great deal of room within which the curriculum developer can move freely. There is need, however, for such decision points to be made explicit and for the range of alternatives at each to be explored if this freedom is in fact to be exercised. For if these decision points go unnoticed or if alternatives are not recognized, curricula will be determined in large part by habit or tradition or the tastes of the people who happen to be developing them rather than by free, enlightened, imaginative consideration of the possibilities.

SCIENCE AND THE HUMANITIES

Ernest Nagel

The place of science in a program of liberal education is not a new problem; it has been at the focus of reflection on educational philosophy and practice since Plato. Nevertheless, although the basic issues may not have undergone radical transformation with the passage of the centuries, the problem has acquired new dimensions and fresh complexities in contemporary American society.

Until comparatively recent times, the theoretical sciences were regarded as branches of philosophical inquiry, having for their ultimate objective knowledge of man's supreme good in the light of his place in the universe; education designed for developing enlightened and cultivated minds was reserved for small minorities in relatively small populations; and the organization of human life did not require large groups of highly trained scientific personnel. Under such circumstances, it was easy enough for Plato and his successors to argue persuasively for a conception of liberal education in which the study of science occupied a prominent place. But these circumstances are no longer present. It is in consequence more difficult today to win effective general agreement that a solid grounding in natural and social science is an indispensable part of a humanistically oriented education, and that such grounding is no less essential for the formation of a liberal intelligence than is thorough exposure to the materials traditionally classified as belonging to the humanities.

What are the distinctive contributions the study of science can make toward realizing the objectives of a liberal education? Let me outline what I regard as the three cardinal contributions.

The Theoretical and Moral Value of Science

It has been the perennial aim of theoretical science to make the world intelligible by disclosing fixed patterns of regularity and orders of dependence

From Ernest Nagel's section in Chapter 4, "Science and the Humanities," of *Education in the Age of Science,* edited by Brand Blanshard, © 1959 in *Daedalus* by The American Academy of Arts and Sciences, © 1959 by Basic Books, Inc., Publishers, New York. Reprinted by permission of the author, The American Academy of Arts and Sciences, and Basic Books, Inc., Publishers.

in events. This aim may never be fully realized. But it has been partly realized in the scientific exploration of both animate and inanimate subject matter. The knowledge that is thus progressively achieved — of general truths about various sectors in nature as well as of particular processes and events in them — is intrinsically delightful to many minds. In any event, the quest for such knowledge is an expression of a basic impulse of human nature, and it represents a distinctive variety of human experience. It is a history of magnificent victories as well as of tragic defeats for human intelligence in its endless war against native ignorance, childish superstitions, and baseless fears. If to be a humanist is to respond perceptively to all dimensions of man's life, an informed study of the findings and of the development of science must surely be an integral part of a humanistic education.

There is the further point that knowledge acquired by scientific inquiry is indispensable for a responsible assessment of moral ideals and for a rational ordering of human life. Ideals and values are not self-certifying; they are not established as valid by appeals to dogmatic authority, to intuitions of moral imperatives, or to undisciplined preference. Moral ideals must be congruous with the needs and capacities of human beings, both as biological individuals and as historically conditioned members of cultural groups, if those ideals are to serve as satisfactory guides to a rich and satisfying human life. The adequacy of proposed moral norms must therefore be evaluated on the basis of reliable knowledge acquired through controlled scientific inquiry. It is simply grotesque to imagine that anyone today can exercise genuine wisdom in human affairs without some mastery of the relevant conclusions of natural and social science.

I am not unaware that there have been great moral seers who possessed little if any scientific knowledge of the world or of man, and who nevertheless spoke with understanding about the paths of human virtue. However, though such men may have expressed profound insights into the ways of the human heart, merely to proclaim an insight does not establish its wisdom; and it is by no means self-evident that their vision of the human good, though generous and wise for their time, is really adequate for men living in different climes and with different opportunities for developing their powers. Insight and imagination are undoubtedly necessary conditions for moral wisdom, but they are not sufficient. For insights and visions may differ, and knowledge of the world and human circumstance must be introduced for adjudicating between conflicting moral ideas. It would be absurd to deny the exquisite perceptions and the stimuli to reflection that are often found in the pronouncements of scientifically untutored moral seers. But I do not believe their pronouncements can be taken at face value, or that in the light of the scientific knowledge we now possess those pronouncements are invariably sound. In short, apart from the intellectual joys accompanying the enlarged understanding of the world that scientific knowledge may bring, such knowledge is indispensable if the ideals and the conduct we adopt are to be based neither on illusion nor on uninformed parochial preferences. It is not an exaggeration to claim that the theoretical understanding that the sciences provide is the foundation for a liberal civilization and a humane culture.

Science as Intellectual Method

The conclusions of science are the products of an intellectual method, and in general they cannot be properly understood or evaluated without an adequate grasp of the logic of scientific inquiry. I am not maintaining, of course, that there are fixed rules for devising experiments or making theoretical discoveries. There are no such rules; and it is in large measure because it is commonly supposed that there are, that scientific inquiry is frequently believed to be a routine grubbing for facts, and unlike literature and the arts to require no powers of creative imagination. Indeed, science has fallen into understandable though undeserved disrepute among many humanistic thinkers because students of human affairs have sometimes permitted this misconception to control their inquiries and their literary productions. Nor am I asserting that the sciences share a common set of techniques of inquiry, so that disciplines not employing those techniques are not properly scientific. Except for the ability to use a language, it is doubtful whether there is such a set of common techniques. Certainly the techniques required for making astronomical observations are different from those used in the study of cellular division; mathematically formulated laws are relatively recent developments in chemistry, biology, and the social sciences; and though quantitative distinctions are widely used in many sciences, the techniques of measurement are often quite different for different subject matters.

On the other hand, I am suggesting that what is distinctive of all science, not merely of natural science such as physics, and what assures the general reliability of scientific findings, is the use of a *common intellectual method* for assessing the weight of the available evidence for a proposed solution of a problem, and for accepting or rejecting a tentative conclusion of an inquiry. Scientific method, in my use of this phrase, is a procedure of applying logical canons for *testing* claims to knowledge.

Those logical canons have been adopted neither as arbitrary conventions, nor because there are no conceivable alternatives to them, nor because they can be established by appeals to self-evidence. They are themselves the distilled residue of a long series of attempts to win reliable knowledge, and they may be modified and improved in the course of further inquiries. They owe their authority to the fact that conclusions obtained in accordance with their requirements have agreed better with data of observation, and have in the main withstood further critical testing more successfully, than have conclusions obtained in other ways. The use of scientific method does not guarantee the truth of every conclusion reached by that method. But scientific method does give rational assurance that conclusions conforming to its canons are more likely to approximate the truth than beliefs held on other grounds. To accept the conclusions of science without a thorough familiarity with its method of warranting them is to remain ignorant of the critical spirit that is the life of science. Not every claim to knowledge is a valid claim; and without a clear grasp of the standards that evidence for a conclusion must meet, the risk is large of becoming a slave to every rhetorical appeal, to every plausible though specious argument, and to every intellectual fashion.

A firm grasp of the logical grounds upon which the sciences rest their conclusions serves to show that the sciences can make no dogmatic claims for the finality of their findings; that their procedure nevertheless provides for the progressive corrections of their cognitive claims; that they can achieve reliable knowledge even though they are fallible; and that however impressive the achievements of science have been in giving us intellectual mastery over many segments of existence, we cannot justifiably assume that we have exhaustively surveyed the variety and the depths of nature. The critical temper, the confidently constructive rationality, and the manly intellectual humility that are essential for the practice of scientific method are not simply adornments of a well-balanced mind; they are of its essence.

Science as the Code of a Community

This brings me to the final point I want to make in this context. Viewed in broad perspective, science is an enterprise carried on by a self-governing community of inquirers who conduct themselves in accordance with an unwritten but binding code. Each member of this republic has the right and the obligation to make the most of his capacities for original and inventive research, to make full use of his powers of imagination and insight, to be independent in his analyses and assessments, and to dissent from the views of others if in his judgment the evidence requires him to do so. In return for this he must submit his own investigations to examination by his scientific peers, and he must be prepared to defend his claims by reasoned argument against all competent critics, even if he should believe himself their superior in knowledge and insight. Accordingly, no question of fact or theory is in principle finally closed. The career of science is a continuing free exchange of ideas, and its enduring intellectual products are in the end the fruits of a refining process of mutual criticism. This does not mean that individual scientists do not possess passions and vanities, which are often obstacles to dispassionate judgment and which may hamper the advance of knowledge. It does mean that the institution of science provides a mechanism for discovering the truth irrespective of personal idiosyncrasies, but without curtailing the rights of its members to develop freely their own insights and to dissent from accepted beliefs.

The organization of science as a community of free, tolerant, yet alertly critical inquirers embodies in remarkable measure the ideals of liberal civilization. The discipline that fosters these qualities of mind therefore must have an important place in an educational program designed to develop members for such a society.

I must now discuss some of the obstacles in modern American society that stand in the way of adequate realization of the values that are obtainable from training in science.

The Danger of the Mole's-Eye View

In the first place, there is the high degree of specialization now required for exploration in most branches of science. Much of the indispensable day-by-day work of the scientist, even when he engages in fundamental research, has in consequence a relatively narrow scope. It is work which for the most part can be carried on successfully without thinking about the basic assumptions and issues. Accordingly, most scientists, whether in academic life or in one of the engineering professions, have at best only a perfunctory interest in the philosophical aspects of their discipline.

To be sure, in the course of solving their own technical problems many of the creative minds in science have felt themselves compelled to give close attention to the structure of scientific ideas, to examine the significance of scientific statements, or to analyze the logic of scientific inquiry. Indeed, revolutionary advances in scientific theory sometimes have been the consequences of just such comprehensive reflections. But to a large fraction of practicing scientists, concern with such matters is a luxury for which their immersion in detailed technical problems leaves them little time.

In consequence, the intellectual climate in which the sciences are taught is not generally favorable to the study of science as part of a liberal education. Courses in so-called "general science," designed in the main for those not contemplating a scientific career, are frequently so empty of scientific content, as well as of competent philosophical commentary, that they are viewed with merited contempt by scientists and humanists alike. On the other hand, the more traditional courses in science are normally organized so as to provide training mainly in professional skills. Unless he is guided by an exceptional teacher, it is only an exceptional student who acquires from such courses a just appreciation of the structure of scientific ideas, or of the logic and the civilizing significance of scientific procedure.

A second reason for the current difficulty in developing a satisfactory program of liberal education is rooted in the fact that in the popular, as in the Marxist, image of science, even fundamental research is primarily a handmaiden to technology. The major financial rewards and positions of influence go for the most part to the applied scientist, such as the engineer and the physician, rather than to those engaged in basic research. Under such circumstances it is by no means easy to secure adequate recognition for the conception that the pursuit of pure science is one of the glories of a liberal civilization. I am not suggesting for a moment that the practical values of training in the sciences are of no serious importance and should be ignored in considering the place of science in liberal education; and I have never encountered a good reason for maintaining that there is no room in a humanistically oriented education for anything in the curriculum of scientific studies that will prepare students for some practical profession. I am urging, however, that primary or exclusive emphasis upon the development of specialized skills is a disservice to the student, to the future of both pure and applied science, and to the prospects of a liberal society.

The Fear of Science as Inhumane

While science is currently prized for contributions to technology, paradoxically it is also condemned as the ultimate source of many of our major evils. The invention of the terrifying instruments of mass destruction has evoked widespread distrust of science, and has reinforced deep-seated doubts whether the benefits of scientific progress outweigh the miseries and the fears that apparently must be included in the price for advances in knowledge. Further, many critics of contemporary society attack science for having made possible the rise of so-called "mass culture" and its alleged consequences: the severe restrictions upon individual freedoms, the loss of a sense of individual inner purpose, the use of techniques for manipulating the minds as well as the bodies of men, the decline in standards of human excellence, and the general vulgarization of the quality of human life. Moreover, it is argued that science is inherently amoral and therefore likely to develop in the student a trained incapacity for distinguishing between good and evil and a callous indifference to humane values. In short, many humanistic thinkers view with concern the assignment to science of any large role in liberal education.

I shall try to meet some of the strictures made in the name of humanism against science and its influence; and to suggest what could be done to emphasize the humanistic and philosophic import of science, without depriving science instruction of substantive content.

It is undoubtedly true that the existence of mass cultures depends upon the technical fruits of theoretical and engineering research. It is also undoubtedly the case that many of these techniques have been put to reprehensible uses. On the other hand, it is absurdly unilluminating to make science therefore responsible for the failings of contemporary society, as unilluminating as it would be to place the blame for Hitler's moral inadequacies upon the procreative act of his parents. Scientific discoveries and inventions indeed have created opportunities which frequently have been misused, whether by design or by inadvertence. But an opportunity does not determine the use that men make of it. It is childish to bewail the expansion of science as the chief source of our current evils, and sheer sentimentality to look with longing to earlier days when science played a less conspicuous role in the human economy — as if living under such earlier conditions were an option now open to us, and as if societies less complex than ours exhibit no failings comparable with those of our own.

It is not possible to deny that, despite improvements in the material conditions of life for an increasing fraction of the populace, much of our energy is directed toward the realization of shoddy ideals, and that relatively few men lead lives of creative self-fulfillment and high satisfaction. It is difficult to demur at such indictments without appearing to act the part of a Philistine. Nevertheless, the failings noted are not unique to our own culture. Critics of American mass culture tend to forget that only comparatively small elite groups in the great civilizations of the past were privileged to share in the high achievements of those cultures, and that even those groups had only limited opportunities for appreciating the supreme products of the human spirit. In our own society, on the other hand, modern science and technology have made available to unprecedented numbers the major resources of the great literature and of the arts of the past and present, never accessible before in such variety to the highly privileged and cultivated members of earlier societies. I do not claim that these benefits are of passionate interest to the great majority. But there seems to me ample evidence that an increasing number in our society has come to value them, and that as a consequence of exposure to such things tastes have become more discriminating and less provincial.

Discriminating tastes cannot be formed overnight. In view of the size and the heterogeneous character of the American population, and of the fact that adequate leisure and training for developing and pursuing rational ideals is a fairly recent acquisition for most of its members, it is perhaps remarkable how rapid has been the growth of sensitivity in our society to the great works of literary, scientific, and artistic imagination. It is simply not the case that the mechanisms of our alleged mass culture are all geared to enforcing meretricious standards of excellence, or that there is today a decreasing number of opportunities for men to cultivate their individual talents. The evidence seems to me overwhelming that the growth of scientific intelligence has helped to bring about not only improvements in the material circumstances of life, but also an enhancement in its quality.

Humanists Not Immune to Provincialism

If thorough exposure to the discipline of science is essential for the development of a liberal intelligence, familiarity with the subjects traditionally classified as the humanities is no less essential. The values implicit in the study of the humanities are too well known to require extended comment. Their study acquaints us with a range of human aspirations and passions to which we can be strangers only if we remain provincial members of the human race; they transmit to us visions of human excellence that have stirred men throughout the centuries and that make men kindred spirits despite accidents of birth and circumstance; and they make us conscious of our cultural heritage, and so potentially more discriminatingly aware of its virtues and limitations. But there is no inherent incompatability between the liberal values implicit in the study of the sciences and those fostered by the humanities.

Nevertheless, professional humanists often display a snobbish traditionalism, a condescension toward everything modern, and an impatience with the critical standards of scientific thought. There have been humanists whose enthusiasm for the aqueducts of ancient Rome had no bounds but for whom contemporary systems of water supply were undeserving of a cultivated man's serious interest. There are self-proclaimed humanists who are profoundly affected by the tragic heroism of the Spartans at Thermopylae but who dismiss the Warsaw uprising against the Nazi oppressor as merely a sordid incident. There are humanists who claim a special kind of truth for knowledge about human values and who reject as sheer presumption the view that ordinary canons of scientific validity are pertinent for assessing the worth of moral insights. Needless to say, I am not suggesting that attachment to the classical tradition of humanistic thought is invariably associated with the narrowness of spirit some of these attitudes exhibit. However, the fact that they are sometimes manifested suffices to show that professional scientists have no monopoly on snobbery and provincialism, and that training in the humanities does not insure breadth of perspective.

Since the claim that the humanities represent a distinctive mode of knowledge is a frequent source of antagonism between scientifically oriented thinkers and spokesmen for the humanities, I must deal with it briefly. The claim seems to me to rest partly on a misunderstanding of what is covered by the label "scientific method," partly on a confusion of knowledge with other forms of experience, and partly on what I regard as a mistaken belief in the efficacy of human reason to establish absolutely certain and necessary truths about empirical subject matter. I have already indicated that the label "scientific method" does not signify either a set of rules for making discoveries or the use of certain techniques in conducting inquiries. In any case, I am in full agreement with those who maintain that distinctive subject matters require distinct modes of investigation; that the techniques employed in the natural sciences are not paradigmatic for the study of human affairs; and that though there are physical, biological, and sociopsychological conditions for the occurrence of preferences and valuations, trustworthy judgments about moral ideals cannot be deduced simply from statements about those conditions.

The disciplines constituting the humanities in some cases supply instruction which is no different in kind, though it is different in specific content, from the knowledge obtained in various special areas of natural science. This is patently the case for history and biography, and for much descriptive literature about the habits, customs, and aspirations of men. The factual claims of such literature must be tested by reference to the available evidence. Though standards of proof in these inquiries may be less stringent than in other areas, cognitive claims are validated through the use of logical canons common to all discursive thought about empirical subject matter. On the other hand, there are other humanistic disciplines, among them poetry, painting, and music, which are sometimes alleged to be sources of a special kind of knowledge, to which the canons of scientific method are said to be irrelevant. Now undoubtedly these disciplines can be instructive, in ways different from the way propositions are instructive. They can provide objects for reflection and perception; they can acquaint us with works of imagination that develop our sensibilities and heighten our powers of discrimination; they can present us with patterns of sound, color, and rhythm which evoke, intensify, and discipline emotional responses; and they can confront us with embodied visions of human virtue and human destiny. These are all important and instructive forms of experience. But since nothing is stated by these objects in propositional form, in no intelligible sense can they be regarded as conveying truth or falsity. They are therefore not sources of a special kind of knowledge, though they may be occasions or subject matters for knowledge.

Men who are equipped by native endowment and training to be successful investigators in one area are usually not equally successful in other areas. In any event, the capacity for making contributions to moral enlightenment is not uniformly distributed; and insofar as humanists are capable conservers and purifiers of the conscience of mankind, they require powers of moral imagination and insight which are as specialized as are the powers of imagination and insight into physical processess that the competent physicist must possess. However, as has already been argued, imagination and insight are not sufficient for establishing a cognitive claim, whether in morals or in physics. For insights must be tested. In a manner analogous to the procedure in physics, a test of a moral insight consists in formulating a hypothesis, comparing the consequences of the hypothesis with alternative assumptions and with empirical data relevant to the problem, and finally evaluating the adequacy of the hypothesis as a solution of the moral problem in the light of the evidence. Those who reject this procedure as not suitable for the adjudication of moral issues, and who also reject authoritarian justifications of moral judgments, attempt to validate moral principles by appealing to an alleged rational intuition of their necessary truth. I do not think this approach is tenable, among other reasons because of the historical fact that men have claimed intuitive certainty for incompatible moral principles. Accordingly, though there are as many distinct true statements as there are situations about which predications can be made, there are not several *kinds* of truth, and there is only one reliable *method* for establishing claims to truth. In short, the contention that the humanities employ a distinctive conception of truth and represent a mode of knowledge different from scientific knowledge seems to me to be the consequence of a failure in analysis.

I have already indicated what I take to be the humanistic values fostered by science. Finally, I want to suggest briefly how some of these values might be conveyed through the teaching of scientific subjects. The prospects for a liberal society depend upon the teaching of science as part of a liberal education which is dominated neither by a narrow utilitarianism nor by a comparably myopic professionalism. We cannot afford the folly of killing the goose that lays the golden eggs. Whatever be the urgencies of foreign or domestic politics, we must not institute a system of science education whose primary aim is to prepare students for careers in applied science. We must aim also to develop capacities which will contribute to the pursuit of the disinterested love of learning along the entire front. But above all, somewhere in their education we must equip the future laymen in science, as well as the future engineers and the future pure scientists, with mature conceptions concerning the nature of the scientific enterprise and the logic of scientific inquiry.

My main suggestion is that the liberal values of science can be best exhibited by teaching science with a strong emphasis upon methodological issues. I most certainly do not mean by this the institution of courses in the methodology of science, separate from or in lieu of work in the substantive materials of the sciences. Such courses, though they have a place in the curriculum, convey little to those unfamiliar with the subject matter of the sciences. I do mean that the materials of a discipline should be so presented that the logical principles controlling the analysis, the organization, the validation, and the modification of scientific statements are kept in full view, and that the findings of the sciences are exhibited as the products of a creative but critical intelligence.

The Importance of Method

The student should be disabused of the common misconception that a collection of facts is either the beginning or the goal of scientific inquiry.

Emphasis must be placed on the theoretical motivations that underlie the gathering of data, upon the selective character of observation and experiment, and upon the need to analyze and interpret the primary data of observation before they can be admitted as significant fact. Moreover, the student should be made to recognize that the concepts to which he is introduced have not been obtained by a process of simple abstraction from empirical data, but that they are intellectual creations, often *suggested* by the data, and are the products of a constructive imagination. Accordingly, the structures and functions of scientific concepts need special attention, and the logical as well as overt operations that relate concepts to crude experience must be discussed. In view of the increasing role that quantitative notions play in modern natural and social sciences, the logic of measurement and the major types of quantitative measures occurring in a given discipline deserve particular consideration. The student should be made aware that the introduction of quantitative distinctions is not a denial of qualitative differences, but on the contrary is a means for identifying such differences in a more discriminating manner than is customary in everyday affairs. The chief objective of these methodological emphases is to make explicit that science is not a mechanical routine, and that even at the most elementary levels of achievement it involves the use of a disciplined but sophisticated imagination.

The Function of Theory in Science

A second group of considerations to which attention needs to be given is the various ways in which the materials of a subject matter are organized and explained. The student should come to understand that natural history is not natural science, and he should be taught to appreciate the difference in this respect between, say, classificatory botany and genetics. Here again the realization should be enforced that theories are not extracted from empirical data, that they are not inductive generalizations or extrapolations from the observed facts, that they are indeed free creations of the mind. On the other hand, it should be made clear that theories are not just arbitrary inventions, and that they must meet a variety of conditions to be satisfactory. Accordingly, attention needs to be given to the function of theories both as guiding principles for further inquiry and as unified systems of explanation and prediction. It is essential in this connection to note the limitations of a crude empiricism and to stress the intellectual and practical advantages that follow from theories which enable us to subsume under a few principles a vast array of apparently disparate facts. Furthermore, the student should be enlightened on what really takes place when a theory, initially adopted to account for a limited range of similar phenomena, eventually absorbs into its scope of application quite different phenomena. Such extensions of theories occur repeatedly in the history of thought, and they effect important unifications in our knowledge. But such unifications are often construed to signify that science has somehow managed to diminish the variety of nature and to destroy apparent distinctions. In consequence, science comes to be conceived as a form of black magic which converts the world into an alien mystery and makes incoherent the procedures of science itself. Surely one thing a student ought not to carry away with him from his exposure to science is the belief that the universe becomes less intelligible the more science advances.

Science as the Discipline of Judgment

Finally — and this seems to me of greatest importance — the substantive materials of every science should be so expounded that the student acquires a habitual sense of the difference between competent and doubtful evidence, and between well-grounded conclusions and those that have a precarious foundation. The basic ideas of the logic of sampling procedure and the rationale of experimental control groups must therefore be brought home to the student. It thus should become clear to him that the mere agreement of a given hypothesis with empirical data does not constitute a sound basis for accepting the hypothesis, and that unless evidence is produced and analyzed with a view to determining what alternative assumptions are compatible with the facts, one has not even begun to think scientifically. It is not an unreasonable conjecture that if these elementary but basic points in the logic of proof were transmitted through the teaching of science, there would not be such a dishearteningly large number of victims to specious claims and preposterous intellectual fads. But however this may be, the student should also become aware that evidence can have different degrees of probative force, depending on the composition and the mode of obtaining the evidence as well as upon the character of the conclusion the evidence is used to support. Accordingly, no one has received an adequate education in science who does not realize not only that science does not claim definitive finality for its conclusions, but also why such claims cannot be made. Those who acquire such a realization also understand the nature of the continuing critical reflection that is essential to scientific inquiry.

Let me add that such methodological emphases in the teaching of science can be achieved only at a price. A large fraction of the price is that such courses cannot be encyclopedic compendia of whatever might be useful for a professional career in science. Some traditional subject matter must therefore be eliminated. I am convinced it can be done without serious loss if the remainder is effectively presented with a stress on those traits that distinguish science as a method of inquiry. But the price is not too high if the teaching of science contributes vitally to a liberal education.

PHILOSOPHY AND THE HUMANITIES

Frederick A. Olafson

Philosophers who have turned their thoughts to the subject of education have most often concerned themselves with the construction of very abstract models of cognition by means of which the activities of teaching and learning are to be understood.[1] Such attention as they have given to the subject matter of instruction has tended to be dominated by a concern with the morally or practically beneficial effects to be expected from a child's acquisition of a certain kind of knowledge. It would appear, too, that the decisive index used in assessing the value of such knowledge has often been the degree to which it approximated to an antecedently established archetype of knowledge. While the primary emphasis that has been given to these matters by Plato and by most of the modern philosophers of education from Locke to Dewey is understandable and has led to the elaboration of important theses in general epistemology, there are good reasons for thinking that this commentary needs to be more broadly based than it has often been in the past. More specifically, it will need to be informed by a better understanding of the distinctive character of the several subjects of instruction. Whatever contribution general epistemology may be able to make to the understanding of teaching and learning, its theses clearly stand in need of the kind of amplification that can come only from a survey of the particular types of knowledge to which the divisions of academic subject matter correspond. In the absence of such a survey, there will be a very strong tendency for a single type of knowledge to be treated as the perfect exemplification of the general model of knowledge produced by our epistemology and for other subjects to be regarded simply as inferior approximations to that epistemic standard which will itself very likely become harder and harder to distinguish from its paradigm instance. What I am suggesting then is that the philosophy of education needs to orient itself to a much greater degree than it has previously done on the various "philosophies of," e.g., the philosophies of science, of history and the social sciences, of law, and of art, which have come to occupy such an important

Reprinted from *The Monist, 52* (January, 1968) with permission of the Open Court Publishing Co., LaSalle, Illinois, and the author.

1. For an interesting discussion of such models, see Israel Scheffler, "Philosophical Models of Teaching," *Harvard Educational Review, 35* (1965), pp. 131–143.

place in contemporary philosophy. My special concern in this paper will be to argue that much discussion of the humanities and of their place within the instructional programs of the schools could benefit from work that has recently been done in the philosophy of language and in the philosophy of history and the social sciences. My guiding assumption which I will try to make as plausible as I can is that a consideration of the distinctive logical and conceptual features of the humanities does not have a merely theoretical interest but offers important clues to the nature of the educational and broadly moral importance which we traditionally impute to these studies.

I

One reason why so much current discussion of the humanities and of liberal or general education casts so little light on its subject is that the concept itself of "the humanities" is not satisfactorily explicated. While no one would presumably wish to dispute such frequently heard statements as that the humanities are the studies that befit a free man or that they somehow exhibit the distinctively human attributes of human beings, these characterizations are not very helpful either since they stand in need of just the same kind of clarification as does the concept of the humanities. Taken literally, the second of them would equate the humanities with the study of human culture in all aspects — scientific, technological, linguistic, political, etc. — and while there may well be a sense of the term in which, like the German '*Geisteswissenschaften*', it comprehends the social sciences, the standard American usage is one that contrasts the humanities with *both* the natural and the social sciences.

This narrower notion of the humanities can be isolated, I suggest, by making a distinction among the disciplines that in one way or another take human culture as their subject matter. The distinction I have in mind is the familiar one between those studies that are primarily historical in their method of inquiry and those — the social sciences — which, however dependent they may be on history for their "raw materials," are mainly concerned to discover the underlying uniformities or laws by means of which human events can in some measure be predicted and controlled. This contrast between the historical or "idiographic" and the generalizing or "nomothetic" disciplines has often been challenged, but usually, I think, because of the broader philosophical implications that have been — or have been thought to be — associated with it. In making use of it I am not implying that the humanist *qua* historian is not dependent in countless ways upon the kind of knowledge that the natural and social sciences seek to acquire. I am only saying that while he may be a consumer of such knowledge he is not himself a producer of it and that like the historian his primary interest addresses itself to particular periods, events and persons in the past.

"The historical study of human culture" is still somewhat too broad a rubric to serve as a definition of the humanities and it would include a good deal of historical work that is only marginally humanistic. I would therefore propose two further restrictions on the concept of the humanities, although I recognize that neither effects an absolutely clean distinction and will therefore have to be used in a tentative and flexible way. With this understanding, then, it seems natural and consistent with familiar usage to interpret the concept of the humanities as having a special affinity with the study of that subclass of human cultural achievements that are thought of as the achievements of assignable individuals or groups of individuals. Thus a language or a kinship system represents a cultural achievement in a perfectly good sense of that term; and both historical linguistics and cultural anthropology accordingly have a strong claim to be included among the humanities. But in the case of a language or a kinship system the achievement is in a special sense collective since it does not seem possible to discriminate the contribution made to them by particular individuals. By contrast, *King Lear* and the paintings in the Brancacci Chapel are the achievements of individual human beings even though the debt of Shakespeare and Masaccio to the artistic traditions in which they worked may have been very great. It is clear, of course, that the study of folklore, myth and early literature and art generally — all of which necessarily have a somewhat anonymous and collective character — is not only an important area of humanistic scholarship but also makes a major contribution to the understanding of later achievements which *are* assignable to definite individual authors. But if Homer seems to us very like the poets we *can* identify, the history of the Greek verb is very hard to think of as a series of individual achievements and the same might be said of the evolution of a system of matrilineal descent. It would appear, then, that in the case of these marginally humanistic areas of study we become progressively more unwilling to describe them as humanistic as the features of human culture with which they deal become harder to think of as involving the voluntary and purposive activity of individual human beings.

The second criterion I propose to incorporate into the concept of the humanities as the historical study of human culture has to do with the standard by which a human achievement is to be judged rather than with the identity — collective or individual — of its author. I suggest that when the production of an individual human mind is of such nature that it calls for appraisal in terms of a reasonably well worked-out and available canon of truth, it is *to that extent* withdrawn from the peculiar sphere of the humanities. The qualifying phrase which I have italicized in the preceding sentence is important since it may well be that a work like Newton's *Principia* will have, over and above the strictly scientific doctrines it propounds, certain features which it shares with other nonscientific works and which may be such as to claim the interest of the humanist. Nevertheless, the force of this last distinction is to mark out as the special province of the humanities those human achievements which have a primarily moral and aesthetic character in a very broad sense of the former term in which it would cover a good deal of what we may otherwise think of as falling into the spheres of politics and religion. I suspect that we have something like this restriction I am proposing in mind when we hesitate, as we sometimes do, to include philosophy and religion among the humanities. Certainly the element of personal synthesis and vision is more evident in these fields than it is in science; but both are, after all, supposed to enunciate truths about God or the world or the human mind. It seems rather incongruous, therefore, to classify them with literature and the other arts. On the other hand, there is little general agreement on a canon for determining the truth or falsity of the assertions made by the classical systems of philosophy and theology; and since both very often have great moral and aesthetic interest we are also moved to include them among the humanities. Sometimes a rather unsatisfactory compromise between these conflicting inclinations is effected, at least in the case of philosophy, by assigning the history of philosophy to the humanities and associating current philosophy more closely with the social and natural sciences.

It will be apparent from the conception of the humanities which I have been outlining that I am neglecting one whole aspect of humanistic education which is of very great importance in the schools. After all, if the humanities are to remain alive and grow in our own time, then young people must be taught to paint, to play musical instruments, and to write, to mention just a few of the relevant skills; and some of these young people must go on to create new work of merit. It could be argued that by interpreting the humanities as a special form of historical study, I am putting forward a consumer's rather than a producer's definition and a backward-looking consumer's at that! I can reply to this criticism only by saying that in applying the term 'the humanities' to studies of the type I have described I have no intention of challenging the importance or indeed the prior educational claim of a practice-oriented conception of the humanities. It does seem clear, however, that practice in this sense will — at least at the higher levels of attainment —increasingly require a measure of understanding of the tradition in which one is working; and that, as a matter of historical fact, the humanities considered as a group of studies within the schools and colleges have been more concerned with keeping alive an understanding of certain intellectual and artistic traditions than they have been with the sponsorship of innovation. If this conservatism has brought the humanities on occasion into justified opprobrium, there does not seem to be any danger that humanistic training along historical lines is paralyzing creative innovation in this country at the present time. The situation in fact appears to be quite the opposite; and the difficulties of the schools in maintaining anything like the older sort of humanistic training are clearly very great. If there is a "crisis in the humanities," as we are told on every hand there is, then it is a crisis that affects both kinds of humanistic training; but in the case of the historical kind there are signs that the crisis has passed and that the patient has slipped into a coma. That fact in itself justifies a special inquiry into the rationale for such training.

On closer inspection, it turns out that the crisis in the humanities is two-fold. First, the schools are, as I have pointed out, experiencing acute difficulties in maintaining anything like the traditional programs of instruction in such subjects as English literature.[2] In most schools that are still making even an effort to give their students some understanding of the English and American literary tradition, virtually everything before the nineteenth century with the sole exception of Shakespeare has disappeared from the curriculum. The crisis here consists quite simply in the fact that larger and larger tracts of the history of Western culture are becoming unavailable for purposes of instruction by virtue of the lack of historical and linguistic preparation on the part of the great mass of students. Since this preparation alone makes possible access to and understanding of the great works of the past and since those works have traditionally been the staple of humanistic education, it is not surprising that training in the humanities should have reached the low ebb at which it presently stands in most of our schools. If this deficiency is being partially made up at the college level for those students who go on, it should also be pointed out that humanities work in the colleges is very severely limited in what it can hope to achieve in the case of the majority of students by the inadequacies of their training in the secondary schools.

The second crisis in the humanities is not so directly related to the situation in the schools as is the first; but it is deeper and more intractable and it directly affects our ability to develop a coherent approach to the educational difficulties just noted. It is in essence a crisis of doubt bearing upon the epistemic status of the humanities themselves and more particularly upon the language of the humanities. This doubt is occasioned in the first instance by a comparison of history and literature with the natural sciences which, as Descartes was among the first to argue, give us clear and proven truths about the world while the humanities seem to deal principally in fictions, hearsay, personal impressions and the like. At a deeper level, this doubt extends to many of the concepts on which the humanist must rely most heavily and especially to evaluative and teleological concepts; and it challenges the assumption that these concepts have any purchase on the world and that by such means any reliable truths can be articulated. In this way a picture develops of the humanist as a kind of primitive artisan who with the makeshift and obsolescent tools at his disposal carries on a task

---

2. Massive evidence in support of this assertion can be found in James J. Lynch and Bertrand Evans, *High School English Textbooks* (Boston: Little, Brown and Co., 1963).

which will one day soon be performed with properly designed scientific instruments. It may be conceded by those who find this picture persuasive that there is a measure of justification for the humanist's perseverance in his quasimythical discourse on human themes since the natural sciences have not yet reached the point at which they have very much to tell us about human beings at those levels of thought and action with which the humanities have typically been concerned. But this concession is not enough to breathe new life into such training as is still given in the humanist's stone age technology; and the steady forward progress of science gives assurance that the crudities incident to the latter's decay are no more than the price that must be paid for the impressive new expertise that is just around the corner.

If all the humanities currently suffer under a suspicion that this picture of their relationship to the exact sciences may be uncomfortably close to the truth, it is the "verbal humanities" whose status is most directly challenged. Unlike music and the visual arts, literature and history use language and enunciate propositions which are after all the sort of thing that can be true or false. This fact about them suggests that they are trying to do something like what the scientist does; but this very *rapprochement* through language with the sciences proves to be just the source of the trouble since both the historian and the poet are, although for somewhat different reasons, often hard put to explain the sense in which what they tell us is true. To be sure, the historian is at least talking about things that actually happened and to that extent has a hold on the "real world" that the poet and even the novelist may seem to lack. On the other hand, if the historian passes moral judgment on the actions he chronicles or if he gives a dramatic form and unity to events instead of simply explaining them by subsumption under approved sociological or economic laws, how is he to be distinguished from the mere fabulist or even from the poet? The plight of the verbal humanities, then, is that they are at once too much like the sciences to claim that they are simply doing something different to which the progress of the sciences offers no competition; and too unlike to be able to pass muster by the standard that acceptance of such competition would impose.

II

This dilemma of the verbal humanities and of the "humanist intellectual" has recently been formulated in very harsh terms by Professor Ernest Gellner.[3] His treatment of this issue emphasizes its sociological aspect much more strongly than I have done; and he argues that the crisis in the humanities is a direct consequence of the advent of universal literacy which

3. In his essay, "The Crisis in the Humanities and the Mainstream of Philosophy" in J. H. Plumb (Ed.), *The Crisis in the Humanities* (Harmondsworth, Eng.: Penguin Books Ltd., 1964), pp. 45–81.

automatically invalidates the claim to special cognitive status of the "clerk," i.e., the person whose education has been primarily linguistic and literary rather than scientific or technological. In spite of this difference in emphasis, however, Gellner's case against what he calls "verbal knowledge" is much the same as the one I have outlined above. As a result of "the towering superiority of science as a source of knowledge of the universe . . . the man sensitive to the meanings of words, to their connections and inferential powers, their histories and recorded alignments in books can no longer claim — whatever else he may claim — that he is, primarily and above all and more than anyone else, a *knower*."[4] The crisis therefore is not, as is sometimes supposed, due to the fact that there are now two cultures where there used to be only one and that dominated by the Masters of the Word. "The real and deeper problem concerns what if anything the humanities have to communicate"[5] in the kind of exchange with the scientific culture that is now so often desiderated. While Gellner's essay ends with an appeal for a new sociologico-philosophical inquiry into the complex relationship between the cultures of science and everyday life, his present judgment that "it is not obvious that the humanities contain, in any serious sense, genuine *knowledge*"[6] tends to throw a chill over any expectation that such an inquiry could prove to be anything but an autopsy on the humanist's claim to be a "knower."

It is not surprising that many humanists have reacted to charges such as these by claiming that the humanities *do* in fact purvey knowledge of a distinctive kind which is most often conceived of as an intuitional apprehension of objective value properties. It has been argued that this "qualitative knowledge" is both fundamentally different from the kind of understanding science can give and in some usually undefined way superior to it. A defense of the humanities' epistemic status through an espousal of an objectivistic theory of value has in fact become one of the commonest general rationales for humanistic study; and while such an interpretation of the humanities has never to my knowledge been developed in any very great philosophical depth, it underlies a great deal of current discussion of the humanities and their place in education. For reasons which I cannot go into here but which would be familiar to any acquainted with recent criticism of value objectivism, I do not think this line of defense is a promising one in spite of the fact that it almost seems to be forced on the humanist by the terms in which the challenge to his cognitive status has been posed. At the same time, however, I would agree that the challenge is a serious one and that it must be met on its own terms and not by some emotivistic account of what the humanities are about. While it would be foolish to expect that the

4. *Ibid.*, p. 78.
5. *Ibid.*, p. 79.
6. *Ibid.*

articulation of a valid philosophical rationale for the humanities would necessarily have an immediate and invigorating effect on our educational practice, it seems equally unlikely that a set of disciplines that are without adequate means of intellectual self-defense will have the morale that is needed even to maintain the present shaky position they occupy within our schools and colleges.

In the essay by Professor Gellner to which I have been referring, there is a passage which offers some important clues as to the quarter in which a satisfactory rationale for the humanities might be sought although it is far from clear that the author himself regards them in this light. In this passage a contrast is made between the language of the humanities and the special technical idioms of the sciences; and the former is declared to be "incomparably closer to what we *are*, to the life we live than is the language of science."[7] There are certain "concepts in terms of which we see ourselves and live our lives",[8] and these concepts with the distinctions they express are also the working capital of the humanities. Unfortunately, there are no logical bridges that lead from this "vernacular of life" to the "Sacred Language of Truth," i.e., science; and it is therefore "the chasm ... between real knowledge and identity which is the fundamental issue."[9]

Now in spite of its somewhat apocalyptic flavor this seems to me to be well stated; and it is surprising that Gellner does not see that he has the makings of an answer to his question in his very statement of it. For if the "vernacular of life" in some sense defines our identity as human beings as Gellner appears – quite rightly, in my view – to be saying it does, then how could there be any knowledge of human beings that abstracted entirely from "the concepts in terms of which we see ourselves and live our lives?" There could of course be, and there in fact already are, many different ways of studying human beings that do so abstract; but it seems fair to say that when an attempt is made to study purposive human action without making any reference to the intentional structure of that action, the subject matter of the inquiry is behavior and not action and that this shift in the nature of the inquiry is due precisely to a principled neglect of the element of intentional structure. Such intentions, in turn, stand in the closest possible relationship to those "concepts in terms of which we see ourselves and live our lives" among which Gellner must surely mean to include concepts of purpose and value and action. Unless it is denied a priori that any inquiry into action as distinct from behavior can claim to produce "genuine knowledge" – and to do this would require a defense of a special interpretation of the concept of knowledge itself and not just a passing reference to "the towering superiority" of science – there is a strong prima facie case to be made in

7. *Ibid.,* p. 79.
8. *Ibid.,* p. 78.
9. *Ibid.,* p. 79.

behalf of the view that there is a perfectly respectable and distinctive way of studying human beings that treats "the vernacular of life" as an integral and centrally important element in the life that is under study.[10]

In this connection there is a crucial ambiguity in Gellner's antithesis of real knowledge and "the vernacular of life" to which I must now draw attention. It is one thing to argue, as Gellner surely means to do, that the evaluative and moral predicates we use in everyday life and in the humanities do not designate objective properties of things and situations which could be discovered by means of any procedure of verification we are likely to recognize; and I would go farther with him and deny, as I think he would be disposed to do, that evaluation as such is a matter of "knowing" at all. It is far from clear to me, however, that the humanities, as distinct from some of their present-day interpreters, are in any way committed to such a claim since their concern has typically been with the human person at a certain level of his relationship to himself and to others and not with some special interpretation of the evaluative and intentional activities in which he characteristically engages. The point I want to make is simply that it is perfectly possible for our evaluative and purposive concepts not to be cognitive in the sense of somehow standing for certain items of reality and yet for our multifarious employment of such concepts to figure in an essential way in a certain kind of knowledge we have of ourselves and of other human beings. There may thus be a "chasm," as Gellner believes, between "real" or scientific knowledge of the world and our human identity to the extent that the latter is not exhausted by those of its aspects which lend themselves to scientific inquiry as Gellner conceives it, but also comprises conceptually mediated activities that are not addressed simply to the discovery of what is the case. As chasms go, however, this one does not appear to be especially sinister or perilous; and the "human identity" that stands on the far side need not be, as Gellner seems to imply, an uninterpretable surd since it can in fact be apprehended and "known" via the kind of reflexive self-knowledge for which men have traditionally looked to the humanities and to philosophy.

Some of the advantages of the definition of the humanities which I outlined earlier should now be apparent. That definition associated the humanities not so much with the actual painting of pictures and writing of novels and poems as with the understanding and appreciation of such works within the context of the historical tradition in which they were produced. This distinction of levels makes it possible to deny that a poem, for example, represents any apprehension of features of reality that are unknown to science while at the same time affirming that the humanities, understood as the study of man as a being capable of feeling and choice and action and as

10. Two recent books that lend support to this general conclusion are A. I. Melden, *Free Action* (London, 1961) and Charles Taylor, *The Explanation of Behaviour* (London: Routledge and Kegan Paul, 1964).

among other things a maker of poems, do embody a distinctive form of knowledge. This knowledge of man is inevitably dependent in countless ways on what can be learned about human beings through both scientific and everyday observation; but it is also distinctive because it recognizes and gives a place of central importance to those configurations of evaluative and purposive meaning that can be elicited from our experience and from the works that formulate that experience. These are in fact the prime materials of humanistic study; and if the humanist considered as a maker or *poietes* is not a "knower" in Gellner's sense — a fact which by no means entails that he is merely expressing his feelings — the humanist, understood as the student of human life at those levels at which works of art and certain other oeuvres provide some of the best evidence of its true nature, still has a special claim to that honorific title.

In attributing a reflexive and second-order character to the humanities, I may seem to be giving support to the currently popular view that a liberal or nonspecialist education is one in which an understanding of the conceptual structure — as distinct from the detailed substance content — of one's own and other disciplines is imparted.[11] In fact I have no such intention. Quite apart from the difficulty of teaching the conceptual structure of a discipline to students who have no real mastery of the materials to which the concepts in question apply, it is not at all easy to see how this interpretation of liberal education would suitably describe the study of works of imaginative literature, to take just one example. No doubt it would be possible to approach the study of works like *Don Quixote* or *Middlemarch* in a purely formal way and to treat them as so many contrasting examples of the ways in which a nonreal world can be articulated in the medium of language. It is clear, however, that while the value of such a phenomenological approach to literature might be considerable, it could well prove to be a rather sterile exercise from the standpoint of humanistic education if the student's attention were thereby diverted from the commentary, direct and indirect, which such works make on human character and society. Through the study of a carefully selected group of such works, the student can be brought to an understanding of a gradually evolving tradition or set of traditions — moral, religious, social, and political — in which he himself stands; and the study of that tradition would be an exercise in historical understanding in the broadest sense rather than in conceptual or logical analysis. This kind of historical study does not have to be a worship of the "great dead" for the story it unfolds is essentially unfinished and invites a critical reaction from the student; and it is emphatically not history in the manner of the potted summaries characteristic of textbook histories of literature either. If I had to give a single example of the kind of historical understanding I have in mind

11. I have in mind such recent books as Philip Phenix, *Realms of Meaning* (New York: McGraw Hill, 1964), and Daniel Bell, *The Reforming of General Education* (New York: Columbia University Press, 1964).

and that brings all the resources of a deeply informed and sensitive mind to bear on a set of texts, I could scarcely do better than to point to the works of Erich Auerbach in which a profound grasp of the moral and broadly human themes of Western literature is combined with a fine appreciation of the formal aspects of a work of literary art.[12] In a sense of the word which is now almost entirely lost, such history is *moral* history; and by comparison with it a conceptual Cook's Tour of otherwise unexplored continents of learning would prove sadly disappointing.

It does not of course follow that because the humanities are not primarily concerned to produce what is now called "conceptual sophistication," philosophy, which is so concerned, can make no contribution to humanistic education. On the contrary, I would fully subscribe to Gellner's statement that while "philosophy may not be the queen of the sciences . . . it *is* at the apex of the 'humanist' disciplines"[13] in the sense that "the most general and fundamental questions that . . . crop up in the course of historiography, jurisprudence, literary study, etc. *are* philosophy and when treated systematically are classed as 'philosophy' rather than as parts of the specific discipline from which they arose."[14] In other words, if the humanities in my sense are at one remove from the actual production of works of art simply by virtue of being the historico-critical study *of* such works, then philosophical interest in the humanities would typically find its point of application at a third level in the form of analyses which, as Gellner puts it, "service the basic conceptual equipment of humanist thought."[15] While it is quite true that the second level in this pyramid is dependent on the third or philosophical level in the sense that any basic challenge to the adequacy of the humanist's conceptual equipment must be met at the level of philosophical analysis, it does not seem wise from a pedagogical standpoint to fuse these two levels as some current theories of the curriculum seem to propose we should, and thus transform all humanistic study into an inquiry into the logical conditions of such study's being possible at all. Aptitude for and interest in the specifically philosophical questions that arise with respect to the humanities seem likely always to be much less widely shared than a capacity for response to the humanities themselves and the works with which they deal.

III

In connection with the foregoing remarks, it is worth noting that the history of humanism in the West offers some useful hints to the philosopher

12. Auerbach's masterpiece is of course his *Mimesis* (Princeton, N. J.: Princeton University Press, 1956).
13. Gellner, *op. cit.,* p. 69.
14. *Ibid.,* p. 70.
15. *Ibid.,* pp. 70–71.

as to what the principal presuppositions of humanistic study have traditionally been and which bits of conceptual equipment in the humanist's tool kit
are most in need of the kind of clarificatory analysis that could establish their
integrity in the face of such challenges as may be made. One such
presupposition which seems particularly clear is the belief that the concept of
the individual human agent yields an interesting and valid unit in terms of
which certain types of explanation can and in fact must be given. In its most
familiar form, this assumption is reflected in the interest we take in all
manner of stories, in *res gestae,* ranging all the way from everyday gossip to
history and cosmic myth. So strong and inveterate is this attachment to the
dramatic and dialectical structure of human action that men have often quite
naturally seen the whole cosmic scene in terms of the tensions and resolutions
that are typical of the stories we tell about ourselves; and speculative
"philosophies of nature" have also projected the categories of dramatic
explanation on the world at large. At the present time, however, not only
have such extravagances been suppressed, but the very notion of human
agency itself has become problematical. A substantial unwillingness has
developed, not just among behavioral scientists where it would be expectable
and even appropriate, but among some analysts of historical knowledge and
perhaps some historians as well, ever to accept as the last step in an historical
explanation a statement to the effect that an individual human agent did x
because he believed it would lead to result y which he desired, unless the
relationship of these desires and beliefs to doing x has been explained through
subsumption under a general law. Now, without entering here into the very
complex issues that are involved, I would propose as a priority item for the
agenda of a philosophy of the humanities an examination of the concept of
human action as it is deployed in the description and explanation of action in
narrative history and imaginative literature. Whether the logical integrity of
this concept can be demonstrated in the face of the criticisms that have been
directed against it is a matter that only the progress of such an investigation
can reveal. What is clear is that the humanities have a major stake in such
inquiries, however they may turn out.

The importance of the concepts of personality and agency for the
humanities is connected with another "presupposition" of a more general
kind. Humanism has always been closely associated with a concern for
language; and to be a humanist was once virtually identical with being able to
write Latin in an elegant classical style. This emphasis on the style of
expression as distinct from the substance of one's thought has brought down
a great deal of deserved ridicule on the heads of the humanists; and yet it is
not too difficult to discern a more serious intellectual concern beneath their
traditional interest in literary style. In seeking to develop an instrument of
expression characterized by a high degree of intelligibility and clarity and
elegance, the humanists were attempting to provide a language in which all

members of the republic of letters could communicate effectively with one another.[16] In our own day, when a host of technical jargons with their debased popular versions appear to have won an almost complete victory over the ideal of a common idiom of expression, the humanists' concern for the latter takes on a special significance that it can hardly have had for them. It is generally acknowledged that we face a serious problem of communication among the various linguistic communities which scientific inquiry along different and independent lines has brought into being; and this problem can hardly be solved unless the relationship of these technical dialects to the shrunken remnant of common nontechnical speech is clarified and in some measure reconstructed. As one philosopher has put it, diplomatic negotiations between the various principalities of science are necessarily carried on in the *koiné* of everyday, nontechnical language; and the humanist's assumption is that it is both possible and highly desirable to devise a linguistic instrument that will enable us to move perspicuously and easily from the frontiers of one scientific domain to those of another. No such instrument is presently at our disposal; nor can we hope to find one, as the humanists did, in some purer language of the past once the barbarous accretions of the present have been scoured off. Here Gellner's strictures on at least one influential wing of the analytical movement in philosophy are much to the point since there has certainly been a tendency in some quarters to deny or to ignore the problematical character of the relationship between the natural sciences and the common sense understanding of the world and a failure to appreciate the need for the sort of renovation within the language of everyday life itself that would enable it to perform its task of mediation more effectively than it can at present. But I would also argue that the aspiration to create a common language, however different the context in which it arises may have become, does not simply express a utilitarian demand for a lingua franca of interscientific communication, but also a general human need for a means of encompassing and connecting the discrete departments of practical and cognitive activity. Moreover, that aspiration together with the strong emphasis upon linguistic expression to which it leads seem to me to be characteristically humanistic. While it must now be recast, as I have pointed out, into the optative mood and even then must reckon with the possibility that more or less extensive shifts within ordinary language will be necessary if its function is to be realized, all current philosophical inquiries that seek to cast light on the interdependence of the scientific and common sense understanding of the world seem to me to have a special interest from the standpoint of the humanities; and I would say the same of some of the

16. In saying this I am not unaware of the fact that the Renaissance humanists by insisting on the revival of classical literary styles may well have prevented medieval Latin from serving as the common language of the learned world and thus contributed to the eventual demise of Latin in all forms.

investigations of the *Lebenswelt* that have been carried out under phenomenological auspices. Indeed, even the prevailing complacency of Oxford-style
analytical philosophy with respect to the integrity of the distinctions
enshrined in ordinary language has not prevented it from making contributions of real value to our understanding of that common language on which
the humanities are so heavily dependent. There are promising signs that more
philosophers are becoming interested in work along these lines and also that
more scholars within the humane disciplines themselves are coming to
appreciate the importance for their own studies of the issues to which these
philosophers address themselves.[17] To suggest that the time is ripe for "interdisciplinary cooperation" would be decidedly premature, but the situation
has at least improved to the extent that philosophers, art historians, jurists,
literary scholars, and others can benefit from one another's work. From such
understanding as may be achieved in this way, the humanities themselves can
only profit; and if they do, it seems likely that a more coherent conception of
what the humanities are and of how they can most profitably be taught will
emerge.

17. I have in mind such books as W. B. Gallie, *Philosophy and the Historical
Understanding* (London: Chatto and Windus, 1964) on the philosophical side and
E. Gombrich, *Art and Illusion* (London: Phaidon, 1960) and N. Frye, *Anatomy of
Criticism* (Princeton, N. J.: Princeton University Press, 1957) among recent works of
humanistic scholarship.

THE USES AND ABUSES OF HISTORY

W. B. Gallie

Our account of explanations in history serves to reinforce the more general and familiar thesis that historical understanding is of a basically different kind from that achieved in the natural sciences by the discovery of new laws or by learning how to apply established laws to what seemed to be exceptional cases. At the same time, our account includes — and indeed stresses the indispensable service — of such general laws in supporting any new interpretation of the logic of some particularly puzzling historical situation. And equally, our account of historical understanding — of what it means to follow an evidenced narrative — certainly permits the use of any such narrative as a source of supply from which particular cases can be abstracted to suggest or to support this or that general law of the social (or in some cases the physical) sciences. In both these ways, therefore, historical understanding has important links with the kind of understanding that is gained in the sciences. But to grant this is in no way to subtract from our basic claim that historical understanding is something *sui generis,* inasmuch as it is the understanding of how some particular outcome came to be.

But if historical understanding is essentially of this kind, are we not forced to confess that the long-cherished idea of history as a guide to the future has been a sheer illusion? Must we not concede that history is, in itself, useless, or that its value is confined entirely within itself — to the intellectual satisfaction and self-discipline of those who study it, steeping themselves in a past whose intelligibility offers us no positive guidance for the ever-emerging future? Certainly, it seems to me, we should have to consent to this conclusion if the only way in which knowledge can be used or can prove itself useful were that exemplified by the application of scientific laws and formulae to help us meet the problems of practical life. Engineering, medicine, and the rapidly developing social sciences are in action every day before our eyes, to remind us of the importance — and indeed of the magnificence and the, humanly speaking, providential character — of this sort of "useful knowledge." But perhaps because of the very massiveness, as well as the comparative novelty, of what we owe to and expect from the applied sciences, we are all of us today liable to neglect other forms of useful knowledge: and to neglect them to our peril. Historical understanding, I shall now argue, can be of use to us, and needs must be used by us, in a variety of ways that are of the first importance to any form of civilised life.

In the first place, historical understanding can teach us, especially with regard to the institutional sides of life, what we are or where we stand in the light of where we have come from; more particularly understanding of what we are in the light of whence we have come can explain why there are certain things which we *cannot* do, let the future develop as it may. Secondly, historical understanding can assist us, somewhat in the manner of practice for games of skill, not indeed to foresee and forestall the difficulties that will face us, but to meet and cope with them, whatever forms they may take, with a kind of confidence, a kind of necessary carefreeness, such as no degree of scientific preparation can provide. Thirdly (and this will no doubt cause some eyebrows to rise) historical understanding can help us to see and can give us justifiable assurance regarding, not simply what we can or cannot do, but about what we ought to do or must never do in many important kinds of moral situation.

With regard to the first of these claims, that to understand any institution or practice or doctrine it is necessary to know something of how it came to be, it will be useful to glance for a moment at *its* history, at how it has come to be in the very uncertain, ill-defined and rather neglected condition in which we find it today. There are a few suggestive adumbrations of it in Plato, but it is nowhere seriously developed in the thought either of the ancient world or of the renaissance. But early in the eighteenth century it found in Vico its first and still in many ways its incomparable prophet, and in the 1760s it found in Justus Möser its first fully conscious and disciplined exponent. Thereafter it imposed itself rapidly on almost all forms of social thought — legal, political, economic (at least in Germany) and educational — although, curiously enough, despite the efforts of Hegel, it had very little effect on the practice of philosophy; at the same time, it was responsible for that most unphilosophical and unnatural of intellectual abortions *Naturphilosophie*. By the mid-nineteenth century it had become virtually a canon of intellectual orthodoxy: Renan's *The Future of Science* is a prolonged hymn to the historical method; Comte's *Positivist Philosophy* is almost a paradigm of what is today commonly meant by historicism; while Marx's social thinking is quite as much an historical interpretation of economics as an economic interpretation of history. Perhaps this genetic approach (as it came to be called) to all human institutions and conditions reached its apogee in the teachings of Freud; but thereafter, especially in

Anglo-Saxon philosophical circles, a definite reaction against it set in. Here is a good representative statement of the "anti-genetic" attitude – of the attitude which repudiates the claim that we are discussing – written with Freudian teachings particularly in mind. It comes from the introduction to C. D. Broad's *The Mind and its Place in Nature.*

> We are all extremely liable to confuse a history of the becoming of a thing with an analysis of the thing as it has become. Because C *arose out of* B, and B out of A, people are inclined to think that C is *nothing but A in a disguised form.* Thus, suppose we could show that action from a sense of duty developed out of action from fear of public opinion, that this developed out of action from fear of the ghosts of dead ancestors, and that this developed out of action from fear of living chiefs . . . . We should be very liable to think that we had *analysed* the sense of duty as it now exists, and proved that it is just a disguised form of fear of punishment by tribal chiefs. This would be simply a gross mistake. To analyse anything you must examine and reflect upon *it;* and the most elaborate account of what preceded it in the course of history is no substitute for this. At the best a study of the history of a thing may make you look for factors in the thing which you might otherwise have missed. But, on the other hand . . . it is just as likely to make you turn a blind eye to factors in it which were not present in the earlier stages.

At first sight it seems impossible to disagree with anything that Broad says here; and yet, on careful reflection, we can see that his criticism is pertinent only to the most grossly exaggerated examples of the genetic approach. Everyone will agree that to understand a thing you must reflect about *it:* but what is in question is whether such understanding is possible, with regard to any human institution or condition unless some account is taken of how it came to be the way it is – and when and where and how it is. To distinguish *analysis* from *history* as Broad does is simply to remind us that we have two words for two kinds of description or understanding, and to suggest – as yet without any show of proof – that these words stand for altogether different operations, the first of which can proceed adequately in all cases without any assistance from the second. But this is exactly what is in question. Do things – in particular do human institutions, practices, beliefs, creeds, etc. – always lie entirely open to our analytic inspection, revealing all that they are in a single instant, provided that our analytic inspection is powerful enough? Are not institutions, for example, constantly being adapted, so that their identity can hardly be of a simple, directly recognisable kind? Quite often considerable historical study, not to mention great intellectual perceptiveness, is called for before we can establish the identity, or the continuity through remarkable developments, of an institution – or a practice, or a belief, or a creed, or even the meaning of a word. And yet once such an identity or continuity of development has been uncovered, we may be absolutely certain about it: what has been disclosed is so unmistakable that it can be accepted as part of the definition or analysis of the institution in question.

A second latent weakness in Broad's argument is this. In his final sentence he seems to be mixing up a question of intellectual principle (which is here our only concern) with one of prudence in intellectual practice. It is true that we sometimes possess some knowledge of an institution's present condition whilst we as yet know almost nothing of how it came to be in that condition. In cases of this kind it would clearly be absurd to attempt to interpret or explain the former knowledge by the latter ignorance. But what should be considered, with regard to the question of principle, is a case in which we have valuable but imperfect knowledge of a thing's present condition and considerable although no doubt still more imperfect knowledge of its recent development into that condition. And the question to be decided is whether in this kind of case the genetic approach has something of quite special value to contribute to our understanding of the thing's present character and behaviour. More particularly we ought to ask: What sorts of insight, what sorts of otherwise neglected truths about human actions and institutions, can an historical or genetic approach, and only such an approach, provide? What are the kinds of factor which, unless picked out and appreciated in their historical development, are liable to be misjudged or ignored in any direct functional analysis of an actually existing situation? These questions are of crucial importance for the critical philosophy of history: but to date they have never received the attention that they deserve, either from the enthusiastic nineteenth century advocates, or from the somewhat panicky twentieth century detractors, of the genetic approach to human affairs. In the rest of this chapter I shall try to sketch out the broad lines of an answer to them, chiefly in terms of some familiar although all too easily neglected features and problems of political life.

First, then, the historical approach often helps us to see the importance of features of an institution which at first sight seems unjustifiable or arbitrary, since (apparently) they in no way help to fulfil the institution's most obvious functions or purposes. Nevertheless such factors may be among the necessary conditions of the institution's survival or efficiency. They may even — paradoxical though this at first sounds — express the very quick of its existence; that which not only keeps it in being but contains the seeds of its main future developments; that which will be remembered and cherished long after its currently accepted functions and purposes have become outmoded or forgotten.

Thus, for example, every political movement or party embodies, in addition to its official platform and its plans for legislative reforms, a number of vague, emotionally charged reminders of the past from which it has sprung. These may take the form of styles of address, the repetition of slogans and sacred names, ceremonies of remembrance, badges, banners, marching songs — all of which serve as cues for articulate or silent mass affirmations of loyalty and cohesion. The origin of such emotional cues may be remote or forgotten or fantastically misunderstood; or they may enshrine and echo personalities and incidents whose relevance to the practical issues of the day seems almost nil. Hence to practical forward-looking men the retention of these emotional cues may seem to be not simply useless but positively embarrassing and frustrating — it may seem describable only in pathological terms, as the expression of childishly wishful fantasies, or of unacknowledged aggressivenesses and phobias, or at best of ossified survivals from a more ignorant age. But the aptness of such descriptions does not mean that the emotional cues so described can be easily dispensed with. They may be essential to the party's continued existence as a reliable, recognisable unity. For, broadly speaking, every human association is formed to meet some particular need or danger or opportunity; and if it is really successful in uniting men for this first purpose, it will tend to be kept in being and made use of for other related purposes. Again, very broadly speaking, the greater the number of different purposes that a particular association can be used to serve the greater its chances of persistence, despite inward strains and anomalies and contradictions. It would therefore be the height of folly to regard all seemingly arbitrary features of a political movement or institution as negligible. They are there: and they cannot be ignored or disowned or flouted or sneered out of existence. Of course, it may always be possible — indeed, it is often a crucial task of statesmanship — to develop them, to canalise or direct them, to utilise them (or their names) for very strange purposes. But before any of these things can be done, such seemingly arbitrary features need to be understood: in particular the ways in which they have become interwoven with other aspects of the movement need to be understood. And it is difficult to see how such understanding is to be had, except by an historical appreciation of how the movement has developed, and by assessing, in the light of that development, the different relations of its many different strands. Such an appreciation will commonly show that the apparently arbitrary survival of some emblem or dogma from long ago in fact points back to some choice or alignment which was quite essential to the accepted orientation of today's rational and practical policies.

A closely similar point can be made from the other side, i.e., in terms not of popular acceptance and support of a particular institution or movement, but of its first, and subsequently, legendary founders or leaders. Admittedly, every political movement starts from some widely recognised danger or opportunity: but precisely which individual, of all the many individuals who might well give the new movement leadership and direction, will in fact be there and available, on the spot and with exactly the right status and record to meet the call of the hour — this is indeed almost entirely a matter of chance. But, on the other hand, once a first leader is recognised: once the movement has begun to develop under his hand and under his name, to be symbolised by his face or voice or known character and way of life, then commonly it will begin to take on features and qualities which had no necessary connection with the danger or opportunity which first brought it into being. Such personally attributable features, it might be thought, must be superficial and quickly lost and forgotten. But to assume this is to give way to a culpably shallow rationalism. The capacity of mankind, in its political actions, to make legends out of its leaders is a factor of immense historic importance. To admit this is not to subscribe to the foolish doctrine that great men make or determine the histories of the movements they initiate or the nations they lead. Every important chapter in human history is, of course, made by successive generations of men in their thousands or millions. But very commonly in making such a chapter together, and in order that they shall succeed in making it together, men must imprint upon it the image, complete with some arbitrary as well as with politically requisite features, of its first spokesman or protagonist or guide.

Besides helping us to see what we can and what we cannot do with our institutions in view of the ways they have come to be what they are, I believe that a study of their history can assist us in a more direct and positive fashion towards a wise use of them. Not, to be sure, by enabling us to foresee the dangers or difficulties with which our institutions may in future be faced, but rather — paradoxical although this again may sound — by preparing us to maintain and adapt them in the face of changes that are entirely unpredictable. History reveals on its every page the importance of contingencies — accidents, coincidences or other unforeseeable developments — in every human enterprise, relationship and institution: it would therefore be utterly illogical to expect it to aid us in anticipating and forestalling specifically predicted developments. Nevertheless, in spite of the seeming paradox, it can and does assist us to achieve a "masterful manipulation of the unforeseen."

As a rough analogy, to indicate how this can be, I would cite the use of practice in games of skill. To some extent, of course, practice is preparation for broadly predictable situations: it includes the building up of habitual moves and responses which are appropriate to recurrent features or moments of the game. But practice is something much more than this, especially for a player of some skill. Its chief purpose is to get the player into a state of general preparedness — of "form" as we say — which means an all-around readiness, quickness and flexibility of responses which enable him to introduce or combine moves or strokes or feints or what not as occasions demand, and such as he has never tried out before: to prepare him, in a word, so far as this is possible, for *whatever* shall happen. Now the oddness of such practice — and of its effectiveness — deserves far more serious consideration than it has hitherto received from either philosophers or psychologists. Here it will be sufficient to make good its reality by pointing to two of its principles or quasi-principles,[1] which to date have remained nameless, but with which we are all perfectly familiar.

The first of these I shall call the principle of the reserve: the second, which looks, at first glance, the direct opposite of the first, I call the all-or-nothing principle. History affords us innumerable examples of both: indeed, to follow and to appreciate an instance of either principle is to enjoy one of the keenest and most characteristic pleasures that historical study can afford.

First, then, the principle of the reserve. When faced with any task, problem or impasse, we must be prepared for the possibility that the best, the most rationally and scientifically laid plans that we can contrive may go awry. We should therefore, if possible, retain the means and materials — or at the very least keep in mind the possibility — of other methods of pursuing our aim: methods that may be less convenient or less desirable, rougher or costlier, and whose working out we may have only vaguely envisaged. But, whatever their drawbacks, we must have them to hand, to avoid being guilty of that worst of practical shortcomings, being found entirely unequal to the event, being found entirely resourceless before the situation — no matter how freakishly fortuitous — that actually faces us. It is as a safeguard against such a contingency, which always threatens those who put their faith in some theoretically water-tight project, some prediction of how things are bound to turn out, that the principle of reserve is of such great practical value.

It is worth noting that, although this principle is most obviously pertinent to the conduct of public affairs, it has some perfectly good analogues among maxims or considerations which apply to the most personal and private sides of our lives: for example, that we must work, but without allowing ourselves to be entirely used up by our work; that while we should give all that we have to give in many of our personal relationships, we should never, so to speak, identify our lives with a relationship of any one particular kind; and that we should always keep something of our own — despite the principle of frankness and self-giving to others — that we "scarcely tell to ony." Quasi-principles of this kind are most easily stated in negative form: they are essentially vague, and it is inconceivable that we should ever be offered statements of the sufficient conditions of their just or appropriate employment. They have to be discerned and recognised through successive

---

1. I say principles *or quasi-principles* because, of course, there is something strange about an alleged principle which is concerned, not with such and such a kind of case or situation, but expressly with those particular situations which escape the net of our usual classificatory and predictive systems.

examples. Our endeavour to master and apply them is the very antithesis of any habitual or automatic application of a rule. Yet by means of the examples which histories afford, we certainly can create and constantly improve our capacity for dealing with tomorrow's contingencies when they arrive.

The all-or-nothing principle seems, at first, to make altogether contrary demands upon us. It rests upon recognising that, in certain extreme situations, it is necessary to put all one's fortune on a single cast, to dare to put it to the touch to win or lose it all. But how can such heroic recognition be squared with the cautious, the realistically adaptive, the sometimes (inevitably) opportunist spirit of the man who works on the principle of the reserve? This seeming contradiction can be removed, however, if we recall the special character of the two principles — they are expressly intended to deal with the contingent aspect of experience — and if we contrast them, in this respect, with other empirically grounded rules of prudence. The latter, which we find embodied in countless proverbs, maxims, practical tips, etc., are propounded as rules known to be true on the whole, or in the great number of usual or normal or standard cases, if not of this particular case; they are known to be true in the long run even if acceptance of them should prove disappointing in the short run in which we are actually engaged. But practical decision, although it will normally base itself on such generally true maxims, has also its own natural anxiety over the particular case with which it is currently engaged. To the man of action there come moments when the long run and the majority of cases begin to mean nothing, when his whole concern is with this particular case which is proving itself an obvious deviant, a twister, a freak, and upon whose outcome, good or ill, his whole future, his life, the cause he lives for, may depend.

This kind of situation might be illustrated by that of a skilled and usually reliable and indeed conventional card player who for some personal reason must win a particular game, irrespective of distressing his partner, violating the usual conventions, etc., and equally irrespective of the extent of his loss if he loses. We may assume that he will begin play in quite orthodox fashion, e.g., in conformity with his bids if the game is bridge. But after a very few rounds it may be clear that orthodox play, although it may here as always minimise losses, is not going to guarantee victory. What, then, is to be done? If our player has the lead, we can imagine him proceeding to open up the game in a new and quite surprising way, in view of his earlier leads. And should this tactic disappoint, he may change yet again, despite raised eyebrows from partner or opponents. The unorthodoxy of his procedure, his offence against the conventions, may, however, be entirely justified in view of his own peculiar aim. Alternatively, we might imagine him staking all upon one enormous bluff at the outset; a bluff which might well cost him almost every trick in the game, but from which there is a real chance of attaining the narrow victory that he requires. On the former supposition he exemplifies the principle of the reserve; on the latter he exemplifies the all-or-nothing principle. Use of the former principle depends upon the ability to judge, in terms of one particular situation, the relative values of a number of approaches all of which are no doubt theoretically commendable: the latter depends upon the ability to see where the one small chance lies in a complex situation, and upon the ability, which Cardinal de Retz took to be the hallmark of practical genius, to distinguish the chance that is extraordinary from the chance that is truly impossible.

Now it requires no further arguing, I think, to derive from this description the conclusion which history is continually illustrating, although a too narrow logic may dislike it: namely that every successful man of action brings with him a mastery of both the above principles, and an almost instinctive skill in applying them, to any complex and serious situation.

Finally I want to suggest that historical understanding can often help us to decide which courses of action we are morally obliged to follow and which we are obliged to shun. This assistance is particularly important for those moral choices and resolves that arise because of our involvement in institutions, or our adherence to some important movement or cause: in a word, to the institutional side of morality, which contemporary moralists tend either to neglect or else to treat in the most perfunctory and hackneyed manner.

My claim in this connection can be introduced by recalling that we can hardly hope to man or serve an institution worthily unless we believe in it. Now, what does believing in an institution amount to? Not necessarily to believing that it has a future or that the future is with it; but rather that it deserves to have a future, that it has potential life in it and therefore might well have a great future if only we and others give it the support, and apply to it the energy and the intelligence, that it requires and deserves. But how, it may be asked, can historical understanding contribute to such positive, practical beliefs?

Certainly historical understanding will not suffice to ensure loyal support, intelligent service, faithful defence or careful development of any institution or cause. Nor, perhaps, in strictness, is it a logically necessary condition of such service, which conceivably might be given by some simple soul who had virtually no historical understanding of the institution that he was serving. For ultimately, it might be argued, loyal adherence to any institution or cause must be based upon some intuition or revelation of its worth, some direct and original appeal which it exercises upon the practical and imaginative sides of our natures. I am not myself altogether happy with this view, but for the argument's sake let us accept it. But now it must be admitted that the kinds of intuition or revelation that are here alleged, are notoriously — and indeed sometimes cruelly and even hideously — fallible. How, then, are they to be tested and secured? Not simply by a consideration or calculation of the foreseeable consequences of the actions and attachments which they commend; for some of these consequences will themselves have to be judged by the way they will play back upon and affect the future of the institution or cause whose value — or the rightness of our adherence to which — is the very thing that we are trying to confirm. Moreover, there are notorious practical difficulties in the way of such calculations of foreseeable consequences, unless made on the broadest and crudest scales. But by what other means can our moral intuitions and revelations be tested or confirmed? It is here, I believe, that historical understanding can make its contribution.

This can best be explained by an example. Suppose one had had the extraordinarily good fortune to be one of the original disciples of Socrates, considered as the first exemplar of the spirit of free criticism deployed to vindicate the autonomy of morals; or of Galileo, conceived as the first clear exemplar of the true method of hypothesis and experiment in physical inquiry. If one had had a modicum of intelligence, one could not but have recognised in either case something of immense importance, something most certainly with life in it and deserving a future. One would certainly have believed *in* what one heard and saw; and one might well have been fired to devote one's life and energies to furthering the aims and methods which either of these intellectual masters had begun, however laboriously and imperfectly, to disclose. Yet, in attempting this task, one would almost inevitably have run into innumerable and enormous difficulties: difficulties of a kind that would not simply have brought progress quickly to a halt, but would have made one feel entirely at a loss, in doubt, and intellectually and morally forlorn. What light, what guidance, one might well then ask, could the first fragmentary findings of either master afford to us when faced with *this* incomparably more complicated problem? How would *he* have envisaged the difficulties of applying here the method which seemed to him so lucidly inevitable in the first chosen simple cases?

But now, contrast this imaginary situation with that which we, in fact, enjoy: we who can look back across centuries of the continuing struggle for freedom of thought, containing so many noble reaffirmations of the autonomy of morals, or at the astonishing developments and successes of the method first descried by the genius of Galileo. Is it not far easier for us to see what Socrates and Galileo were respectively about than it was for the first of their disciples? Looking back along the line of development that stems from either name, surely it is now far easier for us to know what we mean by the spirit of free criticism or by the method of ideal and real experiment. And is it not now, correspondingly, far easier for us to know what it is that we believe *in* when we say that we believe in the spirit of free criticism or in the spirit of experimental inquiry? I do not say that our beliefs in these excellent things are necessarily stronger or more effective in producing appropriate attitudes and actions, or that they are more trustworthy, more deserving of faith and hope, than were the original beliefs first fired by the examples of Socrates and Galileo. What I claim is that any such belief, when it has been to some extent articulated through the history of its vicissitudes and revivals, its unexpected implications, its revolutionary extensions and triumphant reaffir- mations, has one immense advantage over any direct, original acceptance of it — no matter how powerful, how penetrating, how full of prophetic promise the original apprehension and acceptance of that belief may have been. When our beliefs have been to some extent historically articulated we are in a very much better position to *describe* them, to indicate the differences — perhaps the many ranges of differences — that an acceptance of them makes to the rest of our conduct or view of the world. We are thus not only better equipped to defend the institutions and causes we believe in against polemical attacks, we are also in a better position to defend and discuss and reaffirm them *to ourselves,* to our critical perplexed selves, in moments — or decades or centuries — of difficulty, doubt, and discouragement. In a word, it is often easier for us to act rightly because we have historical understanding to help us; or, conversely, historically understanding can sometimes help us to decide what we ought to do and to do it.

I do not think it is necessary to pursue this argument beyond the example I have given. Certainly it is a form of argument that might admit of grave abuse, since it presupposes that we can distinguish those traditions which embody and develop an idea of unquestionable value, from those which may simply express some deep-seated and perhaps evil tendency in human nature. But despite this possible danger there can be no question in my mind, of the moral illumination which historical understanding can sometimes provide.

THE LAW AND THE SCHOOLS

Paul A. Freund

If you were to look at a book on law and the schools, the chances are that you would find a discussion of the contract rights of teachers, tax exemption of school property, disciplinary powers over pupils, and similar issues on which lawyers might give advice to school administrators. Law, that is, comes in from the outside, and is to be left, a useful but esoteric art, in the hands of the professionals. It is as if science were relevant to the schools only as the basis for the design of buildings, or government only as the source of administrative regulations. The root cause of this comparative neglect of law as an appropriate subject for general education is, I believe, that law is regarded as a system of rules to be mastered by those self-doomed to work with them, and not, like science or government, as an enterprise, an ongoing process, whose study contributes to an enlarged understanding of, and participation in, the world around us.

In the colleges, to be sure, law as a subject of undergraduate study is receiving increasing attention. Surprisingly, perhaps, the most heavily subscribed kind of undergraduate course in law is that in business law. The older and still prevalent form of such a course is one devoted to rules: the requirements of valid contract, the liability of the various signers of a check, and the like — a how-to-keep-the-lawyer-away, or what-to-do-till-the-lawyer-comes sort of exposition. Happily, there is growing dissatisfaction with this conception of legal study, and the younger generation of business law teachers is striving to give the subject the intellectual content and stimulus that would warrant its place in a university curriculum.

In liberal arts programs, a variety of approaches is taken, often conditioned by the departmental niche to which the course is allotted and by the general orientation of the department itself. Law in Society is a familiar offering in sociology. It has the virtues and the hazards of any such overview. It has the virtue of seeing law as more than simply a system of punishments designed to keep order in society. Rather, it shows law to be a system that facilitates organization, association, transactions; that resolves conflicts or deliberately leaves a certain amount of friction; that operates as an

From *Harvard Educational Review*, Vol. *36,* No. 4 (Fall, 1966), pp. 470–476. Reprinted by permission of the author and the *Harvard Educational Review.*

educational force; and that can yet be dysfunctional in some of its operations. The hazard of the course is that any attempt at a systematic, functional analysis may compress too much into too few or too general categories and may, as in anthropology, require more refined differentiations. A political science oriented approach can take a variety of forms. Law may be brought within the fold, domesticated and subdued, as it were, by the pressure group theorist who assimilates the judicial process to the legislative; or it might be captured by the operations analyst who equates understanding with predictive power and so, programming judicial decisions, gets out of a computer, as from a major premise, all that was put into it, elaborating the obvious by methods that are obscure. These are caricatures, of course, though it is hard to avoid the impression that the work of some of the grimmer practitioners of behavioralism is a caricature of itself. There are partial insights to be gained from all these approaches, and from others; what is intolerable is the claim of any of them to constitute the one true faith, the only road to intellectual salvation. Their tactical legitimacy may well depend on the polemic context in which they are employed: whether to insist that a pitcher is half full or half empty may turn on whether you are combating the illusion that it is completely empty or completely full.

Aside from these rather special approaches, there is a view of law from the inside of the process that seems to me highly fruitful for general education, whether at the university or the school level. What I have in mind is more than a view: it is a vicarious participation in the process of legal thinking through immersion in some of the problems and the literature of the common law.

There is probably no more systematic literature of justification than the reports of decided cases extending back for several hundred years, with conflicting claims and interests laid bare and judgments rendered in the light of reasoned opinions and dissenting opinions, taking account in varying measure of precedent, analogy, logic, history, custom, morality, and social utility. For educational purposes the problem is to extract from this abundant quarry a set of materials that will be intrinsically interesting and comprehensible to particular age groups, that will link themselves to the students' own range of experience and observation. The problem is not as formidable as it may seem, inasmuch as the stuff of law can be related to such normal experiences of school children as association in clubs, disciplinary proceedings, engaging in simple commercial transactions at the neighborhood shops, and reading facts, opinions, gossip, and untruths in newspapers. The art is to hold the legal materials in a double focus: to see them as significant for their own sake, developments in the rationalizing of certain areas of human experience, and also as exemplifications of the rational process itself, with a wider significance for the developing intellectual style (to use a too pretentious phrase) of the student.

Let me try to be more concrete, setting out in summary form certain modes of thought that are almost inescapably called for in legal reasoning, together with sectors of the law that might appropriately evoke these responses.

1. Dialectical thinking

There is a built-in dialectic in law, not merely because of the adversary procedure in litigation but because of the nature of the issues. When Justice Holmes would jauntily enter his study, fling his hat on the rack, and turn to his law clerk with the challenge, "State any proposition and I'll deny it," he was embodying the spirit of the common law, the rubbing of blade against blade in the scissors of the mind, making a truer and finer line. When Columbia University, a decade ago, celebrated its bicentennial, the theme of the celebration was "The Right to Knowledge and the Free Use Thereof." It is a noble theme, but one that challenges the legal mind to produce countervailing nobilities. Does it matter how the knowledge is acquired, whether by resort to eavesdropping or unauthorized search and seizure of private papers? Does it matter how the knowledge is used, whether by plagiarism or indiscriminate tale tattling? The legal problems of illegal search and seizure and interference with a right of privacy call for accommodations of a sensitive sort; these are richly documented in the literature and hardly beyond the appreciation of the schoolboy.

In this connection, it seems to me that courses in the Bill of Rights, admirable as they are in intent, lose much of their value unless they are conceived in a dialectical way. Granted that it is important to know about the guarantee of a fair trial under the Fifth Amendment and the guarantee of a free press under the First. What is more important is to see the two in confrontation, in the context of the problem of press coverage of pretrial investigations and trial reporting, and to try to resolve the clash by more refined principles than either of them alone. It is important pragmatically if we are to learn to mute the clangor of clashing isms; it is important for learning because we do not really "know" a principle until we know its opposing principles and reshape them all in the process. Better that students be encouraged to feel this implicitly, kinesthetically, than that they be taught from outside, as it were, the theories of scholasticism, Hegelianism, or Morris R. Cohen's principle of polarity.

2. Contextual thinking

Questions like "What caused the Civil War?" are a staple of the schools. Would it be thought an impertinence if a student, before responding further, were to put a question of his own: "What exactly do you mean by 'caused'?" or "Why should we want an answer to that question?" This kind of response, pertinent or impertinent, is endemic in legal analysis. Consider, for example, the problem of legal cause in the law of torts. If a child is drowning offshore while two observers watch passively on the beach, one the child's nursemaid and the other a stranger, has either "caused" the child's death? If an intoxicated man, having been served by a too compliant bartender, playfully slaps the head of a companion who has an abnormally thin skill, who or what caused the resulting injury to the victim? It will surely be evident that to answer the question some decision on the purpose of the inquiry will have to be taken. The question may be asked of a lawyer, a moralist, a sociologist, or a physician, and the answer may vary accordingly. Was the question asked to assess legal liability, to affix moral blame, to promote understanding of human actions, or to aid in taking corrective or preventive measures? In the process, such concepts as concurrent cause, proximate cause, cause versus condition, and purposive identification of cause will have emerged without their formidable labels. Ideally, a discussion of this kind could end with this interchange between teacher and student: "Have you ever heard of Mill's theory of cause in history?" "No, sir." "Well, you've just discovered it."

3. Ethical thinking

The concept of commutative justice is central to much of our treatment of social issues. It is also central to that great corpus known as the law of contracts, which deals essentially with the making, keeping, and breaking of promises. What kinds of promises should be binding and what not binding? What circumstances should qualify as excuses for non-performance? What remedies should be available in case of breach? — these are the major classes of issues raised in this branch of the law. In considering them, the student will have to consider questions of public policy regarding illegal or odious undertakings, the extent to which supervening unforeseen events ought to release one from an undertaking, and the rationale of enforcing promises at all, as reflected in the law of damages — whether it be based on the reliance by the promisee upon the expected benefits that performance by the promisor would bring him, or on the promisor's having received a *quid pro quo* for his promise. The meaning of just expectations, on which the social order ultimately rests, can here be explored in considerable depth, without ranging beyond the students' personal field of reference.

4. Genetic thinking

The responsiveness of the social organization to changes in modes of production, distribution, and labor is a recurring theme in social studies. The pace, the pains, and the progress in this adaptive process are documented in quite human terms in the law reports. The subject of industrial accidents is a notable example, moving from the plight of the injured worker whose claim would be defeated by the employer's defense — either of the worker's contributory negligence, his assumption of the risk of the job, or the causative conduct of a fellow-employee – through the abolition of these defenses by legislation, to the provision for workmen's compensation as a cost of the business irrespective of the negligence of employer or employee. A comparable evolution emerges from a study of the manufacturer's liability for defective products in the hands of the consumer, a progression that eventually enabled the consumer to sue the remote manufacturer and that has tended to supplant the criterion of proof of negligent manufacture with an implied absolute warranty on the manufacturer's part. These responses to changing patterns of industrial and commercial life give point to the remark of the late Professor Hocking, the Harvard philosopher, that to teach social studies without law is like teaching vertebrate anatomy without the backbone.

5. Associative thinking

Movement occurs not only through organic institutional changes but through the adaptive and assimilative processes of the mind. We live by metaphor; we advance by simile; we rise by concepts. The legal right of privacy is a fairly recent notion, which can be traced, in one sense, from protection against eavesdropping (itself a metaphor), through offensive shadowing (a metaphor but also "like eavesdropping"), to the gossip sheet and unauthorized use of name or photograph (the general concept of privacy). Related to this process is the human addiction to fictions, to thinking "as if" one thing were another, an addiction particularly strong, no doubt too strong, in the law. Legal fictions (the "white lies of the law," von Jhering called them) can be looked at in many ways, but for purposes of comparing them with fictions elsewhere two categories suggest themselves: (a) normative fictions, like models or ideal types: the "reasonable man," or "everyone is presumed to know the law"; (b) categorizing fictions, whereby the new is assimilated to the familiar, the tribute that change pays to continuity – for example, the protection of interests of personality, such as privacy, as if they were "property rights," and the treatment of corporations as if they were legal "persons."

The conspicuousness of fictions in the law may serve to point to their prevalence in other more respectable disciplines – political science or economics or the natural sciences – and to suggest their uses and abuses and their relation to hypotheses and myths.

6. Institutional thinking

Perhaps the most distinctive feature of a legal system is the central position of a procedural framework, with specialized organs and ways of operation, underscoring the interrelation of ends and means. The amenability of a given problem to resolution by codified rules, or by generalized principles and *ad hoc* decision, or by unstructured nonlegal methods, is an inquiry that serves to sharpen an understanding of the problem itself. Given an apparent agreement in the abstract on an issue, say, of mercy killing or the right of privacy, the effort to put the agreement into an institutional form with attention to who decides disputes, by what procedures, under what standards, with what sanctions, may uncover some latent differences and some consequent reshaping of the ends themselves. The effort may, at the same time, suggest some ways of resolving or bypassing initial differences through agreement on procedures. A simple exercise in negotiating and drafting an uncomplicated contract can prove illuminating for an understanding of international disputes and constitution making.

7. Self-critical thinking

Occasions arise when old doctrine has been so radically reinterpreted, when fictions have become so attenuated, that an abandonment of the old in favor of a fresh formulation seems inescapable. The phenomenon of judicial overrulings is familiar enough and is almost always accompanied by a reasoned articulation. The factors that lead judges to reach such conclusions are not very different, *mutatis mutandis,* from those that lead theoretical scientists to opt, at a certain point, for change over continuity. Every experiment, we are told, implicates in principle not only the postulate under investigation but the whole system of postulates of which this one is a part; and so it is with the novel case in law. The decision whether to continue the process of assimilation and adjustment or to abandon antecedent positions is in either field a quasi-ethical judgment. The elements that ought to enter into such a choice can be analyzed in notable episodes of the judicial, no less than the scientific, process.

If these seven intellectual traits, or some of them, seem worthy of more deliberate cultivation in the schools, and if the law appears to offer some particularly apt opportunities in this direction, the mechanics of the educational enterprise (the preparation of teachers, the assembling of materials and their sequential use) can be explored by teachers and lawyers together. I should confess, finally, that this essay, like the approaches to which I alluded at the outset, should be taken in a polemic context: that the cardinal sin of our classrooms is one-dimensional thinking, all warp and no woof, making for glibness of mind that knows the answers without really knowing the questions. It is the cardinal sin, I would maintain, because it characterizes some of the most academically successful products of the system. What I have tried to suggest is essentially an antidote to glibness that can be ingested without tears.

ON THE ROLE OF CHOICE
IN AESTHETIC EDUCATION

Walter H. Clark, Jr.

The simplest statement of the goal of moral education is that it wants to turn out good *choosers*; people who will choose good and choose well. One wonders whether a similar simplification will do for aesthetic education. Should such education aim for the inculcation of taste? Is the successful teacher one whose students not only discriminate between good and bad works of art, but also consistently *choose* the good or better works of art? Such questions have a disingenuous sound. Sensing their aura of superficial right thinking, we suspect that the most essential commerce with art must lie somewhere east of discrimination. Nevertheless, the fact that we do admit some virtue to these questions suggests that choice must have at least a subsidiary role to play in what it is that we do with works of art. I shall try to establish the role of choice in the realm of aesthetics because I believe that showing what can be expected of it and what cannot must inevitably suggest avenues along which we may make a freer and more natural approach to the teaching of art and appreciation.

I

For a start we should ask about choice itself. This is best done in terms of the verb, since it is the relation between the doer and the thing done which occupies the attention of the moralist. What is it 'to choose'? First and most obviously we can say that to choose is to do something, less obviously, to do anything in the appropriate context. Second, we can say that alternative is joined to choice with hoops of steel. Where there is choosing, alternatives must exist. Where there is no alternative, there can be no choice. Third, we should note with Webster that, in contrast to a synonym such as 'prefer,' "choose implies a decision of the judgment." To choose, thus, is to do something for which we can give reasons. It is also, in the case of moral choices, and some others as well, an action resting on principle.

We shall have to dive more deeply into these three aspects of the

From *The Journal of Aesthetic Education*, Vol. *II*, No. 3 (July, 1968), pp. 79-91. Reprinted by permission of the author and *The Journal of Aesthetic Education*.

definition. 'To choose' is fascinating in its own right and may lead us away from the more basic reason for pursuing it, namely, the wish to establish its place in the realm of the aesthetic. The writer will try to check such inclinations in himself, and hopes that the reader will look forward to the ultimate uses which can be made of the distinctions that follow.

To choose is to do. How can it be contrasted to other doings, and what does it have in common with them? In the first place there belongs to it no identifying behavior. We can talk of someone running, walking, swinging his arms. Each of these calls to mind a picture of the doer engaged in the act. But if you tell me that a man in the next room is choosing I am no wiser as to the movements of his body. Does this mean that choice does not involve behavior? In most cases choice does indeed involve behavior. But a particular behavior (pointing, for example; saying "I'll have *that* one."), if it is to constitute choosing, must occur within the appropriate context. Part of the purpose of this extended definition is to indicate some conditions governing the contexts within which we choose. At present I simply wish to differentiate kinds of action (running, walking, arm swinging) which are relatively context free, from choosing, which has in common with breaking laws, hitting home runs, and a great many other "actions" considerable dependence on context. (Hitting a home run does not just consist in hitting a ball over a fence; it must be a certain kind of ball, over a certain fence, on a particular kind of field: the elaborate rules of baseball must be satisfied.) To point, to say, "I'll have *that* one," is not in itself to make a choice.

What of choices that do not involve behavior? The immobile batsman chooses to take a strike. Obedience to the Decalogue shows itself in terms of what we do not do. This raises the question, "When is a not doing a doing?" to which the answer suggests itself, "When it is deliberate." Behavior, clearly, is not a satisfactory criterion for choice. Deliberate action, or restraint from action, on the other hand, would seem to be involved in every case where choices are made. May I urge this upon the reader as one provisional criterion of choice. It helps, for example, in distinguishing the verb 'to choose' from a broad range of verbs such as 'to stroll' or 'to blink one's eye' which name things we sometimes do deliberately and sometimes do not.

There is one more question to ask about choosing as doing before going on to consider other aspects of its definition. I have already said that choice sometimes manifests itself in terms of the chooser's deliberate abstention from external behavior. This prompts a related question. Is choosing something we do, or can do, in our heads? Is it correct to say, for example, "I have chosen my car for next spring — but I shan't buy it until then?" If it is proper to speak in this way, then perhaps choosing is one kind of doing which precedes another kind of doing (buying the car), that of putting the choice into execution. I should certainly not wish to maintain this latter view — though choosing can no doubt be done in one's head. The best way to get at this problem is in terms of a distinction between choosing and deciding. Is there a difference between choosing a course of action and deciding upon a course of action? I maintain that choosing a course of action implies embarking upon it (committing oneself to it absolutely), whereas deciding upon a course of action does not *per se* imply embarking upon it (in fact the implication generally is that the decider has *not* embarked upon the action). A decision having been made, we are safely out of doubt, but there is no guarantee that the matter will not be reopened. With choice, things have gotten beyond the matter of reopening. The ironbound earnest of this is adoption of the action under consideration. J. L. Austin in "A Plea for Excuses,"[1] distinguishes what he calls *stages* of an action. "We can dismantle the machinery of the act, and describe (and excuse) separately the intelligence, the appreciation, the planning, the decision, the execution and so forth." The emphasis in choice is upon what Austin calls the executive element. The question of whether choosing is something we do in our heads or outside them thus depends upon whether we are involved in mental or physical acts. The executive element of a physical act involves behavior. The executive element of a mental act need not. When I *choose* to think about one problem rather than another the choice consists just in thinking about the problem (in the context of choice). From this vantage point we can return to the example, "I have chosen my car for next spring – but I shan't buy it until then." What is happening here is that the speaker is treating the element of decision as if it were executive – and simultaneously downgrading the executive element as of relatively little importance. A story helps make the point clear. Imagine the speaker as an effete aristocrat with vast quantities of money, a P. G. Wodehouse character. The real work for him lies in determining upon which car. Once this is done it's as good as bought – literally. For this man choosing a car *is* head work rather than hand or bank book work. Of course one need not be an effete aristocrat to talk this way. It's a matter of how one slices one's action – which stage one wishes to emphasize. Vagaries of usage aside, I maintain that in its fundamental sense 'to choose' implies execution of a constitutive act.

Another aspect of choosing concerns alternative. The obvious but significant point to make is that where there are no alternatives there can be no choice. The thing done, the execution, requires the existence of the thing not done. The sheer beauty of this formulation dims somewhat when we reflect that, from a logical point of view, *any* doing has alternatives, if only the minimal one of not doing. Therefore we amend this criterion to read that not only must there be alternatives, but the chooser must be aware of them as alternatives. Where the agent is ignorant of alternatives it would not be correct to say that he has been choosing (though we might indeed want to say

1. J. L. Austin, "A Plea for Excuses," *Philosophical Papers,* ed. J. O. Urmson and G. J. Warnock (Oxford, Eng.: Oxford Press, 1961), p. 149.

that a choice has been made). On the other hand we can conceive of a case where the agent thinks certain alternatives exist, though in point of fact they do not. His misconception leads him to describe his act as a choice, but the onlooker will not agree. From these examples we can see the importance of the dual criteria, (1) that the agent see himself as having alternatives[2] and (2) that what he *sees* as an alternative truly be one. The satisfaction of these two criteria is essential to the establishment of the context within which the doing 'to choose' takes place.

Judgment is the final aspect of choosing to be examined here. It is difficult to talk about, being more general and harder to pin down than aspects already dealt with. Yet it is important in that it distinguishes choice from other words that look much like it (for example, 'to prefer'). Perhaps the simplest way to start is to go back to the point that choice is deliberate. Judgment carries this qualification a step further. To choose is not only to do freely; it is furthermore to do something which the chooser can justify (or which others expect him to be able to justify). As Aristotle says, "Children and animals have a share in the voluntary, but not in choice. . . . For choice is not shared by irrational creatures."[3] When we say that an element of judgment is involved in making choices we mean that the chooser should be able to explain his doing. I do not wish to claim that wherever a choice has been made the chooser has consciously acted in accordance with the laws of reason. Further, one can certainly make a choice based on faulty reasoning. And still further, it appears conceivable that we might want to describe a particular act as "a choice" even though the agent might not be able to provide rational justification for the act. That is, we may feel that the agent *should* be able to offer a justification, though in fact he does not. This situation would be analagous to one in which there was disagreement between agent and onlooker as to whether the executive stage took place within a valid choosing context.

II

I should now like to see whether a place can be found for choice in art. Before retracing the steps of the previous section, however, there are a few words to say about doing and happening, and we should briefly recall John Dewey's triadic relationship. Dewey urges us to keep in mind the threefold entities of artist, work of art, and experiencer. It is to the relationship between artist and work on the one hand, experiencer and work on the other, that I shall particularly attend. Creating a work of art is primarily a matter of

2. What of a case where alternatives exist, but are not discernible as such — as in choosing (?) between identical objects? An interesting, but side, issue.
3. *Nicomachean Ethics,* II, 2.

doing. Experiencing a work of art, Dewey's own views to the contrary notwithstanding, is something that happens to us, just as a visual perception happens to us. This is not to deny that experience plays a role in creating a work of art, or (as Dewey points out) that an active element is involved in experience. It is to say that in creation the weight falls on doing; in experience of art the weight falls upon a certain kind of internal happening. This happening is what the experience of art is all about. It is what the work of art exists *for,* to provide us with a certain range of internal happenings collectively labeled "aesthetic experience." We may put ourselves in the way of experiences or encourage their advent by doing various things. But these doings subsist as means. The experience itself is the end. This pairing of creating-doing and experiencing-happening is important to keep in mind when we talk about art education. In teaching someone to create art (insofar as this notion makes sense) we are primarily concerned with what it is that he *does* (produces), including particularly those doings which fall in the context of choice. To paraphrase the opening remark, the teacher of artists wants to turn out people who will choose the combinations of elements which make good art and who will choose well.[4] The teacher of art appreciation, on the other hand, wants to turn out people to whom, aesthetically speaking, good things happen. It is perhaps not necessary to point out that the teacher who wishes to influence doings is somewhat more confined in his operations than the teacher of appreciation. If we want somebody to *do* something of his own free will we must be prepared to offer arguments that will secure his free assent.[5] If, on the other hand, we want to induce a certain kind of mental happening — want someone to see a reversing diagram in a particular way, for example — we may try to induce free assent ("See it as a duck.") or, contrariwise, we may simply place it in such a position that the student cannot help seeing it, and rely on the processes of the brain to do the rest. We might talk about ducks to him, or show him other pictures of ducks before showing him a diagram which we wish him to see in this way. In none of these cases, however, do we worry about securing his free assent and subsequent action.

The foregoing argument leads me to distinguish sharply between the education of artists and the education of experiencers. The former are to be exempted from further consideration herè. For one thing artists are few, experiencers many. There is a general suspicion, moreover, that artists are

4. Suppose, however, that there was a way of circumventing choice in the making of art; that artists could be taught to turn out good art without making choices. We would not object, would we? I suggest that the case would be quite other with respect to moral education.

5. While Pavlovian conditioning may have a role to play (for example, toilet training) in the education of a moral agent, he must pass beyond it to reach autonomy. Conditioning, insofar as it deprives the agent of freedom, strips him of responsibility without which there can be no moral conduct.

born, not made. And finally, the education of an artist more nearly parallels that of a moral agent, whereas it is *differences* in aesthetic and moral education which are our particular concern in this paper. Then let us attempt to find a place for choosing in art experience. I shall consider two kinds of choosing and try to show that they are, at best, peripheral to it. Call these, "choices about art" on the one hand and "choices in art" on the other.

Choices about art are similar in most ways to choices we make about all sorts of things. If we decide to go to a movie tonight the problem remains of just which movie to attend. If we are to buy a picture for the living room wall there remains the question, "Which picture?" The criticism of the movie or book reviewer, or of the newspaper art critic helps us to solve these problems of practical living, much as *Consumer's Guide* aids in making economic choices. The choice is *about* the object rather than within the object since the executive action apprehends the object only in a superficial sense. To choose one book over another is to pick it up and start to read it. To choose one movie over another is to buy a ticket and take one's seat. To choose a picture is to take it home, or to stand in front of it rather than in front of another. In the same way, to choose any economic good is to pay for it and take possession. There is nothing peculiarly aesthetic about choosing a picture any more than there is anything peculiarly sporty about choosing a baseball glove, though considerations of an aesthetic or athletic nature may enter into such choices. The movie reviewer ranks or grades movies in the same way that *Consumer's Guide* ranks baseball gloves. (The criteria of *Consumer's Guide,* however, are perhaps easier to state. The measurement of the object in terms of the criteria is more objective, easier to perform.) Choices *about* works of art make dispositions of them based on the indications of the chooser's own value criteria, or those of an accepted authority. These dispositions are of two sorts. There are those which deal with the object in some sense not directly associated with its aesthetic potential (for example, choosing a picture to cover a crack in the wall or investing in an old master). And there are those which deal with the object as a potential source of aesthetic experience. These latter dispositions include the cases where the action chosen is such as to put us into contact with the work of art in an anticipatory frame of mind (i.e., anticipating some form of aesthetic experience). Buying a recommended book or painting or paying our way into a theater come under the heading of such dispositions. Clearly the first sort of disposition is not aesthetic. The second sort might be termed propaedeutic in that it puts one in the way of aesthetic experience. The most basic thing (i.e., the first thing) that an aesthetic education can teach us is to make the choices that put us in the way of aesthetic objects, hopefully better aesthetic objects. But to be in the presence of the art object, however necessary a condition of aesthetic experience, is not sufficient for it. An aesthetic education curriculum which is intended simply to teach the student to make choices *about* works of art cannot be assured of success, no matter how good the choices or how well they are made. For the mere presence of the art object provides no guarantee of an aesthetic experience (or of the "right" aesthetic experience, if there be such a thing). And it is aesthetic experience which is the ultimate end and justification of our commerce with works of art. We must look further if we seek a role for choice at the center of aesthetic experience and education.

There is yet another kind of choice which I have called "choice in art." It differs from choice about art in that the experiencer chooses in the process of apprehending the work of art. Typically choices *about* art take place before or after, choices *in* art take place *during* the experience of a work of art. The acts here are mental or involve only the movement of the sensory organs. Let us start by considering the latter. Imagine a teacher or a piece of criticism giving us directions as to *how* to look at a painting. "Look first at the figures in the lower right foreground, then let your eye travel along the line of perspective toward the clump of trees in the middle ground, and proceed on toward the upper left and the line of the horizon." These directions prescribe a series of eye movements which it is hoped will lead to a certain sort of experience of the work of art. Through them the critic or teacher can, to some degree, shape the viewer's experience. He can, for example, single out elements of the painting and decree a temporal sequence for viewing them. The viewer then has a choice of viewing or not viewing the elements in this sequence. In so doing he is making choices *in* his experience of the work of art. Is he not, then, choosing aesthetic experience? Alas, no, for the same objection that applied to the case of *choosing about* applies here. It is true that in each case the prescribed actions must result in a perception, but mere perception does not amount to aesthetic experience. Making such choices, no matter how refined or explicit they may be, does not entail aesthetic experience. At best we can term them facilitative. We may, of course, distinguish between different sets of choices and judge some more likely than others to lead to aesthetic experience. In the same way we can assess different strategies as more or less likely to lead to success in games. But neither a game strategy nor a set of directions for perceiving parts of a work amount to a guarantee of winning, or of having an aesthetic experience.

Let us turn to the case of mental acts and choices in art. If we can focus our eyes on one or another facet of a painting, or move them from one element to another, is it equally true that we can choose to look at the painting or its elements with attention; i.e., can we listen to the melody at the expense of the counterpoint, or can we attend to the metre and ignore the imagery, and so on? The constituents of these examples are mental acts, and if what we have described is possible, then it can be said that we are capable of making choices *in* (the course of experience of) the work of art. It must be clear to the reader that the same sorts of objection already raised can be raised again. Choosing to attend to a work of art in a certain way will not guarantee an aesthetic experience. And again, certain mental acts or series of acts are, no doubt, more likely to lead to an aesthetic experience than others. Thus, if we are looking at a work of art and our aim is to attain an aesthetic experience, significance does attach to the way in which we choose to look at it. Wherein do these mental acts differ from the physical acts of *choices about* art? I would say that the former allow of more sophisticated yet perhaps less precise control on the part of the critic or teacher. When I look at a picture (in the minimal sense) there is little doubt in my mind as to what I am doing. But what about such similar verbs as 'looking carefully', 'attending', 'contemplating'? I may decide upon one of these yet feel unsure later as to whether or not I have succeeded in doing it. The following dialogue cannot but sound odd to us: Teacher: "Look (i.e., merely look) at that painting." Student: "I'm trying as hard as I can." I do not think the student's reply would sound odd if we substituted for (merely) "Look" either "Look carefully," "Attend," or "Contemplate." What I am getting at here, then, is that in addition to the difficulties which the mental acts of *choices in* share with the previous cases we have discussed, there is also the problem that many mental acts are themselves matters of trial and success. This means that while we can choose to try to do them, we cannot choose them in their own right.

Before going on to talk briefly about alternative and judgment in aesthetic matters, let us summarize and extend what we have said about the doing aspect of choice and aesthetic experience. I want to talk in terms of three pairs of opposed terms. These are trying-succeeding and doing-happening, which have already been mentioned, as well as a pair of terms introduced by Gilbert Ryle in his book *The Concept of Mind.*[6] Ryle distinguishes between *observing* and *having a sensation.* The former is a kind of activity, the latter is not, "Observing entails having at least one sensation, though having sensations does not entail observing."[7] Observing, further, may or may not have an outcome.

Although I have been using the expression "aesthetic experience" throughout this paper, I have not tried to explain it, nor shall I here. What I will say, for purposes of clarification, is that I regard aesthetic experience as something very like a perception (what Ryle would call a sensation) of a complex sort, or else a series of perceptions. Indeed, this may be a literal description of aesthetic experience of the fine arts; literature, clearly, presents additional problems. Having an aesthetic experience is, or is analogous to, having a sensation of a particular sort. Just what sort I do not wish to attempt to describe. Suffice it to say that not any garden variety of perception will do. This we already know by implication from the fact that it is not

6. Gilbert Ryle, *The Concept of Mind* (New York: Barnes and Noble, Inc., 1949), Chap. VIII.
7. *Ibid.,* p. 223.

necessarily sufficient for the critic to get us to have a (mere) sensation of a work of art, or even a fairly complex structure of sensations, for us to have an aesthetic experience of it.

If this linkage of aesthetic experience with perception be accepted, we can make a clear distinction between the executive element of choice and aesthetic experience. Aesthetic experience, to borrow the language of Ryle, belongs to a category not susceptible of choice. We can choose to try but we cannot choose to succeed. We can within limits choose our doings, but only in a negligible sense our happenings. We can choose to observe and in a sense we can choose the most simple of sensations, but not the more complex, elusive ones — to which category aesthetic experiences would belong. From a logical point of view, therefore, choice must remain at a distance from aesthetic experience. At best we can choose only strategies of action which it is hoped will facilitate the having of aesthetic experience.

Let us now consider alternative. The point has already been made that where there are no alternatives there can be no choice. Imagine that we wish to destroy alternative in order to do away with the possibility of choosing. One way in which this might be done is to eliminate the possibility of adopting alternative courses of action until only one remains (in which case no alternative would exist). Another way would be to alter the situation so that existing alternatives are no longer mutually exclusive. In this latter case choice is eliminated by virtue of the agent's being able to embrace both courses of action.

To my way of thinking, choice about and in aesthetic matters moves in this latter direction. Its alternatives are less firmly polarized than is the case in moral contexts. There is no real aesthetic equivalent of moral obligation, for one thing. Teachers, it is true, sometimes talk as if they feel their students *ought* to choose good art over bad, but no one (artists perhaps excepted?) gets as exercised over "wrong" aesthetic choice as over wrong moral choice. Secondly, though art is something we experience for its own sake, moral choices have consequences which must be taken into consideration. The consequences of a moral action may destroy the very basis upon which an alternative action had rested. Reading a Joyce Kilmer poem does not close off the alternative of reading a Shakespeare poem in the way that killing a man closes off the alternative of not killing him.

Thus far we have considered two aspects of choice — the element of doing and the element of alternative, insofar as they bear on aesthetic experience and the possibility of aesthetic choice. These two aspects may also be seen as helping to define the total context within which choice takes place. Judgment too, aids in this definition. We have already said that where someone chooses we expect him to be able to justify his choice. But what relevance has justification for aesthetic situations and choosing? Justification is something we do *after* making a choice, or it is something offered to us *before* by someone who is recommending a particular choice to us. With regard to the first case the thing to point out is that we justify doings, not happenings. The notion of justification depends on the prior notion of an agent. An aesthetic experience, viewed as a happening, is not the sort of thing that can be justified, though choices *about* or *in* aesthetic objects may be. Presumably what makes it worthwhile, from the point of view of inducing experience, to offer justifications in support of aesthetic choices, is the fact that the justification may serve as a means of amplifying the rather limited *facilitation* of aesthetic experience provided by choices alone. This will come out more clearly if we go on to consider the case of justifying a recommendation. Let me offer a model of critical justification in order to make certain problems clear.[8]

The major premise of such an argument would make reference to some general critical principle; joining it to an imperative. The minor premise would attribute to the object properties specified in the principle cited in the major premise. For example:

> Major Premise: Art objects with unity are art objects to choose. (i.e., Choose art objects with unity.)
> Minor Premise: X is an art object with unity.
> Conclusion: X is an art object to choose. (i.e., Choose X.)

Is it not more likely that we will lead someone to an aesthetic experience of a work of art by telling him that it has unity than by ordering him to choose it? I think so. Taking exhortations to choose, and ascriptions of value, terms such as 'good' (which may be treated as choice-commands) are mere shorthand (from the point of view of inducing experience) for such justifications. Though in logic these premises are subservient to the conclusion, in teaching and nonnormative criticism they take precedence over it.

In summary of this paragraph on justification I want to suggest that once having played down the role of choice in aesthetic situations, it becomes possible to treat certain justifications of choice as if they were directions for ways of experiencing the art object.

III

In the foregoing sections we have addressed ourselves to the question of how things are, what choice is, and what role it has to play in aesthetic experience. Now is the time to say a few words on how things ought to be. If

8. The reader who desires a clearer account of the nature of aesthetic justification and the logic of imperatives is referred to the following: Monroe C. Beardsley, *Aesthetics: Problems in the Philosophy of Criticism* (New York: Harcourt, Brace & Co., 1958), pp. 470–473, and R. M. Hare, *The Language of Morals* (Oxford: Clarendon Press, 1952), Chap. II.

what has been said about choice is correct, does it tell us anything about how to go about aesthetic education or what its goals should be? In literal terms, of course, we cannot expect descriptions to provide us with programs. We may, however, cite descriptions as evidence in attacking or advocating various goals, methods, and curricula. This is what I want to do — attack certain aims and practices in aesthetic education and to suggest alternative ends and means.

Returning to the opening remarks of this paper, I deny once more, and emphatically, that the proper goal of aesthetic education is to turn out good choosers. Fundamental to art, I maintain, is aesthetic experience and it is toward this end that educators must turn. Whatever sort of thing aesthetic experience may be, it is at least perceptual, and perceptual, moreover, in a certain sort of way such that we can point out the importance, not so much of seeing the art object, but how it is seen. The question, then, is how to get people to see in peculiarly aesthetic ways, or how to teach people to see in these ways.

Aesthetic experience is a happening, not a doing. It is, in Ryle's language, an upshot, something that comes about. We may stumble across it, as in finding a rose on a path, or we may strive for it, as in winning a game. It seems to me that educators should be concerned both with students' stumblings across (getting them to see) and with their strivings for (teaching them how to try to see). Under the former heading we would include such activities as the planning of architecture and decor, school libraries, the hanging of art works, as well as the sorts of classroom activity directed to the end of aesthetic experience, but without the students' knowing participation.

Where we are striving to have an aesthetic experience, or where we are teaching students to try, the element of doing (and choosing) enters in, but only in a secondary sense. We choose certain art objects, or we choose to attend to them in certain ways, for the sake of the hoped-for upshot, just as we make certain choices of strategy or tactics in a tennis game for the sake of winning. We cannot choose aesthetic experience any more than we can choose to win. So, in teaching, we seek to affect those choices of the student which we feel are most likely to lead to the upshot, just as a coach attempts to encourage the choices which he feels maximize his players' chances of a winning.

Much the same sort of point can be made with respect to knowledge. There is no choice that can be *equated* with aesthetic experience; neither can any knowledge, even the knowledge which most completely comprehends the desired experience. To know that a given painting is unified is *not* the same thing as to experience it as unified, though if we experience it as unified we may well *know that* it is unified as a result. Still, if we are teaching someone to experience art, telling him that a painting is unified may have the effect that he sees the painting as unified (and then it may not).

It is a mistake to suppose that *telling to* (guiding choices) or *teaching that* (informing) comprise the only possible activities for someone who is trying to teach students to have aesthetic experiences (i.e., to try to put themselves in the way of having aesthetic experiences). Without going into details I should like to point out that coaches and trainers, who face somewhat similar problems, engage in a wide variety of activities with respect to their charges. In a sense, their understanding of what education comprises has much to recommend it to the teacher of art appreciation. Diet and morale are important concerns. They constantly evaluate means in terms of ends (or the alumni do it for them). They are often quite flexible and experimental when it comes to teaching methods. (How many teachers of poetry make as sophisticated use of imitation and memorization as does the college football coach?)

What I am trying to say, in summary, is that choice — either about or in works of art — is but one tool among many which can be used in the process of trying to have an aesthetic experience. The teacher who focuses too sharply on his students' choices (doings) or cognitive states (knowings) runs the risk of confusing means with ends. He is like the coach or the general who accepts his own strategy without question.

Only take care how to taste, one might say, and the question of what to taste will take care of itself.

ON MAKING MORALITY OPERATIONAL

Nancy Gayer

Moral education is inevitably with us. Since we cannot eliminate it, the school's responsibility is to find out more about it and improve it, so that it will result in a moral people.

If the phrase "a moral people" makes you wince, never mind. Morality doesn't necessarily imply adherence to a repressive, rigid, narrow code of behavior. The morality concept is large enough to include freedom and innovation, liberation and progress, rationality and discipline. Remember that its crucial criterion is goodness — whatever is good for man.

It is time that we stop identifying the moral man with the bore and the prig, or the prying censor, and understand that he can be anyone whose character exemplifies the values that we truly admire, that he can epitomize a way of life we think pleasant and rewarding for ourselves and desirable for those whose futures we are helping to shape. 'Morality' need not be a nasty word.

The Overt and the Covert

Values, as everybody knows, are culturally transmitted. The nature of the interaction between human beings is such that moral attitudes are instilled by means of the very words used in communicating. Nonmoral values are no different from moral values in this respect. Both are as much imbedded in the terms of everyday language as the experience of color is in our seeing.

Instead, then, of asking the fruitless question whether moral education *should* be given, we must inquire what values and moral outlooks actually *are* being given and investigate the *manner* in which they are being given. Then, when we become aware of the mechanism and content of the moral instruction which actually permeates all of our educational activities, we shall

From *Phi Delta Kappan, Vol. XLVI,* No. 2 (October, 1964), pp. 42-47. Reprinted by permission of the author and *Phi Delta Kappan.*

NOTE: *The author gratefully acknowledges her debt to Norman and Susan Buder and to Myles Burnyeat for their criticisms and contributions while this article was in preparation.*

be in a better position to answer such questions as what values *ought* the schools to teach. A still further problem is the need to justify whatever values we decide are good. But before we discuss what ought to be done, we should find out what we are actually doing. For this preliminary purpose, I want to illustrate some of the ways in which teachers, in using the ordinary language of subject and skill instruction and classroom management, also succeed, somewhat unconsciously, in passing on to their pupils certain moral values as well.

Planned Moral Teaching

There are, of course, many methods of deliberately teaching moral values. I shall summarize some in passing for the sake of clarifying the distinction between planned and unplanned moral education. My categories are rough and ready and are not meant to be definitive.

> *Direct,* as when a teacher lectures or conducts a discussion on why one ought to be honest.
> By *example,* as when a teacher influences his pupils to be trustworthy by conscientiously being a model of reliability himself.
> By *intended by-product,* as when a teacher, in using problem-solving techniques to teach his subject, also instills an appreciation of critical thinking in his pupils.
> By *training,* as when children become democratic through being in classrooms specifically designed to give guided experiences in self-government and in the common loyalties.
> By *discovery,* as when a teacher uses role-playing procedures to help pupils examine and create their own values as well as to discover the values held by others.

Unplanned Moral Teaching

I made a contrast between two modes of moral education, the conscious or planned, and the unplanned or linguistic. Words take on a characteristic import or force from the way they are used within a context. Although both modes are linguistic, I am confining 'linguistic' to the latter, the unplanned mode, for the sake of emphasizing that the largely unintended and unnoticed transmission of values which characterizes it is derived from the logical function of language. Unplanned moral instruction comes about in the very act of speaking, whether one is actually talking about values or not.

When one describes a pupil as being alert, one is also expressing a *favorable attitude* towards alertness and *commending* the pupil for being alert. Certain values are imbedded in the words we use in ways that we mistakenly suppose are purely descriptive (evaluatively neutral) and are passed over and absorbed without either party being aware of the nature of the transaction. For instance, an apparently ordinary word like 'clean' is value-laden in our schools. It has connotations both of approval and prescriptivity. Implicit in the way the word is used are both "It is good to be clean" and "One ought to do things which lead to cleanliness." The phrase that comes almost automatically to the lips is "*nice* and clean"; and never "*nasty* and clean." That the latter seems a contradiction in terms illustrates how much being clean is, for us, something to be praised. By contrast, in various other cultures and times cleanliness has been a matter of comparative indifference.

It is because we have such a value that when parents, leaving school at open house, remark, "Such a clean school!" no one supposes them to be finding fault. Nor are building principals unaware of this important criterion of judgment as to how well the school is fulfilling its task.

Rock-Bottom Values

I am not advocating that we should stop putting cleanliness next to godliness, but simply asking you to imagine the enormous changes in routine and ways of talking which would be needed to foster an opposing or indifferent attitude towards cleanliness. That it seems absurd even to want to make such a change testifies to the strength of our attachment to whatever values we happen to hold. It would take quite an overhauling to become neutral enough about cleanliness to leave it to the pupils to decide for themselves whether to be clean or not. Similarly, what would it be like to run a school that was neutral in such values as learning, truth-telling, or friendliness? And how can we do without generally shared rules for the protection of life, health, and property?

It would be very difficult indeed, for these values are so much part of our thinking. We would need to be able to say sincerely things like "So what, it was only a lie" as readily as "Never mind, she didn't really mean to hurt your feelings" comes to our lips now. The fabric of the school is woven with the thread of many values, some so basic that we are completely unaware that they are there and that they are values which are continuously being transmitted.

When people get worried about the moral situation, they often talk as if the younger generation were questioning the whole foundation of our life, but in fact there is a substratum of accepted moral standards which are so taken for granted that they are not even noticed. Next time someone starts talking about the crisis in values, ask him *which* values he is talking about. It's very likely that it isn't truth-telling as such, but rather cheating or sex behavior – and this narrow range of questioned values delimits the problem considerably. It's not that all of our values are going out of fashion at the same time, but that specific problems are arising for specific reasons. It isn't as if we're confronted with an abyss in the face of which we have to construct a complete value system; we have a foundation upon which we can't help but build, and these values which we already have *preclude* certain answers to the problems; e.g., to approve wholeheartedly of cheating, we would have to modify the value we place on truthfulness and to abandon the use of exams for grading and diagnosis. Those who justify cheating do so on the basis of certain other overriding values, such as loyalty to a friend who needs help, the desire to be successful, etc. None of these values is *prima facie* despicable. All of them were learned or strengthened at school.

Unplanned Value Sabotage

In cases such as truth-telling, cleanliness, honesty, etc., our habitual uses of language are working on our side, in that the values imbedded in these words and usages are ones we want the young to have anyway. But there are also cases in which language is working against our interests and where, therefore, it is important to become aware of what we are saying and doing in order to prevent damage. I shall lead into this topic by means of the little word 'may.' Although the meaning of 'may' is unambiguous, it is unnecessarily made ambiguous by the way it is used in the schoolroom – with undesirable consequences. Our language has few words to express the notion that one is being given a choice, and 'may' is one of the most natural and simple ways of doing it. On the other hand, the means of politely telling someone to act in a specific manner are infinitely varied and do not require the use of 'may.'

I choose this little word deliberately. Although we are all aware of the importance of such educational objectives as "enlarging the scope of individual freedom" and "teaching to make good choices," we are apt to forget that in ordinary everyday life these high-sounding concepts are expressed by such humble phrases as "you may," "I invite you to," and "would you like to"; and negated by actions whose appropriate verbal expressions are, "you must," "it is necessary to," "this is the rule," and "I want you to." All too often, teachers use the expressions of freedom for eliciting nonchoice responses, and follow them up by actions which belie the true meaning of their words. They thus violate the big concepts of freedom, choice, and responsibility which they suppose are the organizing principles for their classroom practices.

'May' and 'Must'

When the teacher says "You may line up, children," she means "You *must* line up." If Robbie takes 'may' as meaning *may* and goes on painting, he will soon find out that he is not doing the right thing. The teacher will tell him to line up, or she may even rebuke him for not having listened! We are so accustomed to swaddling commands in the soft garments of requests that it may be forgotten that "You may" does not even make a request. It offers a choice; it gives an option to do otherwise.

An objection may be made that "You may" does not offer a choice; rather, that it is a giving of permission. The children are being permitted to line up. But giving permission entails giving the right not to perform the act in question. If I am given permission to do something but am not allowed to refrain from doing it, then I am not being *permitted* at all; I am being *compelled*. I have no choice but to do it.

Or you may say that this usage is all right because the pupils *want* to line up; they want to go out to play. The children are being given permission to do something they already want to do; their teacher is responding to a request as yet unuttered; there's no question of their being compelled to do something that they don't want to do. This is a questionable assumption. Does "You may take out your arithmetic books" signal your pupils that they are now being allowed to do something which they have been just dying to do all morning? But whether they actually do or don't want to take out their books is immaterial; your use of 'may' is unjustified unless you intend your pupils to be equally free not to take them out.

Sowing Seeds of Conformity

Now, contrast telling the same children who were told that they might line up, "You may play on the jungle gym today." Does this mean "Play on the jungle gym and nowhere else," or, alternatively, "One of the places you may play at is the jungle gym"? It could mean either. In the case of lining up, the children soon learn that 'may' *means* 'must.' In cases like that of the jungle gym the teacher's intent in using 'may' is unclear.

How is Robbie to handle this troublesome state of affairs? He can respond by looking around to see what everybody else is doing. This, of course, sows a seed of "other-directedness." Or, he can play it safe by going to the jungle gym. Or perhaps he will continue taking 'may' as indicating an option to refuse — earning the reputation of being anti-social, stubborn, or not-quite-bright.

The Banishment of 'Obedience'

Observe, however, that he is not likely to be called 'disobedient'. That term and 'obedience,' its counterpart on the report card, went out with the coming in of the mythology surrounding the democratic classroom. The same conceptual framework which has led to the use of 'may' for 'must' — a fallacious identification of giving orders with being authoritarian, and the ensuing masquerading of orders into something less reprehensible — also disguises the use of obedience as a behavior criterion. 'Disobeying' implies the existence of a rule, command, or order. One is not disobedient if there is nothing to disobey. Within a frame of reference where teacher-made rules and teacher orders are thought to be undemocratic, and democracy is highly valued, a disobedient child is an implicit reflection on the teacher. She has not been "democratic." Far better to shift the onus on the pupil by calling him 'uncooperative'. His offense thus is against the group and not against an "authoritarian" teacher, guilty by virtue of the nature of the child's crime.

Using 'may' for 'must' helps to perpetuate a widespread and pervasive myth among American teachers that they don't give orders and that doing so is undemocratic. Such beliefs are unwarranted. They are relics from an unrealistic and misconceived educational theory which envisaged the teacher as a sort of grown-up peer member rather than as the person in charge. Giving orders is an integral part of almost any leadership function. We may disguise the essential nature of the orders, serving them up as polite requests or indirectly expressed desires for certain responses, and this is a separate, although relevant problem. But when we clothe what are actually commands in the vocabulary of choice, we violate truth just as much as if we were to tell our pupils that the earth is flat. Both of these verbal acts are deceptions about reality, about what is the case.

There are times when 'may' does mean 'must,' and they should be mentioned for the sake of completeness. These are when 'may' is used ironically. Irony often assumes its unique character by the inverted use of a word, by putting it in invisible quotation marks, so to speak. With unmistakeable coldness and emphasis a mother will tell her naughty child that he " 'may' go to bed." If teachers took that tone when using 'may' for 'must,' there would be no need for this discussion. But, alas, their musting 'mays' are as unstressed and dulcet as their permissive 'mays.'

The Mandatory and the Permissive

In order to do any kind of moral thinking, one needs to be able to distinguish between mandatory rules and permissive rules. "One ought to do such-and-such" and "It is wrong to do so-and-so" take the form of mandatory rules. These require obedience. "It is not wrong to do so-and-so," "It is all right to do so-and-so," and "One may do such-and-such" take the form of permissive rules. These permit choice. One is free to do x or not to do it as one wishes. If adults use 'may' to mean both 'may' and 'must' when they direct children, they thereby make it that much more difficult for the children to learn the all-important distinction between the two concepts, between what they are allowed to choose to do or not do, and what is not being left up to them to decide.

Of course, those children who understand what the teacher has in mind by "You may" know that they *must.* The damage is not *per se* in being told what to do (although this can be overdone), but in having the *telling* disguised. Pupils are not so much deceived by the teacher stratagem as enlightened in respect to the real authoritarianism lurking beneath the sweetness and light.

I have explored the use of 'may' in some depth but other examples are available; some may have occurred to the reader. For example, teachers often say, "Would you *like* to come in now?" when they mean "Playtime is over. Come in!" Although their utterance seems to ask the wishes of the class, seems to be giving the pupils a choice, it is actually an order. Just the other day a nine-year-old pupil told me of her substitute primary teacher, who "invited us to do everything. She'd say 'I invite you to be quiet; I invite you to go to recess; I invite you to sit down.' She was sure mean. The kids called her 'Mrs. Invite' behind her back."

The connection between the misuse of 'may' for 'must,' etc., and the mystique which has grown up around the democratic classroom underlines how an apparently insignificant verbal matter has ramifications which lead to a systematic misrepresentation of the classroom situation. In other words, our *practice* has been confused and misdirected — not just our talk; it's not a matter of words alone, but of actions going astray *because* of confusion in thinking and speaking, which, after all, are done with words. A realistic moral education should sharpen and not blur the distinction between 'may' and 'must,' between the permissive and the mandatory, and thus prepare the pupil for a world in which he will find both positive laws enjoining or forbidding certain courses of action and areas in which he is expected to exercise a responsible choice for himself. This is the area of moral freedom.

The Area of Moral Freedom

We want pupils to develop into autonomous moral agents, but we should keep in mind that the areas in which we can permit them to exercise their judgment without restriction are circumscribed by values which are too basic to relax, just as in society at large moral autonomy is only permitted within an area circumscribed by law. The teacher's role as the mentor of children and young persons is not unlike the role of law itself in setting up the prohibitions and permissions regulating conduct. If this seems to conflict with our democratic presuppositions, it is because we confuse authoritarianism with authority — misconstrue as authoritarianism the authority of leadership which inevitably goes with positions of responsibility. It is not rules as such which constitute authoritarianism, but rules arbitrarily and unjustly formulated and enforced. The teacher who says "Clean up because I tell you to" is being overtly authoritarian, just as the teacher who says "You may clean up now" is covertly so. But the teacher who says "Clean up, so that our classroom will be nice for tomorrow" is giving a reason why it is desirable to behave in a certain way. And this is the crucial difference between arbitrary and rational leadership, between good and bad ways of exercising control over others.

In routine cases such as cleaning up, it isn't necessary to add one's reasons to the telling.That would be boring to the pupils and a waste of time. The pupils already know the reasons. However, teachers must be *prepared* to give reasons justifying their orders, rules, or requests, as well as to volunteer them at the relevant times. The reasons must be sound, and, ideally, the persons to whom they are addressed should be given every practicable opportunity to offer counterarguments. But the nature of even the most democratically administered authority is such that when neither party is persuaded of the rightness of the other's view, the decision of the one in authority prevails, for that is what it means to be "in authority." This is not authoritarianism, but rather a nonauthoritarian exercise of authority. Often, the authority resides in the vote of the majority   but not in the schoolroom, except in certain specified areas. Only thus can teachers, administrators, parents, and managers exercise the kind of leadership indigenous to their role without abdicating from its crucial characteristic — that of making decisions affecting their charges when there are basic disagreements as to what is right.

The reason why it is important to be aware of what values are being inculcated through our use of language is that we can then decide which of these values we hold to be basic and mandatory. These can be explained to our pupils, and the enforcement of them justified, in rational terms. Within the limits of the mandatory we can extend as much as possible the area in which we invite the pupil to use his own judgment and decide on a course for himself. In this way we can avoid the familiar paradox of moral education by combining both the teaching of positive values and the teaching of independent critical reflection.

Ventriloquism

Moral reflection in the classroom is just a shadow of the real thing unless it leads up to actions in which the pupil has a genuine free choice. If the answer which pupils are to give to the question of what the standards of classroom behavior should be is predetermined by the teacher, the pupils can't help but catch on to the strategy and feed back the expected answer. This isn't a sample of real moral reflection; it isn't education for the burden of real moral choice and for the responsibility of choosing and justifying one's own actions. I have reference to the practice of asking elementary school pupils to volunteer the specific rules by which they want to live in the classroom and then rigging the answers by means of teacher comments on unwanted suggestions, so that what is given back by the pupils are the very rules the teacher would herself have made. I have yet to see among the "pupil-made" rules displayed on chart-racks such a rule as, "If someone hits first, it is all right to hit back." No sensible teacher would include such a rule – and quite rightly – because we can't have schools where pupils are allowed to fight each other, just as we can't allow persons within society itself to settle their disputes by physical force.

The fault lies in pretending that the teacher has not used the pupil as a ventriloquist's dummy to give voice to her own intended rules and to con her pupils into thinking that they ought to obey these rules because they made them up themselves. And this in the name of antiauthoritarianism! This is no preparation for autonomous rule making. Teacher-made rules against physical aggression can be explained without authoritarian overtones and without intellectual dishonesty. There is much scope for pupil-made rules, even with young children, e.g., on the playground, within a system of free choice game areas open to all, led by eight-and nine-year-old play-leaders. And the wider the scope the better. But we should not ask pupils to make up rules in any domain unless we are prepared to accept whatever they come up with. We can avoid the onset of a *Lord of the Flies* situation by clearly circumscribing with mandatory rules the children's area of freedom.

Morality can be made operational by teachers who understand clearly what their basic values are, so that they can teach them deliberately and rationally instead of unconsciously. The next move is to encourage the pupil to make his own rules and choices, within the area of freedom – but these must be genuine, and not induced by manipulation. The blurring of the distinction between the mandatory and the permissive can only have the effect of shielding the pupil from the full meaning of moral responsibility and giving the teacher a disguise for restricting the scope of the pupils' own decisions. The point of being clear about the distinction is to widen the area of pupil responsibility as much as possible, while giving pupils those basic values in the light of which they can make their own decisions.

When the teacher says to Robbie that he should obey the rules listed on the chart-rack because he and his friends made them up, it isn't only that the teacher is being dishonest but that this isn't a good enough reason for Robbie. They aren't his rules, and in one way or another he knows it. If she had said,

"Do it because I say so," he *would* have a good enough reason, even though she was being authoritarian, because *she is the teacher.* If she had said, "Do it because we will have a much better time if we obey the rules, and the rules are good ones, the result of much thought and experience on my part," Robbie would have a reason for obeying them twice over, once because a recognized authority says he has to and then again because a recognized authority says there's happiness ahead in following good rules.

Moral Argument

As pupils grow older they may come to question society's basic values. This is the time when rational explanation by teachers becomes even more crucial, for it is unlikely that pupils will challenge all of the values at once. They will have internalized most of them, even as you and I. Pupil-teacher arguments — or discussions, if you like — will be conducted in terms of other values, and pupils will learn how moral differences arise within a framework of general standards accepted by both sides.

It is the outcome of such moral argument that is productive of innovation and progress, stability and sanity in an ever-changing world. Education for such a world must be education for the exercise of genuine moral responsibility in conditions of genuine moral freedom. Such is the task and the obligation of the school, and the moral responsibility of its teachers. 'Morality' need not be a nasty word. But it needs to be made operational for the here and now, and for all of us who live in it.

TAMPERING WITH NATURE IN ELEMENTARY SCHOOL SCIENCE

Joanne Reynolds Bronars

The science program in the elementary school generally includes a unit on plant and animal life. Many such units include one or more of the following recommended learning experiences:[1]

(1) Enclosing flies, crickets, or grasshoppers in jars and cutting off the air supply in order to prove that living things need air in order to stay alive.

(2) Catching, chloroforming, and mounting insects, moths, and butterflies in order to study their structure.

(3) Withdrawing light and water from selected plants in order to prove that these are necessary factors in plant growth.

(4) Dropping acid on live meal worms in order to observe reactions to outside stimuli.

(5) Controlling the diet of white mice so that some of them will display the effects of malnutrition.

(6) Putting frogs in ice water in order to slow down bodily processes and simulate hibernation.

(7) Incubating hens' eggs, which are broken open at various stages in order to examine developing embryos.

(8) Dissecting plants, flowers, starfish, frogs, and other small creatures. The McGraw-Hill Book Company will now supply through the mail live crayfish, guppies, mice, and other small animals for use in elementary school classroom experiments and demonstrations.[2]

All of these activities involve having children control, distort, or stop the life processes of some kind of living organism in order to learn something

From *The Educational Forum, XXXIII* (November, 1968), pp. 71-75. Reprinted by permission of the author and Kappa Delta Pi, an honor society in education, owners of the copyright.

1. See, for example, such science texts as June Lewis and Irene Potter, *The Teaching of Science in the Elementary School* (Englewood Cliffs, N. J.: Prentice-Hall, 1961); Wilbur Beauchamp and Helen Challand, *Basic Science Handbook K-3* (Chicago: Scott, Foresman & Co., 1961); Edward Victor, *Science for the Elementary School* (New York: The Macmillan Co., 1965).

2. *The New York Times,* March 27, 1966.

about its functioning. Two assumptions underlie these activities: first, that the concepts and facts to be learned constitute necessary additions to the child's store of knowledge and secondly, that children learn more easily, thoroughly, and with a higher degree of interest through first-hand experiences involving direct manipulation of concrete materials.

The question as to which specific learnings should be a part of the curriculum will not be explored here, nor will any objection be raised against the general learning principle stated above. There are, however, some related assumptions regarding the acceptability of these classroom experiences which need to be examined, both in terms of their intellectual grounds and of their moral implications. Three assumptions will be examined here:

(1) School children share in the right of human beings to control and alter the natural environment in order to satisfy curiosity, add to our store of knowledge, or to make life more safe and comfortable.

For most men the realm of value deals with human values – with a concern for man's desires and needs. However, as we have increased our understanding of the ways in which man is integrally related to the web of nature, we have come to see that man's control over the natural world must be subject to limitations. Wholesale destruction or exploitation of other forms of life imperils our own life on this planet as will the uncontrollable multiplication of man as a species. Rachel Carson reminds us:

The balance of nature is not the same today as it was in Pleistocene times, but it is still there: a complex, precise, and highly integrated system of relationships between living things which cannot safely be ignored any more than the law of gravity can be defied with impunity by a man perched on the edge of a cliff. The balance of nature is not a *status quo;* it is fluid, ever shifting, in a constant state of adjustment. Man, too, is part of this balance. Sometimes the balance is in his favor; sometimes – and all too often through his own activities – it is shifted to his disadvantage.[3]

Furthermore, sociologists, anthropologists, and others increasingly point up the fact that we are part of one human race, and that we need to discard tribal concepts in favor of a concern for the welfare of all members of the human family. It is more and more the case, then, that decisions involving the control or destruction of any form of life must be made on the basis of sober and intelligent assessment of long range and far reaching consequences.

It seems reasonable to assert that such decision making belongs in the hands of mature adults who not only possess a large body of data upon which to base their decisions, but who also are capable of being moved by what has been termed "a reverence for life." It is in childhood that such a sense of

---

3. Rachel Carson, *Silent Spring* (New York: Fawcett World Library, 1964), p. 218.

reverence will need to be developed, as well as an understanding of man's interrelatedness with nature. We need to consider the kind of school science program which will best accomplish this.

This purpose is not being served when the focus is upon experimentation with living things which have been wrenched from an ecological system. Rather, the focus might better be upon an understanding and appreciation of our world gained through *observation,* so that children, like the ancient Greeks, might behold its workings with a sense of wonder.

Focusing science study upon observation of living things in their natural habitat would require a program built upon field trips, rather than upon the importation of separate items from a site into the artificial environment of the classroom. If observations are planned carefully, children can witness all aspects of the life cycle including, if it is thought to be important, such phenomena as malnutrition and death. Children can be taught to make careful sketches of plants and animals out in the field. They can observe and record on film seasonal changes or changes in the life cycle of an organism. They can listen to woodland sounds and capture them with a tape recorder. Furthermore, children can be helped to make decisions regarding which items might be removed from a field site without disturbing its ecology (fallen leaves, but not leaves pulled from trees; abandoned nests of birds, but not those in use, etc.) as an initial stage in their understanding that there is privilege, purpose, and responsibility involved in man's control of his environment. The privilege is one to be earned by individuals possessed of emotional and intellectual maturity; the purpose must be clearly defined and justified; the responsibility must be knowingly and willingly assumed. We need to ask whether all three of these criteria have been satisfied when we allow children to cut off a grasshopper's life in a glass jar.

(2) All children do or should have similar value orientations toward forms of life which some adults consider to be worthless.

A current science text introduces an experiment involving the killing of flies and grasshoppers with the injunction, "Make sure that the children regard the animals used in the following experiments as pests and that they understand that these animals do not feel pain as humans do."[4] What is the meaning of the term 'pest'? It is generally used to designate something which causes inconvenience to the one employing the term. Some adults consider flies to be pests because they deposit germs on food or because they buzz around in an annoying way. But where houses are well screened, flies do not pose the same kind of threat, and from an aesthetic point of view might be considered to be quite beautiful and to be appropriate subjects for poetry along with the dragon fly or the Japanese beetle. Grasshoppers may be considered to be pests because in great numbers they destroy crops. A few

4. Lewis and Potter, *op. cit.,* p. 177.

grasshoppers in the city, however, do not pose that kind of danger, but rather may be admired for their remarkable athletic feats. Some children may regard bees as pests because they sting; others may regard them as friends because they make honey. What is being suggested here is that the term 'pest' is a value term, not a descriptive one. We cannot describe certain living things as pests *per se,* nor can we expect that all children will or should agree with the way in which we employ the term in the classroom. All that we can do is to state a value position and invite children to consider it. The teacher's right to compel children to accept it is a moral question that needs to be explored.

Just as the concept of what constitutes a pest needs analysis, so does the concept of pain as it applies to animals. Pain is a philosophical concept, not a publicly observable phenomenon. We can only assume that other human beings feel pain as we do when they say, "I have a toothache," or when we make certain inferences from their overt behavior. Since we cannot communicate with fish, insects, trees, or grass, the question was to whether these forms of life experience anything that we could designate as pain becomes even harder to deal with. Again, we cannot assert to children in the classroom that grasshoppers feel no pain; we can only state it as a debatable assumption, and may expect that some children will not regard it as a sufficient ground for permitting experiments upon them.

The fact that a variety of attitudes, feelings, and values about living things may be expressed by children in any one class is often not recognized, much less hoped for. This writer has asked a number of groups of college students to respond to the question, "At what point along the following continuum would it bother you to injure, kill, or dissect the form of life indicated?" The continuum consisted of the following items: grass, flowers, ants, flies, worms, goldfish, mice, cats, pigs, horses, and human beings.

There was at least one student in every group who was disturbed by the thought of trampling down grass or picking flowers. Other students ranged along the continuum which extended to those who had witnessed and were interested in various forms of surgery, including autopsies. When we examined the grounds for the feelings or attitudes expressed, they were based upon concerns such as the following:

A religious sense of the sacredness of all forms of life; aesthetic sensitivity toward all forms of life in their natural state; acute distress at the thought of inflicting pain on any living thing; revulsion at the thought of handling maimed or dead things (Sometimes this depended upon size: "I could kill or dissect a mouse but not a hamster"); emotional identification with animals that are conventionally regarded as pets; and interest in the structure and functions of organisms and in experimentation which will improve life for man.

It might be argued that it is the job of the school to change attitudes through a broadening of the child's experience, in which case the child would be compelled to participate in all of the planned classroom experiences. On the other hand, it might be argued that respect must be given to the feelings and points of view expressed by the children and genuine options accorded them regarding the activities in which they will participate. Thus the child who does not wish to kill flies or mount butterflies would not be penalized or condescended to by the teacher or by his classmates. In any case, we need to explore with children the variety of emotional, philosophical, and religious stances that are taken toward various forms of life and examine the meanings attached to such concepts as "pest," "useful form of life," "purposeful behavior," or "consciousness."

(3) Examination of the actual object will result in better learning than the use of representative materials.

A general acceptance of the value of firsthand experience does not preclude the necessity for making some qualifications regarding specific learning experiences. For example, when students dissect a frog in order to study its internal organs, how much do they actually see? Unless a dissection is skillfully performed the organs may be mangled. If a student is numbed by revulsion, he may be blocked from an objective contemplation of the object before him. Perhaps in these cases much more could be learned from an examination of enlarged color slides or even carefully drawn diagrams. Some of the excellent models of human anatomy are becoming more widely used in schools and seem to be regarded as adequate substitutes for human corpses. When flowers are being studied, some of the large, beautifully constructed models of flower parts, which can be taken apart and reassembled, may provide a more effective means of studying about the reproductive function of the flower than an examination of actual pistils and ovaries. Some natural processes cannot really be observed at all by the naked eye, as, for example, the opening of a bud into a fully opened flower. Separate stages in the process may be witnessed, but the use of films employing time-lapse photography provides a learning experience which no amount of firsthand examination of flowers can duplicate.

What is being suggested is that we must be clear about the aim of a particular science activity and intelligent in our selection of the most effective form of learning experience, be it the actual object, photographs, diagrams, models, television viewing, or a live demonstration. If this were done, we might find that the tradition bound one-shot lesson on the dissection of a frog has little to commend it beyond the fact that it has always been a part of the syllabus.

In summary, we need to undertake a careful examination of the assumptions underlying experimentation with living things in the elementary school science program. The position is taken here that it should be the job of the elementary school to help children develop observational techniques with which to study the natural world. Furthermore, they should be helped to develop a respect for various life processes and an understanding of their own interrelatedness with nature. It is recognized that some educators may consider experimentation with living things to be a legitimate part of the science program, but it is believed that such activities must be carried out in a sensitive, intelligent manner with full awareness of the philosophical, moral, and psychological implications.

ON BOTTLENECKS IN MATHEMATICS EDUCATION

Stephen I. Brown

The low intellectual level at which arguments and counterarguments for reform in school mathematics are pitched is distressing, to say the least. In general, opposing camps seem to talk *at* and not *to* each other. There is very little effort to clarify what people *mean,* and attempts at taking a philosophical stand, meagre as they have been, have been squelched with invectives such as "put up or shut up." Morris Kline has often been the butt of such remarks, for the premium nowadays seems to be on "producing material" — which means writing curricula for the schools. Twice within the last decade he has written lead articles in *The Mathematics Teacher,* only to be chastised in a response article on each occasion either for being factually incorrect, or for not putting his ideas down in the form of a text, where (according to Zant — his most recent respondent) they can be "judged and tried out by teachers in the schools."[1]

In the second "debate" Zant further asserts, "The time has passed for merely talking about what should be done. It seems that a pattern has evolved for producing materials." He then suggests the following five-point pattern for writing curriculum materials.

1. The material should be produced by a team effort. Certainly the team of writers should include mathematicians, mathematics educators, and teachers. Valuable assistance can be furnished by learning theorists and measurement specialists.
2. The material should be written so that the student for whom it is intended can read it.
3. The material should be used experimentally in the schools. If it does not teach — that is, if the students do not attain the stated

From *Teachers College Record, 70* (December, 1968), pp. 199‑212 with changes made by the author. Reprinted by permission of the author and *Teachers College Record.*

1. Morris Kline, "The Ancients Versus the Moderns, A New Battle of Books," and Albert E. Meder Jr., "The Ancients Versus the Moderns — A Reply." *The Mathematics Teacher, LI,* No. 6, 1958, pp. 418‑433; Morris Kline, "A Proposal for the High School Mathematics Curriculum," and James H. Zant, "A Proposal for the High School Mathematics Curriculum — What Does It Mean?" *The Mathematics Teacher, LIX,* 4, 1966, pp. 322‑334.

behavioral objectives (there are also other kinds of worthy objectives) — the material should be rewritten and retested experimentally until the students do learn.

4. Meaning and understanding of the fundamental concepts of mathematics are essential; hence the material should be written from this point of view.

5. If there are so-called modern concepts of mathematics which are useful in teaching and understanding of the mathematics included, they should be used.[2]

I am not at all convinced that this list of truisms, vague assertions and oversimplifications would be the least bit helpful to Kline or anyone else concerned with curriculum revision. Furthermore, I should like to stress one obvious point that seems to have been missed by reformers' reactions to Kline. Though *the production of a curriculum* may tend to clarify what a man means by claims such as "to get a student to understand mathematics, he must re-create it," there are other ways of clarifying meaning. Furthermore, no amount of curriculum experimentation in schools is going to answer rather fundamental questions like:

(1) What is mathematics and how does it relate to science? to reality?

(2) Why should mathematics be taught?

(3) How does the "creative mathematician" generate mathematical ideas?

That is, there are certain points made by Kline, and by others, that are worth arguing about and capable of fruitful analysis even without the existence of a crash program to substantiate them.

It is indeed unfortunate that in his more recent article Morris Kline once more creates so many caricatures and commits so many factual errors.[3] In addition, as with previous articles on both sides of the fence, he tends to make — without justifying or clarifying — sweeping assertions in the area of mathematics education. Still, there are serious philosophical and experimental questions embedded in his article, and I should like to unearth some of them. I shall ignore a number of factual errors (and urge others concerned with questions of substance to do likewise) over which opponents will gloat. Instead I shall raise what seem to me to be some basic questions suggested by the article, questions to which I would like to see the math-education community address itself.[4] The primary object here will not be to take a stand on the

2. Zant, p. 333, *loc. cit.*

3. Kline, "Intellectuals and The Schools: A Case History," *Harvard Educational Review, 36,* 1966, pp. 505–511.

4. For a discussion of the "factual" errors see the original version of this article in the December, 1968 issue of *Teachers College Record.*

issues, nor to draw distinctions between (and to make a case for) "modern" vs. "traditional" approaches to mathematics. I merely wish to open questions that ought to be met head-on by the various factions.

I should stress that I pretend to be no expert in the politics of curriculum innovation, and make no claims about appropriate ways of proceeding. It seems to me, however, that there exist basic questions of a philosophical and experimental nature that ought to be (and in fact are not) being considered by those concerned with curriculum development. The questions will be generated from the following four categories that Kline alludes to in his recent article: Mathematics and Intuition, Creation of Mathematical Ideas, Mathematics and Science, and Goals of Teaching Mathematics.

Mathematics and Intuition

Professor Kline asserts, "Mathematics is understood intuitively, that is, through pictorial, physical and experiential evidence," rather than through logical arguments.[5] The implication here is that *all* of mathematics is understood this way. It seems to me that there are many fairly elementary mathematical ideas (that jar one's intuition), for which there are no *pictorial* or *physical* (I'm not sure what he means by "experiential" here) methods of persuasion. How (especially before one is familiar with the theory of equations) does one come to understand intuitively that $\sqrt{2}$ is irrational (cannot be expressed in the form a/b for a and b integers)? How does one come to appreciate intuitively that though *all* the rational numbers can be put in a one-to-one correspondence with the natural numbers $(1, 2, 3, 4, \ldots)$, the real numbers (all nonimaginary numbers) are so "huge" that there is no such correspondence for them on as short an interval as one wishes to name (i.e., the rationals are countable, while the reals are uncountable)? How does one intuitively see that (using ruler and compass) it is, in general, impossible to trisect an angle? I suggest a serious analysis of the following kinds of questions:

(1) What mathematical concepts lend themselves to particular kinds of intuitive explanations? Which do not? I suggest that a close analysis be given to "impossibility" concepts in mathematics, and more generally to ideas that seem to require proof by contradiction.

(2) What kind of teaching tends to develop one's sense of intuition? (It is worth pointing out the rather obvious fact that a phenomenon which is "intuitively obvious" to one person is nonsense to another.) There seems to be a move among several curriculum designers (especially for early elementary grades) *away* from a rigorous, deductive approach, and *towards* a more "playful" spirit —referred to by exponents of Educational Services Incorpo-

5. Kline, *loc. cit.,* p. 508 (3).

rated (now known as E. D. C.) as a "pre-mathematical" experience. The emphasis is in fact on working with "things" (pendula, blocks, cards, etc.) under very minimal direction from a teacher. The claim is that there is little need (at least from the logical point of view of supplying information) for reinforcement by a teacher under such a scheme because the youngster's hunches are easily verifiable through manipulation of materials.

Though psychological evidence — Piaget in particular — would seem to suggest such an approach especially at pre-operational and concrete stages of development, Friedlander has pointed out that the generation of hypotheses and their simultaneous evaluation, i.e., production and editing, are behaviors which, though pedagogically desirable, may not be (in the absence of training) psychologically compatible.[6]

What in fact is the impact on one's sense of intuition of such concrete experience? Does an early approach of intensive experience of this sort yield powerful pay-off when the child is prepared to conceive of the world in more abstract terms, or does it hinder his development by wedding him to the need for concrete representations? It is worth recalling a notion that has begun to dawn on those who are anxious to interpret Piaget's results for the classroom. As enlightening as his scheme may be, Piaget (concerned as much with epistemological issues as with psychological ones) was essentially *testing* and not attempting to *teach* youngsters what his tests indicated they in fact could not grasp. In addition, the existence of cognitive stages of development from infancy to adolescence does not in and of itself imply that at any given stage ideas must be presented in an order which reflects the chronological growth of the individual.

(3) How does one's facility in understanding ideas intuitively affect his inclination to *prove* conjectures? to generate conjectures?

(4) What do we mean by an *intuitive understanding?* Is an intuitive understanding one which merely engenders greater belief in a concept, or need it represent the skeleton of a formal proof? (In the case of irrationality of $\sqrt{2}$, the former is much easier to come by than the latter.)

(5) Historically, what were the circumstances surrounding the generation and clarification of anti-intuitive mathematical ideas? What (if any) pedagogical implications can we draw? What kinds of pedagogical questions ought we ask? With perhaps a correction factor of ϵ (and ϵ clearly approaches 0) none of the curriculum programs in mathematics ("traditional," "modern," or otherwise) places in historical perspective any of the significant (intuitive or otherwise) ideas introduced. The modern programs are especially guilty of giving the illusion that the beautiful "structural" development of the subject arrived full-blown like Athena from the top of Zeus' head. Perhaps

6. B. Z. Friedlander, "A Psychologist's Second Thoughts on Concepts, Curiosity, and Discovery in Teaching and Learning," *Harvard Educational Review, 35,* 1965, pp. 18-38.

more significant is the fact that (and this hardly needs documentation) very few teachers of mathematics are even the least bit familiar with the history of the subject. One need not be committed to a "genetic" principle in the teaching of mathematics to appreciate that historical analysis may shed some light on the intellectual hurdles that one must overcome in order to appropriately understand an idea.

The difficulties involved in using negative numbers (referred to as "numeri ficti" — fictitious numbers) during the Renaissance might indicate that the concept has more substance than appears on the surface, and that a cavalier extension of a number line "to the left" glosses over a multitude of sins. Might the student and the teacher *both* learn something significant about how perceptions of the "real world" may simultaneously *suggest* and *hinder* the development of mathematical ideas (especially anti-intuitive ones) through a close analysis of the evolution of the derivative and definite integral in the calculus?

That there were great debates among scholars in the 17th century over the sum of the simple-looking infinite expression $1 - 1 + 1 - 1 + 1 - 1 + 1 - 1 + \ldots$ suggests that the idea of an infinite sum is far from intuitive, and as a matter of fact requires some fancy and rather arbitrary machinery. The fact that it took two centuries to arithmetize the very vague geometric concept of the infinitely small ("atoms," which are neither finite nor zero), which neither Newton nor Leibniz was able to really clarify, suggests not only that the ideas are anti-intuitive, but that their clarification required an intellectual *tour de force* which is hardly conveyed to a beginning calculus student by a slick ϵ, δ definition of limit.

(6) How ought intuition and rigor to interrelate in the attempt to codify what one already strongly believes in mathematics? The problem is both philosophical and pedagogical. How should one conceive of mathematics? How should he teach it?

(7) We have been speaking of intuition simultaneously as an attribute of *explanation* and of *understanding*. How do these two ideas relate?

Creation of Mathematical Ideas

Kline comments, "Moreover, in the creation of mathematics the thinking consists not of logical arguments but by guessing, conjecturing, generalizing from specific examples, and imagining a plan of attack. To get students to grasp mathematics thoroughly, they must re-create it, of course with the guidance of a teacher ... "[7] As far as I know, there is very little evidence on how mathematical ideas were originally conceived. Jacques Hadamard presents some insight on the basis of after-the-fact introspection by famous mathematicians, but this is barely a beginning.[8] I suspect that the

7. Kline, *loc. cit.,* p. 508 (3).
8. Jacques Hadamard. *Psychology of Invention in the Mathematical Field.* Princeton: Princeton University Press, 1945.

"creative moment" in most cases is arrived at through a much less rational process than even the essentially inductive procedure that Kline describes, and that Polya has popularized so well.[9] It would certainly be enlightening to find out how, in fact, ideas are "created" by research mathematicians. In particular, it would be interesting to see if there is a significant difference depending upon the branch of mathematics. What kinds of "pictures" inspire the algebraist?

Interesting as this information would be, it seems to me that we ought to be cautious about drawing pedagogical imperatives from it. Must we also re-create the social milieu together with all the "irrational" attributes that led to the genesis of an hypothesis? Why *must* students re-create mathematics in order to understand it thoroughly? Towards what end? Perhaps by "understand thoroughly," Kline means that they ought to conceive of their task in the same way that the originator of the idea did. If this is the case, however, his remark is essentially tautologous.

What kind of worthwhile experimentation can be conducted in which students do in fact re-create mathematics? How is their grasp of the mathematical ideas as well as transfer to other tasks affected by the process? Most of the experimentation as well as text material on student discovery requires such a trivial amount of organization and clarification on the part of the student, that one would hardly be said to be re-creating the mathematics — even with the guidance of a teacher.[10]

Mathematics and Science

Kline comments that mathematics is "not self-generating and in any case not self-justifying to students. Motivation for the study must be given, and the most appealing and historically most justified motivation is the use of mathematics to help man understand and master natural phenomena. This interconnection with the sciences would, beyond supplying motivation, give meaning to concepts and theorems, because these are abstractions from reality." [11] Below are a few experimental and philosophical questions that his assertion raises and that ought to be analyzed.

(1) The fact that Professor Kline finds the usefulness of mathematics in helping man understand and master natural phenomena as the most appealing motivation for the study of mathematics is no reason to make the unqualified assertion that the subject is *not* self-justifying for students. For what kinds of students are what kinds of motivations appropriate? Certainly many people are intrigued by puzzles of all sorts regardless of their relationship to

9. George Polya. *How to Solve It.* Princeton University Press, 1948. *Induction and Analogy in Mathematics.* Princeton, 1954.

10. For a further analysis of the sense in which 'discovery' is used in some of the modern mathematics programs, see S. Brown, *Selected Issues Related to Structure in the Learning of Mathematics,* unpublished doctoral dissertation, Harvard Graduate School of Education, 1967.

11. Kline, *loc. cit.,* p. 508 (3).

problems in the mastery of "natural phenomena."[12] Perhaps more to the point, regardless of what in fact *does* motivate students, do we wish to engender an attitude of *inquiry for its own sake* and not necessarily for answering some pressing "wordly" problems? If the answer is yes, then what in fact *does* motivate students may be something we attempt to influence (how?) rather than something we (as the jargon goes) "capitalize on."

(2) There is a clear implication that mathematical theorems and concepts are abstractions from reality, while science is more concrete. As with *intuition* vs. *rigor,* the dichotomy is obviously in need of clarification. Science, it seems to me, may be as "abstract" as mathematics. Perhaps more to the point, what kinds of explanations (scientific or mathematical, or both) are concrete (or abstract) for what students at what levels of sophistication? It has become a truism that in teaching mathematics (and perhaps in teaching in general), one ought to proceed from the concrete to the abstract. What is concrete for whom? Do positive instances of a generalization represent something concrete? Is a model (scientific or mathematical) necessary as a concrete representation? What are the consequences of proceeding from the abstract to the concrete? It is worth clarifying what we mean by these very abused terms. It may be necessary to distinguish between philosophical (abstract, being more general), and psychological (abstract, being harder) uses of the terms.

(3) Regardless of motivational and clarifying value of science in the learning of mathematics *per se,* should math and science (together with perhaps other disciplines) be taught as interrelated subjects? That is, is there something valuable (aesthetically or from the viewpoint of intellectual "potency") about perceiving the world in an *interdisciplinary spirit?* Here clarification of meaning is once more required.

(i) In the name of "integration" of various branches of mathematics, there exist some school systems which "unite" algebra and geometry by using two different texts (each independently conceived) — one for each subject — and alternate their use from one day to the next. This "layer cake" approach would seem on the surface to have very little value above teaching the subjects independently. One could of course plan to cover related topics (as is generally *not* done in the above case) in mathematics and science (like differentiation in mathematics and laws for falling bodies in physics) at the same time in two different courses.

(ii) Another possible interpretation of interdisciplinary might be the one that Kline seems to be suggesting. We could use science as a

12. Most of the modern programs as well as the traditional ones seem to conceive of problems in a very narrow sense. That is, regardless of the extent to which mathematics is viewed as a structure, it is very rare that problems are posed whose solutions do not follow from the context of the immediately preceding section.

tool for motivating and clarifying mathematics (or of course vice versa).

(iii) One could — in a Progressive Education spirit — bring several disciplines to bear on a particular theme (like "occupations serving the household," "European backgrounds of the colonists," as in Dewey's "Laboratory School"). There, of course, is no guarantee that there will emerge any worthwhile mathematics (for example) in a unit on "occupations serving the household," but then Dewey did supplement these units with more formal work in several of the disciplines, and perhaps one can think of more pervasive foci.

(iv) Another possibility would be to select underlying philosophical type themes that represent the concern (on a "meta" level) of all disciplines.

(a) One might take a comparative look at the meaning and role of definition, proof, doubt, evidence, consistency, explanation, etc., among the various subjects. What is there about the nature of mathematics which accounts for the fact that *most* mathematical "truths" tend to sustain the wisdom of the ages (becoming reshuffled and reorganized but not invalidated with the passage of time) while science and most other disciplines have more frequent and sudden deaths? Can we make the above claim about *all* mathematical truths? In what sense is mathematics revisable (over the long haul) — discounting those obvious cases in which formal logical errors have been commited?[13] I am not sure how proficient one has to be in a subject before he can gain from such an analysis. Professor Olafson, in reviewing Daniel Bell's *The Reformation of General Education,* takes a dim view of the feasibility of such "conceptual inquiry" within just one discipline as a general education requirement for college students.[14] I should think that an even superficial go at *some* of these philosophical questions would yield greater dividends than he concedes. That an intellectual counterpart of Heisenberg's uncertainty principle exists in mathematics (Gödel's incompleteness theorem), which places the foundations of the subject on a bed of quicksand, might give pause to those who feel that the only way to respectability in a discipline is through quantifica-

13. For a conception of mathematics as "immortal" see David Eugene Smith, "Religio Mathematici," *American Mathematical Monthly,* October 1921. For a counter-argument that much of mathematics may be both *a priori* (and thus not empirical in the sense in which science is) *and revisable* see Robert Rogers, "Mathematical and Philosophical Analyses," *Philosophy of Science,* July 1964.

14. *Harvard Educational Review,* 36, 1966, pp. 537-42.

tion and the building of mathematical models. One of Gödel's major conclusions is that, given any system within which arithmetic can be developed (which of course excludes finite systems), there exist true statements not derivable within the system.[15] In general, a curriculum designed to analyze the limitations of various disciplines in answering (or asking, for that matter) significant questions would seem to warrant serious consideration as a general education requirement.

(b) Regardless of the value of explicitly incorporating some of these philosophical considerations into the curriculum *per se,* those who are responsible for instruction in the schools might gain considerably from an analysis of these themes. Let us choose the problem of explaining rules of multiplication of signed numbers as a case study for purposes of illustrating how a close analysis of two ostensibly different *explanations* might reveal important common threads. The intention here is less to look at the *legitimacy* of alleged explanations or their definition than it is to compare the nature of their *appeal*.

The SMSG explanation for why we define the product of a negative and positive as negative is based primarily upon a desire to preserve the distributive principle in our new system (signed numbers). The distributive principle asserts:

$$\text{For all } x, y, z, x \cdot (y + x) = x \cdot y + x \cdot z.$$

The SMSG explanation for why $(2) \cdot (-3)$ has to be -6 is as follows:[16]

$(2) \cdot (0) = 0$, because of the *multiplication property* for 0

$(2) \cdot [3 + (-3)] = 0$, by writing $0 = 3 + (-3)$

$(2) \cdot (3) + (2)(-3) = 0$, if the *distributive principle* is to hold
　　　　　　　　　　for signed numbers

$6 + (2)(-3) = 0$, since $(2)(3) = 6$.

Now since $(2)(-3)$ must be the opposite of (6), it must equal -6.

Morris Kline, criticizing the SMSG approach on grounds that it presents mathematics as an axiomatic, ahistorical discipline comments, "Extending the distributive law to negative numbers will be of no help at all in understanding negative numbers. . . .The essential point here is that we

---

15. For an intelligent layman's discussion of Gödel's work, see Ernest Nagel and James Newman, *Gödel's Proof* (New York: New York University Press, 1960).
16. See School Mathematic Study Group, *First Course in Algebra,* Yale University Press (1961), pp. 145 ff. For a detailed mathematical criticism of their approach, see Stephen I. Brown, "Signed Numbers: A 'Product' of Misconceptions," *The Mathematics Teacher,* March 1969, pp. 183-195.

human beings agree to operate with negative numbers in such a way as to make our formulas more useful."[17]

He then proposes that we teach rules for multiplication of signed numbers by using formulas such as: $T = 5t$ where T is the temperature after the passage of t hours. If we ask for the temperature three hours ago, we are, he asserts, led to consider $5(-3)$ and supposedly would be inclined to conclude that it is -15. His argument here is vague, but he most likely is suggesting that we select -15 as the answer based upon extrapolation from a table such as the one below:

$$
\begin{aligned}
5(3) &= 15 \\
5(2) &= 10 \\
5(1) &= 5 \\
5(0) &= 0 \\
5(-1) &= ? \\
5(-2) &= ? \\
5(-3) &= ?
\end{aligned}
$$

To fill in the question marks, note that in each case as we proceed (multiplying by 5 in each case) from one positive integer to the next lower one, the product is 5 less. If $5(-1)$ then is to be 5 less than $5(0)$ it must be -5. Such reasoning suggests that $5(-3) = -15$.

In Kline's alleged explanation let us for the moment disregard the fact that the formula and pattern might have been suggested by a physical phenomenon. Though the students might be highly motivated by explanations that "come from" science, the allegation of "real worldliness" is somewhat contrived here since we do not have to refer at all to the "real world" in the analysis of the problem.

How does Kline's proposed explanation compare with that of SMSG? It looks on the surface as if they are miles apart. One is based upon axiomatic deductive structure and the other upon the observation of a pattern.[18]

Do they share common ground? It is perhaps easier to analyze this question if we ask a rather obvious question with regard to the SMSG explanation. Why must the distributive principle hold in the extended system? In particular, why must $(2)(3 + (-3)) = (2)(3) + (2)(-3)$? The answer is simple: There is no *logical* reason. We are motivated by an *aesthetic* principle which we might characterize as a "wishful thinking" argument. The

17. See Kline, "A Proposal for the High School Mathematics Curriculum," *loc. cit.*, p. 322 ff.
18. It would be a worthwhile exercise to attempt to relate arguments by "patterns" and those based upon deductive structure. I suspect the relationship is much more complicated than merely the distinction between induction and deduction.

aesthetic principle asserts: "Wouldn't it be nice if many of the properties we had before held in our new system."

At first glance it looks as though Kline is presenting an entirely different kind of justification. Doesn't every fool see "intuitively" that if $T = 5t$ relates time to temperature, then the temperature 3 hours ago $((5)(-3))$ must have been -15 degrees? The answer is: There is nothing predestined about the relationship between $5(-3)$ and -15 given this setup.

A graph of the linear relationship $T = 5t$ will enable us to clarify the point. Let us first plot a few points for the case of the positive integers. Now what should $5(-3)$ be if we do not yet know how to multiply signed numbers? The answer that Kline seems to suggest is motivated by the following picture:

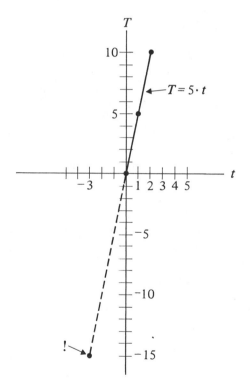

But what does that picture argue implicitly? The graph makes a plea for the continuation of a *linear* relationship as we progess through the negative numbers? Why must the points along $T = 5t$ for the case of negative t remain collinear with those for which t is positive? The answer obviously *once* more is that though this need *not* logically be so, it would be nice if the properties we ascribe to positive integers were to remain intact as we extend to a new set. Again, the argument is based upon *"wishful thinking"*. If we want collinearity preserved, then $5(-3)$ must equal -15, just as we argued in the SMSG case that if we want the *distributive principle* preserved, then $(2)(-3)$ must equal -6.

It may very well be that the subtleties of argument by "wishful thinking" represent an "intellectual hurdle" for the student that is itself more overpowering than the distinction between *axiomatics* and patterns.[19] The force of the above assertion is not to "wash out" an important philosophical distinction. It is rather to point out that there is a subtle and substantial thread that unites the two alleged explanations.

Recall that the purpose of this long digression was *not* to examine the validity of an explanation nor to characterize explanations in mathematics (valuable as such an enterprise would be). We are concerned instead with examining alleged inharmonious explanations with the intention of searching for common ground. We do *not* claim, as Kline does, that one leads to better understanding than the other. We do claim, however, to have exposed an epistemological kind of issue that it would be unwise for researchers and curriculum writers to ignore.

Goals of Teaching Mathematics

Professor Kline bemoans the fact that no one of the curriculum groups sought to understand the goals of elementary and high school education. He comments, "In view of the large number of students who attend the lower schools, most of whom never get to college, and of the relative ignorance of these students, surely the objectives of education at these levels are different from those of the liberal arts colleges. Nevertheless, no group prefaced its recommendations by an analysis of what the elementary and high schools should be seeking to achieve and how the new curricula contributed to these goals."[20]

I think his point is a very good one. One can teach mathematics as an end in itself, and this seems to be the direction of most of the curriculum groups. Designers of curricula then need only ask themselves questions like: Given this student's level of maturity, what is the most elegant and powerful way of conceiving of a mathematical idea? One can, of course, argue the relative merits of teaching Euclidean geometry through a vector approach, or Hilbert's axioms, but *the goal* is essentially to ensure that the students gain proficiency in mathematics as well as a feeling for what mathematics is about.

19. It is worth stressing that there are other explanations, e.g., Beberman and Vaughan, *High School Mathematics Course 1*. (Boston: D. C. Heath and Co., 1964), Revision of University of Illinois Committee on School Mathematics – UICSM, pp. 42–47, which do *not* require that the student reason by "wishful thinking" in order to appreciate the "rule" for multiplication of signed numbers.

20. Kline, *loc. cit.*, p. 508 (3).

A case in point is the pamphlet put out by Educational Services Incorporated entitled *Goals for School Mathematics.*[21] Though there are a few sweeping assertions in the section entitled "Broad Goals of the School Mathematics Curriculum," which hint at extra-systemic reasons for teaching mathematics (e.g., "The building of confidence in one's own analytic powers is another major goal of mathematics education"), the justification is for the most part self-contained. The authors claim, "A mere recital of the topics proposed for the future curriculum does scant justice to our goals. *Familiarity* is our real objective."[22]

There are of course methodological discussions on how best to introduce these ideas.[23] Witness the fact that there is barely a modern mathematics text in existence which does not "advertise" the fact that it is committed to "discovery" or "structure" somewhere in its title. "Learning by discovery," however, is conceived by curriculum designers as a means to achieving a very self-contained end — proficiency in (and perhaps enjoyment of) mathematics *per se.* We might mention that even as far as *this* goal is concerned, there is much need for clarification of terms, and there seems to be very little justification for drawing *any* conclusion on the basis of what appears to be contradictory experimental evidence.[24]

There seems to be very little talk nowadays, especially among curriculum designers, on broader justification for teaching mathematics than "familiarity" with the content. What kinds of transfer benefits do we desire? The fact that mathematics was shown years ago not to have an impact on "training of the mind" was perhaps a reflection on the teaching strategy more than on the subject. What kind of intellectual power *beyond* the ability to handle and understand mathematics do we hope that the learning of mathematics will generate? The fact that the achievement of such goals may be hard (or perhaps impossible) to measure is no reason not to state them and to argue over them. Once the goals are stated, they themselves will obviously not imply (logically) any pedagogical strategy, but we may have some reason to question the criterion of "elegant" or "good" mathematics as the almost sole judge of what should be taught.

Professor Kline criticizes the appointment of mathematics professors as professors of mathematics education. He feels that though they may know their subject matter better than the educators, the problem of curriculum in the schools is primarily pedagogical, and therefore ought to be the domain of

21. *Goals for School Mathematics: The Report of the Cambridge Conference on School Mathematics* (Boston: Houghton Mifflin, 1963).

22. *Ibid,* p. 8.

23. See, for example, Robert Davis, *Discovery in Mathematics: A Text for Teachers* (Reading: Addison-Wesley, 1964); Z. P. Dienes, *Building Up Mathematics* (London: Hutchinson Educational Ltd., 1961).

24. Brown, *loc. cit.,* p. 17.

education professors (perhaps working in conjunction with mathematicians) who demonstrate superiority in this area.

If by pedagogical expertise Professor Kline means that education professors are better than mathematicians at knowing *what* mathematical ideas youngsters *can* grasp, and at what age they can do so best, I think the issue is highly debatable. If nothing else, the modern curricula have demonstrated — contrary to the expectation of many educators — that youngsters are capable of dealing with some very sophisticated ideas quite early in their development.

I think it is unfortunate that mathematics educators persist in the role they do. The prevailing attitude among mathematics educators seems to be that they are middlemen who wait for the word from "on high" (i.e. from mathematicians) in order to find out what ought to be taught. Their job then is to interpret and implement for the education community what mathematicians feel is an appropriate curriculum.

This attitude is clearly expressed by Professor Max Beberman of the University of Illinois Committee on School Mathematics (UICSM) and a major figure in the area of mathematics curriculum revision.

> My point of view has always been that I, personally, have very little responsibility for the selection of the content to be tried out experimentally. My job is to find out what things can be taught and what things can't be taught. So, if someone makes a suggestion about a topic to be taught and it turns out that, when I give my best efforts to this, I still can't get it across to children, maybe it can't be taught — maybe. I don't know how much harm we do to students if we select good mathematical content in the first place and then exert our best efforts to get it across. I'm perfectly content, as a professor of education, to devote all of my attention to finding the right kind of pedagogy to get mathematical ideas across to children. . . .[25]

It seems to me that the problem of design, implementation and evaluation of a curriculum in the schools is much deeper than pedagogical in the sense I have interpreted Kline's use of the word. (How to teach X to Y? At what age can X be taught to Y?). The deeper role is one that mathematicians seem notoriously anxious to avoid. If mathematics educators persist in being "middlemen," they ought at least to have mobility in both directions (from the schools to the scholars as well as the other way), and ought to broaden their scholarly communications to include psychologists and philosophers as well.

I do not mean to take the naive position of assuming that unless goals are clearly stated at the onset, nothing reasonable can follow. I am well aware

25. *The Role of Applications in a Secondary School Mathematics Curriculum.* Proceedings of a UICSM Conference at the University of Illinois, Urbana, 1964.

of the fact that difficult problems are frequently stated only after they have been solved. I merely urge that we begin to establish *some interaction* between content and more broadly conceived goals in the design of curriculum. Without such interaction, I do not see how we can make very much sense out of the controversy over intuition vs. rigor, concrete vs. abstract, mathematics through science vs. deduction. With such interaction, perhaps we will not only begin to generate some worthwhile questions, but to carry on some nontrivial research as well.

NAME INDEX

SUBJECT INDEX